NOLAN MIDDLE SCHOOL

Level 6

Perseverance

•

Ancient Civilizations

•

Taking a Stand

•

Beyond the Notes

•

Ecology

•

A Question of Value

SRA OpenCourt READING

Level 6

— PROGRAM AUTHORS —

Marilyn Jager Adams   Jan Hirshberg   Marlene Scardamalia

Carl Bereiter   Anne McKeough   Gerald H. Treadway, Jr.

Joe Campione   Michael Pressley

Iva Carruthers   Marsha Roit

SRA

A Division of The McGraw-Hill Companies

Columbus, Ohio

Grateful acknowledgment is given to the following publishers and copyright owners for permissions granted to reprint selections from their publications. All possible care has been taken to trace ownership and secure permission for each selection included. In case of any errors or omissions, the Publisher will be pleased to make suitable acknowledgments in future editions.

Acknowledgments

PERSEVERANCE
"The Fire Builder" reprinted with the permission of Simon & Schuster Books for Young Readers, an imprint of Simon & Schuster Children's Publishing Division from HATCHET by Gary Paulsen. Copyright © 1987 Gary Paulsen. "Amaroq, the Wolf" from JULIE OF THE WOLVES. TEXT COPYRIGHT © 1972 BY JEAN CRAIGHEAD GEORGE. Used by permission of HarperCollins Publishers. ON TOP OF THE WORLD: THE CONQUEST OF MT. EVEREST by MARY ANN FRASER, © 1991 by MARY ANN FRASER, text and illustrations. Reprinted by permission of Henry Holt and Company, LLC. From SAINT GEORGE AND THE DRAGON by Margaret Hodges. Copyright © 1984 by Margaret Hodges (text); copyright © 1994 by Trina Schart Hyman (illustrations). By permission of Little, Brown and Company (Inc.). Text copyright © 1992 by David A. Adler. Illustrations copyright © 1992 by Robert Casilla. All rights reserved. Reprinted from A PICTURE BOOK OF JESSE OWENS by permission of Holiday House, Inc. "Mother to Son" from COLLECTED POEMS by Langston Hughes. Copyright ©

1994 by the Estate of Langston Hughes. Reprinted by permission of Alfred A. Knopf, a Division of Random House, Inc. "Back to the Drawing Board" Copyright © 1991 by Russell Freedman. All rights reserved. Reprinted from THE WRIGHT BROTHERS: HOW THEY INVENTED THE AIRPLANE by permission of Holiday House, Inc. "Crazy Boys" by Beverly McLoughland in Lee Bennett Hopkin's HAND IN HAND: AN AMERICAN HISTORY THROUGH POETRY, c. 1994, Simon & Schuster, New York. Reprinted by permission of the author.

ANCIENT CIVILIZATIONS
From DIGGING UP THE PAST, text copyright © 1989 by Carolyn James and S.D. Schindler. Reprinted by permission of Franklin Watts, a division of Grolier Publishing. "The Search for Early Americans" reprinted with the permission of Margaret K. McElderry Books, an imprint of Simon & Schuster Children's Publishing Division from SEARCHES IN THE AMERICAN DESERT by Sheila Cowing. Copyright © 1989 Sheila Cowing. "The Island of Bulls" from Lost Cities by Roy A. Gallant. Copyright © 1985 by

Roy A. Gallant. Used with permission of the publisher Franklin Watts, Inc. "The People on the Beach" from THE SECRETS OF VESUVIUS by Sara Bisel. Copyright © 1990 by Sara C. Bisel and Family and The Madison Press Ltd. Reprinted by permission of Scholastic, Inc. HIS MAJESTY, QUEEN HATSHEPSUT, TEXT COPYRIGHT © 1987 BY DOROTHY SHARP CARTER. Used by permission of HarperCollins Publishers. "To the Not Impossible Him" by Edna St. Vincent Millay. From COLLECTED POEMS, HarperCollins. Copyright 1922, 1950 by Edna St. Vincent Millay. All rights reserved. Used by permission of Elizabeth Barnett, literary executor. From THE RIDDLE OF THE ROSETTA STONE, COPYRIGHT © 1990 by JAMES CROSS GIBLIN. ARTWORK © 1990 BY HARPERCOLLINS PUBLISHERS. Used by permission of HarperCollins Publishers. THE SILK ROUTE TEXT COPYRIGHT © 1995 BY JOHN S. MAJOR. ILLUSTRATIONS COPYRIGHT © 1995 BY STEPHEN FIESER. Used by permission of HarperCollins Publishers.

TAKING A STAND
"The Pretty Pennies Picket", from PHILIP HALL LIKES ME, I RECKON MAYBE by Bette Greene, copyright © 1974 by Bette Greene. Used by permission of Dial Books for Young Readers, an imprint of Penguin Putnam Books for Young Readers, a division of Penguin Punam Inc. "Class Discussion" from SCHOOL SPIRIT by Johanna Hurwitz. TEXT COPYRIGHT © 1994 by JOHANNA HURWITZ. Used by permission of HarperCollins Publishers. "The Grimke Sisters" reprinted with the permission of Atheneum Books for Young Readers, an imprint of Simon & Schuster Children's Publishing Division from GREAT LIVES: HUMAN RIGHTS by William Jay Jacobs. Copyright © 1990 William Jay Jacobs. "I Have a Dream" reprinted by arrangement with The Heirs to the Estate of Martin Luther King, Jr., c/o Writers House, Inc. as agent for the proprietor. Copyright 1968 by Martin Luther King, Jr., copyright renewed 1991 by Coretta Scott King. "Martin Luther King, Jr." by Gwendolyn Brooks (from Black Out Loud, edited by Arnold Adoff,

www.sra4kids.com

SRA/McGraw-Hill
A Division of The McGraw-Hill Companies

Send all inquiries to:
SRA/McGraw-Hill
8787 Orion Place
Columbus, Ohio 43240-4027

Printed in the United States of America.

ISBN 0-07-569250-3

5 6 7 8 9 RRW 05 04 03

— Program Authors —

Marilyn Jager Adams, Ph.D.
BBN Technologies

Carl Bereiter, Ph.D.
University of Toronto

Joe Campione, Ph.D.
University of California at Berkeley

Iva Carruthers, Ph.D.
Northeastern Illinois University

Jan Hirshberg, Ed.D.
Reading Specialist

Anne McKeough, Ph.D.
University of Calgary

Michael Pressley, Ph.D.
University of Notre Dame

Marsha Roit, Ph.D.
National Reading Consultant

Marlene Scardamalia, Ph.D.
University of Toronto

Gerald H. Treadway, Jr., Ed.D.
San Diego State University

Table of Contents
Perseverance

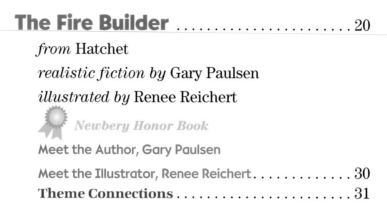

Table of Contents

Ancient Civilizations

Table of Contents
Taking a Stand

UNIT 4

Table of Contents

Beyond the Notes

UNIT 5

Table of Contents

Ecology

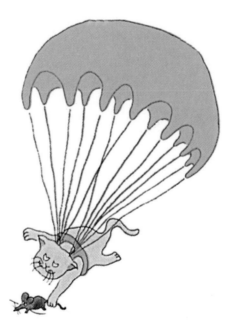

UNIT 6

Table of Contents
A Question of Value 568

Have you ever tried to learn something really, really hard for you? How long did it take? Did you keep trying until you got it? How important is perseverance? What can the ability to keep trying do for our lives?

Focus Questions How will Brian deal with the physical and emotional challenges of being alone in the wilderness?
What might you do if you were faced with Brian's situation?

The Fire Builder

from *Hatchet*
by Gary Paulsen
illustrated by Renee Reichert

Three days ago, Brian Robeson, age thirteen, boarded a Cessna 406 airplane to visit his father who lives in the Canadian wilderness. During the flight, the pilot suffered a heart attack and died. Despite Brian's desperate attempts to make radio contact and to land the plane safely, the plane crashed into a lake in the northern Canadian woods. Brian, the only passenger, survived.

Now that he has survived the crash, he must survive the Canadian wilderness. In the past three days, he has been attacked by hordes of vicious mosquitos and flies, has been racked with hunger, and has seen a bear. The only tool he has is the hatchet his mother gave him before he boarded the airplane in New York. So far he has found a rock shelter and has managed to satisfy some of his hunger with berries.

It is the third night of Brian's ordeal and he is sleeping in his shelter.

At first he thought it was a growl. In the still darkness of the shelter in the middle of the night his eyes came open and he was awake and he thought there was a growl. But it was the wind, a medium wind in the pines had made some sound that brought him up, brought him awake. He sat up and was hit with the smell.

It terrified him. The smell was one of rot, some musty rot that made him think only of graves with cobwebs and dust and old death. His nostrils widened and he opened his eyes wider but he could see nothing. It was too dark, too hard dark with clouds covering even the small light from the stars, and he could not see. But the smell was alive, alive and full and in the shelter. He thought of the bear, thought of Bigfoot and every monster he had ever seen in every fright movie he had ever watched, and his heart hammered in his throat.

Then he heard the slithering. A brushing sound, a slithering brushing sound near his feet——and he kicked out as hard as he could, kicked out and threw the hatchet at the sound, a noise coming from his throat. But the hatchet missed, sailed into the wall where it hit the rocks with a shower of sparks, and his leg was instantly torn with pain, as if a hundred needles had been driven into it. "Unnnngh!"

Now he screamed, with the pain and fear, and skittered on his backside up into the corner of the shelter, breathing through his mouth, straining to see, to hear.

The slithering moved again, he thought toward him at first, and terror took him, stopping his breath. He felt he could see a low dark form, a bulk in the darkness, a shadow that lived, but now it moved away, slithering and scraping it moved away and he saw or thought he saw it go out of the door opening.

He lay on his side for a moment, then pulled a rasping breath in and held it, listening for the attacker to return. When it was apparent that the shadow wasn't coming back he felt the calf of his leg, where the pain was centered and spreading to fill the whole leg.

His fingers gingerly touched a group of needles that had been driven through his pants and into the fleshy part of his calf. They were stiff and very sharp on the ends that stuck out, and he knew then what the attacker had been. A porcupine had stumbled into his shelter and when he had kicked it the thing had slapped him with its tail of quills.

He touched each quill carefully. The pain made it seem as if dozens of them had been slammed into his leg, but there were only eight, pinning the cloth against his skin. He leaned back against the wall for a minute. He couldn't leave them in, they had to come out, but just touching them made the pain more intense.

So fast, he thought. So fast things change. When he'd gone to sleep he had satisfaction and in just a moment it was all different. He grasped one of the quills, held his breath, and jerked. It sent pain signals to his brain in tight waves, but he grabbed another, pulled it, then another quill. When he had pulled four of them he stopped for a moment. The pain had gone from being a pointed injury pain to spreading in a hot smear up his leg and it made him catch his breath.

Some of the quills were driven in deeper than others and they tore when they came out. He breathed deeply twice, let half of the breath out, and went back to work. Jerk, pause, jerk——and three more times before he lay back in the darkness, done. The pain filled his leg now, and with it came new waves of self-pity. Sitting alone in the dark, his leg aching, some mosquitos finding him again, he started crying. It was all too much, just too much, and he couldn't take it. Not the way it was.

I can't take it this way, alone with no fire and in the dark, and next time it might be something worse, maybe a bear, and it wouldn't be just quills in the leg, it would be worse. I can't do this, he thought, again and again. I can't. Brian pulled himself up until he was sitting upright back in the corner of the cave. He put his head down on his arms across his knees, with stiffness taking his left leg, and cried until he was cried out.

He did not know how long it took, but later he looked back on this time of crying in the corner of the dark cave and thought of it as when he learned the most important rule of survival, which was that feeling sorry for yourself didn't work. It wasn't just that it was wrong to do, or that it was considered incorrect. It was more than that——it didn't work. When he sat alone in the darkness and cried and was done, was all done with it, nothing had changed. His leg still hurt, it was still dark, he was still alone and the self-pity had accomplished nothing.

At last he slept again, but already his patterns were changing and the sleep was light, a resting doze more than a deep sleep, with small sounds awakening him twice in the rest of the night. In the last doze period before daylight, before he awakened finally with the morning light and the clouds of new mosquitos, he dreamed, of his father at first and then of his friend Terry.

In the initial segment of the dream his father was standing at the side of a living room looking at him and it was clear from his expression that he was trying to tell Brian something. His lips moved but there was no sound, not a whisper. He waved his hands at Brian, made gestures in front of his face as if he were scratching something, and he worked to make a word with his mouth but at first Brian could not see it. Then the lips made an *mmmmm* shape but no sound came. *Mmmmm——maaaa.* Brian could not hear it, could not understand it and he wanted to so badly; it was so important to understand his father, to know what he was saying. He was trying to help, trying so hard, and when Brian couldn't understand he looked cross, the way he did when Brian asked questions more than once, and he faded. Brian's father faded into a fog place Brian could not see and the dream was almost over, or seemed to be, when Terry came.

He was not gesturing to Brian but was sitting in the park at a bench looking at a barbecue pit and for a time nothing happened. Then he got up and poured some charcoal from a bag into the cooker, then some starter fluid, and he took a flick type of lighter and lit the fluid. When it was burning and the charcoal was at last getting hot he turned, noticing Brian for the first time in the dream. He turned and smiled and pointed to the fire as if to say, see, a fire.

But it meant nothing to Brian, except that he wished he had a fire. He saw a grocery sack on the table next to Terry. Brian thought it must contain hot dogs and chips and mustard and he could think only of the food. But Terry shook his head and pointed again to the fire, and twice more he pointed to the fire, made Brian see the flames, and Brian felt his frustration and anger rise and he thought all right, all right, I see the fire but so what? I don't have a fire. I know about fire; I know I need a fire.

I know that.

His eyes opened and there was light in the cave, a gray dim light of morning. He wiped his mouth and tried to move his leg, which had stiffened like wood. There was thirst, and hunger, and he ate some raspberries from the jacket. They had spoiled a bit, seemed softer and mushier, but still had a rich sweetness. He crushed the berries against the roof of his mouth with his tongue and drank the sweet juice as it ran down his throat. A flash of metal caught his eye and he saw his hatchet in the sand where he had thrown it at the porcupine in the dark.

He scootched up, wincing a bit when he bent his stiff leg, and crawled to where the hatchet lay. He picked it up and examined it and saw a chip in the top of the head.

The nick wasn't large, but the hatchet was important to him, was his only tool, and he should not have thrown it. He should keep it in his hand, and make a tool of some kind to help push an animal away. Make a staff, he thought, or a lance, and save the hatchet. Something came then, a thought as he held the hatchet, something about the dream and his father and Terry, but he couldn't pin it down.

"Ahhh . . ." He scrambled out and stood in the morning sun and stretched his back muscles and his sore leg. The hatchet was still in his hand, and as he stretched and raised it over his head it caught the first

rays of the morning sun. The first faint light hit the silver of the hatchet and it flashed a brilliant gold in the light. Like fire. That is it, he thought. What they were trying to tell me.

Fire. The hatchet was the key to it all. When he threw the hatchet at the porcupine in the cave and missed and hit the stone wall it had showered sparks, a golden shower of sparks in the dark, as golden with fire as the sun was now.

The hatchet was the answer. That's what his father and Terry had been trying to tell him. Somehow he could get fire from the hatchet. The sparks would make fire.

Brian went back into the shelter and studied the wall. It was some form of chalky granite, or a sandstone, but imbedded in it were large pieces of a darker stone, a harder and darker stone. It only took him a moment to find where the hatchet had struck. The steel had nicked into the edge of one of the darker stone pieces. Brian turned the head backward so he would strike with the flat rear of the hatchet and hit the black rock gently. Too gently, and nothing happened. He struck harder, a glancing blow, and two or three weak sparks skipped off the rock and died immediately.

He swung harder, held the hatchet so it would hit a longer, sliding blow, and the black rock exploded in fire. Sparks flew so heavily that several of them skittered and jumped on the sand beneath the rock and he smiled and struck again and again.

There could be fire here, he thought. I will have a fire here, he thought, and struck again——I will have fire from the hatchet.

Brian found it was a long way from sparks to fire.

Clearly there had to be something for the sparks to ignite, some kind of tinder or kindling——but what? He brought some dried grass in, tapped sparks into it and watched them die. He tried small twigs, breaking them into little pieces, but that was worse than the grass. Then he tried a combination of the two, grass and twigs.

Nothing. He had no trouble getting sparks, but the tiny bits of hot stone or metal——he couldn't tell which they were——just sputtered and died.

He settled back on his haunches in exasperation, looking at the pitiful clump of grass and twigs.

He needed something finer, something soft and fine and fluffy to catch the bits of fire.

Shredded paper would be nice, but he had no paper.

"So close," he said aloud, "so close . . ."

He put the hatchet back in his belt and went out of the shelter, limping on his sore leg. There had to be something, had to be. Man had made fire. There had been fire for thousands, millions of years. There had to be a way. He dug in his pockets and found a twenty-dollar bill in his wallet. Paper. Worthless paper out here. But if he could get a fire going . . .

He ripped the twenty into tiny pieces, made a pile of pieces, and hit sparks into them. Nothing happened. They just wouldn't take the sparks. But there had to be a way——some way to do it.

Not twenty feet to his right, leaning out over the water were birches and he stood looking at them for a full half-minute before they registered on his mind. They were a beautiful white with bark like clean, slightly speckled paper.

Paper.

He moved to the trees. Where the bark was peeling from the trunks it lifted in tiny tendrils, almost fluffs. Brian plucked some of them loose, rolled them in his fingers. They seemed flammable, dry and nearly powdery. He pulled and twisted bits off the trees, packing them in one hand while he picked them with the other, picking and gathering until he had a wad close to the size of a baseball.

Then he went back into the shelter and arranged the ball of birchbark peelings at the base of the black rock. As an afterthought he threw in the remains of the twenty-dollar bill. He struck and a stream of sparks fell into the bark and quickly died. But this time one spark fell on one small hair of dry bark——almost a thread of bark——and seemed to glow a bit brighter before it died.

The material had to be finer. There had to be a soft and incredibly fine nest for the sparks.

I must make a home for the sparks, he thought. A perfect home or they won't stay, they won't make fire.

He started ripping the bark, using his fingernails at first, and when that didn't work he used the sharp edge of the hatchet, cutting the bark in thin slivers, hairs so fine they were almost not there. It was painstaking work, slow work, and he stayed with it for over two hours. Twice he stopped for a handful of berries and once to go to the lake for a drink. Then back to work, the sun on his back, until at last he had a ball of fluff as big as a grapefruit——dry birchbark fluff.

He positioned his spark nest——as he thought of it——at the base of the rock, used his thumb to make a small depression in the middle, and slammed the back of the hatchet down across the black rock. A cloud of sparks rained down, most of them missing the nest, but some, perhaps thirty or so, hit in the depression and of those six or seven found fuel and grew, smoldered and caused the bark to take on the red glow.

Then they went out.

Close——he was close. He repositioned the nest, made a new and smaller dent with his thumb, and struck again.

More sparks, a slight glow, then nothing.

It's me, he thought. I'm doing something wrong. I do not know this——a cave dweller would have had a fire by now, a Cro-Magnon man would have a fire by now——but I don't know this. I don't know how to make a fire.

Maybe not enough sparks. He settled the nest in place once more and hit the rock with a series of blows, as fast as he could. The sparks poured like a golden waterfall. At first they seemed to take, there were several, many sparks that found life and took briefly, but they all died.

Starved.

He leaned back. They are like me. They are starving. It wasn't quantity, there were plenty of sparks, but they needed more.

I would kill, he thought suddenly, for a book of matches. Just one book. Just one match. I would kill.

What makes fire? He thought back to school. To all those science classes. Had he ever learned what made a fire? Did a teacher ever stand up there and say, "This is what makes a fire . . ."

He shook his head, tried to focus his thoughts. What did it take? You have to have fuel, he thought——and he had that. The bark was fuel. Oxygen——there had to be air.

He needed to add air. He had to fan on it, blow on it.

He made the nest ready again, held the hatchet backward, tensed, and struck four quick blows. Sparks came down and he leaned forward as fast as he could and blew.

Too hard. There was a bright, almost intense glow, then it was gone. He had blown it out.

Another set of strikes, more sparks. He leaned and blew, but gently this time, holding back and aiming the stream of air from his mouth to hit the brightest spot. Five or six sparks had fallen in a tight mass of bark hair and Brian centered his efforts there.

The sparks grew with his gentle breath. The red glow moved from the sparks themselves into the bark, moved and grew and became worms, glowing red worms that crawled up the bark hairs and caught other threads of bark and grew until there was a pocket of red as big as a quarter, a glowing red coal of heat.

And when he ran out of breath and paused to inhale, the red ball suddenly burst into flame.

"Fire!" He yelled. "I've got fire! I've got it, I've got it, I've got it . . ."

But the flames were thick and oily and burning fast, consuming the ball of bark as fast as if it were gasoline. He had to feed the flames, keep them going. Working as fast as he could he carefully placed the dried grass and wood pieces he had tried at first on top of the bark and was gratified to see them take.

But they would go fast. He needed more, and more. He could not let the flames go out.

He ran from the shelter to the pines and started breaking off the low, dead small limbs. These he threw in the shelter, went back for more, threw those in, and squatted to break and feed the hungry flames. When the small wood was going well he went out and found larger wood and did not relax until that was going. Then he leaned back against the wood brace of his door opening and smiled.

I have a friend, he thought——I have a friend now. A hungry friend, but a good one. I have a friend named fire.

"Hello, fire . . ."

The curve of the rock back made an almost perfect drawing flue that carried the smoke up through the cracks of the roof but held the heat. If he kept the fire small it would be perfect and would keep anything like the porcupine from coming through the door again.

A friend and a guard, he thought.

So much from a little spark. A friend and a guard from a tiny spark.

The Fire Builder

Meet the Author

Gary Paulsen was an "Army brat," so his family moved around a lot. Nature became an escape for Paulsen. He is very proud to have finished the Iditarod, a 1,200-mile dog-sled race in Alaska, twice. Says Paulsen, "The overriding concern among kids is honesty." He thinks that to protect kids from the truth is unfair to them. For this reason, his stories are often about tough reality and tough children.

Meet the Illustrator

Renee Reichert received her degree in art from the University of Massachusetts at Amherst. Her work has been displayed at the Society of Illustrators 41st Annual Exhibition, and the Vincent Louis Galleries in Greenwich Village. It has also been included in numerous other exhibitions on Long Island. Ms. Reichert says she is "inspired by both the beautiful and the absurd." She shares her home on Long Island with her husband, two children, and their pets.

Theme Connections

Within the Selection

Writer's Notebook Record your answers to the questions below in the Response Journal section of your Writer's Notebook. In small groups, report the ideas you wrote. Discuss your ideas with the rest of your group. Then choose a person to report your group's answers to the class.

- What were the conditions Brian faced inside the cave?
- What actions did Brian take that show his determination to survive?
- Perseverance often requires being resourceful. How did Brian's resourcefulness help him build his fire?

Across Selections

- Now that you know what this theme is about, look ahead in the unit and start thinking, How many ways are there to persevere? Brian persevered both physically and mentally, but are some kinds of perseverance more physical or more mental than others?

Beyond the Selection

- Think of a time when you had to be resourceful. Maybe you had to fix something that was broken or use your resources to solve a problem. How did your resourcefulness help you persevere? Get into small groups and share your experiences. Then pick one or two stories from your group and share them with the class.

31

Amaroq, the Wolf

from *Julie of the Wolves*
by Jean Craighead George
illustrated by Anthony Carnabuci

Miyax pushed back the hood of her sealskin parka and looked at the Arctic sun. It was a yellow disc in a lime-green sky, the colors of six o'clock in the evening and the time when the wolves awoke. Quietly she put down her cooking pot and crept to the top of a dome-shaped frost heave, one of the many earth buckles that rise and fall in the crackling cold of the Arctic winter. Lying on her stomach, she looked across a vast lawn of grass and moss and focused her attention on the wolves she had come upon two sleeps ago. They were wagging their tails as they awoke and saw each other.

Her hands trembled and her heartbeat quickened, for she was frightened, not so much of the wolves, who were shy and many harpoon-shots away, but because of her desperate predicament. Miyax was lost. She had been lost without food for many sleeps on the North Slope of Alaska. The barren slope stretches for three hundred miles from the Brooks Range to the Arctic Ocean, and for more than eight hundred miles from the Chukchi to the Beaufort Sea. No roads cross it; ponds and lakes freckle its immensity. Winds scream across it, and the view in every direction is exactly the same. Somewhere in this cosmos was Miyax; and the very life in her body, its spark and warmth, depended upon these wolves for survival. And she was not so sure they would help.

Miyax stared hard at the regal black wolf, hoping to catch his eye. She must somehow tell him that she was starving and ask him for food. This could be done she knew, for her father, an Eskimo hunter, had done so. One year he had camped near a wolf den while on a hunt. When a month had passed and her father had seen no game, he told the leader of the wolves that he was hungry and needed food. The next night the wolf called him from far away and her father went to him and found a freshly killed caribou. Unfortunately, Miyax's father never explained to her how he had told the wolf of his needs. And not long afterward he paddled his kayak into the Bering Sea to hunt for seal, and he never returned.

She had been watching the wolves for two days, trying to discern which of their sounds and movements expressed goodwill and friendship. Most animals had such signals. The little Arctic ground squirrels flicked their tails sideways to notify others of their kind that they were friendly. By imitating this signal with her forefinger, Miyax had lured many a squirrel to

her hand. If she could discover such a gesture for the wolves she would be able to make friends with them and share their food, like a bird or a fox.

Propped on her elbows with her chin in her fists, she stared at the black wolf, trying to catch his eye. She had chosen him because he was much larger than the others, and because he walked like her father, Kapugen, with his head high and his chest out. The black wolf also possessed wisdom, she had observed. The pack looked to him when the wind carried strange scents or the birds cried nervously. If he was alarmed, they were alarmed. If he was calm, they were calm.

Long minutes passed, and the black wolf did not look at her. He had ignored her since she first came upon them, two sleeps ago. True, she moved slowly and quietly, so as not to alarm him; yet she did wish he would see the kindness in her eyes. Many animals could tell the difference between hostile hunters and friendly people by merely looking at them. But the big black wolf would not even glance her way.

A bird stretched in the grass. The wolf looked at it. A flower twisted in the wind. He glanced at that. Then the breeze rippled the wolverine ruff on Miyax's parka and it glistened in the light. He did not look at that. She waited. Patience with the ways of nature had been instilled in her by her father. And so she knew better than to move or shout. Yet she must get food or die. Her hands shook slightly and she swallowed hard to keep calm.

Miyax was a classic Eskimo beauty, small of bone and delicately wired with strong muscles. Her face was pearl-round and her nose was flat. Her black eyes, which slanted gracefully, were moist and sparkling. Like the beautifully formed polar bears and foxes of the north, she was slightly short-limbed. The frigid environment of the Arctic has sculptured life into compact shapes. Unlike the long-limbed, long-bodied animals of the south that are cooled by dispensing heat on extended surfaces, all live things in the Arctic tend toward compactness, to conserve heat.

The length of her limbs and the beauty of her face were of no use to Miyax as she lay on the lichen-speckled frost heave in the midst of the bleak tundra. Her stomach ached and the royal black wolf was carefully ignoring her.

"*Amaroq, ilaya,* wolf, my friend," she finally called. "Look at me. Look at me."

She spoke half in Eskimo and half in English, as if the instincts of her father and the science of the *gussaks,* the white-faced, might evoke some magical combination that would help her get her message through to the wolf.

Amaroq glanced at his paw and slowly turned his head her way without lifting his eyes. He licked his shoulder. A few matted hairs sprang apart and twinkled individually. Then his eyes sped to each of the three adult wolves that made up his pack and finally to the five pups who were sleeping in a fuzzy mass near the den entrance. The great wolf's eyes softened at the sight of the little wolves, then quickly hardened into brittle yellow jewels as he scanned the flat tundra.

Not a tree grew anywhere to break the monotony of the gold-green plain, for the soils of the tundra are permanently frozen. Only moss, grass, lichens, and a few hardy flowers take root in the thin upper layer that thaws briefly in summer. Nor do many

species of animals live in this rigorous land, but those creatures that do dwell here exist in bountiful numbers. Amaroq watched a large cloud of Lapland longspurs wheel up into the sky, then alight in the grasses. Swarms of crane flies, one of the few insects that can survive the cold, darkened the tips of the mosses. Birds wheeled, turned, and called. Thousands sprang up from the ground like leaves in a wind.

The wolf's ears cupped forward and tuned in on some distant message from the tundra. Miyax tensed and listened, too. Did he hear some brewing storm, some approaching enemy? Apparently not. His ears relaxed and he rolled to his side. She sighed, glanced at the vaulting sky, and was painfully aware of her predicament.

Here she was, watching wolves——she, Miyax, daughter of Kapugen, adopted child of Martha, citizen of the United States, pupil at the Bureau of Indian Affairs School in Barrow, Alaska, and thirteen-year-old wife of the boy Daniel. She shivered at the thought of Daniel, for it was he who had driven her to this fate. She had run away from him exactly seven sleeps ago, and because of this she had one more title by gussak standards—— the child divorcée.

The wolf rolled to his belly.

"Amaroq," she whispered. "I am lost and the sun will not set for a month. There is no North Star to guide me."

Amaroq did not stir.

"And there are no berry bushes here to bend under the polar wind and point to the south. Nor are there any birds I can follow." She looked up. "Here the birds are buntings and longspurs. They do not fly to the sea twice a day like the puffins and sandpipers that my father followed."

The wolf groomed his chest with his tongue.

"I never dreamed I could get lost, Amaroq," she went on, talking out loud to ease her fear. "At home on Nunivak Island where I was born, the plants and birds pointed the way for wanderers. I thought they did so everywhere . . . and so, great black Amaroq, I'm without a compass."

It had been a frightening moment when two days ago she realized that the tundra was an ocean of grass on which she was circling around and around. Now as that fear overcame her again she closed her eyes. When she opened them her heart skipped excitedly. Amaroq was looking at her!

"*Ee-lie*," she called and scrambled to her feet. The wolf arched his neck and narrowed his eyes. He pressed his ears forward. She waved. He drew back his lips and showed his teeth. Frightened by what seemed a snarl, she lay down again. When she was flat on her stomach, Amaroq flattened his ears and wagged his tail once. Then he tossed his head and looked away.

Discouraged, she wriggled backward down the frost heave and arrived at her camp feet first. The heave was between herself and the wolf pack and so she relaxed, stood up, and took stock of her home. It was a simple affair, for she had not been able to carry much when she ran away; she took just those things she would need for the journey——a backpack, food for a week or so, needles to mend clothes, matches, her sleeping skin, and ground cloth to go under it, two knives, and a pot.

She had intended to walk to Point Hope. There she would meet the *North Star*, the ship that brings supplies from the States to the towns on the Arctic Ocean in August when the ice pack breaks up. The ship could always use dishwashers or laundresses, she had heard, and so she would work her way to San Francisco where Amy, her pen pal, lived. At the end of every letter Amy always wrote: "When are you coming to San Francisco?" Seven days ago she had been on her way——on her way to the glittering, white, postcard city that sat on a hill among trees, those enormous plants she had never seen. She had been on her way to see the television and carpeting in Amy's school, the glass buildings, traffic lights, and stores full of fruits; on her way to the harbor that never froze and the Golden Gate Bridge. But primarily she was on her way to be rid of Daniel, her terrifying husband.

She kicked the sod at the thought of her marriage; then shaking her head to forget, she surveyed her camp. It was nice. Upon discovering the wolves, she had settled down to live near them in the hope of sharing their food, until the sun set and the stars came out to guide her. She had built a house of sod, like the summer homes of the old Eskimos. Each brick had been cut with her *ulo*, the half-moon shaped woman's knife, so versatile it can trim a baby's hair, slice a tough bear, or chip an iceberg.

Her house was not well built for she had never made one before, but it was cozy inside. She had windproofed it by sealing the sod bricks with mud from the pond at her door, and she had made it beautiful by spreading her caribou ground cloth on the floor. On this she had placed her sleeping skin, a moosehide bag lined with soft white rabbit skins. Next to her bed she had built a low table of sod on which to put her clothes when she slept. To decorate the house she had made three flowers of bird feathers and stuck them in the top of the table. Then she had built a fireplace outdoors and placed her pot beside it. The pot was empty, for she had not found even a lemming to eat.

Last winter, when she had walked to school in Barrow, these mice-like rodents were so numerous they ran out from under her feet wherever she stepped. There were thousands and thousands of them until December, when they suddenly vanished. Her teacher said that the lemmings had a chemical similar to antifreeze in their blood, that kept them active all winter when other little mammals were hibernating. "They eat grass and multiply all winter," Mrs. Franklin had said in her singsong voice. "When there are too many, they grow nervous at the sight of each other. Somehow this shoots too much antifreeze into their bloodstreams and it begins to poison them. They become restless, then crazy. They run in a frenzy until they die."

Of this phenomenon Miyax's father had simply said, "The hour of the lemming is over for four years."

Unfortunately for Miyax, the hour of the animals that prey on the lemmings was also over. The white fox, the snowy owl, the weasel, the jaeger, and the siskin had virtually disappeared. They had no food to eat and bore few or no young. Those that lived preyed on each other. With the passing of the lemmings, however, the grasses had grown high again and the hour of the caribou was upon the land. Healthy fat caribou cows gave birth to many calves. The caribou population increased, and this in turn increased the number of wolves who prey on the caribou. The abundance of the big deer of the north did Miyax no good, for she had not brought a gun on her trip. It had never occurred to her that she would not reach Point Hope before her food ran out.

A dull pain seized her stomach. She pulled blades of grass from their sheaths and ate the sweet ends. They were not very satisfying, so she picked a handful of caribou moss, a lichen. If the deer could survive in winter on this food, why not she? She munched, decided the plant might taste better if cooked, and went to the pond for water.

As she dipped her pot in, she thought about Amaroq. Why had he bared his teeth at her? Because she was young and he knew she couldn't hurt him? No, she said to herself, it was because he was speaking to her! He had told her to lie down. She had even understood and obeyed him. He had talked to her not with his voice, but with his ears, eyes, and lips; and he had even commended her with a wag of his tail.

She dropped her pot, scrambled up the frost heave and stretched out on her stomach.

"Amaroq," she called softly, "I understand what you said. Can you understand me? I'm hungry——very, very hungry. Please bring me some meat."

The great wolf did not look her way and she began to doubt her reasoning. After all, flattened ears and a tail-wag were scarcely a conversation. She dropped her forehead against the lichens and rethought what had gone between them.

"Then why did I lie down?" she asked, lifting her head and looking at Amaroq. "Why did I?" she called to the yawning wolves. Not one turned her way.

Amaroq got to his feet, and as he slowly arose he seemed to fill the sky and blot out the sun. He was enormous. He could swallow her without even chewing.

"But he won't," she reminded herself. "Wolves do not eat people. That's gussak talk. Kapugen said wolves are gentle brothers."

The black puppy was looking at her and wagging his tail. Hopefully, Miyax held out a pleading hand to him. His tail wagged harder. The mother rushed to him and stood above him sternly. When he licked her cheek apologetically, she pulled back her lips from her fine white teeth. They flashed as she smiled and forgave her cub.

"But don't let it happen again," said Miyax sarcastically, mimicking her own elders. The mother walked toward Amaroq.

"I should call you Martha after my stepmother," Miyax whispered. "But you're much too beautiful. I shall call you Silver instead."

Silver moved in a halo of light, for the sun sparkled on the guard hairs that grew out over the dense underfur and she seemed to glow.

The reprimanded pup snapped at a crane fly and shook himself. Bits of lichen and grass spun off his fur. He reeled unsteadily, took a wider stance, and looked down at his sleeping sister. With a yap he jumped on her and rolled her to her feet. She whined. He barked and picked up a bone. When he was sure she was watching, he ran down the slope with it. The sister tagged after him. He stopped and she grabbed the bone, too. She pulled; he pulled; then he pulled and she yanked.

Miyax could not help laughing. The puppies played with bones like Eskimo children played with leather ropes.

"I understand *that*," she said to the pups. "That's tug-o-war. Now how do you say, 'I'm hungry'?"

Amaroq was pacing restlessly along the crest of the frost heave as if something were about to happen. His eyes shot to Silver, then to the gray wolf Miyax had named Nails. These glances seemed to be a summons, for Silver and Nails glided to him, spanked the ground with their forepaws, and bit him gently under the chin. He wagged his tail furiously and took Silver's slender nose in his mouth. She crouched before him, licked his cheek, and lovingly bit his lower jaw. Amaroq's tail flashed high as her mouthing charged him with vitality. He nosed her affectionately. Unlike the fox who met his mate only in the breeding season, Amaroq lived with his mate all year.

Next, Nails took Amaroq's jaw in his mouth and the leader bit the top of his nose. A third adult, a small male, came slinking up. He got down on his belly before Amaroq, rolled trembling to his back, and wriggled.

"Hello, Jello," Miyax whispered, for he reminded her of the quivering gussak dessert her mother-in-law made.

She had seen the wolves mouth Amaroq's chin twice before and so she concluded that it was a ceremony, a sort of "Hail to the Chief." He must indeed be their leader for he was clearly the wealthy wolf; that is, wealthy as she had known the meaning of the word on Nunivak Island. There the old Eskimo hunters she

had known in her childhood thought the riches of life were intelligence, fearlessness, and love. A man with these gifts was rich and was a great spirit who was admired in the same way that the gussaks admired a man with money and goods.

The three adults paid tribute to Amaroq until he was almost smothered with love; then he bayed a wild note that sounded like the wind on the frozen sea. With that the others sat around him, the puppies scattered between them. Jello hunched forward and Silver shot a fierce glance at him. Intimidated, Jello pulled his ears together and back. He drew himself down until he looked smaller than ever.

Amaroq wailed again, stretching his neck until his head was high above the others. They gazed at him affectionately and it was plain to see that he was their great spirit, a royal leader who held his group together with love and wisdom.

Any fear Miyax had of the wolves was dispelled by their affection for each other. They were friendly animals and so devoted to Amaroq that she needed only to be accepted by him to be accepted by all. She even knew how to achieve this—bite him under the chin. But how was she going to do that?

She studied the pups hoping they had a simpler way of expressing their love for him. The black puppy approached the leader, sat, then lay down and wagged his tail vigorously.

He gazed up at Amaroq in pure adoration, and the royal eyes softened.

Well, that's what I'm doing! Miyax thought. She called to Amaroq. "I'm lying down gazing at you, too, but you don't look at *me* that way!"

When all the puppies were wagging his praises, Amaroq yipped, hit a high note, and crooned. As his voice rose and fell, the other adults sang out and the puppies yipped and bounced.

The song ended abruptly. Amaroq arose and trotted swiftly down the slope. Nails followed, and behind him ran Silver, then Jello. But Jello did not run far. Silver turned and looked him straight in the eye. She pressed her ears forward aggressively and lifted her tail. With that, Jello went back to the puppies and the three sped away like dark birds.

Miyax hunched forward on her elbows, the better to see and learn. She now knew how to be a good puppy, pay tribute to the leader, and even to be a leader by biting others on the top of the nose. She also knew how to tell Jello to baby-sit. If only she had big ears and a tail, she could lecture and talk to them all.

Flapping her hands on her head for ears, she flattened her fingers to make friends, pulled them together and back to express fear, and shot them forward to display her aggression and dominance. Then she folded her arms and studied the puppies again.

The black one greeted Jello by tackling his feet. Another jumped on his tail, and before he could discipline either, all five were upon him. He rolled and tumbled with them for almost an hour; then he ran down the slope, turned, and stopped. The pursuing pups plowed into him, tumbled, fell, and lay still. During a minute of surprised recovery there was no action. Then the black pup flashed his tail like a semaphore signal and they all jumped on Jello again.

Miyax rolled over and laughed aloud. "That's funny. They're really like kids."

When she looked back, Jello's tongue was hanging from his mouth and his sides were heaving. Four of the puppies had collapsed at his feet and were asleep. Jello flopped down, too, but the black pup still looked around. He was not the least bit tired. Miyax watched him, for there was something special about him.

He ran to the top of the den and barked. The smallest pup, whom Miyax called Sister, lifted her head, saw her favorite brother in action and, struggling to her feet, followed him devotedly. While they romped, Jello took the opportunity to rest behind a clump of sedge, a moisture-loving plant of the tundra. But hardly was he settled before a pup tracked him to his hideout and pounced on him. Jello narrowed his eyes, pressed his ears forward, and showed his teeth.

"I know what you're saying," she called to him. "You're saying, 'lie down.'" The puppy lay down, and Miyax got on all fours and looked for the nearest pup to speak to. It was Sister.

"Ummmm," she whined, and when Sister turned around she narrowed her eyes and showed her white teeth. Obediently, Sister lay down.

"I'm talking wolf! I'm talking wolf!" Miyax clapped, and tossing her head like a pup, crawled in a happy circle. As she was coming back she saw all five puppies sitting in a row watching her, their heads cocked in curiosity. Boldly the black pup came toward her, his fat backside swinging as he trotted to the bottom of her frost heave, and barked.

"You are *very* fearless and *very* smart," she said. "Now I know why you are special. You are wealthy and the leader of the puppies. There is no doubt what you'll grow up to be. So I shall name you after my father Kapugen, and I shall call you Kapu for short."

Kapu wrinkled his brow and turned an ear to tune in more acutely on her voice.

"You don't understand, do you?"

Hardly had she spoken than his tail went up, his mouth opened slightly, and he fairly grinned.

"Ee-lie!" she gasped. "You do understand. And that scares me." She perched on her heels. Jello whined an undulating note and Kapu turned back to the den.

Miyax imitated the call to come home. Kapu looked back over his shoulder in surprise. She giggled. He wagged his tail and jumped on Jello.

She clapped her hands and settled down to watch this language of jumps and tumbles, elated that she was at last breaking the wolf code. After a long time she decided they were not talking but roughhousing, and so she started home. Later she changed her mind. Roughhousing was very important to wolves. It occupied almost the entire night for the pups.

"Ee-lie, okay," she said. "I'll learn to roughhouse. Maybe then you'll accept me and feed me." She pranced, jumped, and whimpered; she growled, snarled, and rolled. But nobody came to roughhouse.

Sliding back to her camp, she heard the grass swish and looked up to see Amaroq and his hunters sweep around her frost heave and stop about five feet away. She could smell the sweet scent of their fur.

The hairs on her neck rose and her eyes widened. Amaroq's ears went forward aggressively and she remembered that wide eyes meant fear to him. It was not good to show him she was afraid. Animals attacked the fearful. She tried to narrow them, but remembered that was not right either. Narrowed eyes were mean. In desperation she recalled that Kapu had moved forward when challenged. She pranced right up to Amaroq. Her heart beat furiously as she grunt-whined the sound of the puppy

46

begging adoringly for attention. Then she got down on her belly and gazed at him with fondness.

The great wolf backed up and avoided her eyes. She had said something wrong! Perhaps even offended him. Some slight gesture that meant nothing to her had apparently meant something to the wolf. His ears shot forward angrily and it seemed all was lost. She wanted to get up and run, but she gathered her courage and pranced closer to him. Swiftly she patted him under the chin.

The signal went off. It sped through his body and triggered emotions of love. Amaroq's ears flattened and his tail wagged in friendship. He could not react in any other way to the chin pat, for the roots of this signal lay deep in wolf history. It was inherited from generations and generations of leaders before him. As his eyes softened, the sweet odor of ambrosia arose from the gland on the top of his tail and she was drenched lightly in wolf scent. Miyax was one of the pack.

Amaroq, the Wolf

Meet the Author

Jean Craighead George's family owned a beautiful Pennsylvania farm where George and her twin brothers spent their summers swimming and fishing in its ponds. She and her brothers used to go into the woods with their father, who was a forester. He taught them how to catch catfish and find plants and roots that were good to eat. Many of her books are about kids who use their knowledge of nature and wildlife to survive on their own in the wilds.

Meet the Illustrator

Anthony Carnabuci was always encouraged by his family to create. They used to visit the museum every Sunday when he was young. His mother painted, and he remembers a still life she had done that looked incredibly real. He says, "I thought that I could reach out and touch the objects in the painting." Carnabuci graduated from the Rhode Island School of Design with a degree in art, and his work has been recognized by the Society of Illustrators and *Parents* magazine. He believes that "art is really communication" and he hopes his work is able to accomplish this.

Theme Connections

Within the Selection

Record your answers to the questions below in the Response Journal section of your Writer's Notebook. In small groups, report the ideas you wrote. Discuss your ideas with the rest of your group. Then choose a person to report your group's answers to the class.

- How had Miyax tried to prepare for her journey?
- At what point did Miyax realize she could understand the wolves' signals?
- How did understanding their signals help her win over Amaroq?

Across Selections

- What are some similarities and differences between Miyax's predicament and Brian's predicament in "The Fire Builder"?
- Do Brian and Miyax go about solving their problems the same way?

Beyond the Selection

- Think about how "Amaroq, the Wolf" adds to what you know about perseverance.
- Add items to the Concept/Question Board about perseverance.

On Top of the World

The Conquest of Mount Everest
by Mary Ann Fraser

It was May 28th, 1953. With feelings of loneliness and excitement, Edmund Hillary and Tenzing Norgay watched the last of their companions head down the mountain. It had taken eight months, an army of men, and three tons of supplies to get them to where they now stood, 1,100 feet from the summit. In the morning they hoped to be the first ever to climb the highest mountain in the world——Mount Everest.

As their companions faded from view, Hillary and Tenzing began preparations for the night. Already they had climbed many miles from Katmandu, the expedition's starting point. But over the next twenty-four hours would come their greatest obstacles.

Straddling the border between Tibet and Nepal, Everest rises 29,028 feet out of the world's youngest——and highest——mountain range, the Himalayas. Near the top of the world, the air has only one third the oxygen found at sea level. Breathing the thin air, climbers can suffer physically and mentally. But the weight of oxygen tanks and frames also makes climbing more difficult.

Hillary counted their remaining oxygen canisters. They had fewer than they had hoped for. But the men knew that if they were ever to make it to the top, this was their best chance. In winter, the fierce winds called monsoons that scoured Everest's sides would defeat the best of climbers. Summer monsoons brought heavy snows that increased the risk of an avalanche or a fatal slip. Only during a few days in late spring and early autumn was Everest climbable at all. But even in May, the weather could change at any moment and crush all hopes of success.

For four hours Hillary and Tenzing scraped the frozen ground to make a platform and pitch their cotton-and-nylon tent. At five miles above sea level, it was the highest anyone had ever camped.

Both men were experienced mountaineers. Edmund Hillary, a beekeeper from New Zealand, had proven his mountain-climbing skills in the Himalayas in 1951 and 1952. This was his first attempt at Mount Everest.

Tenzing Norgay, a Sherpa born in Nepal, had spent most of his life in Everest's shadow. The Sherpas are a people who came to eastern Nepal from Tibet. They call the mountain Chomolungma, which means "Mother Goddess of the Earth." Because they are adapted to the high altitude and extreme weather of their homeland, Sherpas are born mountaineers.

But no one had seen more of the world's highest mountain than Tenzing. He had first explored Everest as a porter in 1935, and had been a member of five more expeditions. For this reason Colonel John Hunt, head of the 1953 British attempt, had asked Tenzing to be his guide and *sirdar,* or leader of the Sherpas hired to assist the expedition.

After dinner of canned apricots, dates, and sardines, Hillary and Tenzing drifted into restless sleep.

All night long icy gusts of wind tried to snatch their tent from its ledge. But the gods of Chomolungma were with them. By four in the morning, when they crawled from their sleeping bags, it was calm. The thermometer read -27 degrees Fahrenheit.

The men drank melted snow mixed with lemon juice and sugar, and ate their last can of sardines on biscuits. Then Hillary thawed his frozen boots over the kerosene stove.

Peering from their tent, they looked down the side of the mountain. Below them lay the rest of the world. Tenzing pointed beyond the Khumbu Glacier to the old monastery of Thyangboche. They were comforted knowing the monastery's Buddhist monks were praying for their safe return.

At 6:30 A.M. Tenzing and Hillary strapped on their thirty-pound oxygen packs. They knew that without them they could die. They would have only four and a half hours to reach the top and return before their oxygen ran out.

Linked by a nylon rope, they began their final ascent. Each wore a down suit protected by another windproof layer of clothing, three pairs of gloves, a hat, and snow goggles. To help them climb, they had strapped steel spikes called crampons to the soles of their boots. Each boot had an inner waterproof lining and inch-thick insulation, and weighed over two pounds.

Hillary and Tenzing were not the first to attempt to reach the summit. The first expedition was in 1922, a year after Tibet opened its borders to foreigners. Eight times since then, the monstrous peak had sent the world's best mountaineers back in defeat. It had taken the lives of at least thirteen men. Each time, the effects of extreme cold, altitude, and terrain had won. Only the year before, Tenzing and Swiss mountaineer and guide Raymond Lambert had been just a thousand feet from the summit when fierce winds and cold turned them back.

But on the clear, frosty morning of May 29th, Tenzing and Hillary had the strongest start yet. From the start of the 1953 expedition, all fifty-three members had worked to advance supplies from camp to camp up the mountain. They knew that the higher the final camp was, the more likely the men would reach the summit before their oxygen ran out.

Colonel John Hunt had decided to send Tom Bourdillon, an excellent rock climber, and Charles Evans, an experienced mountaineer, to try for the summit first. On May 23, this First Team left for Camp VIII, at the South Col. In the meantime, the remaining men moved supplies farther up the mountain. If the First Team failed, Tenzing and Hillary would try for the top from an even higher location.

Three days later Bourdillon and Evans stumbled back to the South Col, where the others were waiting. They had run out of oxygen, energy, and time three hundred feet from the top of Everest.

The next day the Second Team was moved into position, at Camp IX. It was now up to them alone to climb the last 1,100 feet.

Steadily they kicked steps in the snow, breathing from the oxygen canisters secured to their backs. The strain of each movement prevented them from speaking, yet they worked together as a team.

About four hundred feet from the South Peak's face, the men came to an abrupt stop. Which way should they go? Bourdillon and Evans had taken the ridge, but its loose snow made it dangerous. Hillary and Tenzing decided to take the face route. Cautiously they chipped steps straight up the mountainside, knowing that if they zigzagged, the undercut snow could avalanche.

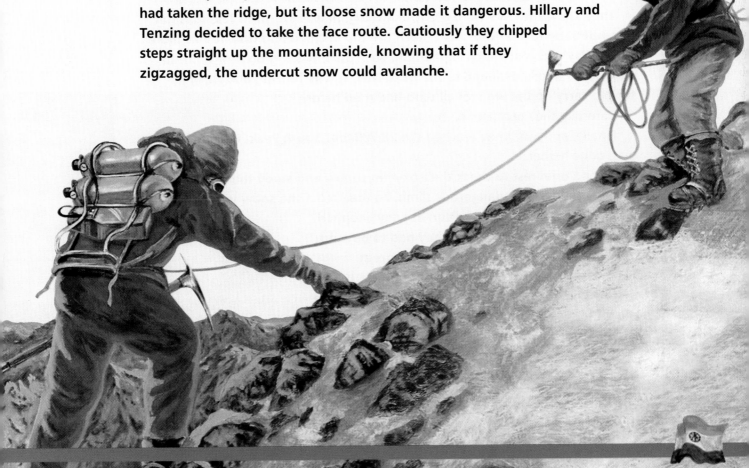

They were halfway up Everest's treacherous Southeast Ridge when suddenly the powdery snow broke away. Hillary slid several feet before he could stop his fall with his ice ax.

"I don't like this," he gasped. "Shall we go on?"

Tenzing replied, "Just as you wish."

They knew the risks were great, but the goal was worth it. This was not a competition to see who could reach the top of the world first. It was more like a relay race, with each expedition, each man, passing on new gains in experience and knowledge to the next. Now it was Tenzing and Hillary's turn to carry on the work of all who had tried before.

Carefully they pushed on.

Finally, at 9 A.M., they reached the 28,700-foot South Peak. No one had ever gone higher.

After a brief rest to check their oxygen supply and study the ridge ahead, they continued their dangerous climb. To their relief the snow was firm.

Their axes rang out in unison as they chopped steps up the razor-like ridge. They had to be more careful than ever now. To their right, great overhanging cornices of snow stuck out like twisted fingers above a 10,000-foot drop. To their left were plunging cliffs of windswept rock.

They could see the tents of Camp IV more than a mile below. Like a giant bird Hillary flapped his arms, but he knew he was too far away for the men at the camp to see him.

As they continued on, step by icy step, Tenzing began fumbling with his oxygen equipment. Hillary stopped, and discovered that ice had completely blocked the tube through which Tenzing was exhaling. Quickly Hillary cleared it so his partner could get fresh oxygen again. He then checked his own equipment and cleaned out the ice from the exhaust tubes.

But with one danger averted, they found themselves staring at an even greater barrier: A giant rock, forty feet high, blocked the ridge. There seemed to be no way over it and no way around it. Had Everest won again?

Then they noticed a small crack that rose like a chimney between the rock and cornice of ice. Hillary wedged himself into the chimney. Pushing with each part of his body and kicking with his boots, he slowly wriggled his way upward. At any moment the cornice could split away. His only safety lay in the rope Tenzing had wrapped around his ax and driven into the snow.

At last Hillary dragged himself over the top of the rock and onto a wide ledge. Then, securing his end of the rope, he motioned for Tenzing to follow.

Hillary heaved with all his might until Tenzing, too, collapsed at the top of the chimney.

At the height of almost twenty Empire State Buildings, any movement was very tiring. It took several minutes for them to catch their breaths.

Ahead, the ridge rolled in a series of seemingly never-ending humps. As the men climbed over one, another always loomed ahead. Their boots felt like lead, and their packs grew heavier with each step. Time was quickly passing, and there was still no sign of the summit. With each bite of the ax, shards of ice and rock were hurled into the air.

It was now 11:30 A.M. Their oxygen supply was dwindling, and in a few minutes they would have to turn back defeated.

Once more Hillary looked ahead, and suddenly realized the ridge didn't rise up, but fell sharply away. With a glimmer of hope the two climbers whacked more steps in the firm snow.

Beyond them lay a dome of ice. It stood like an island surrounded by an ocean of snow-capped peaks. The summit. But was it safe? Could it break away?

Probing with their axes, they cautiously staggered the last few yards. At last they stood on the highest point on earth, 29,028 feet above the sea. From the top of the world, they could see four countries: Tibet to the north, Sikkim to the east, India to the south, and Nepal to the south and west.

The moment was too great for words. Tenzing threw his arms around Hillary and thumped him on the back.

Then Tenzing unwound from his ax a string of flags: one for the United Nations, one for Britain, one for Nepal, and one for India. Hillary turned off his oxygen and removed his mask. Then he pulled out the camera he had kept warm beneath his shirt and took some pictures. These would be proof that they had made it. They were on top of the world!

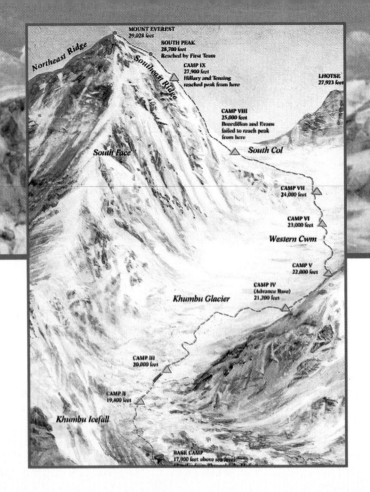

MOUNT EVEREST
29,028 feet

SOUTH PEAK
28,700 feet
Reached by First Team

CAMP IX
27,900 feet
Hillary and Tenzing
reached peak from here

LHOTSE
27,923 feet

CAMP VIII
25,000 feet
Bourdillon and Evans
failed to reach peak
from here

South Face

South Col

Northeast Ridge

Southeast Ridge

CAMP VII
24,000 feet

CAMP VI
23,000 feet

Western Cwm

CAMP V
22,000 feet

CAMP IV
(Advance Base)
21,200 feet

Khumbu Glacier

CAMP III
20,000 feet

CAMP II
19,400 feet

Khumbu Icefall

BASE CAMP
17,900 feet above sea level

A Final Note

Hillary and Tenzing spent only fifteen minutes on Everest's peak because of their limited oxygen supply. But before their return to camp, they left gifts of thanks to the Buddhist gods the Sherpas believe live on Chomolungma. Buried on top of the world are a small blue pencil that belonged to Tenzing's daughter, biscuits, lollipops, a chocolate bar, and a cross from Colonel Hunt.

When Hillary and Tenzing reached Camp VIII, their friends rushed out to greet them with oxygen, hot drinks, and shouts of "Everest has had it!" It was a victory for all the members of the mountaineering party.

But why was this expedition successful when all others had failed? One reason was that climbers from the eleven previous Everest expeditions had willingly shared their experience and knowledge.

Access to Mt. Everest was first allowed in 1921 by the government of Tibet. Two of the most famous early climbers were George Leigh-Mallory and Andrew Irvine, who in 1924 vanished along the Northeast Ridge. No one knows how high they were able to climb before they died. It was Mallory who, when asked why he wanted to climb Mt. Everest, replied, "Because it is there."

Bad weather, avalanches, and lack of oxygen turned back the expeditions that followed. Southern access to the peak was made possible in 1949, when Nepal opened its borders to foreigners. The most helpful of the later expeditions was made by the Swiss. It was on their climb in 1952 that Tenzing and Raymond Lambert came within a thousand feet of the summit.

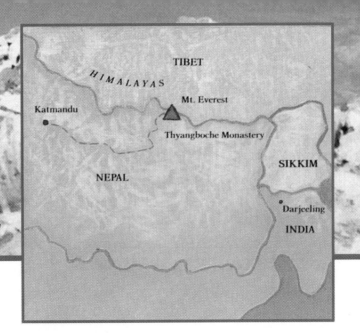

Another reason for Hillary and Tenzing's success was the superior planning by Colonel Hunt, the expedition's leader. When selecting climbers, he looked for men between the ages of twenty-five and forty with experience scaling the Himalayas and the ability to work selflessly with others. Fourteen men were chosen, including Michael Ward, who was to be the doctor. It was his responsibility to help prevent the illnesses that had plagued earlier expeditions. In addition, thirty-eight Sherpas were hired to carry supplies up the mountain.

Colonel Hunt had the men make practice climbs in Wales, the Alps, and the Himalayas. These treks enabled them to come together as a team and test new equipment and rations.

Superior supplies also gave the 1953 expedition an advantage over earlier teams. Improvements included tents made of a new cotton-nylon weave, two new styles of boots designed to prevent frostbite, and sleeping bags with both an inner and outer layer of down.

The use of more efficient and reliable oxygen sets, both closed circuit and open circuit, was the greatest improvement of all. Hillary and Tenzing used the open circuit, which mixed oxygen with the outside air. The closed circuit, used by Evans and Bourdillon, fed pure oxygen through a bag. The new systems allowed the climbers to conserve energy and climb faster, with less risk of depleting their oxygen supply.

Many countries have since sent people to Mt. Everest's summit, using further technological advancements. In 1963, Americans made the first traverse of the mountain, and six men reached the summit. Twenty-five years later, the Japanese made the first television broadcast from the top. In 1989, the first two women, both Americans, reached the peak. And in 1990, Sir Edmund Hillary's son, Peter, followed in his father's footsteps to stand on the world's highest point.

The conquest of Mt. Everest was the ultimate mountaineering test for Hillary and Tenzing. But it was also the fulfillment of a dream for those who had tried before, and an inspiration for all mountain adventurers to follow.

On Top of the World

Meet the Author and Illustrator

Mary Ann Fraser is both a writer and an illustrator. She wrote *On Top of the World: The Conquest of Mount Everest* because of the "amazement [she] felt for people's ability to reach new goals."

Theme Connections

Within the Selection

Record your answers to the questions below in the Response Journal section of your Writer's Notebook. In small groups, report the ideas you wrote. Discuss your ideas with the rest of your group. Then choose a person to report your group's answers to the class.

- What obstacles did Hillary and Tenzing encounter on their climb to the top of Everest?
- How did Hillary and Tenzing overcome these obstacles?
- Was there any point along the way where it looked like they might not be able to go on?

Across Selections

- How were the obstacles Hillary and Tenzing faced similar to those faced by Miyax in "Amaroq, the Wolf"?
- What role did tools play in Hillary and Tenzing's success? Compare that role with the role tools played in "The Fire Builder."

Beyond the Selection

- Think about how "On Top of the World" adds to what you know about perseverance.
- Add items to the Concept/Question Board about perseverance.

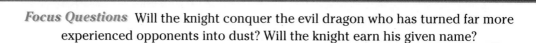

Focus Questions Will the knight conquer the evil dragon who has turned far more experienced opponents into dust? Will the knight earn his given name?

Saint George and the Dragon

from ***The Faerie Queene*** by Edmund Spenser
retold by Margaret Hodges
illustrated by Trina Schart Hyman

In the days when monsters and giants and fairy folk lived in England, a noble knight was riding across a plain. He wore heavy armor and carried an ancient silver shield marked with a red cross. It was dented with the blows of many battles fought long ago by other brave knights.

The Red Cross Knight had never yet faced a foe, and did not even know his name or where he had been born. But now he was bound on a great adventure, sent by the Queen of the Fairies to try his young strength against a deadly enemy, a dragon grim and horrible.

Beside him, on a little white donkey, rode a princess leading a white lamb, and behind her came a dwarf carrying a small bundle of food. The lady's lovely face was veiled and her shoulders were covered with a black cloak, as if she had a hidden sorrow in her heart. Her name was Una.

The dreadful dragon was the cause of her sorrow. He was laying waste to her land so that many frightened people had left their homes and run away. Others had shut themselves inside the walls of a castle with Una's father and mother, the king and queen of the country. But Una had set out alone from the safety of the castle walls to look for a champion who would face the terrible dragon. She had traveled a long, long way before she found the Red Cross Knight.

Like a sailor long at sea, under stormy winds and fierce sun, who begins to whistle merrily when he sees land, so Una was thankful.

Now the travelers rode together, through wild woods and wilderness, perils and dangers, toward Una's kingdom. The path they had to follow was straight and narrow, but not easy to see. Sometimes the Red Cross Knight rode too far ahead of Una and lost his way. Then she had to find him and guide him back to the path. So they journeyed on. With Una by his side, fair and faithful, no monster or giant could stand before the knight's bright sword.

After many days the path became thorny and led up a steep hillside, where a good old hermit lived in a little house by himself. While Una rested, the Red Cross Knight climbed with the hermit to the top of the hill and looked out across the valley. There against the evening sky they saw a mountaintop that touched the highest heavens. It was crowned with a glorious palace, sparkling like stars and circled with walls and towers of pearls and precious stones. Joyful angels were coming and going between heaven and the High City.

Then the Red Cross Knight saw that a little path led up the distant mountain to that city, and he said, "I thought that the fairest palace in the world was the crystal tower in the city of the Fairy Queen. Now I see a palace far more lovely. Una and I should go there at once."

But the old hermit said, "The Fairy Queen has sent you to do brave deeds in this world. That High City that you see is in another world. Before you climb the path to it and hang your shield on its wall, go down into the valley and fight the dragon that you were sent to fight.

"It is time for me to tell you that you were not born of fairy folk, but of English earth. The fairies stole you away as a baby while you slept in your cradle. They hid you in a farmer's field, where a plowman found you. He called you George, which means 'Plow the Earth' and 'Fight the Good Fight.' For you were born to be England's friend and patron saint, Saint George of Merry England."

Then George, the Red Cross Knight, returned to Una, and when morning came, they went together down into the valley. They rode through farmlands, where men and women working in their fields looked up and cheered because a champion had come to fight the dragon, and children clapped their hands to see the brave knight and the lovely lady ride by.

"Now we have come to my own country," said Una. "Be on your guard. See, there is the city and the great brass tower that my parents built strong enough to stand against the brassy-scaled dragon. There are my father and mother looking out from the walls, and the watchman stands at the top, waiting to call out the good news if help is coming."

Then they heard a hideous roaring that filled the air with terror and seemed to shake the ground. The dreadful dragon lay stretched on the sunny side of a great hill, like a great hill himself, and when he saw the knight's armor glistening in the sunlight, he came eagerly to do battle. The knight bade his lady stand apart, out of danger, to watch the fight, while the beast drew near, half flying, half running. His great size made a wide shadow under his huge body as a mountain casts a shadow on a valley. He reared high, monstrous, horrible, and vast, armed all over with scales of brass fitted so closely that no sword or spear could pierce them. They clashed with every movement. The dragon's wings stretched out like two sails when the wind fills them. The clouds fled before him. His huge, long tail, speckled red and black, wound in a hundred folds over his scaly back and swept the land behind him for almost half a mile. In his tail's end, two sharp stings were fixed. But sharper still were his cruel claws. Whatever he touched or drew within those claws was in deadly danger. His head was more hideous than tongue can tell, for his deep jaws gaped wide, showing three rows of iron teeth ready to devour his prey. A cloud of smothering smoke and burning sulfur poured from his throat, filling the air with its stench. His blazing eyes, flaming with rage, glared out from deep in his head. So he came toward the knight, raising his speckled breast, clashing his scales, as he leaped to greet his newest victim.

The knight on horseback fiercely rode at the dragon with all his might and couched his spear, but as they passed, the pointed steel glanced off the dragon's hard hide. The wrathful beast, surprised at the strength of the blow, turned quickly, and, passing the knight again, brushed him with his long tail so that horse and man fell to the ground.

Once more the Red Cross Knight mounted and attacked the dragon. Once more in vain. Yet the beast had never before felt such a mighty stroke from the hand of any man, and he was furious for revenge. With his waving wings spread wide, he lifted himself high from the ground, then, stooping low, snatched up both horse and man to carry them away. High above the plain he bore them as far as a bow can shoot an arrow, but even then the knight still struggled until the monster was forced to lower his paws so that both horse

and rider fought free. With the strength of three men, again the knight struck. The spear glanced off the scaly neck, but it pierced the dragon's left wing, spread broad above him, and the beast roared like a raging sea in a winter storm. Furious, he snatched the spear in his claws and broke it off, throwing forth flames of fire from his nostrils. Then he hurled his hideous tail about and wrapped it around the legs of the horse, until, striving to loose the knot, the horse threw its rider to the ground.

Quickly, the knight rose. He drew his sharp sword and struck the dragon's head so fiercely that it seemed nothing could withstand the blow. The dragon's crest was too hard to take a cut, but he wanted no more such blows. He tried to fly away and could not because of his wounded wing.

Loudly he bellowed——the like was never heard before——and from his body, like a wide devouring oven, sent a flame of fire that scorched the knight's face and heated his armor red-hot. Faint, weary, sore, burning with heat and wounds, the knight fell to the ground, ready to die, and the dragon clapped his iron wings in victory, while the lady, watching from afar, fell to her knees. She thought that her champion had lost the battle.

But it happened that where the knight fell, an ancient spring of silvery water bubbled from the ground. In that cool water the knight lay resting until the sun rose. Then he, too, rose to do battle again. And when the dragon saw him, he could hardly believe his eyes. Could this be the same knight, he wondered, or another who had come to take his place?

The knight brandished his bright blade, and it seemed sharper than ever, his hands even stronger. He smote the crested head with a blow so mighty that the dragon reared up like a hundred raging lions. His long, stinging tail threw down high trees and tore rocks to pieces. Lashing forward, it pierced the knight's shield and its point stuck fast in his shoulder. He tried to free himself from that barbed sting, but when he saw that his struggles were in vain, he raised his fighting sword and struck a blow that cut off the end of the dragon's tail.

Heart cannot think what outrage and what cries, with black smoke and flashing fire, the beast threw forth, turning the whole world to darkness. Gathering himself up, wild for revenge, he fiercely fell upon the sunbright shield and gripped it fast with his paws. Three times the knight tried and failed to pull the shield free. Then, laying about him with his trusty sword, he struck so many blows that fire flew from the dragon's coat like sparks from an anvil, and the beast raised one paw to defend himself. Striking with might and main, the knight severed the other paw, which still clung to the shield.

Now from the furnace inside himself, the dragon threw huge flames that covered all the heavens with smoke and brimstone so that the knight was forced to retreat to save his body from the scorching fire. Again, weary and wounded with his long fight, he fell. When gentle Una saw him lying motionless, she trembled with fear and prayed for his safety.

But he had fallen beneath a fair apple tree, its spreading branches covered with red fruit, and from that tree dropped a healing dew that the deadly dragon did not dare to come near. Once more the daylight faded and night spread over the earth. Under the apple tree the knight slept.

Then dawn chased away the dark, a lark mounted up to heaven, and up rose the brave knight with all his hurts and wounds healed, ready to fight again. When the dragon saw him, he began to be afraid. Still he rushed upon the knight, mouth gaping wide to swallow him whole. And the knight's bright weapon, taking advantage of that open

jaw, ran it through with such strength that the dragon fell dead, breathing his last in smoke and cloud. Like a mountain he fell, and lay still. The knight himself trembled to see that fall, and his dear lady did not dare to come near to thank her faithful knight until she saw that the dragon would stir no more.

Now our ship comes into port. Furl the sails and drop anchor. Safe from storm, Una is at her journey's end.

The watchman on the castle wall called out to the king and queen that the dragon was dead, and when the old king saw that it was true, he ordered the castle's great brass gates to be opened so that the tidings of peace and joy might spread through all the land. Trumpets sounded the news that the great beast had fallen. Then the king and queen came out of the city with all their nobles to meet the Red Cross Knight. Tall young men led the way, carrying laurel branches to lay at the hero's feet. Pretty girls wore wreaths of flowers and made music on tambourines. The children came dancing, laughing and singing, with a crown of flowers for Una. They gazed in wonder at the victorious knight.

But when the people saw where the dead dragon lay, they dared not come near to touch him. Some ran away, some pretended not to be afraid. One said the dragon might still be alive; one said he saw fire in the eyes. Another said the eyes were moving. When a foolish child ran forward to touch the dragon's claws, his mother scolded him. "How can I tell?" she said. "Those claws might scratch my son, or tear his tender hand." At last someone of the bolder men began to measure the dragon to prove how many acres his body covered.

The old king embraced and kissed his daughter. He gave gifts of gold and ivory and a thousand thanks to the dragonslayer. But the knight told the king never to forget the poor people, and gave the rich gifts to them. Then back to the palace all the people went, still singing, to feast and to hear the story of the knight's adventures with Una.

When the tale ended the king said, "Never did living man sail through such a sea of deadly dangers. Since you are now safely come to shore, stay here and live happily ever after. You have earned your rest."

But the brave knight answered, "No, my lord, I have sworn to give knight's service to the Fairy Queen for six years. Until then, I cannot rest."

The king said, "I have promised that the dragonslayer should have Una for his wife, and be king after me. If you love each other, my daughter is yours now. My kingdom shall be yours when you have done your service for the Fairy Queen and returned to us."

Then he called Una, who came no longer wearing her black cloak and her veil, but dressed in a lily-white gown that shimmered like silver. Never had the knight seen her so beautiful. Whenever he looked at the brightness of her sunshiny face, his heart melted with pleasure.

So Una and the Red Cross Knight were married and lived together joyfully. But the knight did not forget his promise to serve the Fairy Queen, and when she called him into service, off he rode on brave adventures until at last he earned his name, Saint George of Merry England.

That is how it is when jolly sailors come into a quiet harbor. They unload their cargo, mend ship, and take on fresh supplies. Then away they sail on another long voyage, while we are left on shore, waving good-bye and wishing them Godspeed.

Saint George and the Dragon

Meet the Author

Margaret Hodges' father asked her older cousin, Margaret Carlisle, to move in with the family after his wife died. It was Cousin Margaret and Hodges' father who helped lead Hodges down the path to writing by giving her many books to read. While at public school Number 60 in Indianapolis, Indiana, she wrote a poem. It was published in the children's magazine, *St. Nicholas*. Hodges even had her own television show for ten years as the storyteller on "Tell Me a Story." It aired locally in Pittsburgh, Pennsylvania.

Meet the Illustrator

Trina Shart Hyman worked many years before she became a famous children's illustrator. She started drawing when she was young and went on to art schools in her hometown of Philadelphia, Pennsylvania. While living in Sweden, Hyman got her first job illustrating *Pippi Longstocking*. It took her only two weeks. She later returned to the United States and had many rejections before getting work as an illustrator. She won a Caldecott Award, one of the most important awards for children's books, for *Saint George and the Dragon*. Hyman is known for using people from her life, including her neighbors, friends, their children, and her own children, in her illustrations.

Theme Connections

Within the Selection

Record your answers to the questions below in the Response Journal section of your Writer's Notebook. In small groups, report the ideas you wrote. Discuss your ideas with the rest of your group. Then choose a person to report your group's answers to the class.

- What makes this dragon so fierce and hard to defeat?
- Sometimes it takes bravery to persevere. How does the knight's bravery help him defeat the dragon?

Across Selections

- How is the kind of perseverance found in "Saint George and the Dragon" different from that found in the other stories you have read? How is it the same?
- Saint George receives help from a spring of water and from an apple tree. Name another story in which a character receives help from nature.

Beyond the Selection

- Think of a time when you were physically challenged. Maybe you were challenged by playing a sport or by suffering an injury. How was your challenge similar to Saint George's challenge? Were you able to persevere? Take a few minutes to write down your story, then share your story with the class.

Brittany Children. c.1892. **Enella Benedict.** Oil on canvas. 31 $\frac{5}{8}$ × 24 $\frac{1}{8}$ in. The National Museum of Women in the Arts, Washington, DC.

On the Dogger Bank. William Clarkson Stanfield. Oil on canvas. Victoria and Albert Museum, London.

Four Jockeys Riding Hard. c.1815. **Théodore Géricault.** Museé Bonnat, Bayonne, France.

Focus Questions What obstacles did Jesse encounter during his lifetime? How did he overcome these obstacles?

A PICTURE BOOK OF
JESSE OWENS

David A. Adler

illustrated by Robert Casilla

Jesse Owens was born on September 12, 1913, on a small farm in Oakville, Alabama. His given name was James Cleveland. His nickname was J.C.

J.C.'s grandparents had been slaves. His parents, Henry and Mary Emma Owens, were sharecroppers. They farmed on another man's land and shared with him their small crop of corn and cotton.

76

J.C.'s parents lived with their many children in a house that J.C. later described as "wooden planks thrown together." The roof leaked. In winter, cold wind blew through the walls. In summer, the house was so hot, J.C. felt he could hardly breathe.

J.C. was skinny and often sick with what his family called a "devil's cold." It was probably pneumonia. There was no money for doctors or medicine, so to cure J.C.'s illness, his mother wrapped him in cloth and put him by the fireplace.

A large lump once appeared on J.C.'s leg. His mother cut it out with a hot kitchen knife. J.C. said later that's when he learned "the meaning of pain."

When J.C. was about nine his family moved to what his mother said would be "a better life." They moved north to Cleveland, Ohio.

On J.C.'s first day of school in Cleveland, his teacher asked him his name. "J.C. Owens," he said. She thought he said "Jesse" and wrote that in her book. From then on he was known as Jesse Owens.

In Cleveland Jesse's father and older brothers worked in a steel mill. His mother worked washing clothes and cleaning

houses. Jesse worked, too——sweeping floors, shining shoes, watering plants, and delivering groceries. Even with the whole family working, the Owenses were still very poor.

In 1927 Jesse entered Fairmount Junior High School. There he met Charles Riley, a gym teacher and coach of the track team. Riley saw Jesse run in gym class and asked him to train for the track team. Because Jesse worked afternoons, he met the coach every morning before school. Jesse felt very close to Coach Riley and called him "Pop."

Coach Riley taught Jesse to run as if the ground were on fire. He said Jesse should train not just for the next race, but to be the best runner he could be. He told Jesse to always train for the future——"for four years from next Friday."

With a lot of work and with what Jesse later called his "lucky legs," he ran so fast and with such grace that he was called a "floating wonder." One newspaper reporter wrote that when Jesse Owens ran, it seemed like he was about to "soar into the air."

In 1928 Jesse Owens set the junior high school record for the long jump and the high jump. In 1933 he set high school records for the long jump and for the 220-yard dash.

He went to Ohio State University and was on the track team there, too. On May 25, 1935, at the Big Ten Championship meet, Jesse had what has been called the greatest day in track-and-field history. He set three world records and tied a fourth, all within forty-five minutes.

Several weeks later, on July 5, 1935, Jesse Owens married Minnie Ruth Solomon, a young woman he had met at Fairmount Junior High School. He said later, "I fell in love with her the first time we talked, and a little more every time after that." She was quiet, smart, a loving and supportive wife for Jesse, and a good mother to their three daughters, Gloria, Marlene, and Beverly.

In 1936 the Olympic games were held in Berlin, Germany. Adolf Hitler, the German Nazi leader at the time, said native Germans were part of a "master race"; that blacks and especially Jews were inferior. Jesse Owens and other athletes proved he was wrong. Jesse Owens won four gold medals and was the hero of the 1936 Olympics.

He tied the Olympic record of 10.3 seconds for the 100-meter race, set a new world record of 20.7 seconds for 200 meters around a curve, and was part of the team to set a record for the 400-meter relays.

With a long jump of 26 feet, 5 5/16 inches (8.06 meters), Jesse Owens set a new Olympic record, too.

He "seemed to be jumping clear out of Germany," wrote one reporter.

Lutz Long, the popular German jumper who came in second, ran over to shake Jesse's hand. The picture of the two athletes——a black American and a white German in the midst of all the hate and prejudice around them——is one of the lasting images of the 1936 Olympics.

There was a parade in Cleveland to welcome Jesse Owens home, and in New York City, he rode at the head of a ticker-tape parade of the entire Olympic team. But there was prejudice, too, and Jesse said later that when he returned to the United States, "I couldn't ride in the front of the bus . . . I couldn't live where I wanted."

In the years following Jesse's great victories at the 1936 Olympics, he worked as a playground director, made speeches, appeared on radio programs, and led a band of black musicians. He started the Jesse Owens Dry Cleaning

Company in 1938, but it went out of business a year later. He continued to run, too, in exhibition races against baseball players, cars, motorcycles, dogs, and horses. Years later he wrote that sometimes those races made him feel more like a spectacle than an athlete, but he also wrote, "At least it was an honest living. I had to eat."

Jesse Owens gave hundreds of speeches on the value of family, religion, and hard work. He was warm and friendly, and audiences loved to listen to him.

Jesse Owens also wrote his autobiography and two books on issues facing the black community. In the first one, *Blackthink: My Life as Black Man and White Man,* he wrote, "If the Negro doesn't succeed in today's America, it is because he has chosen to fail." Two years later, in *I Have Changed,* he seemed more aware of the prejudice blacks faced every day and showed more understanding for those who fought for equality.

For many years, Jesse Owens was called the "World's Fastest Human," and he won many awards. In 1950 he was named the all-time greatest track-and-field athlete by the Associated Press. In 1976 President Gerald R. Ford gave him the Presidential Medal of Freedom. In 1979 President Jimmy Carter gave him the Living Legends Award.

Jesse Owens died of lung cancer on March 31, 1980, in Tucson, Arizona. People all over the world were saddened as they remembered his great victories and his warm smile. The races Jesse Owens ran were over in seconds, but the story of his rise from a poor sharecropper's son to a world hero has inspired young people to dream and to work hard to make their dreams come true.

A PICTURE BOOK OF
JESSE OWENS

Meet the Author

David Adler was born into a family with five brothers and sisters. They all had their own hobbies. One brother liked to make rock candy. Another brother made dirt clean. As a group, the Adler children liked to collect things, including baseball cards, bottle caps, and autographs. Being raised in this kind of family helped mold Adler into a very successful writer of stories for children.

Meet the Illustrator

Robert Casilla was born in Jersey City, New Jersey. He began illustrating after graduating from the School of Visual Arts. He said, "I find great rewards and satisfaction in illustrating for children." He enjoys working with watercolors for his illustrations. Many of his illustrations are for biographies. When he illustrates a biography, he tries to learn a lot about the person. Knowing the person very well helps him when he works on the art.

Theme Connections

Within the Selection

Record your answers to the questions below in the Response Journal section of your Writer's Notebook. In small groups, report the ideas you wrote. Discuss your ideas with the rest of your group. Then choose a person to report your group's answers to the class.

- What challenges did Jesse Owens have to overcome as a boy?
- When Jesse started running track in junior high, how did his hard work on the track pay off?
- At the 1936 Olympics, what did Jesse's outstanding track performance prove?

Across Selections

- Perseverance doesn't always involve emergencies or unusual situations. With this in mind, how would you say Jesse Owens's story is different from the others you have read in this unit?
- Jesse Owens's perseverance changed his life. How are the changes in his life similar to those you've seen with other characters in this unit?

Beyond the Selection

- Think about how "A Picture Book of Jesse Owens" adds to what you know about perseverance.
- Add items to the Concept/Question Board about perseverance.

Mother to Son

Langston Hughes
illustrated by Anna Rich

Well, son, I'll tell you:
Life for me ain't been no crystal stair.
It's had tacks in it,
And splinters,
And boards torn up,
And places with no carpet on the floor——
Bare.
But all the time
I'se been a-climbin' on,
And reachin' landin's,
And turnin' corners,
And sometimes goin' in the dark
Where there ain't been no light.
So boy, don't you turn back.
Don't you set down on the steps
'Cause you finds it's kinder hard.
Don't you fall now——
For I'se still goin', honey,
I'se still climbin',
And life for me ain't been no crystal stair.

Focus Questions What difficulties did the Wright brothers encounter before their first flight? How did they react to defeat and disappointment?

Back to the Drawing Board

from *The Wright Brothers: How They Invented the Airplane*
by Russell Freedman
with original photographs by Wilbur and Orville Wright

The year was 1899. In the workroom of their bicycle shop in Dayton, Ohio, two brothers designed and built their first experimental aircraft——a biplane glider flown as a kite. With its successful flight, Wilbur and Orville Wright's next step was to build a man-carrying glider. The performance of this glider, which they tested at Kitty Hawk, North Carolina, in the fall of 1900, left the brothers hopeful. They returned to Kitty Hawk in July 1901, to test a bigger, newly designed glider, but experienced one problem after another. By the end of August, Wilbur and Orville, puzzled and discouraged, went back to Dayton. Wilbur later wrote, "We doubted that we would ever resume our experiments. When we looked at the time and money which we had expended, and considered the progress made and the distance yet to go, we considered our experiments a failure. At this time I made the prediction that man would sometime fly, but that it would not be in our lifetime."

Flying a glider
as a kite.

A replica of the Wrights' pioneering wind tunnel.

The experiments that Wilbur and Orville had carried out with their latest glider in 1901 were far from encouraging. Reflecting on their problems, Wilbur observed: "We saw that the calculations upon which all flying machines had been based were unreliable, and that all were simply groping in the dark. Having set out with absolute faith in the existing scientific data, we were driven to doubt one thing after another, till finally, after two years of experiment, we cast it all aside, and decided to rely entirely on our own investigations."

In the gaslit workroom behind their bicycle shop, Wilbur and Orville began to compile their own data. They wanted to test different types of wing surfaces and obtain accurate air-pressure tables. To do this, they built a wind tunnel ——a wooden box 6 feet long with a glass viewing window on top and a fan at one end. It wasn't the world's first wind tunnel, but it would be the first to yield valuable results for the construction of a practical airplane.

The materials needed to make model wings, or airfoils, and the tools to shape them were right at hand. Using tin shears, hammers, files, and a soldering iron, the brothers fashioned as many as two hundred miniature wings out of tin, galvanized iron, steel, solder, and wax. They made wings that were thick or thin, curved or flat, wings with rounded tips and pointed tips, slender wings and stubby wings. They attached these experimental airfoils to balances made of bicycle spokes and old hacksaw blades. Then they tested the wings in their wind tunnel to see how they behaved in a moving airstream.

For several weeks they were absorbed in painstaking and systematic lab work——testing, measuring, and calculating as they tried to unlock the secrets of an aircraft wing. The work was tedious. It was repetitious. Yet they would look back on that winter as a time of great excitement, when each new day promised discoveries waiting to be made. "Wilbur and I could hardly wait for morning to come," Orville declared, "to get at something that interested us. *That's* happiness."

The Wrights knew that they were exploring uncharted territory with their wind-tunnel tests. Each new bit of data jotted down in their notebooks added to their understanding of how an airfoil works. Gradually they replaced the calculations of others with facts and figures of their own. Their doubts vanished, and their faith in themselves grew. When their lab tests were finally completed, they felt confident that they could calculate in advance the performance of an aircraft's wings with far greater accuracy than had ever before been possible.

Armed with this new knowledge, they designed their biggest glider yet. Its wings, longer and narrower than before, measured 32 feet from tip to tip and 5 feet from front to rear. For the first time, the new glider had a tail——two 6-foot-high vertical fins, designed to help stabilize the machine during turns. The hip cradle developed the year before to control wing warping was retained. The craft weighed just under 120 pounds.

With growing anticipation, Wilbur and Orville prepared for their 1902 trip to the Outer Banks of North Carolina. "They really ought to get away for a while," their sister Katharine wrote to her father. "Will is thin and nervous and so is Orv. They will be all right when they get down in the sand where the salt breezes blow. . . . They think that life at Kitty Hawk cures all ills, you know.

"The flying machine is in process of making now. Will spins the sewing machine around by the hour while Orv squats around marking the places to sew [the cotton wing covering]. There is no place in the house to live but I'll be lonesome enough by this time next week and wish I could have some of their racket around."

The brothers reached the Outer Banks at the end of August with their trunks, baggage, and crates carrying the glider parts. At Kill Devil Hills, their launching site, they found that their wooden shed from the year before had been battered by winter storms. They set to work making repairs and remodeling the building, so they could use it instead of a tent as their new living quarters.

"We fitted up our living arrangements much more comfortably than last year," Wilbur reported. "Our kitchen is immensely improved, and then we have made beds on the second floor and now sleep aloft. It is an improvement over cots. We also have a bicycle which runs much better over the sand than we hoped, so

"Our kitchen is immensely improved..."

"...we have made beds on the second floor and now sleep aloft."

95

Wilbur and Dan Tate launch the 1902
glider with Orville at the controls.

that it takes only about an hour to make the round trip to Kitty
Hawk instead of three hours as before. There are other
improvements . . . so we are having a splendid time."

By the middle of September they had assembled their new
glider and were ready to try it out. This year they took turns in
the pilot's position, giving Orville a chance to fly for the first
time. To begin with, they were very cautious. They would
launch the machine from the slope on Big Hill and glide only a
short distance as they practiced working the controls. Steering
to the right or left was accomplished by warping the wings, with
the glider always turning toward the lower wing. Up-and-down
movements were controlled by the forward elevator.

In a few days they made dozens of short but successful test
glides. At this point, things looked more promising than ever.
The only mishap occurred one afternoon when Orville was at
the controls. That evening he recorded the incident in his diary:

"I was sailing along smoothly without any trouble . . . when I noticed that one wing was getting a little too high and that the machine was slowly sliding off in the opposite direction. . . . The next thing I knew was that the wing was very high in the air, a great deal higher than before, and I thought I must have worked the twisting apparatus the wrong way. Thinking of nothing else . . . I threw the wingtips to their greatest angle. By this time I found suddenly that I was making a descent backwards toward the low wing, from a height of 25 or 30 feet. . . . The result was a heap of flying machine, cloth and sticks in a heap, with me in the center without a bruise or scratch. The experiments thereupon suddenly came to a close till repairs can be made. In spite of this sad catastrophe we are tonight in a hilarious mood as a result of the encouraging performance of the machine."

A few days' labor made the glider as good as new. It wasn't seriously damaged again during hundreds of test glides, and it repeatedly withstood rough landings at full speed. Wilbur and Orville became more and more confident. "Our new machine is a very great improvement over anything we had built before and over anything anyone has built," Wilbur told his father. "Everything is so much more satisfactory that we now believe that the flying problem is really nearing its solution."

And yet the solution was not yet quite at hand. As they continued their test flights, a baffling new problem arose. On most flights, the glider performed almost perfectly. But every so often——in about one flight out of fifty——it would spin out of control as the pilot tried to level off after a turn.

"We were at a loss to know what the cause might be," wrote Wilbur. "The new machine . . . had a vertical tail while the earlier ones were tailless; and the wing tips were on a line with the center while the old machines had the tips drawn down like a gull's wings. The trouble might be due to either of these differences."

First they altered the wingtips and went back to Big Hill for more test flights. Again, the glider spun out of control during a turn. Then they focused their attention to the machine's 6-foot-high double-vaned tail, which was fixed rigidly in place. They had installed this tail to help stabilize the glider during turns, but now, it seemed, something was wrong.

97

Lying in bed one sleepless night, Orville figured out what the problem was. The fixed tail worked perfectly well most of the time. During some turns, however——when the airspeed was low and the pilot failed to level off soon enough——pressure was built up on the tail, throwing the glider off balance and into a spin. That's just what happened to Orville the day of his accident. The cure was to make the tail movable——like a ship's rudder or a bird's tail.

The next morning at breakfast, Orville told Wilbur about his idea. After thinking it over for a few minutes, Wilbur agreed. Then he offered an idea of his own. Why not connect the new movable tail to the wing-warping wires? This would allow the pilot to twist the wings and turn the tail at the same time, simply by shifting his hips. With the wings and tail coordinated, the glider would always make a smooth banked turn.

They removed the original tail and installed a movable single-vaned tail 5 feet high. From then on, there were no more problems. The movable tail rudder finally gave the Wright brothers complete control of their glider. "With this improvement our serious troubles ended," wrote Wilbur, "and thereafter we devoted ourselves to the work of gaining skill by continued practice."

As the brothers worked on their glider, their camp was filling up with visitors again. Their older brother Lorin arrived at the end of September to see what Wilbur and Orville were up to. Then Octave Chanute, a civil engineer who had also conducted gliding experiments, showed up, along with two other gliding enthusiasts. Now six bunks were jammed into the narrow sleeping quarters up in the rafters. At night, the sounds of Wilbur's harmonica, Orville's mandolin, and a chorus of male voices drifted across the lonely dunes.

With their movable tail rudder, the Wrights felt confident that their glider could master the winds. They practiced flying at every opportunity, staying on at their camp until late in October, long after all their visitors had left. "Glides were made whenever weather conditions were favorable," Wilbur recalled. "Many days were lost on account of rain. Still more were lost on account of light winds. Whenever the breeze fell below six miles an hour, very hard running was required to get the machine started, and the task of carrying it back up the hill was real labor . . . but when the wind rose to 20 miles an hour, gliding was a real sport, for starting was easy and the labor of carrying the machine back uphill was performed by the wind."

98

One day they had a wind of about 30 miles an hour and were able to glide in it without any trouble. "That was the highest wind a gliding machine was ever in, so that we now hold all the records!" Orville wrote home. "The largest machine ever handled . . . the longest distance glide (American), the longest time in the air, the smallest angle of descent, and the highest wind!!! Well, I'll leave the rest of the 'blow' till we get home."

That season the Wrights had designed, built, and flown the world's first fully controllable aircraft. The three-dimensional system of aircraft control worked out by the brothers is the basic system used even today in all winged vehicles that depend on the atmosphere for support.

Except for an engine, their 1902 glider flew just as a Boeing 747 airliner or a jet fighter flies. A modern plane "warps" its wings in order to turn or level off by moving the ailerons on the

Lorin Wright took this photo of his brothers and their visitors at Kill Devil Hills in October 1902. From left: Octave Chanute, Orville, Wilbur, Augustus M. Herring, George A. Spratt, Dan Tate.

rear edges of the wings. It makes smooth banking turns with the aid of a movable vertical rudder. And it noses up or down by means of an elevator (usually located at the rear of the plane).

Wilbur and Orville made hundreds of perfectly controlled glides in 1902. They proved that their laboratory tests were accurate. The next step was to build a powered airplane. "Before leaving camp," Orville wrote, "we were already at work on the general design of a new machine which we proposed to propel with a motor."

The Wright brothers could not just take a motor and put it into one of their gliders. First they needed a motor that was light yet powerful. Then they had to design propellers that would produce enough thrust to drive a flying machine through the air. Finally they had to build an aircraft body sturdy enough to carry the weight and withstand the vibrations of the motor and propellers.

Wilbur wrote to several manufacturers of gasoline engines, asking if they could supply an engine that would produce at least 8 horsepower, yet weigh less than 200 pounds. No company was willing to take on the assignment. Wilbur and Orville decided to build the motor themselves with the help of Charlie Taylor, a mechanic they had hired to help out in the bicycle shop.

"We didn't make any drawings," Taylor later recalled. "One of us would sketch out the part we were talking about on a piece of scratch paper and I'd spike the sketch over my bench." In just six weeks, they had the motor on the block testing its power. A marvel of lightness and efficiency, it weighed 179 pounds and generated more than 12 horsepower.

The propellers were much more difficult, since no reliable data on aerial propellers existed. "What at first seemed a simple problem became more complex the longer we studied it," wrote Orville. "With the machine moving forward, the air flying backward, the propellers turning sideways, and nothing standing still, it seemed impossible to find a starting point from which to trace the various simultaneous reactions. . . . Our minds became so obsessed with it that we could do little other work."

During several months of study, experiments, and discussion, Wilbur and Orville filled no less than five notebooks with formulas, diagrams, tables of data, and computations. They were

"They decided to use two propellers turning in opposite directions …"

the first to understand that an aerial propeller works like a rotary wing. The same physical laws that produce upward lift when a curved wing slices through the air will also produce forward thrust when a curved propeller blade rotates. Once they had grasped this idea, the Wrights were able to design propeller blades with the right diameter, pitch, and area for their needs.

"Isn't it astonishing that all these secrets have been preserved for so many years just so that we could discover them!!!" Orville told a friend. "Well, our propellers are so different from any that have been used before that they will have to either be a good deal better, or a good deal worse."

They decided to use two propellers turning in opposite directions, so that any twisting effect on the aircraft would be neutralized. The propellers were connected to the motor through a sprocket-and-chain transmission, like the kind used to drive a bicycle. The motor rested on the lower wing, to the right of the pilot, so it would not fall on him in case of a headlong crash. To balance the motor's extra weight, the right wing was 4 inches longer than the left.

In the Wright brothers' gliders, the wing-warping wires had twisted the entire wing up or down. In their new powered machine, the front edge of each wing was fixed rigidly in place. Only the rear outer edges of the wingtips could now be flexed, much like the movements of ailerons on a modern aircraft. The controls were similar to those in the 1902 glider——a padded hip cradle to operate the wing warping and the tail rudder, and a wooden hand lever to control the forward elevator. With a wingspan of just over 40 feet, the new machine was their biggest yet. They called it their first "Flyer."

There wasn't enough space in the bicycle shop workroom to assemble the entire machine. The center section alone was so big that it blocked the passage leading to the front of the shop.

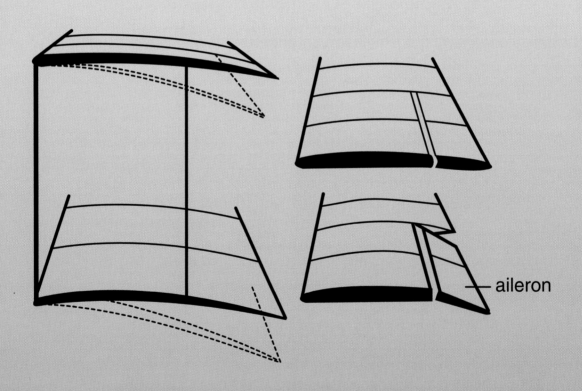

aileron

Wing warping in the 1903 Wright Flyer served the
same function as ailerons on a modern aircraft.

When a customer walked in, one of the brothers had to go out a side door and walk around to the front to wait on the customer. They didn't see their Flyer in one piece until the parts were shipped to the Outer Banks and assembled there.

Wilbur and Orville returned to their camp at Kill Devil Hills on September 25, 1903, and again found a storm-ravaged camp building. They made repairs and put up a second building to use as a workshop for assembling and housing their Flyer. On days with good winds, they took out their old 1902 glider for practice flights. On calm or rainy days, they worked on the new machine indoors.

Their progress was slowed by frustrating problems with the propeller shafts and the transmission sprocket wheels, which kept coming loose as the motor was being tested. Meanwhile, winter arrived early. Rain, snow, and freezing winds buffeted their camp. The water in their washbasin was frozen solid in the morning. They converted an old carbide can into a woodburning stove and piled on the blankets when they went to bed.

"We have no trouble keeping warm at nights," Wilbur wrote home. "In addition to the classifications of last year, to wit, 1, 2, 3 and 4 blanket nights, we now have 5 blanket nights, & 5 blankets & 2 quilts. Next come 5 blankets, 2 quilts & fire; then 5, 2, fire, & hot-water jug. This is as far as we have got so far. Next come the addition of sleeping without undressing, then shoes & hats, and finally overcoats. We intend to be comfortable while we are here."

The propeller shafts gave them so much trouble that Orville had to go all the way back to Dayton to have new ones made. He was returning to North Carolina on the train when he read a newspaper story about Samuel Pierpont Langley's second and last attempt to launch a man-carrying airplane on December 8, 1903. Once again, the *Great Aerodrome* and its pilot had crashed into the Potomac——and so had the $73,000 Langley had spent on it. So far, the Wrights had spent less than $1,000 on their still untested Flyer.

Orville reached Kill Devil Hills with the new propeller shafts on December 11. The brothers were anxious to test their Flyer before the weather got any worse. To launch the machine, they had built a movable starting track——a 60-foot-long wooden rail made of four 15-foot sections. The top of the rail was covered with a thin metal strip. For takeoff, the Flyer would be placed

The flyer sits atop its movable 60-foot starting track.

over this track with its landing skids resting on a small two-wheeled dolly, or "truck" as the Wrights called it, which ran freely along the rail. When the propellers started to turn, the Flyer would ride down the monorail on its truck, heading into the wind until it gained enough airspeed to lift off and fly. The Wrights called this starting track their "Grand Junction Railroad."

They were ready for their first trial on Monday, December 14, but the wind that day wasn't strong enough to permit a launching from level ground. Instead of waiting any longer, they decided to try a downhill launching from the side of Big Kill Devil Hill.

They hoisted a red signal flag to the top of a pole, alerting the lifesaving station a mile away. Before long, five men, two small boys, and a dog came trudging up the beach. The lifesavers had agreed to act as witnesses and help move more than 700 pounds of flying machine over the sand.

Everyone pitched in. Balancing the Flyer by hand, they rolled it along the starting rail, moving each 15-foot section of track from the rear to the front as they went along. When they reached the bottom of Big Hill, the entire 60-foot track was laid on the hillside. Then the Flyer was pulled up the rail and placed in position. "With the slope of the track, the thrust of the propellers, and the machine starting directly into the wind, we did not anticipate any trouble in getting up flying speed on the 60-foot monorail track," Orville recalled.

They started the motor. The propellers turned over, paddling loudly. The transmission chains clattered. The motor popped and coughed, and the whole machine seemed to shudder and shake. The two small boys took one look, backed away, and went racing across the sand dunes with the dog at their heels.

Wilbur and Orville tossed a coin to decide who should try first. Wilbur won. He lay down on the lower wing, sliding his hips into the padded wing-warping cradle. Orville took a position at one of the wings to help balance the machine as it roared down the starting track. Then Wilbur loosened the restraining rope that held the Flyer in place. The machine shot down the track with such speed that Orville was left behind, gasping for breath.

After a 35- to 40-foot run, the Flyer lifted up from the rail. Once in the air, Wilbur tried to point the machine up at too steep an angle. It climbed a few feet, stalled, settled backward, and smashed into the sand on its left wing. Orville's stopwatch showed that the Flyer had flown for just $3\frac{1}{2}$ seconds.

Wilbur wasn't hurt, but it took two days to repair the damage to the Flyer. They were ready to try again on Thursday, December 17, 1903.

They woke up that morning to freezing temperatures and a blustery 27-mile-an-hour wind. Puddles of rainwater in the sand hollows around their camp were crusted with ice. They spent the early part of the morning indoors, hoping the wind would die down a little. At 10 o'clock, with the wind as brisk as ever, they decided to attempt a flight. "The conditions were very unfavorable," wrote Wilbur. "Nevertheless, as we had set our minds on being home by Christmas, we determined to go ahead."

They hoisted the signal flag to summon the lifesavers. Then, in the biting wind, they laid down all four sections of the starting track on a level stretch of sand just below their camp. They had to go inside frequently to warm their hands by the carbide-can stove.

By the time the starting track was in place, five witnesses had shown up——four men from the lifesaving station and a teenage boy from the nearby village of Nags Head. They helped haul the Flyer over to the launching site.

Now it was Orville's turn at the controls. First he set up his big box camera, focused on a point near the end of the track, and inserted a glass-plate negative. Then he placed the rubber bulb that tripped the shutter in the big hand of John Daniels, one of the lifesaving men, and asked him to squeeze the bulb just as the Flyer took off.

The brothers shook hands. "We couldn't help but notice how they held onto each other's hand," one of the lifesavers recalled, "sort of like two folks parting who weren't sure they'd ever see one another again."

Orville took the pilot's position, his hips in the wing-warping cradle, the toes of his shoes hooked over a small supporting rack behind him. Like his brother, he was wearing a dark suit, a stiff collar, a necktie, and a cap. Wilbur turned to the lifesaving men and told them "not to look so sad, but to . . . laugh and holler and clap . . . and try to cheer Orville up when he started."

"After running the motor a few minutes to heat it up," Orville recalled, "I released the wire that held the machine to the track, and the machine started forward into the wind. Wilbur ran at the side of the machine, holding the wing to balance it on the track. Unlike the start on the 14th, made in a calm, the machine, facing a 27-mile-per-hour wind, started very slowly. Wilbur was able to stay with it till it lifted from the track after a forty-foot run. [John] snapped the camera for us, taking a picture just as the machine had reached the end of the track and had risen to a height of about two feet."

Wilbur had just let go of the wing when John Daniels tripped the shutter. The lifesavers broke into a ragged cheer. The Flyer was flying!

Orville couldn't hear them. He hung on to the control lever and stared straight ahead as the icy wind whistled past his ears and the motor clattered beside him. Buffeted by gusts, the Flyer lurched forward like a drunken bird. "The course of the flight up and down was exceedingly erratic," wrote Orville, "partly due to the irregularity of the air, and partly to lack of experience in handling this machine. . . . As a result the machine would rise suddenly to about ten feet, and then as suddenly dart for the ground. A sudden dart when a little over a hundred feet from the end of the track, or a little over 120 feet from the point at which it rose into the air, ended the flight. . . .

"This flight lasted only 12 seconds, but it was nevertheless the first in the history of the world in which a machine carrying a man had raised itself by its own power into the air in full flight, had sailed forward without reduction of speed, and had finally landed at a point as high as that from which it had started."

It had happened so quickly. A boy could have thrown a ball as far as the Flyer had flown. But the Wright brothers were elated. They had launched a flying machine that could actually fly.

The Wright brothers' first flight.

Back to the Drawing Board

Meet the Author

Russell Freedman grew up in San Francisco, California. His parents were good friends with several authors. Many of these authors came over to discuss the news of the day with the Freedmans. Hearing these discussions helped Freedman learn to develop his own ideas, a skill he would use well as an author. He took the idea for his first book from an article in *The New York Times* about teenagers who had already done amazing things in their lives. He called it *Teenagers Who Made History*.

Theme Connections

Within the Selection

Record your answers to the questions below in the Response Journal section of your Writer's Notebook. In small groups, report the ideas you wrote. Discuss your ideas with the rest of your group. Then choose a person to report your group's answers to the class.

- What were some of the problems the Wright brothers encountered while trying to build their airplane?
- How did they overcome some of these obstacles?
- In order to persevere, it's important to be good humored sometimes. In what ways did the Wright brothers' good humor help them deal with setbacks?

Across Selections

- The perseverance of one or two people can sometimes benefit many people. With this in mind, what other story in this unit is similar to the Wright brothers' story?
- How is the type of perseverance found in "Back to the Drawing Board" different from that found in "Saint George and the Dragon?"

Beyond the Selection

- Think about how "Back to the Drawing Board" adds to what you know about perseverance.
- Add items to the Concept/Question Board about perseverance.

 Why does the author refer
to the Wright brothers as "crazy boys?" How
do the choppy lines and offbeat rhythms
affect the tone of the poem?

Crazy Boys

by Beverly McLoughland

Watching buzzards,
Flying kites,
Lazy, crazy boys
The Wrights. They

Tried to fly
Just like a bird
Foolish dreamers
Strange. Absurd. We

Scoffed and scorned
Their dreams of flight
But we were wrong
And they were Wright.

Ancient Civilizations

Have you ever wondered how we know anything about people who lived so long ago that there were no books or other written records? What can we learn from old bones and broken pots? Quite a bit, if you know how. It's a kind of detective work called archaeology. In this unit you can learn both how archaeologists work and what they have figured out about some of the fascinating civilizations that existed before there was written history.

Digging Up the Past

from *Digging Up the Past:*
The Story of an Archaeological Adventure
by Carollyn James
illustrated by Ed Tadiello

Walking up the hill to his friend Joe's, Damien Shea was thinking about Rocky Mountain sheep and what he was going to do for the last three days of spring break. With one foot on the sidewalk and the other in the road, Damien pretended he was a Rocky Mountain sheep climbing up a rock slide. One false move, one loose rock, and he would tumble off the mountain. He kept his eyes on his feet.

"Ah, ha!" he said. Next to his left shoe, poking out of the leaves at the curb, was a quarter. Before putting it in his pocket along with the two large bolts, the pen, and the screwdriver he'd found since breakfast, Damien looked at the coin closely. It was dated 1973. This quarter is older than I am, he said to himself, thinking it was better to spend it before it got any older.

Before seeing Joe, Damien bought gum at the 7-Eleven. He and Joe would need something to chew on while they explored the woods behind Joe's house.

Joe was lucky to have the town's park for a backyard. The park was all wooded, with a crayfish stream sandwiched between two hills. It was the kind of place two ten-year-olds like Damien and Joe could spend whole days exploring nature on their own. And they often did.

This particular day, Damien and Joe made another secret path to the fort they had made out of scrap pieces of wood a week ago. While they worked, they were on the lookout for anything curious. By sunset, their pockets were full of the day's finds.

Before dinner, Damien showed his mother his discoveries.

"The screwdriver's a little bent," Damien said, "but it'll still work."

"I like this rock," Mrs. Shea said. "Do you think those green veins might be gold?"

"Get real, Mom. It's just copper," he said.

Mrs. Shea held a small piece of blue glass up to the light. "Where did you find this?" she asked. The top was round and fluted, with a bubble of clear glass in the middle. As the light passed through it, the fluted points shone like an exploding star. "This is cobalt blue glass. It might be a hundred years old."

Damien told her he found it in the woods behind Joe's house.

"I think you found yourself an old perfume bottle stopper." She held the glass to her nose. "You can almost smell the perfume."

Damien told her that he found lots of old things in the woods. Last week he found a brown bottle with a medicine label.

"You know what," Mrs. Shea said, "you may have found an *archaeological site.*"

Damien's mother was an archaeologist. Archaeology is the science of studying the life and culture of people of the past. Part of Damien's mother's work as an archaeologist was finding buried places where people had lived and worked hundreds, sometimes thousands, of years ago. She found many of these places, or sites, by carefully looking for archaeological clues lying on the ground's surface. The clues might be things people made long ago——things called artifacts——like a broken piece of a bowl or a nail or an arrowhead. Another clue might be an interesting way rocks are arranged, as if around a campfire. Like Damien, she had to be a keen observer.

"Wow, Mom!" Damien yelled. "You mean like I might have found an old Indian village or Egyptian tomb?"

"No. I mean like an old junkyard," said Damien's mother. "Often junk can tell archaeologists more than treasure can. A long time ago," his mother continued, "our town may have been a farm. It's hard to tell that now, with all the houses and streets and the interstate highway. But maybe what you found is evidence of what it used to be."

Damien slapped his thigh and thought, Well, I'll be doggoned. He wanted to find more clues about his town's past life.

"If we go into the woods as scientists," she told him, "we'll find a whole lot more than just neat stuff, Damien. We'll find out about the people who left all that neat stuff there. And maybe even why they left it there."

But his mother said she wouldn't help unless he promised that he was going to behave like an archaeologist. She explained that there are rules and methods archaeologists follow.

"Without rules," she said, "you destroy the meaning of everything you find and the things you'll find will have no meaning."

Damien nodded and promised he'd behave like a scientist.

"The first step in archaeology is to ask the right questions," his mother said. "All science is a way of looking for answers, Damien. What question do you think we should ask first?"

"Uh . . . why did the farmer dump his garbage in the woods?"

"We're too far ahead of ourselves. We still don't know for sure if there was a farm here. Right now we're simply asking, Did people live or work around here before this was a town? If we can find out that they did, our knowledge of archaeology will help us to ask more questions. Where did they come from? What was their life like? Why did they leave? We'll start looking for answers later. Right now, let's set the table."

After dinner, Damien and his mother went to the library. The town kept its special records at the library in acid-free folders and boxes that preserved the paper from rotting. The town's old photographs, original land deeds, subdivision and tax records, and maps were its history. These documents were like pictures in a family album. They were proof of how the town had grown and changed, and changed some more before it became the place where Damien lived today.

At the librarian's desk, Damien asked if he could see the town's historical documents. He told the librarian he was looking for an archaeological site in the woods, but first he needed to know if anyone used to live there.

The librarian left and came back with a box of old documents. Damien and his mother began to search through them. After a while, Damien found an old picture of Joe's house. It looked different. Instead of a garage, there was a barn, and the big oak in Joe's front yard was much smaller in the photograph.

"In 1867," the librarian told Damien, "a farmer named Matthew Abbott built that house on fifty-five acres of land. It was his grandson who sold the farm to the people who built our town."

In the photograph, the woods looked bigger.

"Damien," Mrs. Shea looked at the photograph, "I think this answers our first archaeological question. Now we're ready to ask another question."

"Right, Mom. What's for dessert?"

The next morning, Damien was over at Joe's before sunrise.

"Wake up!" Damien yelled up at Joe's bedroom window. "You're living in Matthew Abbott's house!"

Joe's father came to the window. "Damien," he said, "do you know what time it is?"

"Sure. Five, six o'clock," Damien said. "Did you know your house is more than a hundred years old?"

"Damien, go home. Now."

When Damien got home, he made his breakfast and read comic books until seven. Then he woke up his mother, who also asked him if he knew what time it was.

At nine o'clock, Damien called the mayor's office. The woods officially belonged to the town, and Damien had to get permission to work there. When the mayor said, "My dear little boy," Damien knew the mayor wasn't taking him seriously. The mayor said that he couldn't possibly give him permission because then every little boy in town would want to dig up the parks. Damien said that he didn't want to dig up the park. He wanted to excavate it!

"This is not a game, sir. Archaeology is a science!" Damien nearly shouted into the telephone.

Then Damien's mother got on the telephone. She told the mayor that as an archaeologist she would make sure that proper archaeological methods were followed in excavating the site if the town gave them permission. She apologized for her son calling him but said she would write him later that day to request permission.

"Today we want to go and surface collect, to make sure that a site exists. If you give us temporary permission," she told the mayor, "we'd like to start mapping it out. And, if there's time, we could start a test pit."

She promised that when they were finished digging and studying their findings, they would give whatever they found to the town. She also promised that they would fill in any holes they created. And she invited the mayor to come and watch.

The mayor said he might like to visit the site and that, yes, they had his permission, temporarily.

By this time Joe had come over to Damien's house, and Damien was talking real fast. Did Joe know there used to be a barn behind his house? That his house used to be a farm? Did he want to see a picture of it? Did he want to be an archaeologist?

Joe said, sure, he wouldn't mind being an archaeologist. But first he'd like to be a pitcher for the Orioles.

"Forget baseball, Joe," Damien said. "Starting today you're going to be an archaeologist."

With Mrs. Shea's help, the boys began collecting the tools they would need for their field kits to map out the site. Into their backpacks they put pencils, markers, graph paper, balls of string, measuring tape, a compass, and a bunch of wooden stakes. "Aahhhgg, ze Count Dracula dies," Damien said, holding one of the stakes to his chest and pretending to faint on the couch.

"All those stakes are going to be useful," his mother said. "You'll need them for marking off the areas you'll be digging in." She added Band-Aids to their kits, and then gave each boy a mason's trowel. "Don't lose these. These trowels are your most important tools," she said.

They went into the garage for a couple of square shovels and the screen they would use to sift the dirt. The loose dirt would be put on top of a window screen table that they would shake back and forth, Damien's mother explained. "If there's something in the dirt we miss seeing when we dig, we'll shake it out with this."

After putting the trowels in their field kits, Joe and Damien carried them along with the screen down to the site. Damien's mother brought the shovels and the buckets.

"Before we begin," she asked, "what question do we try to answer now? What exactly are we looking for in the woods?"

"That's easy. Did Farmer Abbott dump his trash in the woods?" Damien said.

"Well, what you're really asking is, is there any evidence left of the Abbott family in the woods? Probably it will be their trash," she said.

They went across the street, down the block, and through Joe's backyard into the woods. Damien's mother asked where they had found the old medicine bottle and they showed her the spot near a small mound.

"And over there," Damien said, pointing to the right, about ten feet away, "is where I found the perfume stopper."

His mother pointed to a row of daffodils behind them. "How did daffodils get out here?" she asked. "And why do you think they're growing in a long, straight line like that?"

"Because someone planted them that way?" Damien said.

"That's possible," she said. "People often plant daffodils along fence lines. Perhaps the Abbotts did, too." Looking at the mound, and then looking up at Joe's house, Damien realized this looked like a good place to have a backyard fence . . . and a very good place to put a junk pile.

Walking in a line behind the flowers, Joe found a rotted wooden post sticking out of the ground. In the opposite direction, Damien found another. Walking back toward Joe, Damien stumbled over the stub of another post. It was an old fence line, all right.

"When we get back home," Mrs. Shea said, "I have to contact the state historical society, to let them know about this place. But for now, boys, let's start mapping."

"I don't see why we have to draw a map when we already know where the site is," Damien said.

"Because archaeology is about *where* you find things as much as it is about *what* you find," Mrs. Shea answered. "Without a map, nothing will have a place. And archaeologists map what they find vertically as well as horizontally. We're going to be working

up and down as well as across. Trust me, we're going to need a record for that. But, like any map, we first need a name for this place."

They decided to call the site Matthew Abbott's Dump One, in case there might be more than one trash pile in the woods. Or "M.A.D. 1" for short.

That settled, they had to figure out where to begin their map. Damien's mother explained, "We can't just draw a map, willy nilly, because then the map could be of any place. We need what's called a datum point for this site. A datum point is something peculiar to this site, and permanent. It will be the map's reference point, the place that we measure everything else on the map from. That way, after we're finished digging, anyone who wants to know where our site was can use maps and our datum point to find it. Let's see . . . is there something around here we can use as a datum point?"

"The daffodils?" Damien asked. Mrs. Shea said that while the daffodils were very noticeable now, archaeologists needed something more permanent. Not only couldn't they find the daffodils in winter, but someone might pull them up.

"How about a tree?" Joe asked.

There was a big oak tree about 15 feet from the center of the mound. They decided to make the tree their datum point.

"Don't you think we should dress up our datum point?" Damien asked. "Like tie a red scarf around it or something?"

"How about tying my sister to it?" Joe laughed and Damien pretended he was Joe's sister begging to be untied.

Damien's mother had drawn a black dot in the middle of a piece of graph paper and marked it Large Oak Tree. "What we really need for our datum point are directions."

Damien took out the compass and stood under the tree. Walking around the tree, he pointed out north, south, east, and west. On the map, his mother drew four straight lines from the datum point. The map was now divided into four squares.

Avoiding the tree's roots, Damien pounded four stakes into the ground in a 10-foot square from the tree. On each stake he tied a long piece of string and gave the other end to Joe. Joe walked straight out from each stake. At the end of the string, he pounded another stake in the ground and tied the string to it. Now, north, south, east, and west were lined out from their datum point.

Working together, they began crisscrossing their string lines with more strings and stakes. First working along the north and south lines, they marked off every 5 feet with a stake. Then going along their east and west lines, they again staked out every five feet. Once the string was tied to their stakes, they had created eighteen squares, five feet by five feet.

"How come five feet, Mom?"

"The squares could have been any size, but I think five by five squares will give you enough room to sit down and work comfortably," she answered.

The squares went beyond where Damien had already found artifacts. But most of them were on and around the mound.

"These squares indicate where we will be digging," Mrs. Shea said. "If we need more squares, we can always make more."

On the map, Mrs. Shea marked off the squares just as they were laid on the ground. She made a note that each square was five by five feet, and then, inside of each mapped square, she wrote two letters and two numbers——using N, S, E, W and 1, 2, 3, 4.

The first letter in each square was an N or S. This meant the square was either north or south of the tree. The other letter was an E or W, for east or west of the tree. The numbers told how close the square was to the tree, with the lowest numbers closest to it.

Each square had its own name, like a town on a map. Damien was standing in a square right on top of the mound. It was in the first row of squares south of the datum point and in the second row of squares west of the datum point. "What's this square called?" he asked. On his mother's map, this was square S1 W2. The square next to this one and right next to the tree was S1 W1. The square on the other side of Damien was called S1 W3.

"Archaeologists name each square for where it is from their datum point," Damien's mother explained. "Otherwise, it would take too long to figure out what square they were talking about. Okay, boys. Let's get ready to dig."

"We need a test pit," said Mrs. Shea. "Let's dig it here." It was a square northeast of the tree, called N4 E3. The closest mapped square was N3 E2. "We can't expect to find any artifacts in this square, though."

"Then why dig it up?" Damien thought that was dumb. Who'd want to dig up a square with nothing in it?

"Because N4 E3 is going to teach us how to dig. And——more important——N4 E3 will help us compare the layers, or strata, of soil in the other squares to this one."

"I don't get it."

"Well, it's like comparing two dishes of ice cream. Let's say you have one dish with a scoop of vanilla and a little bit of chocolate sauce on top. And in another dish, you also have one scoop of vanilla and a little bit of chocolate, except that someone has mushed and mixed the sauce in with the ice cream. You only know what the mixed ice cream used to look like by looking at the first dish. . . . "

"You're making me hungry, Mom."

"The Abbots probably didn't dump their trash here, and probably didn't dig up any of the dirt here, either. So we'll learn what the natural ground looks like. This dirt is undisturbed, and it will let us know how much digging the Abbotts did. If they dug a hole to put their trash in, and then if they dug up more dirt to cover their trash, we'll know that because we'll compare it to how the layers of dirt look in this test pit."

The ground was covered with leaves. There were bits and pieces of old wet leaves stuck together under the dry leaves. Using her fingers, Damien's mother picked through the leaves and rubbed them. She found nothing. She piled them outside of the square. The boys did the same.

About an inch under the leaves, they hit dirt. They measured the depth of leaf covering. Damien's mother recorded it in their field notes. She wrote, "M.A.D. 1, N4 E3, leaf cover 0.0 ft–0.1 ft B.S." Then she wrote the date and her initials and showed it to Joe and Damien.

"Archaeologists always put their initials and date on everything they record," she told them. "That's so anyone who looks at their records will know who to talk to if they have any questions."

She told them that B.S. meant below the surface. "But why didn't you just write the leaves covered the square for about an inch?" Damien asked.

"As scientists," his mother said, "we're using scientific measurements and language. We change inches into decimals. And leaf cover 0.0 ft–0.1 ft B.S. is the way archaeologists write down that the leaves did cover the square for about an inch. Now that we've drawn a map of the top of the site, from here on we'll be mapping the *depth* of the site. The very top of the site is 0.0 ft. From there, we measure down."

Once all the leaves were cleared from the square, Damien's mother showed the boys how to dig with a trowel. The flat side of the trowel was used to scrape the ground, a quarter of an inch at a time. "Never use the point to pry anything up," she said. "I can't stress that enough. If there is something in the ground too big to loosen by scraping, you scrape the dirt around it."

With the flat side of the trowel, the boys dug carefully, scooping the dirt into their buckets. Damien's mother used the square shovel the same way they used their trowels. When they had a bucketful of dirt from their square, they poured it over the processing screen. Joe and Damien took turns shaking the dirt through the screen.

"Mom! I think we found something!" Damien yelled every time they sifted the dirt. But the "something" always turned out to be just pebbles. Damien decided to save the rocks in a pile.

They dug carefully in N4 E3 all morning. By lunchtime, they had dug down two feet. It took a lot longer than they had thought it would. And as they dug, they noticed changes in the dirt. Under the leaves, the top layer of dirt was the blackest. This was the topsoil formed from years of plants and animals rotting on the ground. Below that was yellow clay. There was a band of sand under the clay. By late afternoon, they hit gravelly dirt.

Working together, it took them all day to dig down five feet. Damien's mother then took pictures of the square's walls. The different colors and textures of dirt made the walls look like waves of ribbons. It was starting to get dark, and everyone was hungry and tired.

"This is harder work than I thought, Damien," Joe said. "I think I'd rather pitch for the O's."

"Yeah," Damien agreed. "But think about how much better it will be when we find something."

"The mayor called last night," Damien's mother said. "He had good news. The City Council supports our dig."

For the rest of the site, they would dig each square in six-inch levels. Everything they found in one level would be recorded before they could begin digging up the next level. Each level of each square would have its own bag for artifacts.

Damien began digging in N1 W1 near the tree. Joe worked next to him in N1 E1. And Damien's mother took N1 W4.

"I bet I find more stuff than you, Joe," Damien said.

"Guys," Damien's mother said, "this is not a contest. We're all in this together. We're a team. We're here to find the Abbotts, not stuff."

"If we find the Abbotts, I'm out of here! Fast!" Damien said. As they started digging, the boys made jokes about finding old Abbott's bones.

leaves

topsoil

clay

sand

gravelly dirt

In their first levels, they found only pebbles and roots. But soon after work began at the second level, Damien was jumping up and down at the processing screen.

"I got something! I got something!" he yelled.

He carefully picked the dirt off it with his fingers. It looked round and tinny, with something red written on it. Damien rubbed the tin hard against his pants.

He held it up to see if he could read it. "Coca-cola . . . Ah, it's just a dumb ol' bottle cap." Damien looked disappointed and started to throw it away.

"Hey, not so fast," his mother said. "When was the last time you had a Coke that wasn't a twist-off cap. Someone sat under this tree years ago and drank a Coke. It's an artifact. Put it in the bag. Everything interesting goes into the bags. When we get into the lab, then we'll decide what's important." The bottle cap went into the second-level paper bag marked, M.A.D. 1, N1 W1, 0.5–1.0 ft. B.S., Damien.

Joe found three cigarette filters and a piece of rusted tin in his second level. He put them in his second-level bag.

There was now a large pile of dirt under the processing screen from the first and second levels. Joe and Damien moved the dirt away to get ready for the third level. Damien's mother took pictures of the boys as they measured levels one and two in their squares.

As they worked level three, Damien's trowel hit something hard. He thought it was probably a rock, so he didn't get excited. As he scraped away the ground around it, though, he saw that it was white. Damien used a whisk broom to brush it clean. As more dirt fell off it, he spotted what looked like a set of teeth.

"Joe," he whispered. "Joe! I think I found Farmer Abbott."

Joe went over and looked. They both stared in silence at the jawbone in the dirt. They were so quiet that Damien's mother got suspicious. She went over and found the boys sitting perfectly still and looking at the ground.

"You boys look like you've seen a ghost," she said. Joe's mouth was open, but he wasn't saying a thing. He pointed to the jawbone jutting up at Damien's knees.

"May I?" she asked, and bent down and began carefully sweeping and troweling the area around the bone until it was completely uncovered. She picked up the bone and studied it. She looked at the teeth and said, "What a pretty set of teeth."

"Mom, that's a disgusting thing to say about the dead!"

"Why? Whose teeth do you think these are?"

"Farmer Abbott's. I bet this is where he died."

"Damien, look at these teeth a little more carefully. Do these look like human teeth? Are they the same size and shape as your teeth? Count them. Hold the bone next to your chin. Do you think this bone came from a human being?" she asked.

Damien looked at it closely and said, "Maybe it came from a real ugly human. . . ."

"A sheep is more likely," his mother said. "We'll find out for sure later. But I'm glad you didn't pry it out of the ground. If you had, it might have broken."

In the notebook she wrote where the bone was found and who found it. Damien put the jawbone back exactly in its place in the pit. He measured how far down it was from the surface and how far it was from the pit's walls. His mother took a picture of it.

"Does anyone know if this jawbone is an artifact?" she asked them.

Both of them said it sure was.

"Why do you say that?"

They knew then it was the wrong answer.

"Did someone make this jawbone or use this jawbone? Just because we're saving it doesn't make it an artifact," Damien's mother said.

"It's not an artifact," Damien tried bluffing. "We meant to say it's a . . . it's a . . ."

". . . a bone!" Joe said for him.

"Archaeological sites have artifacts and non-artifacts," she said. "Artifacts are things people made or used. Non-artifacts are things people didn't make——like seeds, shells, and bones. But non-artifacts can tell us as much as artifacts about the people who made a site. What could this jawbone tell us about Farmer Abbott?"

"That he had a sheep," Joe said right away.

"And our job as archaeologists," she went on, "will be to find out why he had a sheep. Maybe sheep were pretty common on nineteenth-century farms. But, then again, maybe they weren't."

"Yeah. And we have to find out where he put the rest of the sheep," Joe said.

As Damien soon discovered, more of the sheep was buried in his third and fourth levels. Once the bones were measured and photographed in the square, they were bagged for the lab.

From the second level down, everyone was finding interesting things. Joe found the top part of a light blue jar. Damien's mom said it might have come from a canning jar. Then Joe found more glass pieces of the same color. Damien's mother found the handle of a blue and white teacup and part of a leather strap.

As Joe was taking his dirt to the screen, a man came walking through the woods, waving his arms over his head.

"Hello! Are there any archaeologists out here?" he yelled from across the stream.

"It's the mayor. Be nice, Damien," Damien's mother said. She stood up, wiped her hands on her jeans, then crossed the stream to greet the mayor. Damien and Joe couldn't hear them, but they saw her pointing to them. The mayor started waving some more. The mayor and Damien's mother walked over to the site.

"So this is Damien," the mayor said. "It's a pleasure to meet such a nice little boy."

Damien shook the mayor's hand and introduced Joe. When the mayor said Joe was a nice little boy, too, Damien and Joe looked at each other and rolled their eyes.

Damien's mother explained how they were excavating the site and recording their findings. Then she asked the mayor if he'd like to watch Joe work the screen.

The mayor asked if he could try it. As he sifted Joe's dirt, he said this reminded him of helping his mother make cakes. He kept shaking the screen and talking about her triple-layer double-dutch chocolate cake that was as light as air. He paid little attention as the little rocks bounced on and off the screen. By Joe's account what happened next wasn't fair. It was Joe's dirt, after all.

After the dirt was shaken off, the screen held about a cup of small rocks. The mayor said, "My, my, that was fun. . . . And what have we here?" He reached over and picked a small coin out of the rocks.

It was the size of a dime, the color of a dime, but it wasn't a dime. On one side was a woman's head with "United States of America" and "1874" written around it. On the other side was the Roman Numeral III. "I found a three-cent piece!" the mayor shouted. "I found a three-cent piece!"

Everyone but Joe was real excited. Damien's mother said this could help them date what they found in their third levels. Unless they found something with a different date on it, the levels 1.0 to 1.5 B.S. were buried around 1874. The mayor kept saying how lucky he was and how much fun archaeology was.

Damien said, "Three cents? Three cents? There's no such thing as a three-cent coin!"

To himself, Joe said that was his three-cent piece, that was his dirt——and that he wanted to go home.

The mayor turned to Damien's mother and told her, "The whole City Council will hear about this." He told her to let him know if they needed anything, anything at all. She thanked him and said they certainly would.

After the mayor left——Damien checked to make sure he left without the coin——Damien's mother went to talk with Joe.

She agreed that it didn't seem fair that the mayor found the coin. But, she told him, "Working a site is a lot like being on a baseball team. Everyone works for the same goal. Whether it's winning the game or digging the best site possible. And that coin did something very special for this site. Since the mayor thinks he found it, we now have the community's support. Thanks, Joe."

Joe felt better. And, anyway, the coin went into the bag marked with his name, not the mayor's.

It had been a long day, but time had passed fast. In less than eight hours they had dug into the nineteenth century.

132

133

Digging Up the Past

Meet the Author

Carollyn James lives in Takoma Park, Maryland, and is managing editor of *Science and Children* magazine. She is also a freelance writer whose articles have been published in many national magazines.

Meet the Illustrator

Ed Tadiello has completely immersed himself in the study of art. He has been a student at two New York City art schools. He also has held memberships in associations especially for artists and illustrators. The focus of his studies has been the human form. According to Tadiello, one of the biggest challenges in drawing characters is that they have a "natural quality to them." It is when this "natural quality" is achieved that he feels he has created a work of art, one he hopes "will touch and inspire the viewer."

134

Theme Connections

Within the Selection

Record your answers to the questions below in the Response Journal section of your Writer's Notebook. In small groups, report the ideas you wrote. Discuss your ideas with the rest of your group. Then choose a person to report your group's answers to the class.

- What did Damien and his mother gain by visiting the library?
- What purpose did the masonry trowels and the window screen serve?
- According to Damien's mother, what is the difference between an artifact and a nonartifact?

Across the Selections

- As you saw in "Digging Up the Past," a lot of archaeology involves research and piecing together clues. How is this process similar to the one the Wright brothers used to invent their plane in the last unit?

Beyond the Selection

- Was there ever a time when you found something of interest lying in the grass or buried in the ground? What was it? What did you do with it? Get into small groups and share your stories. Then pick one or two stories from your group and share them with the class.

The Search for Early Americans

from *Searches in the American Desert*
by Sheila Cowing

In 1888, the Civil War had been over for twenty years. Thousands of eastern Americans had traveled west in covered wagons, looking for new land to farm, new homes, new ways of life. Roads and railroads were being built across the nation.

In the mountains and on the high desert plateaus, the frantic search for gold and silver was over, too. Most mines were run by big companies digging deep under the earth with heavy machinery.

On the plains, on grassy mountain slopes, and in the desert, wherever grass grew, new settlers drove cattle and sheep, searching constantly for fresh grass and water. The miners and the western settlers clashed with the native Americans. On the Great Plains, the Indians were forced to move onto reservations or to engage in war.

In the Rocky Mountains, most native Americans had been killed or driven onto small, isolated reservations where many died of diseases they caught from the white man. Often the Indians found the land set aside for them already occupied by miners or settlers who refused to move. The native Americans were left impoverished and heartsick.

In the Mancos Valley of southern Colorado, which belonged traditionally to the Ute Indians, new ranchers herded their cattle out of the wide treeless valleys up steep, narrow canyons for the winter. There the animals were safe from the terrible icy winds and could be guarded more easily against wolves and mountain lions.

Richard Wetherill and his family had been raising cattle in Mancos for eight years. The Utes were not always friendly toward settlers. But Richard and his family, who were Quakers, had befriended them and had cared for several Indians when they were ill.

Richard was thirty years old, and he and his four younger brothers still lived with their parents. Their married sister lived close by.

Sometimes, during the winter, Richard and his brothers would build a small cabin so they could stay near the cattle. Then they would often ride into the branch canyons looking for ruined cliff dwellings. An old Ute had told them that in the canyons there were the abandoned dwellings of many people——the "ancient ones." One of the dwellings was larger than the others, and the Utes never went there, as it was a sacred place. Richard and his brothers had found only small dwellings.

On December 18, 1888, Richard and his sister's husband, Charlie Mason, rode to the top of Mesa Verde looking for stray cattle and found themselves in a place they had never been before. It was snowing lightly, and they rode close to the edges of the steep cliffs. Thick mesquite underbrush scratched their horses' legs and sometimes snared their hooves.

Late in the morning, they climbed down to rest the horses and walked out on a point of bare rock. Below them, a snowy canyon opened out. Suddenly, Richard grabbed Charlie's arm and pointed. About a half mile away, across the canyon, was a long, deep cave. Inside, blurred like a mirage in the falling snow, was a man-made wall. It was several stories high, with black window and door holes watching the canyon like eyes. Near the center rose a round, tapered tower.

Cattle ranchers Richard Wetherill and Charlie Mason saw this snowy canyon from the top of Mesa Verde for the first time in December 1888.

Keeping their horses as close to the rim as they dared, they started around the canyon. Winding through prickly bushes, they reached a clearing. The cliff dropped away at their feet. Beneath them was the mysterious city in the canyon wall.

Richard climbed down from his horse. He took out his bowie knife and began to slice at the thick branch of a dead piñon tree.

They made a ladder, looping branches with their lariats, and tied it to piñon trunks. When they lowered the ladder over the cliff, it reached the ruins.

There stood a ghost city. This must be the large sacred dwelling the Ute had spoken of. Walls of the rooms had broken, but their remains stood straight, built of stone the red-brown color of oak leaves in winter. Little houses perched one on top of the other. The tower rose near the center, as though uniting the houses. At some point, Richard thought of the name "Cliff Palace" for this place, and the largest ruin at Mesa Verde is still called by that name.

For hours they explored, ducking through low doorways and climbing tumbled walls, searching room after room, leaving footprints in dust perhaps for centuries undisturbed. When they spoke to each other, their voices echoed.

Clay bowls, mugs, and jars for carrying water stood on ledges and floors as though their owners had just put them down and would come back soon to start supper. They found a stone axe, its handle still lashed to its blade. Hundreds of people must have lived here. What had happened to them?

In a back room, they found bones and three skulls. Had there been a battle? No, there would be many more skeletons.

Snow still fell on the mesa and the men were cold, but they were eager to learn whether other large ruins lay close by. Agreeing to camp near where they had first seen Cliff Palace, Richard and Charlie separated. In the late afternoon light, Richard rode north, then across Mesa Verde, following the curve of a deep canyon. There he saw another cliff dwelling rising in places to three stories. He dared not climb down, as it would soon be dark. The walls of this town were protected from the wind by a fringe of spruce trees across the front of the cave. One tall spruce had grown right through a retaining wall. Richard called this ruin Spruce Tree House.

Cliff Palace is the largest cliff dwelling in Mesa Verde National Park in southwestern Colorado. About 400 people lived there at one time.

When morning came and Richard and Charlie tried to find Spruce Tree House again, they rode out to the edge of a different canyon. Curved in a hollow at the base of a cliff lay a third ancient village. It was smaller than Spruce Tree House, built around a square tower four stories high. This ruin they named Square Tower House.

Richard Wetherill and Charlie Mason were not the first to discover cliff dwellings in Mesa Verde. But what they found that December—— Cliff Palace——belonged to a prehistoric civilization no one in the United States had dreamed of. Cliff Palace was an important clue in the mystery surrounding the ruins and the people who once had lived there. The towns these people left behind were preserved in the dry desert air. Richard Wetherill would devote the rest of his life to searching for their story. Charlie Mason would never lose interest in his brother-in-law's search although he moved with his family to Creede, Colorado, where he raised trout in a fish hatchery. Sometimes he even accompanied Richard on explorations.

Richard Wetherill knew that farther south in the open desert, scientists were trying to learn more about the native people who lived in walled adobe villages called pueblos. He felt sure that the Mesa Verde towns belonged to the ancestors of these people, although the walls and towers in the cliffs were more beautiful than any he had seen in pueblos. He wrote to the Smithsonian Institution in Washington, D.C., and the Peabody Museum at Harvard University in Massachusetts, telling them of his discovery. He hoped they would send their scientists to help, or at least sponsor him and his brothers, so that they could hire help for their cattle and be free to explore the canyon dwellings. Both institutions rejected Richard's appeal.

The Smithsonian suggested he ship the artifacts he had found to them. No one would come out to help. They said Richard was not a trained scientist and that he should stop disturbing archeological treasure.

But Richard could not stop. As soon as they moved the cattle out of the summer pasture, he and his brothers climbed back into Mancos Canyon. During the fifteen months after the discovery of Cliff Palace, the Wetherills found one hundred eighty-two large cliff dwellings and many smaller ones. They searched two hundred fifty miles of Mesa Verde's steep cliffs. Richard made maps, marking locations of cliff houses. He drew pictures and took photographs. The men picked up pots, clay figures, and sandals woven from fibers of the yucca plant's long leaves.

When spring came, Richard carried his collection in a ranch cart across the mountains over three hundred sixty miles to Denver, where he sold it to the Historical Society. People did not seem very interested. A few Denver tourists came to the Wetherill ranch to see a cliff dwelling. They told Richard that others thought he was looting graves.

But Baron Gustaf Nordenskiöld, a twenty-three-year-old Swedish archeologist and tourist, saw Richard's collection at the Historical Society and was eager to see more. It took him days to reach the ranch from Denver. First he took a mining train to Durango. Then he bounced all day in a small, rented horsecart, over thirty miles of twisting canyon roads to Mancos. He arrived dirty and tired, but he was still excited. Would Richard allow him to help, he wondered.

It was June. Richard knew that he and his brother Al would be able to explore only a few more days before they would be needed to move the cattle down to the valley. But he was glad to have a scientist interested in his search at last.

In 1889, Baron Nordenskiöld, a Swedish archeologist, worked with the Wetherill brothers excavating prehistoric cave dwellings at Mesa Verde. Here, Richard Wetherill sits on a windowsill of a beautifully made building now called Balcony House.

They set up camp near an alkali spring below a nine-room cliff house Richard had visited only once before. Baron Nordenskiöld described the water's taste as "nauseous." Was this spring, polluted like many desert springs with soda and salt from the soil, the ancient villagers' only water?

The climb to the ruin was steep and slippery. Loaded with digging tools, they struggled through tangled mesquite and then up the open, stony slope.

They began digging inside the red, broken walls of a circular room. Richard found round rooms in most of the cliff dwellings. Many were dug underground, with firepits and stone benches around the walls. He knew that native people farther south used circular underground rooms for meetings of the tribes' religious clans. The Hopis called the rooms *kivas*.

As Richard, Al, and the baron dug, clouds of red dust clogged their mouths and noses. The three men soaked their bandannas in water and tied them around their faces to make breathing easier.

Richard's shovel scraped on something. He began to dig more slowly, so he wouldn't break anything. It was a piece of pottery, black and white like others he had found.

Quickly the baron stopped him. The baron squatted in the rubble and began to pick and scrape the crusted dirt with a mason's trowel. Gently, patiently, he scraped until the pot stood free. Then the baron picked it up as carefully as he would a newborn baby. The pot had not a single crack.

From then on, Richard used a mason's trowel, too. This was how an archeologist collected artifacts. He watched Nordenskiöld measure, take notes, and draw floor plans in each room, marking locations of every pot, bone, or sandal they found. Richard wanted to learn everything he could about this organized way of searching ruins, called archeology.

All summer, while Richard and Al tended cattle, the baron explored other cliff dwellings with Richard and Al's younger brother, John, in the arm of Mancos Canyon the baron named Wetherill Mesa. The baron believed the caves had been inhabited for a long time. The walls and towers could not have been built in a few lifetimes. The people had no horses or machines to help them carry or shape the stones and mix the mortar. How long the construction had taken the baron had no way of knowing. How long ago the ruins had been abandoned he could only guess.

Spruce Tree House, a prehistoric Anasazi dwelling in what is now Mesa Verde National Park, was discovered late one snowy afternoon in 1888 by Richard Wetherill, a cowboy who was so excited by his find that he devoted the rest of his life to archeological exploration.

Near Spruce Tree House, he cut down the spruce growing through the wall. The tree would not have been allowed to push through the wall of a town people lived in. The baron counted the trunk's growth rings and decided Spruce Tree House must be at least one hundred sixty-two years old. He and Richard believed it was actually much older. They thought the cliff dwellings had been built and left before the Spanish arrived in the 1500s, as there were no white man's tools in any of the ruins.

At the Chicago World's Fair in 1893, Richard Wetherill helped represent Colorado. Fairgoers were amazed at his exhibit. It was hard to believe that at least two hundred years before the United States was a country, children in desert caves played inside three-story red and yellow apartment houses built around graceful, tapered towers.

The World's Fair itself was a city of white buildings made to look like ancient Greece and Rome. America did not really have an architectural style of its own. Even the idea of many-storied houses was very new.

Others, too, had been discovering the ancient towns in cliffs, on canyon floors, and in the open desert. At the fair, Richard saw photographs of a cliff dwelling near Grand Gulch, Utah, west of Mesa Verde. Seeing them made him long to explore again. Then he met the Hydes, two wealthy brothers who offered to pay him to explore. He was to give everything he found to the American Museum of Natural History in New York City.

At last Richard Wetherill had a chance to prove he could conduct a scientific search. Even though scientists would not come to help him, he wanted his work to meet their standards. Archeology was a new field, and Richard was determined to be accepted within its ranks. He began to plan. He planned a task for each member of his expedition. He planned exactly how he would describe each artifact he found.

Grand Gulch bends and twists for fifty miles, one of the wildest desert canyons in the country. Yet at one time, it must have been a cultural center, for perched high in the steep cliffs are eighty cliff dwellings. At that point the canyon is so narrow that Richard's pack burros could not pass between its walls. The expedition camped on the cracked white sand wash where once the river flowed among huge rocks shaped like toadstools and dwarves before it entered the canyon.

Each day Richard and his men, carrying heavy packs, climbed the cliffs to the caves on narrow rope-and-branch ladders. Right away, Richard noticed something strange. These people had not used the same articles as the people at Mesa Verde. Digging, he almost never heard the muffled click of his shovel striking pottery. There were not many pottery pieces. Instead, he began to turn up pieces of woven baskets.

Then he found a sandal, woven of yucca fibers like those at Mesa Verde, but much more beautifully. The toe end was round. Mesa Verde sandals were indented at the little toe. He found a spear-throwing stick archeologists called an *atlatl* and spear points, but no bows and arrows. Could these have been different people than those at Mesa Verde?

When he dug into the cave floor, Richard discovered a place where sand had been plastered in a wall around an egg-shaped hole. He knew that Navajos and Utes stored grain this way and began to dig out the hole more carefully, hoping to discover remains of ancient food. Instead, he uncovered a large, finely woven basket. He dug around it until he could lift it out. Underneath lay a man's body.

It was not a skeleton. It was a mummy, a body preserved for centuries by the desert sand's great dryness. With the utmost care, Richard lifted the body out of the hole and laid it on the cave's sand

Richard Wetherill, excavating Pueblo Bonito in Chaco Canyon for the Hyde brothers in 1897, found pottery and baskets at this site.

floor two feet above. He cut away the yucca cloth sack and opened the remains of a rabbit-fur blanket.

The man had died in agony. His black-haired head was thrown up and back. His knees were pulled up tightly. He clutched his belly with his right hand, gripping his wrist with the other hand. He had been slashed across his belly and the whole way across his back.

Someone had tried to sew the terrible wound with a one-eighth-inch-thick cord of black, braided human hair. It must have taken a long time to work a deer-bone awl back and forth through the man's flesh. The stitches in the shriveled, leathery skin were half an inch apart. This must have been the only way to try to stop the gushing blood.

Near the man, Richard found a pair of feet and legs cut off at the knees and a pair of hands and arms sliced at the elbows. The rest of the body was missing. There were seven other mummies buried close by, with spear points in their skulls or backbones.

These people had been killed in battle, Richard thought. Their relatives had buried them with care, wrapping each in rabbit fur or in a cloth woven of turkey feathers, and then in yucca-leaf cloth. They had covered each head with a fine new basket holding new sandals, seed jewelry, and stone knives with wooden handles for each to use in his or her new life.

Later Richard found nearly one hundred men, women, and children buried in graves hollowed out in cave floors near Grand Gulch. Most of their skulls had been crushed, or they had been killed with stone spears. In one skeleton, he found a huge, black volcanic glass blade pinning the hip bones together the way a skewer fastens a roasting turkey. How hard someone must have thrown that blade!

Sitting in the sand at the first burial site, Richard looked around at the low walls the cliff dwellers had built in this cave. These walls were not built as well as those in Mesa Verde. Here, there were no graceful towers or many-storied apartment houses. He had found the bodies buried two to five feet below the tumbled walls.

He picked up a piece of a clay pot. It was rough, and he could see the prints of the fingers that shaped it. There were no pots buried with the bodies he had found, not even broken pieces. The people in Grand Gulch had not used pots, even though pots were more efficient than baskets for carrying water and for cooking. Then Richard remembered something.

He and Baron Nordenskiöld had found pots in a trash mound south of a cliff dwelling in Mancos Canyon. They were gray and coiled, not at all strong and polished like the pots the cliff dwellers there had painted black on white with lightning designs. Perhaps, the baron had suggested, the gray pots belonged to an older race of people.

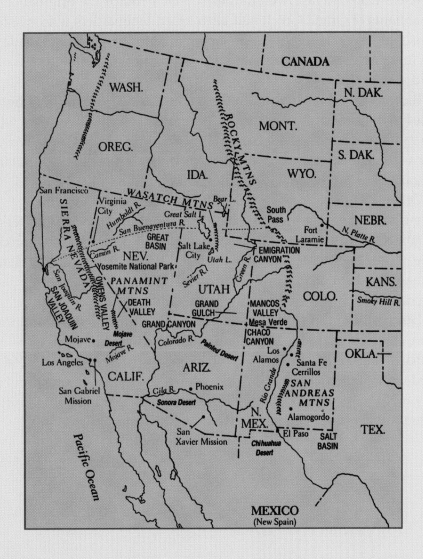

Richard was excited. The heads of these mummies were shaped differently than those of the Mesa Verde people, too. Mesa Verde skulls were short and broad. The baron told Richard that was because they flattened their babies' heads by strapping them to rigid cradleboards, not the padded ones modern native people used. Perhaps the people buried under these cliff dwellings in Grand Gulch belonged to an entirely different, older race of people than the cliff dwellers who had last lived in these caves. Perhaps the original inhabitants of Grand Gulch had been killed by invaders who wanted to use the caves. Possibly the new people built the walls and made the first pots, pressing river mud around baskets to make the baskets hold water longer.

Richard called the older race the Basket Makers. He sent his field notes to the American Museum of Natural History in New York with the mummies and their sandals and baskets. He did not write well, but a scientist friend wrote an article in *Harper's Monthly*, a popular magazine, using the notes and the photographs.

Other scientists did not believe Richard. Because he had no scientific training, they insisted he was a fraud. At Harvard University, an archeology professor told his students that Richard had invented a new people in order to sell more artifacts. This criticism did not deter Richard. He kept on exploring, because he was so fascinated he couldn't stop. He loved exploring more than anything else.

During the summer of 1895, Mr. and Mrs. Sidney Palmer and their three children, Marietta, Edna, and LaVern, set up camp near Richard's ranch. Richard showed them the cave dwellings at Mesa Verde. That fall, Richard and the Palmers traveled south one hundred fifty miles to see a big ruin they'd heard about called Pueblo Bonito, in the Navajo reservation in northern New Mexico.

Pueblo Bonito, in Chaco Canyon, was the largest ruin Richard Wetherill had ever seen. In A.D. 1100, Chaco Canyon was the hub of a major Anasazi complex of towns connected by hand-built roads. In 1988, it was named a prehistoric archeological site of world importance.

For six days they followed a wheel-rut road. The desert was high and flat with no trees and little grass, and the wind blew constantly. The wagon wheels slipped and dragged in the sand.

When the road turned east through a wide canyon wash where once the Chaco River had flowed, they rode past the ruins of a small pueblo. Soon they saw more tumbled walls. Then, to their left, curved against the dark sandstone mesa, lay a ruin that was larger than anything Richard had ever imagined.

Behind the ruin, he found holes in the cliff face, stairs the ancient pueblo dwellers had chipped with stone tools. Climbing, he stepped out on the mesa top overlooking the wide canyon.

Below him, Pueblo Bonito glowed red in the afternoon sun, spread out like a huge half-moon. The whole of Mesa Verde's Cliff Palace would be lost in one small section.

But that was not all. To the east he could see another great ruin. Across Chaco Canyon he could see mounds where several smaller pueblos might be buried. He might be looking down on an enormous city-state, like Rome or Athens!

Why had this civilization died? Where had all its people gone?

With Mr. Palmer, Richard rode across the northern mesa looking for Navajos who might have some of the answers. In the smoky light of hogans Wetherill spoke to the Navajos in their own language.

In 1897, Navajo Indians helped Richard Wetherill dig in Pueblo Bonito.

The older Indian men all gave him the same answer. The great walls looked exactly the same as they had many generations before, when the Navajos first came to the area. At that time more cedar trees and more grass grew on the mesa. The Chaco Wash had water in it and the stream flowed at the surface of the canyon floor, not far down between the eroded banks of an arroyo. But the ancient ones were gone, and no one knew who they were. *Anasazi*, the people called them, which meant "ancient enemy."

Richard and the Palmers explored for a month. They found eleven large pueblos with over one hundred rooms each, and more than one hundred smaller pueblos. Pueblo Bonito alone had more than six hundred rooms. It covered three acres and in some places rose five stories tall.

After they returned to Mancos, Richard could not stop thinking about Chaco Canyon. At one time thousands of people must have lived there. Could the Navajos, poor, wandering sheepherders, have destroyed so great a city? He did not think so. He knew that answers must lie beneath the piles of rubble inside the walls.

Soon after their visit to Chaco, Richard married Marietta Palmer. They tried to settle down to ranch life, but Richard was too restless. He was so fascinated with the Anasazi that he decided to move to Chaco Canyon. He and Marietta opened a trading post for the Navajos, which Richard hoped would support his family.

The Hyde brothers, who had helped finance the Grand Gulch exploration, agreed to send Richard money to excavate in Chaco Canyon. Richard would again give what he found to the American Museum of Natural History in New York City. The first organized search in Chaco Canyon began in 1896.

Over the next four years, Richard dug out nearly two hundred rooms in Pueblo Bonito. Soon he realized that this pueblo had been built differently than those at Mesa Verde. There, rooms were built as people moved in, with the beautiful towers added. But this huge, horseshoe-shaped pueblo had been designed ahead of time to meet a society's needs.

Some rooms were built of thin, flat rocks, others of large stones and mortar. Such different building methods suggested that the rooms had been built at different times and over many years. Walls in Pueblo Bonito lay twelve feet, or two stories, below the level of the main court and rose five stories above.

Without measuring instruments, the Anasazi constructed doorways of the same dimensions between Pueblo Bonita's many rooms.

Rooms were laid over rooms, with huge pine timber ceilings between. The pine trees grew thirty miles away from the canyon. Traveling by foot, how long had it taken these people to haul pine trunks——thousands of them——to Pueblo Bonito? Construction of the pueblo must have taken a long time.

Richard had no way of knowing how long, or when the pueblo had been started. Years later another searcher, A. E. Douglass, discovered a way to find out. He counted the annual growth rings in the ceiling timbers just as Baron Nordenskiöld had done with the tree at Spruce Tree House. Then he compared those rings to many other pine timbers. Pueblo Bonito, he discovered, was begun around A.D. 950. That was five hundred fifty years before Columbus discovered America. Douglass decided that people had lived in Pueblo Bonito until after A.D. 1300. The Mesa Verde cliff dwellings were built later than the main section of Pueblo Bonito and were inhabited a shorter time.

How could people have grown enough food in the open, hot desert for so long with so little rain? The Chaco River bed was hard, dry sand. When he was digging, Richard found only bitter springs.

Then, in July, it rained almost every day for two weeks. Walls of muddy water swept the wash, flooding ditches that Richard hadn't noticed. On the mesas, rainwater channeled into streams that fell over cliffs into shaded rock pools.

Recent research suggests that the Chaco River once flowed in the wash, flooding its banks each spring the way the Nile River did, watering Egyptian crops in ancient times. Did more rain fall in Anasazi times? Did the cliff pools store enough water for drinking and washing all year around? No one knows. People are still searching for answers in Chaco Canyon.

Not only could the Anasazi feed thousands in desert soil, but they also had time to build the largest city in the desert and to become master artists. Richard found pottery and jewelry more beautiful than any he had ever seen. He found hundreds of jars, many like those he'd found at Mesa Verde, but others painted with intricate designs or encrusted with chunks of turquoise. He found necklaces, pendants, bracelets, and carvings, many inlaid with turquoise or made of abalone shell, which shimmered like pearl in the sunlight.

The nearest turquoise mines were two hundred miles away. The nearest abalone lived in the ocean along the California coast, nearly one thousand miles away. Then Richard found the skeletons of fourteen macaws, large parrots with blue, red, yellow, or green feathers. Parrots live in the western Mexican highlands. These people must have traveled great distances!

Perhaps some of these people had moved to Chaco from the cliff houses at Mesa Verde, but Richard knew now that at Chaco the culture was much more advanced. High on the mesas north and west of Chaco were other ruins that looked similar. Could they have been part of Chaco?

Chaco Canyon was a great center, as Richard had suspected. When modern archeologists looked down on the canyon from the air, they discovered that it was connected to at least seventy-five outlying towns by almost five hundred miles of straight roads. Even though they had no wagons or cars, so many people traveled that the Anasazi dug roads thirty feet wide. In some places, low walls or ledges can still be seen edging the road's shallow depression.

Chaco has been called the greatest archeological ruin north of Mexico. An estimated five thousand people lived in four hundred settlements in and around the canyon, dependent on food grown in desert soil. These prehistoric people developed new building techniques. They watched the seasons change with a kind of solar observatory only recently discovered. They were skilled artists. They traded with people over a thousand miles away.

Evening sunlight falls on distant cliffs, while kivas at the ruins of Pueblo Bonita lie in shadow in Chaco Canyon, New Mexico.

Why did they leave Chaco? Where did they go? Richard found no evidence of terrible battles as he had at Grand Gulch. Later searchers believe that groups of people moved all over the desert, as Mesa Verde people had moved into Chaco Canyon. They probably moved in search of water.

When the trees in the forest thirty miles away were cut for ceiling timbers, the underground water those roots drew to the surface may have sunk. Then when the seasonal rains fell, the thirsty desert absorbed the water too fast for the people to catch and store it. The Chaco people, archeologists believe, wandered east to the Rio Grande, where the river flowed all year around, or south to Acoma and Zuñi, or west to Oraibi, home of the Hopis.

All over the southwestern desert, searchers have found abandoned cliff and mesa houses. Some are still unexplored, their floors littered with miniature corn cobs and shards of pottery. Since the ancient ones had no written language, people are still searching for clues to their history.

In the open desert south of Phoenix, Arizona, an ancient people archeologists call the Hohokam, ancestors of the Pima and the Papago, played an Aztec ball game in walled courts. They used a process of etching with acid cactus sap to decorate seashells, five hundred years before European artists "discovered" the method. The Hohokam did not build great adobe or stone cities.

Another ancient people, the Mogollon Mimbres in southwest New Mexico, were the first Americans to decorate pottery with animal, bird, and geometric designs. Their artistic abilities were unknown for centuries because they drilled holes in their pots and jugs and buried them with their dead.

In 1910, Richard Wetherill was shot and killed by a Navajo man, after an argument over a horse. Richard was fifty-two years old. Seven years earlier, archeologists, insisting that he was vandalizing Pueblo Bonito, convinced the federal government to stop his search. For many years, his collection lay in a storeroom at the American Museum of Natural History in New York City. In the summer of 1987, however, the results of Richard Wetherill's searches, the artifacts of the Hyde Expeditions, were displayed in a show at the museum.

Because Richard had no training, scientists did not afford him the recognition he deserved. But Richard's search laid a cornerstone for the science that became American Southwestern archeology. In 1914, when Alfred Kidder and S. J. Guernsey discovered in northeastern Arizona the same kind of remains that Richard had described at Grand Gulch, archeologists acknowledged Richard's discovery of the Basket Maker civilization. Another archeologist, John C. McGregor, pointed out in his book that when Richard dug beneath the cliff dwellers' floor and concluded that the graves were those of an older people, he was the first to use the principle of stratigraphy, which teaches that what is buried deeper is older. Above all, Richard is remembered as one of the first Americans to prove that a great civilization existed in the desert long before Europeans settled there.

Years after Richard Wetherill's death, scientists finally credited him with discovering the remains of a great civilization in the American Southwest.

The Search for Early Americans

Meet the Author

Sheila Cowing taught poetry and short-story writing before she began writing for young people. Her poems have been published in literary journals across the country. She is also an editor for *Shoe Tree*, a literary magazine written by and for young writers. Cowing currently lives in New Mexico where she enjoys hiking in and exploring the desert.

Theme Connections

Within the Selection

Record your answers to the questions below in the Response Journal section of your Writer's Notebook. In small groups, report the ideas you wrote. Discuss your ideas with the rest of your group. Then choose a person to report your group's answers to the class.

- How could Wetherill tell that the people he unearthed had died in battle?
- Which of the three main dwellings mentioned was found to be the oldest?
- How did the scientists use trees to estimate the age of buildings?

Across the Selections

- What similarities are there between Richard Wetherill and the characters in "Digging Up the Past"?
- What archaeological tools and techniques were used in both stories?

Beyond the Selection

- Think about how "The Search for Early Americans" adds to what you know about uncovering the past.
- Add items to the Concept/Questions Board about uncovering the past.

Focus Questions Did the Minotaur exist?
Will Sir Arthur Evans find evidence to support this ancient legend?

The Island of Bulls

from *Lost Cities*
by Roy A. Gallant

According to a Greek myth going back more than 2,500 years, there once was a young man named Theseus, son of the king of the great city of Athens, the capital of Greece. At this time there also lived on the nearby island of Crete a king named Minos. Minos was so powerful and so greatly feared that he was able to demand and get whatever he wished, not only from the people of his island-state but also from the people of nearby Athens on the Greek mainland.

Now it happened, according to the myth, that Minos kept on Crete a fierce monster called the Minotaur, a beast that was half bull and half man and ate human flesh. The word "minotaur" is

built out of two words——King Minos's name and the Greek word *tauros,* meaning "bull." The Minotaur was supposedly kept in a labyrinth, a great maze or place of numerous winding corridors that was so complex that it was impossible to find the way out without help.

From time to time, Minos demanded that the king of Athens send him the seven handsomest young men and the seven most beautiful maidens of the land. These fourteen youths were then led into the labyrinth, where one by one they were found and devoured by the Minotaur.

When Theseus came of age he told his father that he wanted to be one of the youths sent to King Minos so that he might slay the Minotaur and once and for all end this terrible sacrifice the people of Athens were forced to make. Although he feared that his son would never return, Theseus's father granted the young man his wish.

On the appointed day the fourteen youths boarded the ship to Crete, a ship that always flew black sails, a sign of the certain death awaiting its passengers. When they arrived the youths were paraded before King Minos, for him to judge whether all were fair enough for the Minotaur. When the king's daughter, Ariadne, saw Theseus, she fell in love with him. She then managed to see him alone before the youths were led off to the labyrinth. Ariadne told Theseus of her love and gave him a small sword and a ball of thread.

As Theseus led the way into the maze he carefully unwound the ball of thread. On hearing the ferocious roars of the Minotaur as it came charging around a corner of the labyrinth to attack him, Theseus dropped the ball of thread and began slashing at the beast with the sword given to him by Ariadne. He managed to weaken the Minotaur and finally cut off its head. He then picked up the thread and followed it out of the labyrinth, leading his thirteen companions to safety and home.

Before he had departed from Athens, Theseus had agreed to change the black sails to white if all had gone well and he had slain the Minotaur. He forgot to do so. When his father, waiting for the ship's return, saw the black sails, he presumed that his son had been killed. He was so stricken with grief that he killed himself before the ship docked. Theseus then became king.

Was there any truth to the account of Minos and his kingdom on the island of Crete? The Greek poet Homer, who lived about 850 B.C., gave us the first known account of the Cretan king Minos and his palace. Later, in 455 B.C., the Greek scholar Thucydides, who lived in Athens, wrote an account of King Minos and his powerful fleet of ships that ruled the Aegean Sea. Still later, the philosopher Aristotle, born in 384 B.C., also wrote of King Minos dominating the whole Aegean area. And there were some who thought that Crete might have been the legendary kingdom of Atlantis, mentioned by the philosopher Plato about 400 B.C.

So Crete must have had a long history, one that stretched back even before Greek scholars wrote about the land. Crete itself did not have a written history until about 2,500 years ago. Even then the Minoans left very little in writing, unlike the neighboring civilizations of Egypt and Babylonia. The Cretans were called Minoans after King Minos. The legend of King Minos and his Minotaur had existed for centuries before the Minoans used writing. It had been handed down orally in story form from one generation to the next. But because it was only a legend, no one could be certain that there had actually ever been such a kingdom.

In his search for Crete's past, Evans came across several seals. The one at left represents the legendary labyrinth. The seal above shows an athlete leaping over a bull's back.

Fascinated by the Minotaur legend and poetic accounts of a highly developed civilization much older than any other known European civilization, an English scholar from Oxford University named Sir Arthur Evans decided to find out if there was any truth to the Minotaur legend and other accounts of an ancient Cretan civilization. The Minoans had ruled supreme from about 3000 to 1450 B.C., although as a civilization they were still older. The Minoan population at its peak was about 80,000, slightly less than the present population of Portland, Maine.

Evans's interest in Crete began during a visit to Athens where he bought a few moonstones from a Greek merchant. The stones, worn by his wife as lucky charms, had strange writing scratched on them. It was the writing that led Evans to Crete in 1894, where he found more of the stones containing the same writing. He first went to the capital of the island, Knossos, where he noted that many of the women were wearing similar round stones of clay around their necks or wrists as lucky charms. Although some of the stones had simple designs carved on them, others had what appeared to be some form of writing. As he traveled around Crete, Evans saw many such stones. They turned out to be very old indeed, and some had been used as personal identity disks by the ancient Cretans. One such stone had the design of a labyrinth. Another had the shape of a creature half human and half bull.

While in Knossos, Evans became curious about several large blocks of carved stone lying about. He decided to dig a few test trenches near the stones to see if anything might lie buried below. Only a few inches beneath the surface one of his thirty workers struck something hard with a spade. Evans's excitement grew as they continued to dig around the hard object. After only a few hours of digging Evans was almost certain that he had stumbled onto the walls of a large and ancient building, possibly the palace of the mighty Minos. In all, he spent more than twenty-five years working in Crete reconstructing the Minoan remains at Knossos. The hard object just beneath the surface indeed turned out to be the palace of King Minos, built some 3,500 years earlier, even earlier than the time of the great rulers of ancient Egypt just across the sea to the south.

Month after month, year after year, the work continued. The palace of Minos turned out to be enormous, sprawling over an area larger than ten city blocks. It was shaped like a large rectangle, in the center of which was a huge courtyard of red cement. Some sections of the building were five stories high. There were twisting corridors and stairways. There were dead-end passageways and a bewildering number of rooms. Indeed, it was a labyrinth. Evans had no doubt that here was the building described in legend as both the home of Minos and of the dreaded Minotaur.

There was great excitement when the workers uncovered the first fresco. Frescoes are paintings done on walls when the walls are being plastered. In this way the plaster and the colors of the painting dry together, a process that preserves the paintings for a long time. One such fresco was a life-size painting of a young man holding a large cone-shaped cup. His skin was a deep reddish color from exposure to the sun. Other frescoes showed Minoan women, who spent most of the time indoors, as white-skinned. Throughout the palace were images of a two-bladed axe, a symbol associated with the Cretan mother-goddess, whom the Greeks called Rhea. At will she was able to enter the double-axe and vanish. An ancient word for this axe was *labrys*, from which the word labyrinth comes.

As the digging continued, Evans realized that the enormous palace had not all been built at the same time. Hallways, rooms, and storage areas were added on century after century. Minos seems to have been the name of the first Cretan king who constructed the original palace. In his honor, each of the future kings of Crete took the name of Minos and added to the palace to suit his own taste. Evans discovered large storerooms with great jars for wine and olive oil. Some of the jars stood as tall as a man and can be seen in place today. There were also containers lined with stone and with fragments of gold leaf. These were probably from the rooms where the Minoan kings kept their stores of gold, silver, and other precious metals. Nearby were apartments for the royal guards who kept watch over the king's wealth.

Evans again became excited when his workers uncovered what is probably the oldest known royal throne. As described by Evans, there "was a short bench, like that of the outer chamber, and then, separated from it by a small interval, a separate seat of honour or throne. It had a high back, like the seat, of gypsum, which was partly imbedded in the stucco of the wall. It was raised on a square base and had a curious moulding below . . . probably painted to harmonize with the fresco at its side."

As the weeks and months passed, many more discoveries were made——the paved courtyard mentioned earlier, stairways with frescoes of olive branches in flower, a wall painting of a monkey gathering flowers in baskets, and a large fresco of a bull with young acrobats. Paintings and impressions of bulls on vases and other objects were so common that it caused Evans to remark: "What a part these creatures play here!"

Like the people of Spain today, the ancient Minoans seem to have loved a sport involving acrobats and bulls. One large fresco shows a bull in full charge and three young acrobats, two girls and a boy. If we read these frescoes correctly, some sport like this may have taken place: Three youths entered a sports arena containing a bull. As the bull charged, one of the youths would grab the animal's horns, leap over the bull's head, and do a handspring off the bull's back, landing upright on his feet and in the arms of one of the other two youths. This sounds like an impossible trick, but so many Cretan artifacts suggest that some such event took place that it is hard to doubt. Is it possible that this type of event inspired the myth of the fourteen Athenian youths, King Minos, and the deadly Minotaur?

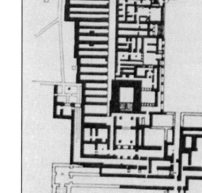

A ground plan reconstruction of the late Minoan palace at Knossos reveals a labyrinth of passageways and hundreds of rooms.

There are frescoes that also show audiences watching the contests in the bull ring. Although in Spain the object of the cruel contest is to kill the bull by plunging a sword into it, in ancient Crete the purpose seemed to be to demonstrate the athletic skills of the acrobats. But surely, from time to time, some of the youths must have been killed during the contests.

With a navy second to none, the Minoan kings ruled the seas. They were wealthy, as suggested by an elaborate game table Evans found, set with crystal, ivory, and gold and silver pieces. And they were enlightened, as evidenced by the modern system of plumbing unearthed at Knossos. Enormous clay pipes, some large enough for a person to stand up in, carried water and sewage away from the palace. There also was a system of pipes for hot and cold water flowing through the palace. After four thousand years, the drainage system at Knossos is still in working order. Nothing equal to it was built in all of Europe

Wall paintings like this one at Knossos suggest that
the Minoans loved a sport in which acrobats vaulted
over the horns and backs of bulls.

until the mid-1800s. Since Evans's time at least three other palaces have been found in other parts of the island, some with as many as 1,500 rooms.

Who were the Minoans, and what happened to bring their splendid civilization down? What they left behind shows them as a people of uncommon grace and elegance who reached an astonishingly high level of craftsmanship. Their vases and bowls of stone and their finely carved gems were unmatched anywhere. And they were apparently a peace-loving people; they had no defense fortifications and none of their art shows scenes of battle, warriors, or weapons, although finely made real weapons of bronze have been found.

Their wealth most likely came from overseas trade. Elegant pottery made by them, and copied by other people, has been unearthed in Egypt, in the Near East, on the Aegean Islands, and in Greece. For many centuries the Minoans enjoyed the good life, but then their civilization collapsed and quickly disappeared.

About the year 1450 B.C. Knossos and other Minoan centers burned. By about 1400 B.C. these cities were completely destroyed. While some scholars have supposed that invaders swept over the island and conquered it, others doubt that this is what happened. They suspect that the catastrophic explosion of the volcanic island of Thera (also called Santorin), 60 miles north of Crete, sent the Minoans and their splendid civilization into oblivion.

The Island of Bulls

Meet the Author

Roy A. Gallant is a well-known science writer who
has written nearly 80 books and more than 200 reviews and
articles. Some of the subjects he enjoys writing about are
astronomy, fossils, extraterrestrial life, dinosaurs, and
astrology. Much of his writing is aimed at young adults
and is written in a down-to-earth, easy-to-understand style.
Gallant's interests include photography, oil painting, skiing,
hiking, and kayaking.

Theme Connections

Within the Selection

Record your answers to the questions below in the Response Journal section of your Writer's Notebook. In small groups, report the ideas you wrote. Discuss your ideas with the rest of your group. Then choose a person to report your group's answers to the class.

- What motivated Sir Arthur Evans to go to Crete in search of an ancient Cretan civilization?
- What artifacts found in the palace of King Minos connect it to the myth of Theseus and the Minotaur?
- What explanations have scholars given for the disappearance of the Minoans?

Across the Selections

- Were the civilizations in "The Island of Bulls" and "The Search for Early Americans" more advanced than you thought they would be? Explain.

Beyond the Selection

- Imagine that you live thousands of years in the future. What do you think archaeologists would find if they were to excavate the dwellings in which you live in the future? How many rooms would they find? How tall is the dwelling? Do you think they would find any personal belongings? Get into groups and discuss what you think archaeologists would find. Then share your thoughts with the class.

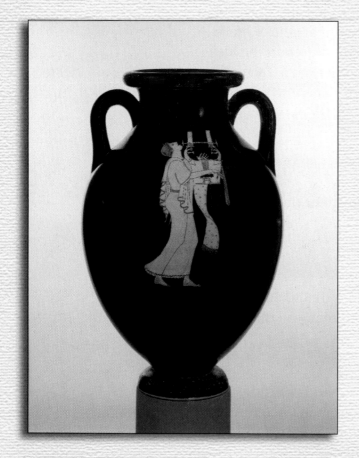

Red Figured Amphora. c.490 B.C. **Attributed to the Berlin Painter.** Terra-cotta and paint. The Metropolitan Museum of Art, New York, NY.

Three Cows and One Horse. Ceiling of the Axial gallery, Lascaux Caves, France. 15,000–13,000 B.C.

The Great Stupa, part of Sanchi ruins in India. 3rd century B.C.–A.D. 1st Century. Stone. Sanchi, Madhya Prades, India.

Ipuy and His Wife receiving offerings from their children. 1275 B.C. Copy of a wall painting from the Tomb of Ipuy. 47.5 × 74 cm. The Metropolitan Museum of Art, New York, NY.

The People on the Beach

from The Secrets of Vesuvius
by Sara C. Bisel
illustrated by Ken Marschall, Laurie McGaw,
Jack McMaster, Margo Stahl

✢———————✢

Athens, Greece, June 1982

The telegram lying at my door was marked "Urgent." As I bent down to
pick it up, I hoped that it wasn't bad news. After spending a long hot
day on my knees in the dusty ruins of an ancient Greek town, I was in
no mood for surprises. When I ripped open the envelope I saw that it
was from the National Geographic Society in Washington, D.C. They
wanted me to telephone them immediately about a special project.

Why are they in such a hurry, I asked myself. As an archaeologist
and anthropologist I have been involved in many expeditions. But my
jobs are almost never emergencies. If something has been lying in the
ground for a few thousand years, another week or two usually doesn't
make much difference.

As I shut the door to my tiny apartment, I calculated the time
difference between Athens, Greece, and Washington, D.C., and then
dialed the long-distance number. My contact at the National Geographic
Society wondered if I could spare a few days to examine some human
skeletons that had just been found at the town of Herculaneum in Italy.
Skeletons in Herculaneum, I thought to myself. Now *that* would be
interesting!

Human bones are my specialty. In fact, I'm often called "the bone lady" because most of my work involves examining and reconstructing old skeletons. Believe it or not, bones are fascinating. They can tell you a great deal about someone, even if the person has been dead for thousands of years.

I can examine a skeleton and find out whether a person was male or female. If she was female, for example, I can tell you about how old she was when she died, whether she had children, what kind of work she might have done and what kind of food she ate. I can even glue dozens of small pieces of a skull back together like a jigsaw puzzle and show you what that person looked like.

The editor at *National Geographic* explained that workmen digging a drainage ditch near the ruins of Herculaneum had accidentally discovered some skeletons lying on what had once been the town's beachfront. Nearby, archaeologists had later uncovered some boat storage chambers in the ancient seawall. Much to their surprise, there

My job is to excavate and study the bones of people who lived and died many centuries ago.

were more skeletons inside these cave-like rooms. Here people had found shelter from the terrifying eruption of Mount Vesuvius in A.D. 79. As they lay huddled together in the dark, they were smothered by an enormous surge of scorching gas and ash from the volcano. Flowing hot ash, rock and pumice then buried them. Today, almost two thousand years later, the tangled remains of these ancient Romans lie as they fell, preserved in the wet volcanic earth.

This was an amazing discovery. Although archaeologists have been digging out Herculaneum for centuries, very few bodies had ever been found. As a result, experts had decided that almost all of the Herculaneans must have escaped before the disaster. We now knew that this was not true.

But even more exciting for me was the chance to study the actual skeletons of real ancient Romans. Because the Romans cremated their dead, they left behind plenty of urns full of human ashes but very few complete remains. So these Herculaneans represented the first large group of Roman skeletons ever found.

"I'll book a seat on the next flight to Naples," I said to the *National Geographic* editor and then slammed the receiver down. I quickly rolled up a few T-shirts and several pairs of jeans and stuffed them into my bag. I knew that I had to leave for Italy right away. Now that the skeletons had been exposed to the air, they had to be properly preserved as soon as possible or they would quickly disintegrate and turn to dust. If that was allowed to happen, a priceless opportunity to find out exactly what the ancient Romans had looked like and how they had lived would be lost.

It was strange, I thought grimly, that Vesuvius, the volcano that had caused one of the biggest natural disasters in the world, was now giving me the most exciting assignment any physical anthropologist could ever dream of. I would be the first person to recreate the lives of these men, women and children who had lived and died so long ago. I knew that bones could talk. If I listened carefully, they would whisper their secrets.

What would these skeletons tell me?

Naples, Italy, June 1982

. . . darkness fell, not the dark of a moonless or cloudy night, but as if the lamp had been put out in a closed room. You could hear the shrieks of women, the wailing of infants, and the shouting of men; some were calling their parents, others their children or their wives, trying to recognize them by their voices. People bewailed their own fate or that of their relatives, and there were some who prayed for death in their terror of dying. Many sought the aid of the gods, but still more imagined there were no gods left, and that the universe was plunged into eternal darkness for evermore.

Pliny the Younger
1st century A.D.

I put down my fork and reread the words that described a group of people trying to escape from the fury of Vesuvius on that August day so many years ago. A chill crept up my neck. I was no longer hungry.

I had been hoping to start examining the new skeletons soon after I arrived. But it was late by the time I checked into my hotel, and I knew that not much could be done until morning. You need good light for excavation work. So I'd had a bath, tucked a few books under my arm and gone down to the hotel restaurant where I ordered a plate of pasta. Then I settled down for a crash review lesson on ancient Herculaneum and how the sudden eruption of Vesuvius had changed its fate forever.

The town of Herculaneum is named after the legendary strongman Hercules. This vase shows Hercules striking Cerebus, the three-headed dog.

177

The descriptions I was reading had been written by Pliny, a seventeen-year-old student who lived in Misenum, across the Bay of Naples. His uncle had sailed across the bay toward Herculaneum to try to help stranded friends, until his ship was cut off by "bits of pumice and blackened stones, charred and cracked by the flames." Did Pliny's uncle have any idea what he was sailing into, I wondered. Or, when he saw from afar the mountain explode and a column of ash and smoke rise twelve miles into the air, could he simply not believe his eyes until he had taken a closer look?

Pliny's uncle eventually landed at Stabiae, several miles south of Herculaneum. Though "great sheets of flame" were flashing out from the peak of Vesuvius, he actually had a bath and went to sleep. But the people with him sat up in terror all night, while the buildings shook as if they were being torn out of the ground. When the door to the uncle's room became choked by a layer of cinder and ash, they woke him up and fled, tying pillows on their heads as protection against the pumice stones that rained around them.

But Vesuvius eventually caught up with Pliny's uncle. In spite of his calm bravery, he was suffocated by sulphur fumes while trying to get back to his ship.

Meanwhile, about twenty miles across the bay at Misenum, Pliny observed the various stages of the eruption, beginning with the appearance of the mushroom-shaped cloud of ash, followed by falling ash, pumice and stones. He described earth shocks so violent it seemed as if the world was not only being shaken, but turned upside down.

I thought it was amazing that the eyewitness account he wrote had come down through the centuries. Only recently did modern scientists realize how accurate Pliny's description was, after they had studied many other volcanoes themselves. I put down my book. From the window I could see Mount Vesuvius, quiet now, looking more like a gentle slumbering hill than a deadly and still-active volcano.

Pliny's description of panicking crowds had been written about the people at Misenum, who had had to shake the ashes off their bodies so they would not be buried alive.

How much worse must it have been for the Herculaneans, who lived closer to the inferno, hemmed in between the mountain and the sea? Vesuvius's blast was so powerful that ash fell as far away as Africa and Syria.

I know many people who get shivers up their spines at the sight of a big lightning storm, or ten-foot waves crashing onto the seashore. But to have the very earth beneath you suddenly gush ash and fire, to have a glowing avalanche of ash and pumice, hotter than an oven, rip over the land at the speed of a galloping horse. . . .

When Vesuvius erupted, ash and gas came spewing out of the summit, forced straight up into the air by the pressure and heat of the blast. Eventually, this cloud cooled, and some of it collapsed, sending ash and hot gas racing down the slopes at speeds of up to seventy miles per hour, ripping the roofs off houses and overturning ships in the bay. These surges were followed by thick and glowing avalanches of fiery ash, rock and pumice——hot magma that has cooled so quickly that it is still full of volcanic gases, like a hard foamy sponge.

Sulphur fumes caused by the eruption of Mount Vesuvius overcome Pliny's uncle in this painting done in 1813.

Vesuvius had not actually erupted for hundreds of years before A.D. 79, and the people of the area believed the volcano was extinct. But they could remember an earthquake seventeen years earlier that had caused much damage to the town. And in the days before the volcano erupted, occasional rumblings and ground tremors were felt, creating the odd crack in a wall, or causing a statue to tumble off its stand. And other strange things happened: wells and springs mysteriously dried up, flocks of birds flew away, and animals were exceptionally restless.

We know now that the dry wells were caused by the increasing heat and pressure that were building deep in the earth, and that animals are always more sensitive than humans to changes in the earth and the atmosphere. But, I wondered, were the people in Herculaneum aware that something was about to happen? Before the mountain actually erupted, did it occur to anyone that it might be a good idea to leave town? How many waited until the streets were so crowded that escape was almost impossible? Were they spooked by the tremors, their suddenly dry wells, or the nervous actions of their animals? Did they think the gods were showing their anger?

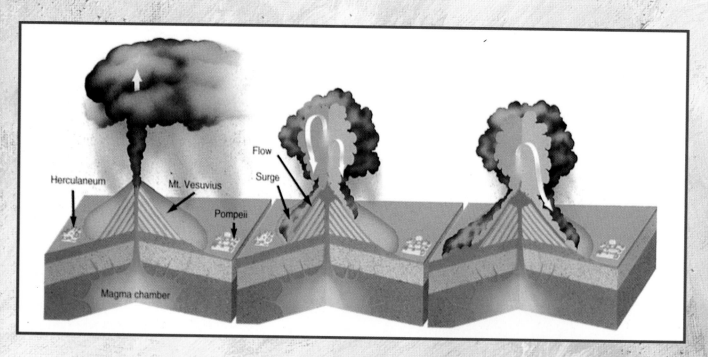

1. At midday on August 24, A.D. 79, Vesuvius erupts, sending a cloud of ash and pumice 12 miles into the air.

2. After midnight, the cloud collapses, sending a surge of ash and hot gas down the mountain, killing the Herculaneans. A flow of hot ash, rock, and pumice eventually buries the town.

3. Early the next morning another surge kills the people of Pompeii. It, too, is followed by a flow of hot debris from the volcano.

We will probably never know exactly what the volcano's victims were thinking in those days before the eruption. We do know that the glowing avalanches that buried Herculaneum and the nearby city of Pompeii created two time capsules of ancient Roman life that have not changed in almost two thousand years.

Sealed by volcanic ash and rock, the buried buildings have been protected from the wind and rain that would have worn down the columns and statues over the centuries. Wooden doors, shutters, stairs, cupboards and tables have not been exposed to the air to rot away, or been destroyed by fire. And unlike other ancient towns, the roads and buildings have not been repaired, or torn down and replaced by something more modern.

Instead, Herculaneum and Pompeii look the way they did so many years ago. The roofs of the houses may be gone, the mosaic floors cracked and the wall paintings faded. But we can still walk down the streets over the same stones that the ancient Romans walked on. We can see a 2,000-year-old loaf of bread, now turned to stone, or eggs still in their shells waiting to be served for lunch.

Although both Herculaneum and Pompeii were buried by the volcano, their fates were quite different. Pompeii, a town of twenty thousand people, lay five miles away from the volcano, but the wind was blowing in its direction when the eruption occurred. Throughout the afternoon and evening of August 24th, ash and pumice rained down on Pompeii. This frightened many people, and some of them fled immediately. But it was not until early the next morning that the first flow of hot gas and ash overwhelmed the town, killing the two thousand people who had failed to escape.

The fallen bodies of the Pompeiians were buried under twelve feet of ash and pumice. When the dead bodies rotted away they left hollow places in the hardened volcanic rock. Archaeologists discovered these cavities in the 1860s and decided to pour in plaster to create lifelike models of the volcano's victims as they lay or crouched in the positions in which they died. Some appear to be gasping or choking in their final moments as they were suffocated by ash so hot that it singed their hair and burned the insides of their mouths. But the plaster also covered up what remained of the skeletons, preventing them from being studied by modern scientists.

Herculaneum, which was less than three miles from Vesuvius, was upwind of the volcano. Most of the falling ash blew in the opposite direction, leaving less than an inch lying over the town by the end of the day. Instead, at about 1:15 early the next morning, a violent surge of ash and hot gas poured over the town. By the time the waves of hot mud followed, everyone was dead. In a few hours, Herculaneum was completely buried under sixty-five feet of hot volcanic matter, which, when it cooled, covered the town like a cement shield.

And so the town lay tightly sealed, for about 1,500 years.

Archaeologists made lifelike models at Pompeii by pouring plaster into the hollow shells of hardened volcanic rock that sealed Vesuvius's victims.

Then in 1709, a well-digger accidentally struck fine polished marble beneath the ground. An Austrian prince who was building a villa in the area realized that the marble was likely just the beginning of a major buried treasure, and he started to dig into the site.

Luckily for the prince, and unhappily for modern archaeologists and historians, the well-digger had found Herculaneum's ancient theater, one of the most luxurious and treasure-filled buildings in the town. The prince wanted art and fine building materials for his villa, so he hired diggers who bored tunnels through the theater, not knowing what it was, and not caring in the least about the damage they were doing to the structure itself.

The prince plundered the building of its bronze and stone statues and vases. Marble was ripped off the walls and pillars, and the treasures were carted off to the prince's own house or those of his rich friends. Before long these valuable artifacts were scattered in museums and private collections all over Europe.

The prince's raiders, burrowing through the site like greedy moles sniffing out treasure, did more damage to Herculaneum than the volcano itself.

More raiding expeditions followed, and it was only in 1860 that serious archaeological work began. But even with many of the most precious objects gone, the excavated town itself told historians a great deal about the ancient Romans and how they lived. Because the ruin had been snugly covered by a wet and heavy layer of earth, Herculaneum was even better preserved than Pompeii (which had suffered more damage under its airy blanket of ash and pumice).

Then just a few years ago came the most amazing discovery of all, when ditch-diggers accidentally found the group of skeletons on the ancient beachfront.

By the time these beach skeletons were found, scientists had discovered that we could learn a great deal about people by examining their bones. We could do much more than make plaster casts. Now we can analyze the bones themselves and reconstruct the skulls to see what the people looked like.

This is where I came in. In the morning, I would help to dig up these bones and begin to study them. For the first time, we would know more about the Romans than what books and paintings and sculptures had shown us. We would be able to see the people themselves.

I would be one of the first modern people to look an ancient Roman in the face.

Herculaneum, June 1982

It was quiet on Herculaneum's ancient beach. Above my head, drying sheets and underwear fluttered from the apartment balconies that now overlook the ruins.

Today this beach is just a narrow dirt corridor that lies several feet below sea level. But thousands of years ago, the waves of the Mediterranean would have lapped where I now stood, and my ears would have been filled with the gentle sound of the surf, rather than the dull roar of midday traffic in modern-day Ercolano, a crowded suburb of Naples.

To one side of me stood the arched entryways of the boat chambers, most of them still plugged by volcanic rock, their secrets locked inside. Only one chamber had been opened so far, and its contents were now hidden behind a padlocked plywood door.

I eyed the wooden door longingly, wishing for a sudden gift of X-ray vision. Dr. Maggi, the director of the excavation and keeper of the key, had been called away to a meeting with some government officials, and would not be back until sometime in the afternoon.

"Dottoressa!"

Ciro Formuola, the foreman of the work crew that was going to help me dig out the skeletons, was calling me from farther down the old beach. He was waving me toward a roped-off area surrounding three ordinary-looking piles of dirt.

I have examined thousands of skeletons in my life, but seeing each one for the first time still fills me with a kind of awe. As I walked over to the mound that Ciro was pointing at, I knew I was about to meet my first Herculanean.

It didn't look like much at first——just a heap of dirt with bits of bone poking out. I knelt down and gently scraped earth off the skeleton, exposing it to the light for the first time in two thousand years. Although the skeleton was badly broken, I had a hunch that it might be female, but I was puzzled by the position of her bones. Her thigh was poking out grotesquely beside a section of skull. It almost looked as if the bones had been carelessly tossed there, they were so broken and tangled.

Then I realized that something dreadful had happened to this woman, and that she had met with a violent death of some kind. Her skull was shattered, her pelvis crushed, and her leg had been thrust up to her neck. Roof tiles were trapped beneath her.

I looked up. Above me was the open terrace where Herculaneans had held sacred ceremonies. Above that was the wall of the town itself, most of the surrounding balustrade now missing.

Had this woman fallen from the wall above? Had some huge force propelled her from the town, perhaps a piece of flying debris, or the blast from the volcano itself, so that she smashed face down onto the ground? What had she been doing on the wall in the first place? Calling down to the people on the beach for help?

The beachfront, the ruins of Herculaneum and Vesuvius as they look today.

I picked up one of the bones and felt its cool smoothness in my hands. Because this was the first Herculanean I got to know, this skeleton was extra special to me. I named her Portia.

By measuring the bones, I could tell that Portia was about 5 feet 1 inch tall. She was about forty-eight when she died——an old woman by Roman standards——and had buck teeth.

Later, after a chemical analysis, we learned that Portia also had very high levels of lead in her bones. Lead is a poison, but in Roman times it was a common substance. It was used in makeup, medicines, paint pigment, pottery glazes, and to line drinking cups and plates. Cheap wine was sweetened with a syrup that had been boiled down in lead pots, so heavy drinkers may have had even more exposure to lead.

I closely examine each bone of a skeleton as I lift it from the wet volcanic earth.

On either side of Portia was a skeleton. One was another female. She lay on her side, almost looking as if she had died in her sleep. As I brushed dirt from her left hand, something shiny caught my eye as it glinted in the sunlight. It was a gold ring.

When we uncovered the rest of the hand, we found a second ring. And in a clump on her hip we found two intricate snakes' head bracelets made of pure gold, a pair of earrings that may have held pearls, and some coins (the cloth purse that had probably once held these valuables had long since rotted away).

We ended up calling her the Ring Lady. She was about forty-five when she died. She was not terribly good-looking; her jaw was large and protruding. There were no cavities in her teeth, but she did have gum disease, which left tiny pits in the bone along her gum line. If she had lived today, her dentist probably would have advised her to floss more often!

We called this skeleton the Ring Lady because of the two gold rings she wears on her left hand. We also found two bracelets, a pair of earrings and some coins by her side.

In fact, most of the Herculaneans I examined had very good teeth, with only about three cavities each. Today, many of us have about sixteen cavities each, in spite of all our fluoride treatments, regular dental checkups and constant nagging to floss and brush! But the Romans had no sugar in their diet. They used honey, but not much, because it was expensive. Instead, the Herculaneans ate a well-balanced diet, including much seafood, which is rich in fluoride. Not only that, but they had strong jaws from chewing and tearing food without using knives and forks. And they did clean their teeth, scrubbing them with the stringy end of a stick rather than using a brush and toothpaste.

On the other side of Portia we dug up the skeleton we called the Soldier. He was found lying down, his hands outstretched, his sword still in his belt. We found carpenter's tools with him, which had perhaps been slung over his back. (Roman soldiers often worked on building projects when they were between wars.) He also had a money belt containing three gold coins. He was quite tall for a Roman, about 5 feet 8 inches.

When I examined the man's skull, I could see that he was missing six teeth, including three at the front, and that he'd had a huge nose. And when I examined the bone of his left thigh, I could see a lump

An archaeologist carefully brushes dirt away from the soldier's skeleton. The soldier's sword still lies by his side.

We found these coins in the soldier's money belt. One of them has the head of the Emperor Nero on it.

where a wound had penetrated the bone and caused a blood clot that eventually had hardened. Near the knee, where the muscle would have been attached, the bone was enlarged slightly. This indicated that he would have had well-developed thighs, possibly due to gripping the sides of a horse with the knees while riding (Romans didn't use saddles).

Had the soldier lost those front teeth in a fight, I wondered. Had he been wounded in the leg during the same fight or another one? His life must have been fairly rough and tumble.

While members of the excavation team poured buckets of water on the three skeletons to loosen the debris, I continued to scrape off the dirt and volcanic matter with a trowel. Later, in the laboratory, each bone and tooth would be washed with a soft brush. Then they would be left to dry before being dipped in an acrylic solution to preserve them. Finally, each bone would be measured, then measured again to prevent errors, and the figures would be carefully recorded.

By late afternoon my back and knees were stiff from crouching, and the back of my neck was tight with the beginning of a sunburn.

I stood up and stretched. There was still much to do before the three skeletons would be free of their volcanic straitjackets. I started to think about heading back to the hotel for a shower and bite to eat. But a flurry of activity down the beach caught my eye, and suddenly I no longer felt tired.

To my right, Dr. Maggi stood outside the locked wooden door I had seen earlier. He was unbolting the padlock. When he saw me, he waved. I put down my trowel, wiped my hands on my jeans and hurried over. Inside, I knew, was the only group of Roman skeletons that had ever been found——the twelve people who had huddled in the shelter and died together when the volcanic avalanches poured down the mountainside into the sea.

I could hear an odd echo from inside the chamber as Dr. Maggi clicked the padlock open. Behind me, a number of the crew members had gathered. We were all very quiet.

189

The plywood door seemed flimsy as Dr. Maggi pulled it open. From inside the chamber came the dank smell of damp earth.

A shiver crept up my neck. We were opening a 2,000-year-old grave. What would we find?

As I entered the cave-like boat chamber, I could barely see, even though the sun flooded through the door. Someone handed me a flashlight, but its light cast greenish shadows, making it feel even more spooky.

The light played over the back of the shelter, no bigger than a single garage and still crusted over with volcanic rock. I saw an oddly shaped, lumpy mound halfway back. I took several steps into the chamber and pointed the light at the mound.

The narrow beam found a skull, the pale face a grimace of death. As my eyes grew accustomed to the dim light, I soon realized there were bones and skulls everywhere. They were all tangled together——clinging to each other for comfort in their final moments——and it was hard to distinguish one from another. But I knew that twelve skeletons had been found in all——three men, four women, and five children. One child had an iron house key near him. Did he think he would be going back home?

I took another step into the cave. At my feet was a skeleton that was almost entirely uncovered. From the pelvis I could see it was a female, a girl, lying face down. Beneath her, we could just see the top of another small skull.

It was a baby.

I knelt down and gently touched the tiny skull. My throat felt tight as I thought about this girl, this baby, and what it must have been like for them in this dark cave in the moments before they died.

"Una madre col suo bambino," whispered Ciro behind me.

"I don't think they're a mother and baby," I said. I could see from the pelvis that the girl was not old enough to have had children. I pointed to my own stomach and outlined a beachball tummy with my arms while I shook my head. "This girl has never given birth."

"Allora, é la sorella?"

I frowned, pulled my Italian-English dictionary out of the back pocket of my jeans and flipped through it. I realized Ciro thought these two skeletons belonged to a baby and its older sister.

"We'll see," I murmured. I knew it was important not to jump to conclusions. You have to question everything about bones, especially ones that have been lying around for two thousand years. I've known cases where people thought bone damage was caused by joint disease, when it was in fact caused by rats gnawing at the dead body.

190

I struggled to free a bronze cupid pin and two little bells from the baby's bones. Whoever the child was, it had been rich enough to wear expensive ornaments. But I knew it would take many more hours of careful study before we knew the real story behind these two skeletons.

Later, in the laboratory, I gained enough information to put together a more likely background for the skeleton of the young girl.

Unlike the baby, she had not come from a wealthy family. She had been about fourteen, and from the shape of her skull I knew she had probably been pretty. When I examined her teeth I could tell that she had been starved or quite ill for a time when she was a baby. She had

Workers reveal an opening to a partially excavated boat chamber in a row with other chambers sealed tight by volcanic rock.

also had two teeth removed about one or two weeks before she died, probably giving her a fair bit of pain. And her life had been very hard. She had done a lot of running up and down stairs or hills, as well as having to lift objects too heavy for her delicate frame.

This girl could not have been the child of a wealthy family, like the baby. She had probably been a slave who died trying to protect the baby of the family she worked for.

And there were many others. Near the slave girl lay the skeleton of a seven-year-old girl whose bones also showed that she had done work far too heavy for a child so young.

We found a sixteen-year-old fisherman, his upper body well developed from rowing boats, his teeth worn from holding cord while he repaired his fishing nets.

Particularly heartbreaking were the two pregnant women I examined, for we were also able to recover their tiny unborn babies, their bones as fragile as eggshells. One woman had been only about sixteen years old.

Though it is fascinating to reconstruct the life of a single person by examining his or her bones, for anthropologists and historians the most useful information comes from examining all of the skeletons of one population. This is one reason why Herculaneum is so important.

During the next few months we opened two more boat chambers. In one we discovered forty tangled human skeletons and one of a horse; in another we found twenty-six skeletons creepily lined up like a row of dominoes, as if heading in single file for the back of the chamber.

The skeletons represented a cross-section of the population of a whole town——old people, children and babies, slaves, rich and poor, men and women, the sick and the healthy. By examining all these skeletons, we can get some ideas about how the townspeople lived and what they were like physically.

We found out, for example, that the average Herculanean man was 5 feet 5 inches tall, the average woman about 5 feet 1 inch. In general, they were well nourished. And we have examined enough people to know that although the rich people had easy lives, the slaves often worked so hard that they were in pain much of the time.

Studying these skeletons closely can also help medical researchers and doctors. In ancient times, many diseases could not be cured by surgery or drugs. Instead, people kept getting sicker, until they eventually died. By examining the bones of these people, we can learn a great deal about how certain diseases progress.

By the end of my stay in Herculaneum, I had examined 139 skeletons. Their bones were sorted into yellow plastic vegetable crates that lined the shelves in my laboratory. And each box of bones has a different story to tell.

Even though I can't tell the good guys from the bad, and I can't tell you whether they were happy or not, I know a great deal about these people. I can see each person plainly. I even imagine them dressed as they might have been, lounging on their terraces or in the baths if they were wealthy, toiling in a mine or in a galley if they were the most unfortunate slaves.

Most of all, I feel that these people have become my friends, and that I have been very lucky to have had a part in bringing their stories to the rest of the world.

Here I am cleaning bones at a long table.

The People on the Beach

Meet the Author

Sara C. Bisel is one of the world's leading specialists in ancient bones. She has worked on skeletons in Greece, Turkey, and Israel. Some of her work has been featured in *Discover* and *National Geographic* magazines and on a National Geographic television program.

Meet the Illustrator

Ken Marschall is well known for his wonderful paintings of the *Titanic*, featured in the best-selling book, *Titanic: An Illustrated History*. He has also created illustrations of the *Hindenburg* and of the *Lusitania*.

Theme Connections

Within the Selection

Record your answers to the questions below in the Response Journal section of your Writer's Notebook. In small groups, report the ideas you wrote. Discuss your ideas with the rest of your group. Then choose a person to report your group's answers to the class.

- Why was the town of Herculaneum so well preserved when the archaeologists found it?
- What was Sara Bisel able to learn from the skeletons she examined?
- What killed the inhabitants of Herculaneum?

Across the Selections

- How is the author of "The People on the Beach" similar to Damien's mother in "Digging Up the Past?"
- How did conducting research beforehand help both Damien's mother and Sara Bisel?

Beyond the Selection

As you've seen in "The People on the Beach," uncovering the past can involve a lot of detective work. Skilled scientists piece together clues in order to determine what happened during a far earlier time. Not all of the past is ancient, though, and most of us have at some time had to piece together clues in order to reconstruct a previous event. Think of a time when you have had to reconstruct an event from its clues. What event was it? Were you able to accurately reconstruct it? Share your stories with the class.

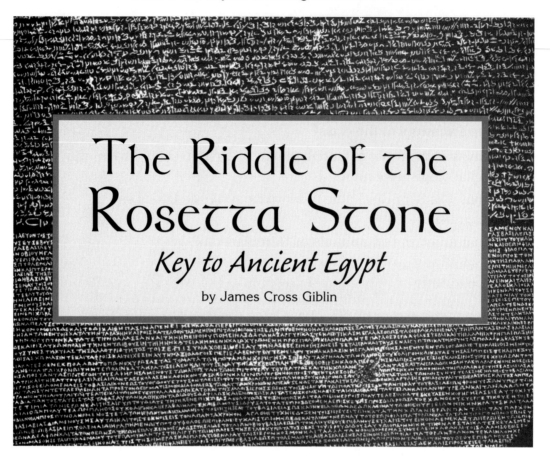

The Riddle of the Rosetta Stone

Key to Ancient Egypt

by James Cross Giblin

I. The Mysterious Hieroglyphs

The scene: The Egyptian Sculpture Gallery of the British Museum in London. The time: Now.

Near the entrance to the long, high-ceilinged room stand two magnificent granite statues of Pharaoh Amenophis III, who ruled Egypt about 1400 B.C. Farther on is a colossal head of Pharaoh Ramesses II dating back to 1250 B.C. And beyond it, resting on a simple base, is a slab of black basalt, a volcanic rock.

Next to the statues and the head, the slab seems unimpressive at first glance. It is roughly the size of a tabletop—three feet nine inches long, two feet four and a half inches wide, and eleven inches thick. But many experts would say that this rather small piece of rock was more valuable than any of the larger objects in the room. For it is the famed Rosetta Stone, which gave nineteenth-century scholars their first key to the secrets of ancient Egypt.

What makes this stone so special? Step closer, and you'll see. Spotlights pick out markings carved into the surface of the stone, and close up you can tell that these marks are writing. At the top are fourteen lines of hieroglyphs—pictures of animals, birds, and geometric shapes. Below them you can make out thirty-two lines written in an unfamiliar script. And below that, at the bottom of the slab, are fifty-four more lines written in the letters of the Greek alphabet.

Before the Rosetta Stone was discovered in 1799, no one knew how to read Egyptian hieroglyphic writing. Its meaning had been lost for almost 1400 years. But countless visitors to Egypt over the centuries had tried to decipher the mysterious symbols. This is the story of their attempts, and of how the Rosetta Stone finally enabled scholars to unlock the Egyptian past.

The story begins in the seventh century A.D., when Greek scholars visiting Egypt first called the symbols "hieroglyphs." They gave them that name, which means "sacred carvings" in Greek, because they found so many of them on the walls of Egyptian tombs and temples.

197

As the Greeks sailed up the Nile River to the ancient cities of Memphis and Thebes, they asked native after native what the hieroglyphs meant. Not even the oldest Egyptians could tell them, for the language expressed in the hieroglyphs had already been dead for several hundred years. It had been replaced by Coptic, the language spoken by Christian Egyptians. And Coptic, in turn, was replaced by Arabic after the Arabs conquered Egypt in A.D. 642. By the time the visitors from Greece arrived, no living Egyptian knew how to read the hieroglyphic writing of his ancestors.

Frustrated in their attempts to get someone to translate the hieroglyphs for them, the Greeks decided on their own that the symbols must be a kind of picture writing. Some thought the pictures were mystical devices used in ancient religious rites, whose meaning was known only to long-dead Egyptian priests.

Others stumbled on the correct definitions of a few hieroglyphs. No one knows exactly where the Greeks obtained this information. Some think it came from craftsmen who made good luck charms based on ancient Egyptian designs and still knew what those symbols meant.

However they obtained it, the Greeks couldn't resist adding their own original "explanations" to the definitions. For example, a Greek writer named Horapollo said correctly that the picture of a goose stood for the word "son." But then he explained that this was because geese took special care of their young, which was completely inaccurate.

The writings of Horapollo circulated widely throughout Europe and influenced the study of hieroglyphs for centuries to come. No one questioned the Greek writer's explanations. Instead, European scholars accepted them as truths and put forward their own mistaken interpretations of the mysterious symbols.

A few genuine advances in understanding the hieroglyphs were made during the 1700s. The French scholar C. J. de Guignes observed that groups of hieroglyphs in Egyptian texts were often enclosed by an oval outline, which he called a cartouche. "Cartouche" is a French word that originally meant a cartridge, and the line around the hieroglyphs had a similar shape. De Guignes guessed rightly that the cartouches in hieroglyphic inscriptions were intended to draw attention to important names, probably the names of Egyptian rulers.

None of these theories brought scholars any closer to a true understanding of the hieroglyphs. As the 1700s came to an end, their meaning was as much of a mystery as ever.

All the secrets of ancient Egypt—its history, its literature, its religious beliefs—remained hidden behind the lines of the mysterious hieroglyphs. And it looked as if they might stay there forever. Then, in 1798, something happened that seemed at first to have nothing to do with the puzzle of the hieroglyphs. The French general Napoleon Bonaparte invaded Egypt with an army of 38,000 soldiers.

France was at war with England, and Napoleon's main goal was to occupy Egypt and then attack British-held India. But like many Europeans of the time, Napoleon was also interested in learning more about Egypt itself. So, along with the soldiers, Napoleon brought with him to Egypt a party of 167 scholars and scientists. Their assignment: to study every aspect of the country and its history.

What neither Napoleon nor the scholars could guess was that their most important discovery would be an odd-shaped black slab with three different kinds of writing on it.

II   The Stone Is Found

Napoleon entered the Egyptian capital, Cairo, on July 21. There he took over an elegant palace to serve as the headquarters for his scholars and scientists.

While the scholars pursued their studies, the tide was turning against Napoleon. On August 1 the British surprised the French fleet at anchor near Alexandria and completely destroyed it. Now Napoleon, his army, and the scholars were trapped in the land the French had conquered.

For the next year, the army fended off attacks by the Turks, who had formerly ruled Egypt. The scholars took measurements of sphinxes, gathered botanical specimens, and made copies of the still-mysterious hieroglyphs they found everywhere. Then, in August 1799, Napoleon evaded the British naval blockade and returned with a few companions to France to deal with problems there.

The French army stayed behind in Egypt—and so did the scholars. In late August, shortly after Napoleon's departure, a large, heavy package arrived at the scholars' palace in Cairo. When they opened it, they found it contained a black stone slab covered with writing in three different scripts.

A note from a French army officer accompanied the package. He told the scholars that the stone had been unearthed in an old fort near the town of Rosetta, thirty-five miles north of Alexandria. French soldiers were tearing down a ruined wall in the fort when they came upon the slab. The top right and left corners were missing, as was the bottom right corner. The soldiers had gone over the rest of the wall carefully in hopes of finding the missing pieces embedded in it, but with no luck.

The scholars labeled the slab the "Rosetta Stone" in honor of the place where it was found, and called in their language experts to examine it. As soon as they glimpsed the writing on the slab, the experts became tremendously excited. This was the first time they had ever seen hieroglyphs carved on the same stone with a passage written in the familiar letters of the Greek alphabet.

Except for the missing corner, the Greek passage seemed to be quite complete. One of the experts set to work at once to translate it into French. He discovered that it was a decree passed by a gathering of priests in the city of Memphis in 196 B.C. The decree praised the accomplishments of the thirteen-year-old pharaoh, Ptolemy V Epiphanes, on the first anniversary of his coronation.

That explained why the passage was carved in Greek. The Greek leader, Alexander the Great, had taken control of Egypt in 332 B.C., and after Alexander's death in 323 B.C. his general, Ptolemy, replaced him. From then until 30 B.C., when Rome conquered Egypt, a long line of pharaohs from the Ptolemy family ruled the country. The Ptolemys kept their Greek culture, including their language, but they also respected the customs and religious beliefs of the native Egyptians. So it was only natural for the priests' statement to have been carved in both Greek and Egyptian on the Rosetta Stone.

After the Greek passage had been translated, the scholars turned their attention to the Egyptian writing on the slab. First they studied the hieroglyphs. Then they puzzled over the second script. They had seen examples of it before on rolls of papyrus, the writing material the Egyptians used instead of paper. Deciding that it was a simpler form of Egyptian writing, the scholars called it demotic, meaning "of the people."

But what did the passages in Egyptian mean? Did they contain exactly the same message as the Greek passage? The last sentence of the Greek text said, "This decree shall be inscribed on a stela [slab] of hard stone in sacred [hieroglyphic] and native [demotic] and Greek characters," so it seemed clear that the inscription was the same in all three languages. That way, the priests' statement could be read by Egyptians who understood Greek, as well as by those who knew only one or both of the Egyptian languages. But the scholars were still far from being able to decipher either the hieroglyphs or the demotic writing.

Meanwhile, the French situation in Egypt was going from bad to worse. In the spring of 1801, British troops landed near Alexandria and a Turkish army marched into Egypt from Syria. Cairo fell to the Turks in June, and the French, under General Jacques Menou, retreated to Alexandria. With the army went the scholars and all the material they had gathered in Egypt, including the Rosetta Stone.

Besieged and outnumbered, the French were finally forced to surrender to the British in September 1801. As part of the settlement, the British ordered the scholars to hand over their treasures. The scholars protested. "Without us," they said, "this material is a dead language that neither you nor your scientists can understand." General Menou went so far as to claim that the Rosetta Stone was his personal property.

At last the British gave in and allowed the scholars to keep the bulk of their collections. But they insisted on taking the Rosetta Stone. Reluctantly, General Menou turned it over to the British general, Hutchinson. "You can have it," he said, "because you are the stronger of us two."

III   Clues to the Puzzle

Fortunately, the French had made a number of copies of the inscriptions on the Rosetta Stone. They did this by covering the surface of the Stone with printer's ink, laying a sheet of paper on it, and rolling rubber rollers over it until good, clear impressions were obtained.

These ink impressions were sent to France, where they were studied closely by many scholars. Each scholar was eager to be the first to decipher the mysterious hieroglyphs, but most of them began by focusing on the demotic inscription, the most complete passage on the slab.

Unlike the hieroglyphs, which were separate units, the demotic script was cursive, which means that the strokes of the letters in each word were joined like handwriting. The scholars guessed that demotic was written with an alphabet, like Western languages. Once they discovered that alphabet, they thought the demotic script would be easier to translate than the pictorial hieroglyphs.

One of the French experts, Sylvestre de Sacy, started with the proper names in the Greek passage and tried to find their equivalents in the demotic version. He believed that, after he'd singled out the names, he would be able to identify the demotic letters in each of them. With these letters in hand, he could then go on to translate other names and words in the demotic passage.

But the process proved to be much more difficult than de Sacy had anticipated. He succeeded in isolating the groups of demotic letters for the names of Ptolemy and Alexander, but found it impossible to identify the individual letters in the names. Eventually he gave up, saying, "The problem is too complicated, scientifically insoluble."

A pupil of de Sacy's, the Swedish diplomat Johan Akerblad, made better progress. Akerblad managed to locate in the demotic passage all the proper names that occurred in the Greek. From them he constructed a "demotic alphabet" of twenty-nine letters, almost half of which later proved to be correct. He went on to demonstrate that the signs used to write the names were also used to write ordinary words like "him," "his," "temple," and "love."

These were impressive achievements. But Akerblad's success in identifying so many demotic characters now led him to make a serious mistake. He became convinced that the demotic script was entirely alphabetic. From then on Akerblad, and other scholars like him, made no further progress in deciphering the demotic passage on the Stone.

In the meantime, the Stone itself had been shipped to England in 1802. There, by order of King George III, it was housed in the British Museum and copies of the writing on the Stone were made available to interested English scholars. In 1814 one of these copies came to the attention of a well-known scientist, Dr. Thomas Young. Immediately his curiosity was aroused.

Young had learned to read before he was two, and by the age of twenty had mastered a dozen foreign languages including Arabic, Persian, and Turkish. An inheritance from an uncle left him free to pursue his scientific interests. At various times, Young studied the habits of spiders, the surface features of the moon, and diseases of the chest. Then, intrigued by the challenge of the Rosetta Stone, he put aside his other studies and concentrated on attempting to decipher the writing on it. Young had read of de Sacy's and Akerblad's work in Paris, and was determined to succeed where they had failed.

Like the French scholars, Young focused first on the demotic section and compared it closely with the Greek passage. He noted that the word "king," or "pharaoh," occurred thirty-seven times in the Greek and could be matched only by a group of demotic characters that was repeated about thirty times.

Similarly, there were eleven mentions of the boy pharaoh, Ptolemy, in the Greek version. Young, like de Sacy and Akerblad before him, decided their demotic equivalent must be a group of characters that occurred fourteen times. Here is how the name Ptolemy looked in the demotic (it reads from right to left):

Young noticed that each time these demotic characters appeared, they were set off at both ends by lines like parentheses. He guessed that the lines were a simplified version of the oval cartouches that surrounded royal names in the hieroglyphs.

Within a few weeks, Young identified most of the groups of characters in the demotic passage that formed individual words. But after that he found it difficult to go further.

Unable to make fresh progress in deciphering the demotic passage, Young turned his attention to the hieroglyphs on the Stone. The beginning of the hieroglyphic inscription was missing, but most of the final lines were complete. Young compared them carefully with the last lines in the demotic version, and made an important discovery. He explained it as follows:

"After completing my analysis, I observed that the characters in the demotic inscription, which expressed the words God, Immortal, Priests, and some others, had a striking resemblance to the corresponding hieroglyphs. And since none of these demotic characters could be reconciled to any imaginable alphabet, I could scarcely doubt that they were imitations of the hieroglyphics . . . ."

Why was this observation of Young's so important? Because it was the first time any scholar had guessed that the demotic script was not completely separate from the hieroglyphic. Instead, as Young correctly noted, the demotic was a simpler form of the hieroglyphic, one that must have been easier for ancient Egyptians to write.

Up until this time, everyone who tried to decipher the hieroglyphs thought they were a form of picture writing. The image of a lion must stand for a lion, or something associated with the animal—his power or his strength. Now Young made a leap of the imagination. It was like the inspired hunches that have led to so many of the great advances in science and technology over the ages.

Young knew that the Ptolemys were of Greek descent, and the name "Ptolemy"—spelled "Ptolemaios" in Greek and pronounced "Puh-tol-uh-may-os"—was an unfamiliar one to the Egyptians. So, instead of trying to picture it in some way, mightn't the Egyptians have written the name with hieroglyphic symbols that represented the sounds, or phonetic values, in it? For example, mightn't the first symbol, ▢ , represent the sound for "P"—"Puh"?

Following through on his hunch, Young assigned letters representing sounds to the symbols in the royal cartouche, as follows:

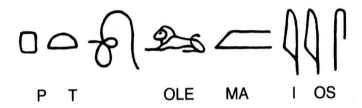

P   T   OLE   MA   I   OS

Young made several mistakes. He thought the third hieroglyph was part of the one for "T," whereas it actually stood for the vowel "O." The fourth hieroglyph, the lion, meant just "L," the fifth meant "M," and the last hieroglyph stood simply for "S." In other words, the spelling in Egyptian was "Ptolmis," not "Ptolemaios."

But Young got three out of the seven symbols right, which was a better score than any scholar before him had achieved.

Like countless other scholars over the centuries, Young still believed that most of the hieroglyphs must have a symbolic meaning. Only in special cases, such as foreign names, did he think that they were used to represent sounds.

Because of this mistaken belief, Young put roadblocks in his own path. However, he had laid a solid groundwork for others in their attempts to decipher the hieroglyphs. And a young Frenchman, Jean-François Champollion, was ready to take up the challenge where Young had left off.

IV "I've Got It! I've Got It!"

Jean-François Champollion, like Thomas Young, had a gift for languages. The son of a bookseller, Champollion was born in a small town in southwestern France in 1790. At five he taught himself to read, and by the time he was ten he showed an unusual interest in the languages of the Middle East.

When Champollion was eleven, his brother took him to the southeastern French city of Grenoble to continue his education. There Champollion was introduced to the famous mathematician Jean-Baptiste Fourier. Fourier had accompanied Napoleon to Egypt, and he showed Champollion his collection of Egyptian antiquities, including a copy of the Rosetta Stone.

The ancient hieroglyphs fascinated the boy. He asked Fourier, "Can anyone read them?" The mathematician shook his head, and Champollion said, "I am going to do it. In a few years—when I am big."

By the time he was seventeen, Champollion had learned Greek, Hebrew, Arabic, Sanskrit, Persian, and other Near Eastern languages, as well as English, German, and Italian. Soon he added Coptic to the list by studying Kircher's grammar and vocabulary. Champollion believed that the Coptic language, which was written with the letters of the Greek alphabet, might have preserved some elements of ancient Egyptian writing.

After graduating in 1807 from the upper school in Grenoble, Champollion went to Paris. There he studied with Sylvestre de Sacy, the scholar who had attempted to decipher the writings on the Rosetta Stone a few years earlier.

For many years Champollion's progress was blocked because, like de Sacy and earlier scholars, he believed the hieroglyphs represented things, not sounds. Then, in 1822, he reversed his position. Some of Champollion's rivals suggested that he had gotten the idea from Thomas Young's *Encyclopedia Britannica* article. There the English scholar explained how the hieroglyphs in Ptolemy's name stood for sounds. Champollion hotly denied these suggestions, claiming that he had arrived at his new position entirely on his own.

However the change came about, it provided Champollion with a new key to the puzzle of the hieroglyphs. He soon made use of it to go a step beyond Young and establish his own worth as a scholar once and for all.

In order to prove his theory about sounds correct, Champollion needed to identify a second name that contained some of the same hieroglyphs as Ptolemy's. There weren't any on the Rosetta Stone, so Champollion turned to copies of hieroglyphic inscriptions from other Egyptian monuments and temples. But no matter how many copies he examined, he couldn't locate a name that met his requirements.

As time passed, Champollion became more and more frustrated. Then one day a colleague sent him a copy of an inscription that had been found in the ruins of a temple on the Nile River island of Philae. Written in both hieroglyphs and Greek, the inscription was a royal decree issued by Pharaoh Ptolemy VII and his Queen, Cleopatra II. (This was not the famous Cleopatra, but an earlier one.)

209

The Greek forms of Ptolemy and Cleopatra, like the English, had several letters in common. However, Champollion corrected Thomas Young's mistake and spelled the first name as "Ptolmis." He also knew that Cleopatra began with a "K" in Greek rather than a "C." Now it was up to the French scholar to show whether or not there was a duplication of hieroglyphs in the Egyptian version of the names. He lined up the two groups of symbols and made a comparison.

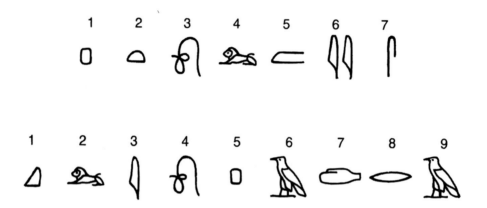

At once it was apparent that three of the hieroglyphs found in the name Ptolemy—the first, third, and fourth—could also be found in their correct places in the name Cleopatra—the fifth, fourth, and second respectively.

Moreover, the symbol that Champollion decided must stand for "A" in Cleopatra appeared where it should in the sixth place and again at the end. Rightly, neither this hieroglyph nor those that he realized must represent "K," "E," and "R" appeared in the name Ptolemy. Nor did the symbols for "M," "I," and "S" appear in the name Cleopatra.

The only hieroglyph that confused Champollion was the one for "T," which was different in the two names. (Later he learned that this represented a difference in pronunciation, for the Egyptians pronounced the "T" in Cleopatra like a "D.")

Having completed his analysis, Champollion assigned letters to all of the hieroglyphs:

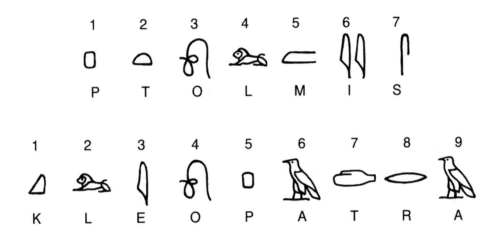

As soon as the last letter was in place, the young Frenchman rushed out of his apartment and ran to the nearby library where his brother was working. "I've got it! I've got it!" he shouted—and fainted.

Champollion had every reason to be excited. He had confirmed that more than one Greek name was expressed phonetically by the hieroglyphs. And he now knew a dozen different hieroglyphic symbols with which he could go about deciphering other Egyptian names and words.

He began with another cartouche from the same inscription and numbered each of the hieroglyphs in it.

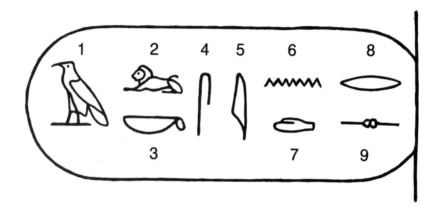

Of the nine symbols, Champollion already knew numbers 1, 2, 4, 5, 7, and 8. When he lined up all the numbers and put the corresponding letters beneath them, he got the following arrangement:

1 2 3 4 5 6 7 8 9
A L   S E   T R

Immediately Champollion thought of the one Greek leader whose name might be identified with this particular combination of letters. It was Alexander the Great, spelled "Alexandros" in Greek, and apparently represented as "Alksentrs" in hieroglyphs.

Champollion filled in the gaps in the arrangement:

1 2 3 4 5 6 7 8 9
A L K S E N T R S

Next he assigned letters to each of the hieroglyphs in the cartouche:

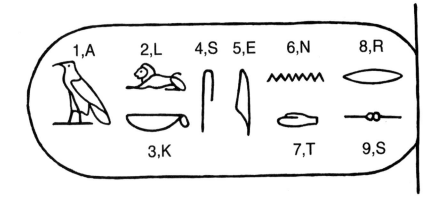

Now he had three more signs to add to his list, those that stood for "K," "N," and "S." (He guessed, and rightly so, that the new hieroglyphs for "K" and "S" indicated that these sounds were pronounced differently in the name "Alksentrs" than they were in the royal names he had deciphered earlier.)

Champollion announced his discovery in a ground-breaking book about hieroglyphs published in 1824. In it he called ancient Egyptian writing a complex system that was "symbolical and phonetic in the same text, the same phrase, the same word."

Champollion must have felt an immense pride when he wrote that. All his years of painstaking and often frustrating attempts at deciphering had been rewarded. "I am going to do it," he had said as a boy when the mathematician Fourier showed him a copy of the Rosetta Stone. Now he had succeeded.

The Riddle of the Rosetta Stone

Meet the Author

James Cross Giblin grew up in Cleveland, Ohio. Although he was a shy child, he decided to pursue an acting career in high school and college, which gave him the confidence to become a writer. After having careers as a playwright and editor, Giblin decided to write children's books because *"They make a special impact on readers."* He has focused his writing on nonfiction, historical subjects from his enjoyment of finding out details about unusual events.

Theme Connections

Within the Selection

Writer's Notebook

Record your answers to the questions below in the Response Journal section of your Writer's Notebook. In small groups, report the ideas you wrote. Discuss your ideas with the rest of your group. Then choose a person to report your group's answers to the class.

- Why was the Rosetta Stone helpful in deciphering Egyptian hieroglyphs?
- What did Napoleon's invasion of Egypt have to do with the Rosetta Stone?
- Before Champollion, how had scholars supposed the hieroglyphs worked?

Across the Selections

- In "The Riddle of the Rosetta Stone," scholars build on each others' work until the riddle is solved. Name a selection you read in Unit 1 that was similar. How was it similar?
- How would you compare Champollion's method of deciphering hieroglyphs with the method used by Sara Bisel to understand the bones she examined in "The People on the Beach"?

Beyond the Selection

- Think about how "The Riddle of the Rosetta Stone" adds to what you know about ancient civilizations.
- Add items to the Concept/Question Board about ancient civilizations.

His Majesty, Queen Hatshepsut

Dorothy Sharp Carter
illustrated by Dave Blanchette

*In Egypt in about the year 1503 B.C., Queen Hatshepsut,
daughter of King Thutmose I, wife of King Thutmose II, ascends
the throne at her husband's death. But it is a throne she shares
as Queen Regent with her nine-year-old stepson, Prince
Thutmose III. Sharing the throne with the prince displeases
Queen Hatshepsut. Two years into her reign, she has a dream
in which the King of Gods, Amon-Re, tells Hatshepsut's mother
that Hatshepsut "shall exercise the excellent kingship of this
whole land."*

*Queen Hatshepsut uses the dream as an excuse to hold a
coronation and have herself declared King of Upper and Lower
Egypt, a bold and audacious act. How can this be? A woman
who is king? Some of the men in her court are angry at her
brazen deed, especially the priests who want Prince Thutmose
to become king as soon as he comes of age. But King
Hatshepsut triumphs and rules Egypt until her death twenty-two
years later.*

*You are about to meet King Hatshepsut and discover what
her life was like in a civilization that no longer exists.*

216

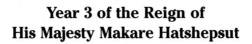

Year 3 of the Reign of
His Majesty Makare Hatshepsut

"Day 14, month 3 of Sowing . . . " While only three months have passed since my coronation, I date my reign as beginning from the death of my husband. It gives a more settled appearance. And in truth I did begin my rule then, for what use was the presence of a nine-year-old boy?

I, Makare Hatshepsut, am Pharaoh of the whole of Egypt, with no fetters, no restraints to hinder me. I know now how a caged bird feels when at long last the door flaps open and it can escape into the limitless blue of heaven.

It is not that I desire power for its own sake. I am not so vainglorious. But to have the authority to do what I know must be done for my country's good——that is ecstasy. Also——to be completely truthful——I desire to demonstrate to Egypt, to the entire world, that a woman can rule every bit as wisely as a man.

Each morning when Henut wakes me, I lie for a moment not thinking at all, only savoring this enormous bubble of happiness. Arching my neck over the cushioned headrest of my bed, I watch a sliver of sunlight enter the high window and light up the curly frieze border of the ceiling. The chariot of Amon begins its journey across the clear sky just as I am about to begin *my* day.

For another moment I ponder my goals as ruler. I will make Egypt stronger than she has ever been——so strong internally that no country will ever dare challenge her.

I will repair all the temples in the land, in particular those which the vagabond foreign rulers of Egypt, the Hyksos, neglected for so long. In addition, I will construct others to be the most beautiful in the world.

And——an idea lodged in a far corner of my mind——I may in time launch a sailing expedition to Punt, that faraway place we know as God's Land, the source of our indispensable frankincense and myrrh. This can in name be a trading expedition, but in fact a purpose just as important will be to explore, to observe the wonders of the Great Green [the Red Sea], of the manners and customs of the Puntites, of the nature of their land. I may command that expedition myself. For I am immensely inquisitive about foreign peoples, how they live and dress and think. Curiosity may be a queenly rather than kingly trait, but in any case, I intend to indulge it.

"It is the hour, Highness."

Henut stands beside my bed, a fresh linen robe in her hands. I slip into the robe, into my sandals. Henut runs a comb through my hair, adjusts a heavy, elaborate wig. I am ready for the first ritual of the morning.

Outside the door wait two high priestesses of Amon, one wearing the mask of Horus, the other the ibis head of Thoth. They bow. We walk in silence down the hall to the House of the Morning, my main chapel.

Inside, the golden ewers of water stand ready on a marble-topped table. Removing my robe, I lave my body, speaking aloud a prayer.

"Great Father God Amon-Re, as thou bathest in the ocean each morning to begin thy journey across the heavens, so bathes thy daughter. Thus we restore our divine vitality for the day's tasks. Guide me, O my father, to live in *maat* for today and always."

The priestesses anointing me, helping to robe me, are a symbol of triumph. They are the result of my first victory as ruler over Amon's priesthood.

The day I ascended the throne, a chief priest informed me, "Each morning two priestesses will accompany Her Majesty to the House of the Morning. As Her Majesty may know, a king is attended by priests wearing the masks of Horus and Thoth. This would of course be unsuitable in the case of Her Majesty." His voice held an edge of superiority.

"Perhaps my proclamation has not reached your ears, Lord," I replied icily. "My Majesty, being king, is referred to by the whole world as *His* Majesty. Furthermore, the priestesses will naturally don the masks of Horus and Thoth."

Shock and indignation so overcame him that he stammered. "S-such a custom is unheard of in the en-entire h-history of the Two Lands!" He glared at me, suddenly realized who——or what——I was, and gulped.

"I beg Her . . . His Majesty's pardon, but for women . . . priestesses to wear the sacred masks defies the holy tradition of Amon's ritual."

"Then we will change tradition. See that the female Thoth and Horus await My Majesty tomorrow." I dismissed him brusquely. He stumbled away, his face pale even for a priest.

They resent me, the priests, and will yet cause me trouble——I sense it. Despite all I do for Amon. However, for the time all goes well. With use customs come quickly to be accepted, and after three months the priestesses and their masks have become routine.

After my ablutions we proceed to another chapel, already occupied by priests and court officials. Here more prayers are said, and a high priest intones, "May a curse be laid, O Amon, on anyone who offends thee, with or without intention."

Later the same priest feels called on to reassure me. "The curse is aimed at His Majesty's ministers, certainly not at His Majesty himself." But he swiftly adds, "His Majesty takes note, I am sure, of all prayers as a guide to royal conduct."

His tone reminds me of Tutami in the classroom: condescending patronage. At times——many times——the priesthood takes on the all-powerful airs of Amon. It could do with a lesson in humility.

Sacrifice and the reading of the entrails follow: A priest spells out the omens. The day is auspicious for the composing of letters, for the holding of audience, for the visiting of friends. Inauspicious for journeys, either by boat or palanquin or foot. (That I could have forecast myself. There is enough work to keep me occupied at home for some time.)

At last I am escorted back to my quarters. After perfuming my mouth with wine and fruit, I submit to being readied. It is a quiet time to think and plan.

Were I a man, I could confer with my officials while being groomed. However, most of my council would die of embarrassment if called on to witness the plucking of my brows, the massage with unguents, the application of kohl and henna. As a dozen corpses would be of no help to me, I think alone.

One problem is that of Prince Thutmose. How he views my dream of divine birth I do not know. Nor do I care. Deep in my mind this lack of interest concerning Thutmose bothers me. Thorough and careful always in my planning, I do not forget the obstacles, however small, which like sharp stones protrude through the path of my life.

The Prince is such an obstacle. He is more than a stone. Rather, he is a vein of rock that appears treacherously now here, now there, for me to stumble over. One day he may loom before me, a high jagged barrier.

Well. The rock lies there, I am aware of it, and there is nothing to do about it. For the time being.

Yesterday Hapusoneb made a suggestion: Why did I not place the Prince under his care as apprentice priest? It is an honor due a prince to serve the Great God of No-Amon. There he would be under the eye of the entire priesthood.

Under *your* eye, O Hapusoneb, perhaps. The entire priesthood may not be so trustworthy. At all events, the idea has merit and I shall consider it.

While my hair is being dressed, I glance over accounts of palace expenditures. To think I once complained (to be truthful not once but many times) of having to learn to read. How thoughtless children are. True it is they do not know what is good for them.

The palace expenses are revealing. So much waste. No doubt kings seldom pay heed to such petty details, but this is a field I can understand and correct. Not only disbursements of the Great House but those made throughout the government can and shall be curtailed. Some officials act as though the lotuses of the Nile were of gold and have only to be plucked. They shall learn.

As an example, I have cut my immediate toilet staff to twenty. My husband had twice that number, including four barbers to shave him when he surely had beard enough for one alone.

I have limited my attendants to one mat spreader, two manicurists and two pedicurists (all four work at once to save time), three hairdressers, two masseuses, four perfumers (well, one to daub on scent and three others to distill the oils and mix the fragrances), one to prepare my bath, two to dress me, two to apply cosmetics, one to adjust my jewelry (my mother used three such, but to her all jewels were lucky or unlucky depending on the day, and this had to be determined by divination). I do not count laundresses, bleachers, pressers, seamstresses.

Today, with one public appearance, and that an informal one, I will dress as a woman. That means a gown instead of a kilt, a light wig, and crown. What an advantage I have over other pharaohs. I can choose my sex as it pleases me.

A whisper. "Majesty?"

The Keeper of Royal Jewelry stands before me, a tray of gold collars in her hands. They are too heavy, appropriate for formal functions. I shake my head and wave her away to fetch other, lighter necklets.

She returns with a necklace of thin gold wires woven about delicate flowers of pearls and amethysts. And with it my favorite earrings, those the Great God Pharaoh, my father, presented me when I was nine. They are butterflies, their wings of lapis lazuli and garnet, fastened to gold loops. I nod. Why cannot one's officials be as eager and amenable as servants?

A discreet cough disturbs my musing. "Your Majesty."

Only Henut dares interrupt my thoughts. I glance up.

My twenty attendants stand in stiff rows like soldiers, their gaze on the floor. Henut stands before them, her eyes plucking their stance, their hands, their expression, as she would pluck feathers from a goose. If any is found wanting, that one will know shortly.

It appears I am readied for the day.

First is scheduled a conference with Chief Treasurer Nehesi. Nehesi is the newest of my councillors, unearthed by Hapusoneb, my faithful minister of a myriad connections.

The Treasurer is a small man, as shriveled as a dried fig. Son of a Nubian brewer, he completely lacks the elegance and assurance of the average courtier. Far more important, he knows and understands value.

For years he was a middleman at the market, dealing in that unit of commerce called the *shat*. Father once explained to me the meaning of the word.

"As an example, my daughter, let us take the seller of a cow. In exchange for it, he is offered so many bushels of corn or lengths of linen or jars of wine. But, being fond of his cow, he decides the animal is worth more than what is offered. The difference then must be calculated in so many *shat*, and an item of that worth agreed on."

"I should not at all mind doing such work," I told him. "To aid seller and purchaser to find articles of equal value——it is a kind of game."

Father chuckled (I was the cause of many of his smiles and laughs). "A kind of game, yes. Didst thou know, Hatshepsut, that some countries base their unit of value on metal, copper or silver or gold?"

I put my nose in the air. "That would be a clumsy system, metal being so heavy and cumbersome."

Father nodded. "A practice to be expected of foreign lands."

Well, what else? In its ideas and practices my Egypt is years in advance of other nations.

Father would have approved of Nehesi: his careful honesty, his tenacity, his precision, his refusal to be intimidated . . . except by *me*. My Treasurer has yet to figure me out and tends to handle me as gingerly as he would an ostrich egg.

Our conference goes well——better for me than for him. After the usual review of revenue and disbursement, he hesitantly broaches a new subject.

"Your Majesty, the Chief Steward brings to my attention"——he pauses, coughs nervously——"a trivial matter. Of very minor importance." He stops again, struggles to heave up the words he wants. He takes a deep breath, and lo, the words come gushing forth. "Your Majesty, there are complaints from the royal household regarding the inadequate ration of bread." He bows his head. (For me to strike it off?)

I allow my arched brows to arch higher. "How is this possible? Do we not provide fourteen hundred loaves a day?"

"Indeed, your Majesty. Oh, indeed. His Majesty may be unaware that Great God-King Thutmose made provision for *two thousand* loaves daily."

"Treasurer, my staff is much reduced from that era. There is now no harem, and fewer personal attendants."

"True, true. But . . . to maintain His Majesty's residence in the appropriate style for a monarch of His Majesty's glorious status, an adequate household staff is absolutely necessary. The staff has grown, of necessity with His Majesty's tremendous responsibilities, to a somewhat greater size than that of the Great God-King Thutmose II. . . ."

Here he marks my frown at mention of my husband's name and leaps to a happier note. "His Majesty will be most gratified to learn that——this from a memorandum of the Chief Steward——the palace has decreased the amount of beer consumed from 200 to 150 jugs a day. Except, of course, when the amount is augmented for holidays."

Which means ten days out of thirty. My subjects live for feast days.

"My Majesty is well pleased about the beer. But back to the bread. My Majesty detests waste and will not provide for gorging."

The Treasurer is unused to women who argue and is thrown off balance. "Your Highness, could we . . . if I may . . . Your Majesty, with the addition of two hundred loaves more, I believe there would be no waste. And no further complaints."

I ponder. An idea sprouts, leafs out, flowers. It is a good idea and has additional merit: It will flick the priesthood's too-haughty nose.

"Lord Nehesi, the state is making major repairs and improvements on Amon's temple. My Majesty has in mind rich gifts, additions to the temple such as statues, obelisks, fine new ceremonial robes for the priests. In return for these, we will request the temple to supply the Great House with two hundred loaves of bread daily."

My Treasurer smiles thinly. Still overawed by a female sovereign, he cannot believe I am serious in demanding bread from Amon's domain. On discovering that I mean what

I say, he wonders if the temple will blame *him* for the proposal, which could have uncomfortable effects; the priesthood can be vindictive in subtle ways.

I have faith in Nehesi's astuteness. Blame can be shared by the Chief Steward, by a dozen other officials. At any rate, I have solved that problem with no increase in my budget. My people will not say of me, "Ah! She flings gold dust about as though it were sand."

Actually Egypt's finances are at present in excellent shape. Our hundreds of granaries in temples and towns are well stocked in the event of a light inundation and the resulting failure of crops. The construction of private buildings is brisk, bringing in good revenue from the state monopoly in brick making; the same is true in papermaking. Fortunately for me, taxation on harvests and ships and property need not be increased this year.

A thought occurs: With my head so full of economies, large and small, I could always find occupation as a simple housewife!

Next on my schedule, I show myself for the first time as Pharaoh at the Window of Appearances. My excuse to the Vizier is that the people adore spectacles of any sort, and a view of Pharaoh is regarded as a grand treat. To be quite honest, I do it for pure pleasure. To distribute largesse in my own name, with no one to nod me permission——ah, I relish that.

Always before, I had stood behind my father or my husband and was handed a small bracelet or two to toss. Today Nefrure alone appears with me. She bounces with anticipation.

"Calm thyself," I chide her.

"Oh, my mother, I do not like to be calm!"

She peers over the railing at the courtyard. It being a hot and windless day, the court is packed with sunshade bearers and fan bearers as well as household officials and relatives of the honorees. A guard marshals the recipients into a queue. On three sides the public, wiping their perspiring faces, strain against the ropes. Even the lowliest wears a clean loincloth for the occasion.

There are seven or eight honorees. As each steps before the balcony and salutes me, I deliver a short speech of praise, ending with "Thou art my faithful servant who hast carried out the orders of My Majesty, who is well pleased with thee. I therefore award thee these gifts with the words 'Thou shalt eat the bread of Pharaoh (Life, Health, Strength!) thy lord, in the temple of Amon.'"

From the tray of gold ornaments I choose necklets, rings, inlaid hatchets, goblets, trinkets in the shapes of bees and lions, to fling to those honored. As the gifts are caught, there are shrieks of delight from the family.

Nefrure is in raptures. She helps to shower "the praise of gold" on her friends Hapusoneb (honored for faithful and meritorious service) and Senmut (for outstanding ideas concerning efficiency and economies in government departments). They will need to grow new necks to wear all the chains she flings to them.

"Senmut needs another bracelet!" Nefrure exclaims, eyes bright with excitement. As I have appointed him her tutor, she sees much of him. They have grown very fond of each other.

"He will not be able to wear so much jewelry or carry it either," I protest. "There will be other opportunities."

"Tomorrow?" she asks hopefully.

I laugh. "Not tomorrow, but very soon."

The last award goes to the Keeper of the Interior Apartments for long and industrious service. "Meritorious" and "outstanding" can certainly not be applied to him, nor I fear, can "faithful." The ceremony will reduce the sting when tomorrow I replace him in office. He is a relic of my husband's rule, disapproves vocally of queen rulers, and treats with no merchant or servant without a fat bribe. His wife is as oily as he, her eyes as shifty as his as she peeps into my face, incredulous that a mere *woman* is capable of filling the throne of the Two Lands. Stupid creature! Ah well, after today I will see little of them. He will be offered the position of Messenger for the Dogs' Food, which he is not likely to accept.

After lunch I escape to my refuge, a chamber furnished with only a long sofa and a small table to hold refreshments. With no other clutter, I can imagine I am on my country estate, the tiles of the floor tinted green as grass, the ceiling molded and painted to resemble a grape arbor, the vines thick with purple fruit.

Here I admit only Henut, to massage my forehead for headache, and my daughter (during those rare moments when she agrees to act like a lady). Today I have invited Senmut——Lord Senmut, as he has been for a month.

Senmut. Ah, Hatshepsut, in spite of thy royal and divine blood and against thy strongest wishes, thou art proved to be all too mortal. To hear the name of Senmut, to glimpse Senmut, to hear Senmut's voice——my breath, my blood cease in their courses, my vision clouds, my ears ring, my head is light.

What does it mean? Surely not that I love him. I have never loved anyone——apart from my dear Egypt——besides my father, and my daughter. I do not allow myself to love anyone. I cannot afford to. Love is weakness. I tell myself that over and over: Love is weakness. Only . . . how do I control my blood, my breath?

I question myself severely. Why do I find this man appealing? He is not handsome, although his face is unique, the features clear cut like his character, mouth thin, eyes both wide and long. The nose is somewhat hooked but not, thanks be to Hathor, as prominent as my own family's nose. The mobility of expression constitutes its charm.

His most significant traits are his boldness of outlook, his self-assurance, his adaptability. As my daughter's tutor he has proved his gentleness, for she can tax one's patience with her teasing.

I say that he is adaptable; already he has adopted the dress, the manners, the carriage, the viewpoint of a nobleman. No. In all frankness he has not done so completely.

With regard to the gods, I have noticed, he is unsophisticated and highly superstitious. And he possesses a peasant's unabashed urge for acquisition. The offices I appoint him to he fulfills without fault. But the titles of those offices he collects and wears as a rustic woman flaunts at one time every string of cheap beads she owns. On all letters, all proclamations, Senmut never fails to include each and every title. Still, modesty is by no means a national characteristic of ours.

Today I confer with Senmut in his new capacity as Controller of Works. We will discuss the reopening of our copper and turquoise mines in the Sinai. (My composure is flawless. No blush, no tremble, no shortness of breath is apparent.)

"The reworking of the mines," I explain, "will require the presence of troops to ensure security from the barbaric sand dwellers. Aside from protection, the project will serve to keep the men occupied. The officers tend to become quickly restless unless they are busy warring and conquering."

Having been at one time a military scribe, Senmut is aware of how the military mind works. He nods.

"The plan is good. The officers will welcome it more than their men."

I look at him inquiringly.

"The common soldiers dislike setting foot on foreign soil. They ask, 'What if we die there? Who will prepare our bodies for burial? Who will recite the ritual over us? Are we to lose eternity because we leave our beloved Egypt?' I fear you must count on some desertions."

An idea comes to mind. These days find me as full of ideas as a palm tree with dates. I make haste to pluck the ideas and put them to work before they rot on the branches. "I will see that a body of priests and two or three embalmers accompany the men. That should allay their fear."

And if I follow Hapusoneb's suggestion of placing the Prince under his supervision as an apprentice priest——which appears most reasonable——then in two or three years' time the boy can himself become part of such an expedition to Sinai. It will provide him training and experience. And it will remove him effectively from the scene of action——for a time.

"That will cheer the men." Senmut's tone approves my decision.

"Have you yourself lived away from Egypt?" I ask.

"At one time. I built a grain warehouse and later the courthouse for the colony that Great Pharaoh Thutmose II"——he bows his head——"established in Cush."

"You engineered those buildings?"

He grimaces slightly. "They were nothing. But seeing them, the general Huy requested me to construct a house in the country for his newly married daughter. *That* I was proud of."

"So you are an architect." Is there no end to this man's talents? "Have you constructed other edifices?"

"A new home for my parents. My tomb and theirs. The deepest joy of life comes from creating a structure——a cottage, a mansion, a palace."

To the Not Impossible Him

Edna St. Vincent Millay
illustrated by Lane Yerkes

How shall I know, unless I go
    To Cairo and Cathay,
Whether or not this blessed spot
    Is blest in every way?

Now it may be, the flower for me
    Is this beneath my nose;
How shall I tell, unless I smell
    The Carthaginian rose?

The fabric of my faithful love
    No power shall dim or ravel
Whilst I stay here,——but oh, my dear,
    If I should ever travel!

241

The Silk Route

7,000 MILES OF HISTORY

John S. Major

illustrated by Stephen Fieser

242

A.D. 700 . . .

The Roman Empire has fallen. Italy, Spain, and northern Europe are controlled by Germanic tribes. London and Paris are small towns; Rome is a half-deserted city of ruins.

In the eastern Mediterranean, the Roman tradition lives on in the Byzantine Empire, with its capital at the great city of Byzantium (also called Constantinople; now Istanbul).

The Christian rulers of Byzantium face a serious challenge from the rapidly expanding world of Islam. Founded by the Prophet Muhammad in 622, Islam has spread throughout Arabia and now also controls Iraq, Armenia, Persia, and much of North Africa.

Meanwhile, on the other side of the world, China is ruled by the glorious Tang Dynasty (618–906), whose emperors have brought China to a high point of power, territorial control, and cultural brilliance. China's capital, Chang'an, is the largest city in the world.

The great empires of the West and the East are linked by the Silk Route, an ancient trade network of caravan tracks across the steppes and deserts of Central Asia.

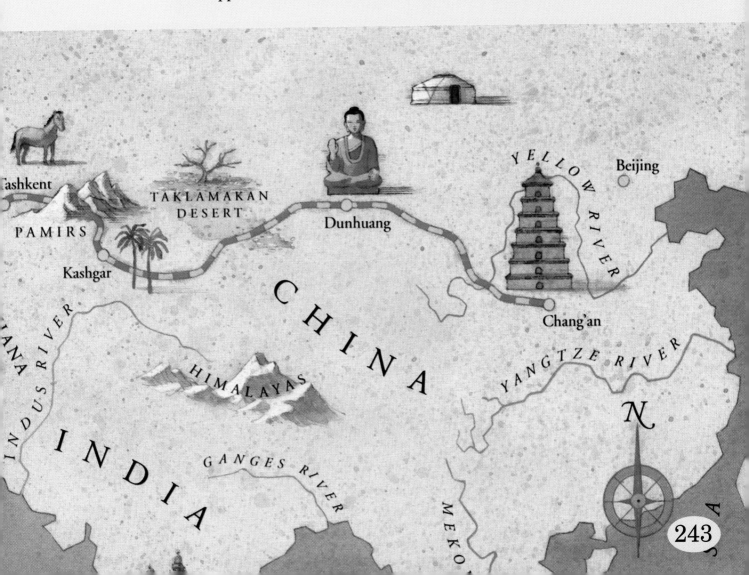

Tang Dynasty China, A.D. 700

The Chinese people called their country the Middle Kingdom. But people in the West called China the Land of Silk. Among all of China's many gifts to world civilization——paper, printing, gunpowder, and a great deal more——silk was the most highly prized in the ancient Western world.

Silk cloth was invented in China around 3000 B.C. No one knows who first made silk cloth. Many Chinese people believed that it was invented by the Silkworm Empress. She was the wife of the Yellow Emperor, the mythical founder of Chinese civilization.

On farms all over China men grow grain while women produce silk. They tend groves of mulberry trees and feed the leaves to silkworms. When the silkworms mature, they make cocoons of silk, which the women collect and boil. Then the women unreel the delicate strand of silk from each cocoon, spin it into thread, and weave it into silk cloth. Farmers pay their taxes in grain and silk.

Chang'an

During the Tang Dynasty, bolts of plain white silk cloth of standard width and length were used as a kind of money. The government used silk to pay officials' salaries, and also exported silk along the Silk Route to Central Asia, where it was traded for fine horses for the imperial army.

In the capital city of Chang'an, merchants get a caravan ready to go to the West. Officials watch while workers take bolts of silk from a government warehouse and load them onto camels. The merchants who will join the caravan buy many things in the city market to trade privately along the way. These trade goods include porcelain, dried rhubarb and other herbal medicines, and fancy silk cloth woven in colors and patterns especially designed to suit the tastes of the Islamic and Byzantine worlds.

The Journey Begins

The caravan includes many private merchants as well as Chinese government officials. Like the covered-wagon trains of the American West, members of the caravan travel together to help one another on the long, dangerous journey. Along the way they will face heat, hunger, thirst, and the ever-present possibility of bandit raids.

Few members of the original caravan will travel all the way to the Mediterranean. The silk and other goods that they are bringing from China will change hands several times along the way.

The caravan begins its journey, which will take many months. It is early spring. The caravan must get beyond the fierce western deserts before the heat of summer arrives. Leaving the city walls of Chang'an behind, it passes through rich farmland. A Buddhist temple is on a nearby hillside.

CHINESE: SI
silk, silk thread

Dunhuang

The Buddhist religion came to China from India along the Silk Route around A.D. 100. The oasis town of Dunhuang, for centuries an important trading and supply center for caravans, soon grew into a great religious center as well. Hundreds of Buddhist cave-temples were cut into the soft rock of a nearby cliff. The cave-temples contain Buddhist statues; the walls are decorated with bright religious paintings.

Some of the merchants go to the cave-temples of Dunhuang to pray for a safe journey, while others buy supplies in the town market. Some Chinese officials take charge of a small herd of horses brought from the west by another caravan. They will escort the horses back to the capital; other officials will continue west to purchase still more of them.

Taklamakan

The Taklamakan is one of the world's driest deserts. Its name means "if you go in, you won't come out" in Uighur Turkish, one of the main languages of Central Asia. The caravan skirts the northern edge of the desert, just south of the snow-capped peaks of the Tian Shan Mountains. The route is very rough, passing around sand dunes, across rocky flats, and through tangled willow thickets along dry riverbeds. But the caravan's two-humped Bactrian camels are strong and hardy. They are used to this difficult country.

Many of the camels and camel drivers that set out from Chang'an turned back at Dunhuang. The merchants hired new ones for this stage of the journey, along with extra animals to carry food and water for crossing the desert. Such changes of men and animals will occur several times along the way from China to Damascus.

Kashgar

Hot and tired after their trip across the Taklamakan Desert,
the men and animals hurry to reach the oasis city of Kashgar.
The pastures near the city are dotted with grazing animals and
the camps of herding peoples: Uighurs in round felt yurts,
Turkomans and Tibetans in black tents.

Kashgar is famous for its fruit. Dates, melons, and grapes are
grown in irrigated fields and vineyards. Everyone in the caravan
looks forward to fresh food and water.

Some of the Chinese members of the caravan will end their
journey here. They trade silk for dried dates, raisins, jade, and
other local products to bring back to China. Others will continue
on toward the west, joined by new merchants, guards, and
camel drivers with fresh animals from Kashgar.

The Pamirs

The Pamirs are a range of high mountains in eastern Afghanistan. Here the route winds through narrow, high-walled valleys beside rushing rivers. The camel drivers call this section of the Silk Route the "Trail of Bones" because of the many men and animals that have died along the way from falls and from sudden storms in the high, cold passes. The westbound caravan meets a caravan heading for China with luxury goods from Western lands and a herd of fine horses from Ferghana.

ابریشم

PERSIAN: ABRASHAM
silk

Tashkent, Kingdom of Ferghana

In the central market of Tashkent, the last remaining Chinese officials in the caravan trade bolts of silk for horses that they will take back to China. The horses of Ferghana are considered by Chinese military leaders to be the strongest and toughest in the world.

Tashkent marks the eastern edge of the Persian cultural world. Some private merchants trade Chinese silk, porcelain, and other goods for Persian metalwork, glass, and musical instruments. They too will head back to China from here.

Transoxiana

After making another stop, in the city of Samarkand, the caravan enters the wild country east of the Oxus (Amu Darya) River. No government rules this land; the nomads who live here will rob caravans if they get a chance to.

Suddenly the caravan is attacked by a group of Turkoman bandits on horseback. After a fierce fight with swords and bows and arrows, the bandits are driven off. But some members of the caravan have been killed or wounded, and the bandits escape with a few heavily laden camels.

Herat

In this thriving Persian city, artisans produce fine metalwork, glassware, carpets, and other goods that can be sold for a high price in China. Herat is also, for the moment, on the eastern edge of the rapidly expanding Islamic world. A newly built mosque looms over the city market.

Merchants from the caravan mingle in the market with local merchants and Turkoman nomads, as well as with Arabs from Baghdad and Damascus. Traders from India are here too, selling spices and brightly dyed Indian cloth. Muslim imams, Zoroastrian priests, Nestorian Christian priests, and Buddhist monks tend to the religious needs of the cosmopolitan city.

The caravan will leave its last Bactrian camels in Herat. For the rest of the journey they will use dromedaries, the one-humped camels of Western Asia.

Baghdad

Baghdad is the greatest city of the Islamic world and a hub of world trade. Caravans crowd the roads leading to the city. An Arab merchant leads a group of African slaves bringing ivory, gold, and spices from Zanzibar. Ships coming upriver from the port at Basra bring spices and printed cotton cloth from India, pearls from the Persian Gulf, and precious stones from Ceylon (now Sri Lanka). Some of these goods will soon be heading east to China.

Only a handful of Chinese merchants remained with the caravan, and they will end their journey here. Most of the silk, porcelain, and other products from China have already changed hands several times along the way, increasing in value each time. The last remaining Chinese merchants will sell their goods for a fortune in Baghdad, but then they face a long, difficult, and dangerous trip home again.

Damascus

Arab merchants have brought bolts of silk from Baghdad to Damascus. Only the finest silk cloth has traveled this far; it includes intricately patterned brocades, brilliantly colored satins, and thin gauze to make nightgowns for aristocratic ladies. Wealthy Muslim women, heavily veiled, admire bolts of finished silk cloth in a shop.

Tyre

In the port city of Tyre, on the Mediterranean coast of Lebanon, goods are loaded on ships bound for cities farther to the west. Some of the silk that was traded in the market at Damascus will be sent to Byzantium, the capital of the Eastern Roman Empire.

ΣΕΡΙΚΟΝ

GREEK: SERIKON
silk cloth

Byzantium

In the main hall of a splendid palace, a Byzantine nobleman receives a visit from a bishop of the Orthodox Christian church. Both are dressed in rich garments of silk brocade. The palace women remain in an inner courtyard, out of sight of the men. A visiting prince from Russia, far to the north, awaits his turn to speak to the nobleman. Perhaps he will receive a small present of silk to take back home with him.

The garments worn by the wealthy people of Byzantium are made of silk cloth brought from China, more than 6,000 miles away. Few people in Byzantium have more than a vague idea of where China is or what its people are like, just as few Chinese know anything about the Eastern Roman Empire. Yet Chinese silk is sold in Byzantium, and Byzantine gold coins circulate in the markets of China. The two empires are linked together by trade, thanks to the brave and enterprising merchants of the Silk Route.

A Closer Look

Silk • For thousands of years the painstaking process of raising silkworms and making cloth from their cocoons had been a Chinese monopoly. But around A.D. 550, during the reign of the Eastern Roman Emperor Justinian, two Nestorian Christian monks who had traveled to China returned to Syria, smuggling back with them silkworm eggs hidden in their hollow bamboo walking sticks. This allowed a silk industry to be established in the Middle East, undercutting the market for ordinary-grade Chinese silk. However, high-quality silk textiles, woven in China especially for the Middle Eastern market, continued to bring high prices in Damascus and Byzantium, and trade along the Silk Route therefore continued as before.

Chang'an • Located in the valley of the Wei River, a tributary of the Yellow River, the Tang capital of Chang'an had been the most important city in China for over 1000 years. Located at the eastern end of the Silk Route as well as near the Great Wall that marked the boundary between China and the nomadic tribes of the north, the city guarded China's most important strategic interests. Chang'an, with a population of well over a million people, was famous throughout East Asia for its palaces, parks, temples, schools, and restaurants. The city was a hub of world trade, and it included resident populations of merchants, scholars, and religious leaders from as far away as Korea, Japan, India, Persia, Armenia, and Syria.

China's Door to the West • The rich agricultural lands of China are isolated from the rest of mainland Asia by high mountains, steep valleys, deserts, and grasslands. The corridor formed by the Wei River and the upper reaches of the Yellow River marked a natural highway that pierced the veil of China's natural isolation. During the Tang Dynasty this corridor was carefully kept under Chinese control and guarded against raids by Tibetans to the south and Turkic tribes to the north. A western extension of the Great Wall was marked by guard towers furnished with beacon fires that could bring news of danger to Chang'an in a matter of hours.

Buddhism • Buddhism was founded in northern India by Gautama, the Buddha ("Enlightened One"), around 550 B.C. Buddhists believed that a life of prayer, meditation, and good works could free the soul from attachment to the sinful world. Buddhism soon spread throughout India and into Central Asia, entering China along the Silk Route around A.D. 100. Over the next few centuries it became established in China and was accepted as one of that country's three major religions (along with Confucianism and Taoism). The early Tang Dynasty marked a time of particular power and influence of Buddhism in China. Cave-temples such as those at Dunhuang (also spelled Tun-huang) attracted pilgrims from all over East Asia.

Caravan Life •
Caravans were made up of many groups of both private merchants and government officials. The travelers hired professional camel drivers, baggage handlers, camp tenders, and other workers, all of whom typically worked only one relatively short stretch of the entire route. Private merchants hired their own armed guards; the Chinese government officials who traveled between Chang'an and Tashkent had military escorts. The caravans carried supplies of food, water, and animal fodder for crossing the deserts that lay in their path. Depending on the terrain, they might go as few as ten or as many as fifty miles in a day. Each night the travelers pitched tents, hobbled their camels, and set out guards to secure their camp against bandit raids.

Oasis Cities •
Within the dry and barren lands between China and the Middle East are a few large oases, isolated pockets of abundant water that make agriculture and urban life possible. Walled cities were surrounded by irrigated fields and pasturelands. Such cities as Kashgar, Bactra (now Balkh), and Samarkand became the capitals of substantial kingdoms as well as great centers of trade along the Silk Route. The Silk Route itself was a network of trails rather than a single highway; branches of the route led from oasis to oasis and to market centers in India, Persia, Russia, and the Middle East.

The oasis cities were surrounded by populations of nomadic herding peoples who traded animal products, such as wool, meat, and hides, for urban goods such as grain and metalware. These nomadic tribes were only loosely under the control of the oasis kingdoms and were feared by townspeople and caravan merchants.

Invasion Routes of Inner Asia •
In some sections of Central Asia geography forced the Silk Route trade to flow through narrow and well-defined corridors. Travelers from China to the Middle East could not avoid the dangerous rivers and high mountain passes of the Pamirs; trade between Afghanistan and India had to cross the Khyber Pass. Many times in history these strategic routes carried invading armies as well as peaceful caravans. Alexander the Great's armies reached the Pamirs in the third century B.C.; the Mongol hordes of Genghis Khan rode through them

1500 years later. As late as the nineteenth century Great Britain and Russia competed to control the invasion routes of inner Asia, the meeting point of the great civilizations of China, India, and the Middle East.

Nomad Warfare •

The various nomadic tribes of Central Asia shared a common culture based on tending herds of grazing animals. The men of the tribes were trained from infancy to become expert fighters and hunters from horseback. Their primary duty was to guard the tribe's herds, but they would also raid towns and caravans whenever the opportunity presented itself. Their main weapon was the short, recurved, composite bow, made of wood and horn, with which they could fire volleys of armor-piercing arrows at full gallop: they used lances and swords for close combat. They specialized in lightning-fast attacks, taking their targets by surprise.

The cavalry units of China's imperial army adopted these nomad techniques of warfare to defend the empire's northern frontier. This led to China's almost insatiable demand for the strong, fast, hardy horses of Ferghana, one of the main items of trade along the Silk Route.

The Religions of Central Asia •

Central Asian trading cities such as Herat were multicultural centers that reflected in population, culture, and religious beliefs the diversity of the peoples of Asia. Buddhists from eastern Afghanistan, Turkestan, and as far away as Nepal and China mingled with Hindus from India. Zoroastrianism, the ancient religion of Persia——whose adherents worshipped the forces of light that struggled against Satanic darkness, and maintained temples with sacred fires——was rapidly giving way to the militant, expanding new religion of Islam. Nestorianism, a Syrian form of Christianity, established churches and cathedrals in all the major cities of Central Asia. Pockets of Greek paganism remained among the colonies left behind by Alexander the Great's conquests almost a thousand years earlier. In the surrounding steppelands, nomads worshipped the Great Blue Sky and communicated with gods and spirits through shamans and healers.

Baghdad and World Trade •

Baghdad, together with the port city of Basra at the mouth of the Tigris River, was a focal point of both maritime and caravan trade. Although some caravans from the Silk Route took a northern route from Merv through Armenia to reach Byzantium overland, many others headed south through Herat to Baghdad and Damascus. Arab sailors from the Persian Gulf dominated shipping in the Indian Ocean, trading in cloth from India, gemstones from Ceylon (Sri Lanka), spices from Indonesia, and gold, ivory, and slaves from the eastern coast of Africa. Baghdad grew rich from trade; it soon became a great political center as well. In 751 the Umayyad Caliphate established its capital at Baghdad and claimed the right to rule the entire Islamic world.

The Islamic Expansion •

Islam, founded by Muhammad in the Arabian cities of Mecca and Medina in 622, makes no distinction between religion and civic life. It considers the world to be divided into the *Dar ol'Islam*, the "world submissive to God," and the *Dar ol'Harb*, the "world at war with God." Those who acknowledge the authority of Allah, the one true God according to the teachings of Muhammad, submit to His rule in every aspect of life.

Islamic armies conquered by force but converted by persuasion; believers in other religions were tolerated, but only Muslims had full civil rights in the Islamic world. The Islamic world grew at a phenomenal pace, and by 700 extended from Tunisia to Afghanistan. For about a century before the establishment of the Umayyad Caliphate at Baghdad, Damascus was the center of the Islamic world. To its ancient status as a hub of north–south and east–west caravan routes was added a new status as a city of mosques and universities, a magnet for merchants and scholars.

Byzantium •

With the gradual decline of Rome, power in the Roman Empire shifted eastward. An eastern capital was established at Byzantium by the Emperor Constantine in 330. The Germanic invasions of the western portion of the Roman Empire in the sixth century left Byzantium in control of what was left of the empire. The Orthodox Christian Byzantine emperors ruled Greece, western Turkey, the Balkan states, and parts of southern Italy and North Africa, but found their power constantly challenged by Germans in the west, Persians in the east, and, after 622, Arab Muslims in the east and south. Nevertheless, Byzantium itself resisted conquest until it was overrun by the Turks in 1453.

The Eastern Roman Empire was rich and cosmopolitan, and many of the goods that traveled across Asia along the Silk Route were destined for its markets. It was also a transfer center for trade to Europe proper, along maritime routes that extended throughout the Mediterranean and via overland routes along the Danube River to central Europe and up the Volga to Russia and the Baltic Sea. A Frankish nobleman in Paris or a Catholic bishop in Spain might well have worn garments of silk that traveled, via Byzantium, the 7,000 miles from China.

The Silk Route

7,000 MILES OF HISTORY

Meet the Author

John S. Major earned his Ph.D. from Harvard University. He lived in Taiwan and Japan before teaching at Dartmouth College for 13 years. He has written such books as *The Land and People of China* and *The Land and People of Mongolia*. Major is currently a senior editor at the Book-of-the-Month Club, Inc.

Meet the Illustrator

Stephen Fieser earned his M.F.A. from Syracuse University after working for 15 years in graphic design. He specializes in picture books with specific geographic and historical settings, including *The Christmas Sky* and *The Wonder Child*. Fieser also teaches drawing and illustrating at Messiah College and Marywood University.

Theme Connections

Within the Selection

Record your answers to the questions below in the Response Journal section of your Writer's Notebook. In small groups, report the ideas you wrote. Discuss your ideas with the rest of your group. Then choose a person to report your group's answers to the class.

- Why do the silk merchants and government officials travel in one large caravan?
- Why do the camel drivers call the portion of the silk route that passes through the Pamirs the "Trail of Bones"?
- Why do the Chinese officials trade silk for horses in the central market of Tashkent?

Across the Selections

- It is not unusual to come across old forms of currency when uncovering the past. As you learned in "The Silk Route," silk was once used as currency in China. What other old forms of currency have you learned about in this unit? In which selections were they mentioned?

Beyond the Selection

- Think about how "The Silk Route" adds to what you know about uncovering the past.
- Add items to the Concept/Question Board about uncovering the past.

Taking a Stand

W hat kinds of things are really important to you? What is worth taking a stand for? Each person would answer these questions differently and each answer would tell us much about the person.

Focus Questions Will the members of the Pretty Pennies Girls Club take a stand against unjust treatment even if it means challenging an authority figure? Can it ever be wrong to take a stand?

The Pretty Pennies Picket

from *Philip Hall Likes Me. I Reckon Maybe.*
Bette Greene
illustrated by Colin Bootman

I no sooner set the ice-cold pitcher of lemonade on the porch when I saw the Blakes' green pickup truck stirring up the dust as it traveled down our rutty road, delivering the members of my girls club. "Ma," I called through the screen door. "Bring out the cookies! The Pretty Pennies are a-coming."

Right away the door opened, but it wasn't Ma. It was my brother Luther wearing a fresh white dress shirt and the blue pants from his Sunday suit. While Susan, Esther, and Bonnie jumped off the truck's back platform, Luther didn't hardly pay no never mind. It wasn't until Ginny the gorgeous climbed down that Luther, wearing a very pleasant expression, took a couple of giant steps toward her and asked, "How y'all getting along, Ginny?"

Ginny didn't get a chance to answer 'cause the one girl who folks say was born into this world talking answered my brother's question. "Fried to a frizzle," said Bonnie Blake. "And that lemonade yonder looks mighty refreshing."

After the lemonade was drunk and the cookies eaten, I performed my duties by rapping on the floor of the porch and saying, "This here meeting of the Pretty Pennies Girls Club is now called to order."

"Trouble with this club," said Bonnie without waiting until we got to new business, "is that we never do nothing but drink lemonade and talk about the boys in the Tiger Hunters' Club."

Heads bobbed up and down in agreement.

Bonnie smiled as though she was onto something big. "What this club needs is somebody with new ideas about things that are fun doing."

266

Then Ginny did something unusual. She found that one sliver of a moment which Bonnie wasn't cramming with words and said, "We just go from one meeting to the next meeting without ever doing anything. Reckon we could use a new president."

Even before Ginny's words were being applauded, I knew there was some truth to be found in them. We do just sit around gabbing——which is fun——but it was the same amount of fun before I got the idea that we had to become a club. "Philip Hall and the Tiger Hunters ain't the only ones can be a club!" And it was also me that told them how it was a known fact that clubs have more fun than friends. Suddenly I felt ashamed of myself for having promised more than I delivered, but mostly I felt angry with the Pretty Pennies, who were fixing to dump their president without as much as a "begging your pardon."

I looked up at the porch ceiling, looking for something like a good idea waiting to bore through my brain. Well, I looked, but I didn't see nothing but ceiling paint. So I closed my eyes and sure enough something came to me. I waved my hands for quiet. "It so happens that I do have a wonderful idea, but I was waiting to tell y'all about it."

Bonnie began, "Is it fun? 'Cause I got me plenty of chores to do at home so if it's——"

I broke right in. "Quiet! Now next month the Old Rugged Cross Church has their yearly picnic, and I've been thinking that we oughta challenge the Tiger Hunters to a relay race."

"Five of them," said Bonnie. "Five of us."

"Yes siree," I agreed. "But they is going to be something special about our five 'cause we're going to be wearing a special uniform which we ourselves made."

Right away I noticed how all the girls came alive when I mentioned the uniform, so I went on to describe it. "With the money we got in our club treasury, we're going to buy big T-shirts and some different-colored embroidery thread for each Pretty Penny. And then"——my finger traced a crescent across my chest——"we could all embroider the words: THE PRETTY PENNIES GIRLS CLUB OF POCAHONTAS, ARKANSAS." I said, really beginning to feel my presidential powers, "And if we were of a mind to, we could also embroider on the names of all the folks we like."

"You going to embroider on the name of Mister Phil Hall?" asked Bonnie in that cutesy-pooh voice of hers.

I laughed just as though I had nary a worry in this world. Oh, sometimes I think that Philip Hall still likes me, but at other times I think he stopped liking me the moment he stopped being the number-one best everything.

But he wouldn't do that, would he? Stop liking me just because I'm smarter than him? I can't help it and, anyway, my teacher, Miss Johnson, herself said that if I'm going to become a veterinarian I'm going to have to become the best student I know how to be.

On Saturday afternoon all us Pennies went into the Busy Bee Bargain Store for white T-shirts big enough to get lost in. After a lot of discussion, we dropped five T-shirts, fifty skeins of embroidery thread, five embroidery hoops, and five packages of needles onto the wrapping counter in front of Mr. Cyrus J. Putterham.

After taking our money, he pulled one tan sack from the counter and began shoveling everything into it.

"Oh, no, sir," I corrected. "We each need our own bags."

His bushy eyebrows made jumpy little elevator rides up and then down. "Don't you girlies have any feeling? Five sacks cost me five times as much as one."

"But we need them," I explained. " 'Cause we're not even related."

He pulled out four more. "Costs me money, each one does. But you wouldn't care nothing about that. Kids never do!"

As we Pretty Pennies embroidered our shirts on the following Wednesday evening, we drank Bonnie Blake's strawberry soda, ate her potato chips, and gabbed on and on about those Tiger Hunters.

We even sent them a letter saying that they ought to get busy practicing their relay running 'cause we Pretty Pennies were aiming to beat them to pieces.

The next meeting was at Ginny's house, where we all sat in a circle on the linoleum floor and talked about our coming victory over the boys while we munched popcorn from a cast-iron skillet and embroidered away. Then from outside:

Bam . . . bam . . . bam-my . . . bam . . . bam!

Our embroidery dropped to our laps as we grabbed onto one another. Bonnie pointed toward the outside while, for the first time in her life, her mouth opened and closed and closed and opened without a single sound coming out.

Finally, Esther, who almost never had a word to say, said, "Wha——— What was that?"

"Let's see," I said, moving cautiously and pulling Esther along with me toward the door. I peeked out just in time to see two figures (both less than man size) race deeper into the halflight before disappearing from sight.

Bonnie, Ginny, and Susan were still sitting like frozen statues.

"It's OK," I told them. "Whoever they were——and I think I know who they were——have already ran away."

Esther followed me out on the porch, where there was a rock the size of a crow's nest and sticking to this rock was a sheet of wide-lined paper. I pulled off the paper, which had been stuck on with a wad of gum, and read aloud:

Dear Pretty Pennies,
You ain't pretty!
You ain't pennies!
And you ain't never going to beat us neither!
> *President Philip Hall*
> *Bravest of all the brave Tiger Hunters*
> *and Lt. Gordon Jennings (also Brave)*

P.S. Why wait for the church picnic to relay race? Meet us at the schoolyard on Saturday and we'll win!

Everybody was really mad and we all began talking at once about those Tiger Hunters who run around scaring the wits out of a person. Bonnie thought we ought to teach them a lesson. "Specially that Phil Hall."

I'd have liked nothing better, but probably for a different reason. It wasn't the scare so much as what he said about not being pretty that ruffled my feathers. Did he mean nobody was pretty? Or was nobody but me pretty? Or . . . or was everybody pretty excepting me? Next thing I knew I was shouting, "We're going to get those low-down polecats!" Then while I had everybody's attention, I gave them their final instructions: "Next Saturday we'll race. Finish embroidering on our club name, front and back. Then everybody wash your shirts so our club name will be clean easy reading. All the folks in Pocahontas is going to know just who it was that beat them Tiger Hunters."

The next morning Philip didn't show up for work at my new business, The Elizabeth Lorraine Lambert & Friend Veg. Stand. Well, he's probably just mad or practicing up his relay running. Or maybe Mr. Hall has him doing chores. But that's the unlikeliest explanation of them all.

Without him there ain't no games or giggles, but today there's not a speck of boredom either 'cause I'm just too busy embroidering my T-shirt and running my business. And with every sale my college money grows. I'm going to become a veterinarian yet.

It was just before bedtime on Friday night that I stitched the last beautiful stitch on my shirt. I held it out for better viewing. Even with the soil from two weeks of handling along with my baby brother Benjamin's mashed-in, smashed-in sweet potato, it was beautiful. Just beautiful!

As I began to draw the wash water, Ma told me to get to bed 'cause I'd be needing my strength for the big race tomorrow. She took the shirt from my hand as she gave me a light shove toward the bedroom. "Reckon I can do the washing if you can do the resting."

When the morning sky came again to Pocahontas, I woke wide awake just as though I hadn't been sleeping at all but only resting up before the big race.

At the kitchen table Ma sat in front of a bowl of peas needing shelling, but her hands sat unmoving in her lap. I tried to remember the last time I had seen my mother just sitting without actually doing anything. All I said was "Morning, Ma," but it was enough to make her look as though she was staring at a spook.

"Reckon I'm going to have to tell you," she said, holding tight to the bowl. "But I don't know how to tell you . . . It's about your shirt. Done shrunk to midget size. Sure did."

As Pa drove down Pocahontas's Main Street, I spotted the rest of the Pennies leaning up against a yellow fireplug. A block away Pa turned his car and angle-parked in front of the E-Z Cash & Carry Market. When the Pennies saw me walking toward them, they all shook their heads just like I was doing something wrong. What does that mean? That I'm not wearing my uniform? No, but I'm carrying it wrapped like a fish in an old newspaper to show them what they'd never believe without seeing. Anyway, they're not wearing theirs either. Too lazy to finish their embroidery probably.

Bonnie began by saying that it was an ordinary washing powder, one of those kinds that they're always talking about over the radio. Then Esther, who would never interrupt anybody, interrupted to say that her water was barely warm.

I was losing patience with everybody talking, everybody understanding but me. "What are you all babbling about mild soap and barely warm water for?"

Suddenly Ginny whipped from a grocery bag a white T-shirt so shrunk that the embroidery's lettering was no longer readable. "We is talking about this."

First we talked about our wasted efforts and then we talked about our wasted money and then we talked about what nobody could understand: what caused the shrinkage.

"Listen here," I said suddenly. "We bought something in good and honest faith that didn't turn out to be a bit of good. Well, if we all go down to the Busy Bee and explain the situation to Mr. Putterham, then he'll give us back our money. Probably even apologize that he can't pay us for our trouble."

"What Mr. Putterham is you talking about?" asked Bonnie, cocking her head like a trained spaniel. "The only Mr. Putterham I know wouldn't apologize to his ma if he ran her down in the broad daylight."

I told her right off. "Trouble with you, Miss Bonnie, is that you ain't got no faith in human nature."

Still, the thought that old bushy eyes ever had a mother was surprising. Reckon I just couldn't see Mr. Putterham having anything that couldn't turn a profit.

Even though I walked into the Busy Bee as slow as I could possibly walk, the others carefully managed to walk even slower. They stayed behind me, pushing me on toward the wrapping counter and the awesome presence of Cyrus J. Putterham. As I watched him tying a piece of string around a shoe box, I got to wishing that one of the other girls had replaced me as president of the Pennies; then they'd be standing here on the firing line instead of me.

The merchant lifted his eyebrows at me, which was a kind of a cheapskate way of asking what I wanted without actually bothering to ask.

"Well, uh . . . Mr. Putterpam——ham! Mr. Putterham, it's uh . . . about what happened two Saturdays ago when we all bought T-shirts from your store. We washed them like we wash anything else," I said, removing the newspaper from my shirt to hold it up. "And they all five shrunk up like this."

He stretched his lips into a hard straight line. "How much you pay for that shirt?"

"Eighty-nine cents."

"See?"

What did he want me to see? "Sir?"

A short blast of air rushed through his nostrils and I came to understand that his patience zipped off on that blast of air. "Something you girls paid only eighty-nine cents for isn't going to last forever. Why, eighty-nine cents for a T-shirt is mighty cheap."

"Oh, no, sir," I corrected him. "Paying eighty-nine cents for something that ain't never been worn is mighty expensive."

He waved his hand as though he was shooing a fly. "All right, I was nice enough to listen to you girls and now y'all get on out of here. I got me a store to run."

274

"Yes, sir," I said pleasantly. "We appreciate your attention, sure do. But what we really want is for you to refund us our money 'cause a shirt that ain't fit to be washed ain't fit to be sold."

"Get on out of here!" Both his hands went flapping in the air. "Now get!"

We may have left the store like scared chicks, but once outside we became more like mad wet hens. Esther kept saying, "Imagine!" Or sometimes she'd vary it with "Would you imagine that!"

Then, as if we didn't have enough trouble, the Tiger Hunters led by the bravest of all the brave Tiger Hunters came up to say that we were going to be beaten so bad that it would be a long time before we showed our face in Pocahontas again.

"Don't fret about it," I told him. " 'Cause I don't think I want to show my face anymore, anyway." A warm tear had begun to worm its way down my cheek.

Philip looked uncomfortable. What's the matter? Hadn't he ever seen a tear before? "We don't have to relay race today," he was saying. "We can put it off until the Sunday of the Old Rugged Cross Church picnic."

We shook hands on it, but I was not able to say any more. Talking took too much effort. So Bonnie explained while Ginny showed Philip and his Tiger Hunters what happened to our shirts. Right away Philip said, "We don't have to let Mr. Putterham get away with that. That's robbery!"

Philip's comment about its being a robbery struck me like one of God's own revelations!

At the far end of Main Street, sitting on a square of grass, is the old red brick courthouse where Sheriff Nathan Miller has a narrow office and two barred cells. As the Pennies and Hunters strode up the courthouse walk, old men sitting out on sunny park benches looked up.

The sheriff told us all to crowd on in. "I'll never forget what good police work you and Phil did in capturing those fowl thieves. You know, no farmer has reported any livestock missing since they left town."

His words encouraged me to tell him about our "robbery" at the hands of the merchant Putterham. I watched the sheriff's face grow more and more thoughtful. Finally he said, "I'm sorry, but there ain't no way I can help you out."

" . . . But why?"

With his booted feet, the sheriff pushed his chair from his desk. "Follow me," he said, already walking with strong strides from his office.

Outside, the men on the benches now seemed doubly surprised to see us kids half-running in order to keep up with Randolph County's long-legged lawman. A block down Main Street and then two blocks down School Street to the last house at the end of the block. The sheriff walked up the driveway and into the backyard. At a backyard sandpile a little boy dressed in diapers and pullover shirt toddled over, saying, "Dadadadada."

The sheriff picked him up and then asked me, "What do you think of my boy's shirt?"

Surely eleven folks didn't walk all the way over here just to look at a tight-fitting baby shirt. It seemed silly, but he really did want my opinion. "I reckon it's a nice enough baby shirt," I told him.

"Uh-hun!" answered the more than six feet of sheriff as though he had suddenly struck gold. "Uh-hun," he repeated. "For a baby shirt it's mighty fine, but it wasn't bought to be no baby's shirt. No Sir! It was bought for me. Last Saturday I paid eighty-nine cents for that T-shirt at the Busy Bee Bargain Store."

"You too!!——Then why don't you——"

"Because selling bad merchandise," he said, "can get a merchant in trouble with his customers without getting him in trouble with the law."

We Pretty Pennies walked with the Tiger Hunters back toward Main Street like a bunch of beaten soldiers. No reason for hurrying. No good left in the day nohow. Then it struck me like a pie in the face. Why are we defeated? Ten of us and only one of them Putterhams. "Stop!" I said, whirling around like a general of the army. "We ain't giving up this battle!"

"We ain't?" asked Philip.

I was the fightingest president the Pretty Pennies would ever have. "No, we ain't, 'cause if we all stood out in front of the Busy Bee Bargain Store showing off our shrunken shirts, then old Mr. Putterham would be so embarrassed he'd have to refund our money."

I broke into a run, followed by Philip Hall, followed by the rest of them. In front of the Busy Bee, we all formed a loose line——a Penny, a Hunter, a Penny, and so forth. "Pretty Pennies and Tiger Hunters. When we're working together we'll call ourselves the great Penny Hunters," I said.

Since Philip Hall didn't look exactly thrilled by my suggestion, I said, "Well, would you rather be called the Pretty Tigers?" His groan gave me his answer.

When a heavy woman with three chilluns slowly made her way toward the Busy Bee door, Bonnie approached her. A moment later she was spreading out her doll-size shirt across her chest while the woman shook her head and said, "I'm going to do my trading at Logan's."

The very next person who was persuaded not to spend money at the Busy Bee was my sister, Anne. She said she could buy fingernail polish at the dime store just as well.

After Anne, there was our preacher, the Reverend Ross, who was going to buy some white handkerchiefs from Putterham, but the Reverend said he'd "be happy to respect your picket line."

"Respect our what?" I asked.

"Folks who is standing like some of God's own soldiers against the world's injustices is," said the Reverend Ross, "a picket line."

Never before in my whole life had I ever felt so important, but then never before had I been on special assignment for God.

Just then a family of five reached for the Busy Bee's door and I called out, "Don't you folks go buying things in there unless"——I held up my shirt——"you don't object to shrinking."

"Lordy," said the wife, coming right over to get a closer look. "Now ain't that a pity?"

Mr. Putterham stepped outside the door. "What's this? What's going on here?"

I turned to watch Philip Hall 'cause I didn't want to miss seeing him speak right up to that old man merchant. But the only thing I saw was the bravest Tiger Hunter of them all with his mouth flung open, looking for all the world like he would never again be able to speak.

The proprietor's eyes now swept past Philip and were looking down the long picket line. "Don't tell me that all you kids have been struck speechless? Somebody better tell me what's going on!"

I took one step forward. "I reckon you oughta know that we is picketing your store, Mr. Putterdam——ham! Mr. Putterham."

His big, bushy eyebrows jumped up and down as though they were skipping rope. "You is doing WHAT? And to WHOM?"

"We is"——my mouth felt too dry for stamp licking——"picketing you," I said, grateful that the words actually sounded.

"Now you listen here, you," he said. "Nobody pickets Cyrus J. Putterham, Pocahontas's leading merchant. Know that?"

"Yes, sir."

"Good," he said, smiling a pretend smile. "Then y'all get on out of here."

"Uh . . . no, sir," I said, trying to remember the Reverend Ross's words about being one of God's own soldiers.

"What do you mean No, sir?" he asked, allowing his voice to rise into a full shout. "You just got through saying Yes, sir."

"Uh, well, sir, that was my answer to your question." Mr. Putterham blinked as though my words were being spoken in a strange new language. I tried again. "What I was saying, Mr. Putterjam . . . ham! Mr. Putterham, was yes, sir, I know all about you being Pocahontas's leading merchant. But no, sir, we ain't moving from our picket line. Not until we get our money back."

His eyes told me how much he wanted me to understand. "But if I give you folks your money back, then everybody who ever bought bad merchandise from me will be wanting their money back too."

From the picket line a single voice called, "Give back the money!" Then more voices, more Pennies and Hunters together calling, "Give back the money!" And I joined my voice with the Penny Hunters and even some folks on the street who were now chanting, *Give back the money!* And taken together the voices sounded as though they were doing a lot more demanding than asking.

The shopkeeper threw up his hands. "All right, all right." He smiled, but it wasn't what you'd call a sincere smile. "Making my customers happy is the only thing that's ever been important to Cyrus J. Putterham. Take your shirts back to the wrapping counter for a full and courteous refund."

After all the shirt money was safely back in the hands of our treasurer, Bonnie Blake, I spoke again to the merchant. "There is one more thing, Mr. Putterpam——ham! Mr. Putterham."

"As long as you girls are satisfied——well, that's thanks enough for me. Why, my very business is built on a foundation of square and fair."

"Yes, sir," I agreed. "Would you mind giving us back our embroidery money?"

"Your what?"

I presented him with the cash register receipt. "Two dollars and fifty cents worth of embroidery thread, ruined when our shirts shrunk."

For a moment I thought his face was growing angry, but then he sighed and placed the additional two-fifty on the counter.

"Thanks, Mr. Putterham."

He smiled and this time it didn't look all that insincere. "You called me Putterham. Finally you did it right."

I smiled back at him. "And finally, Mr. Putterham, so did you."

The Pretty Pennies Picket

Meet the Author

Bette Greene's writing focuses on characters who must learn to stand up for what they know is right. These characters are facing problems that call for moral courage. Greene believes adults need to help young people develop moral courage. Much of her writing is based on memories of growing up in a Jewish family in a small Arkansas town. "My roots, my memories are all Arkansas." She credits much of her success to a teacher who helped her realize she could be anything she wanted to be.

Meet the Illustrator

Colin Bootman is a native of Trinidad who moved to the United States when he was young. He began painting as a child. Bootman still remembers Trinidad, especially the colorful outdoor markets. He now lives in The Bronx, New York, where he works as a freelance artist.

280

Theme Connections

Within the Selection

Record your answers to the questions below in the Response Journal section of your Writer's Notebook. In small groups, report the ideas you wrote. Discuss your ideas with the rest of your group. Then choose a person to report your group's answers to the class.

- Why does Ginny say she thinks the Pretty Pennies need a new president?
- What big event inspired the Pretty Pennies to embroider T-shirts?
- Why did the Pretty Pennies try to return their T-shirts to Mr. Putterham's store?

Across the Selections

- Compare this story with "His Majesty, Queen Hapshepsut" from the last unit. How does Queen Hapshepsut take a stand?
- In "A Picture Book of Jesse Owens," Jesse Owens takes a stand. How is the stand he takes different from that of the Pretty Pennies? How is it the same?

Beyond the Selection

- Think of a time when you have taken a stand for something. What was it for? Did you take your stand alone, or were you part of a group? Did it get you the results you wanted? Looking back, would you say the stand you took was worth it? Get into small groups and share your stories. Then pick one or two stories from each group to share with the class.

Class Discussion

from *School Spirit*
by Johanna Hurwitz
illustrated by Richard Hull

On Fridays, Mr. Flores brought his guitar to school. The last hour of the day was devoted to singing and talk. It was a relaxed and friendly way to end the week, and Julio and all his classmates looked forward to it. In fact, they were almost sorry when the dismissal bell rang and school was over for the week.

This Friday, however, it didn't look as if Mr. Flores would do any guitar playing. The last hour was going to be devoted to a discussion of the fate of their school. It was nothing to sing about. There had been a lengthy article in the newspaper yesterday explaining the decision before the school board. Cricket Kaufman had cut it out and brought it into class. During the lunch hour, Julio had hardly been aware that he was eating his favorite school lunch: pizza squares with pepperoni, tossed salad, fruit cocktail, and chocolate milk. He carefully studied every word of the article. It gave all the details of why the district was considering the proposed closing, and it explained how much money could be saved.

Now Mr. Flores handed out a flyer on yellow paper to each of the students. It had been prepared by the school for the students to take home to their parents. Much of the information from the newspaper article was repeated on the sheet. It also listed the day and date a month off when the school board would next be meeting to discuss the proposed school closing.

Lucas began to fold his copy of the flyer into a paper airplane. A couple of the other boys noticed and did the same thing. Julio was tempted too. A sheet of paper like this was just begging to be transformed into an airplane. But Julio resisted the urge. He was the class president, and his class was discussing something very serious.

282

"I don't see why it's our school that has to be closed," Cricket protested. "If they want to close a school, why don't they close one of the other ones?"

"Yeah," agreed several of the other students.

"Well, aside from the fact that this is the building where you go to school, what makes this place so special?" asked Mr. Flores. "Aren't all schools the same?"

"Oh, no," protested Zoe. She was the expert on this subject. "This school is friendlier. There's a nice feeling here. Even though I'm still new in the community, I think it's great that Cricket's mother went to this school."

"My father went here too," said Sara Jane Cushman.

"So did mine," said Arthur Lewis. "Maybe they were in the same class."

283

"You like the continuity then," said Mr. Flores. He wrote the word CONTINUITY on the chalkboard.

As the teacher turned his back, one of the yellow paper airplanes flew across the room. It was followed by a second one. Mr. Flores turned around and faced the class while the second one was still airborne.

"Now hear this," announced Mr. Flores. "Due to conditions beyond your control the airport is closed and all planes are grounded." He walked over and picked up the two yellow paper planes from the floor. He unfolded them and flattened the sheets out. "This is important information for your parents. If you are missing your notice, I recommend that you come and take one from my desk before you go home."

Julio turned and grinned at Lucas. Mr. Flores was allowing his friend to reclaim his yellow sheet anonymously. No wonder Julio liked their teacher so much.

"I think it's great that this school is old. It's been around here for a long time," said Zoe. "It has a nice old-school smell and feel about it. Not like my last school, which was bright and shiny new and felt more like a hospital than a school."

SENSE OF HISTORY, Mr. Flores wrote on the board.

This time there were no airplanes flying when his back was turned.

"How old is this building anyhow?" asked Arthur.

"It's more than eighty years old," said Cricket before Julio could respond. "It says so in the article."

"Wow. That's how old my great-grandfather is," said Sara Jane.

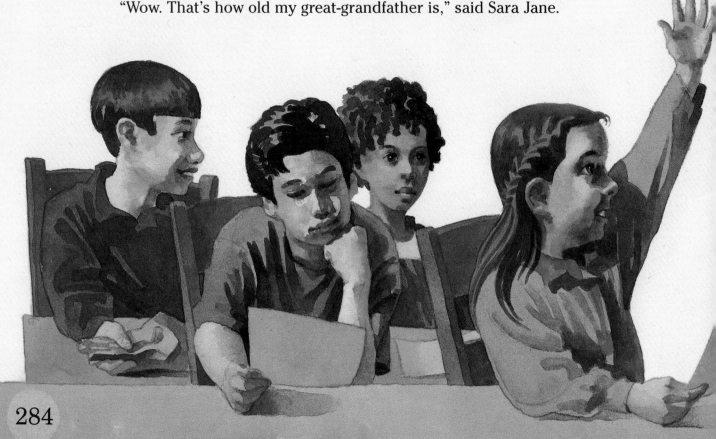

"Maybe Edison went here," suggested Julio. "Maybe that's the way it got his name."

"You could look that up," said the teacher. "And while you're at it, why don't you find out who Armstrong is too."

"I know. I know who that is," shouted Cricket.

Julio looked at Cricket's face. It was red with excitement. She just loved knowing an answer that no one else knew.

"Armstrong is Henrietta Armstrong, who was the first principal of this school. She worked here for forty years. Her picture is in the lobby."

"Oh, right," agreed Julio. He must have passed that picture of the white-haired old lady a hundred thousand times. He saw it and he didn't see it. Now he'd have to make sure to take a good look at it on his way out of the building today. Imagine coming to this building every school day for forty years.

"It doesn't seem nice to honor someone by naming a building after them and then selling the building or tearing it down," said Arthur.

"I sure wouldn't like it if someone did that to me," said Cricket.

"Don't worry, no one is ever going to name a building after you," said Lucas.

"Yes they will," Cricket insisted. "You just wait until I'm the first woman president of the United States. They'll probably want to call this school the Edison-Armstrong-Kaufman School."

"That's too much for anyone to say, and besides, they won't be able to do it if this school is closed," Lucas pointed out.

"I have a suggestion," said Mr. Flores, interrupting Cricket and Lucas. "Who would like to be on a committee to find out what was happening in the world eighty years ago? We can make a time line. Eighty years ago in this community, in the United States, and in the world."

"Ooh, me, me," said Cricket, raising her hand. It was just the type of project she liked.

"Me too," said Zoe.

"Great," said Mr. Flores.

Julio raised his hand.

Mr. Flores nodded in recognition. "Yes, Julio. Do you want to be on the committee too?"

"I want us to do something to rally all the students and to make a difference. Can't we get the school board to change their

minds? How about writing them a letter about how we feel. Maybe all the other classes would write letters too. We should make posters to decorate the halls. Make up a school cheer and a school song. Maybe if we can show the school board that we all have a lot of school spirit, they'll change their minds about sending all of us off to other schools."

Anne Crosby raised her hand. "I want to write a song," she said.

Everyone was surprised by this offer. "Are you a relative of Bing Crosby?" asked Cricket. "I saw him singing in an old movie on TV."

Anne blushed. "No," she said. "But I'd like to make up a song anyway. I like to write poems."

"Great," said Mr. Flores. "If you write a song, I'll accompany you on my guitar." Mr. Flores looked around the room. "Any other ideas?" he asked.

"Maybe we could design T-shirts for everyone in the school," suggested Zoe. "If we all walked around in matching shirts, it would show that we all belong together."

"Blue ones," suggested Cricket.

"No, black," someone else called out.

"It could be like an art project," said Julio. "Maybe the art teacher could help us. If we made a design and everyone brought a plain white shirt to school, we could all make our own shirts in art."

Mr. Flores nodded his head as he wrote TOGETHERNESS on the board.

"I have an idea," offered Sara Jane. "Maybe some of our parents who attended this school would come and tell what it was like in the olden times."

Mr. Flores began a second column of ideas. He wrote LETTER, GUESTS, T-SHIRTS, SONG.

"I think we should plant flowers all around the school yard and do other things to make the school more beautiful," suggested a girl named Joyce Howe. "If we make it look prettier,

287

Continuity
Sense of History
Togetherness
Letter Song
Guests Cleanup
T-Shirts

they will forget that the building is so old. In the newspaper article it said that this school is very shabby."

"It's the wrong season for planting flowers. They'd all die in the cold. But we should be better about picking up trash," suggested Zoe. "I noticed a lot of papers flying around in the yard, during lunch recess. It doesn't look very nice."

"I saw a couple of soda cans too," said Arthur.

"That's not our garbage," Lucas complained. "People waiting at the bus stop on the corner by the school are the ones who throw a lot of that stuff in the yard."

"We still should clean it up," said Zoe. "If someone from the school board comes by, they don't know whose junk it is. They just see it's in our school yard. It looks like we don't care."

"Sometimes there's garbage inside the school too," said Julio, feeling guilty. Just this morning he had kicked a crumpled ball of paper from one end of the hallway to the other without picking it up.

Mr. Flores added the word CLEANUP to his second list. Before he could write anything more, however, the dismissal bell rang.

"Already?" complained Julio. It seemed too soon for the school day to end.

Mr. Flores turned to face the students. "All these ideas are called brainstorming," he said. "Every time one of you made a suggestion, it gave another one of you an idea. You start working on your ideas, and a week from now we'll pick up at this point. If you want, over the weekend you can write a letter to the school board. Next week we can incorporate everyone's ideas and write a class letter for students to sign."

"All right," said Julio. He felt full of energy and excitement from the class discussion. He couldn't wait to speak with some of the other class presidents and the students in the other rooms. In one of the sixth grades there was a tall and very popular girl named Jennifer Harper who was class president. She always had a group of her classmates around her, and they hung on every word she said. Julio had a feeling she would be a good ally for this cause. He'd have to make a point of speaking to her as soon as possible. For the first time in his life Julio regretted that it was Friday afternoon. Now he'd have to wait until school opened again on Monday morning. What a pain!

Class Discussion

Meet the Author

Johanna Hurwitz was born in New York, New York. It's not surprising that Hurwitz knew from the age of ten that she wanted to be a writer. Her parents met in a bookstore. She grew up in a New York City apartment where the walls were lined with books. Her father was a journalist and bookseller, and her mother was a library assistant.

She began her career with books working at the New York City Public Library while still in high school. She then got two degrees in Library Science. She published her first book while in her thirties and has been writing books for children ever since. In one interview she revealed, "It seems as if all my fiction has grown out of real experiences." She has written books about her children's love of baseball, her own childhood and summer vacations, her mother's childhood, and even her cats and their fleas!

Meet the Illustrator

Richard Hull teaches illustration at Brigham Young University. He was also an art director and graphic designer with a magazine for 15 years. Other books Mr. Hull has illustrated include *The Cat & the Fiddle & More*, *My Sister's Rusty Bike*, and *The Alphabet from Z to A (With Much Confusion on the Way)*. He and his wife currently reside in Orem, Utah.

Theme Connections

Within the Selection

Record your answers to the questions below in the Response Journal section of your Writer's Notebook. In small groups, report the ideas you wrote. Discuss your ideas with the rest of your group. Then choose a person to report your group's answers to the class.

- Why does Mr. Flores write the word *continuity* on the chalkboard?
- What are some other reasons the kids want their school to remain open?
- What are some of the ideas they come up with to show support for their school?

Across the Selections

- How is the stand taken in "Class Discussion" similar to the one taken in "The Pretty Pennies Picket?"
- What is something characters in both stories want to do as a way of showing their unity?

Beyond the Selection

- In "Class Discussion" the students hope to make a difference at their school. Have a class discussion of your own, and think of some ways your class can make a difference around your own school. What are some constructive things you can do as a class to help improve your school?

Focus Questions How do the Grimké sisters champion the causes of fairness and justice? What did they endure as a result of taking a stand?

The Grimké Sisters

from *Great Lives: Human Rights*
William Jay Jacobs
illustrated by Stephen Harrington

D ignified, serious, dressed simply, with a white handkerchief framing her delicate features, Angelina Grimké stood calmly at the speaker's stand, preparing to address a committee of the Massachusetts State Legislature.

Outside the State House, men shook their fists in anger. Some hooted and jeered. Others hissed, not the hisses heard at today's sports events, but hisses born of genuine hatred.

It was Wednesday, February 21, 1838. Until that day no American woman ever had addressed a legislative body in this country. The visitors' gallery was packed to capacity. Standees jammed the aisles and the lobby outside the hall. Many in the crowd had come out of curiosity, just to see a woman speak in public, something then considered shameful, even indecent.

Yet as Miss Grimké's powerful voice rang out across the audience, boldly, magnetically, her listeners riveted their attention on her, gripped by the intensity of her message. For there at the lectern stood a white southern woman, born to wealth and aristocratic position, delivering a passionate attack on the South's "peculiar institution"——human slavery.

"I stand before you as a southerner," she declared, "exiled from the land of my birth by the sound of the lash and the piteous cry of the slave. I stand before you as a repentant slave holder.

292

"I stand before you," continued Angelina Grimké, "as a moral being, and as a moral being I feel that I owe it to the suffering slave and to the deluded master . . . to do all that I can to overturn a system . . . built upon the broken hearts and prostrate bodies of my countrymen in chains and cemented by the blood, sweat and tears of my sisters in bonds . . . "

In the audience before her some people openly cried. The chairman of the committee, Miss Grimké later wrote, "was in tears almost the whole time that I was speaking." Sarah, her older sister, was to have been the featured speaker that day. But, ill, she had taken to her bed, persuading young Angelina to substitute for her.

No matter. Before long the names of the two sisters became linked, North and South, as leaders in the forefront of the antislavery movement. Other women, until then hesitant to speak out in public against the curse of slavery, followed their example.

In time the leading women of the age——Lucy Stone, Elizabeth Cady Stanton, Susan B. Anthony——all would express gratitude to the Grimké sisters. It was the Grimkés, they said, who first inspired them to join in battle, crusading for the twin causes of women's rights and the abolition of slavery.

The society into which Sarah and Angelina Grimké had been born could hardly have been a more unlikely setting for the development of social reformers. Charleston, South Carolina, led the South in defending slavery. Wealthy planter aristocrats, including the father of the Grimké sisters, dominated the city's society. The very survival of their gracious and leisurely lifestyle depended on the slave labor system.

It was slaves who planted and harvested their yearly cotton crops——the source of their wealth. It was slaves, too, who built their houses, cooked their meals, cared for their children, stood behind them to fan the flies away as they dined. It was slaves who made possible for the white men their hours of pleasure in hunting and riding, or for the elegant white women the days and evenings filled with tea parties, fancy-dress balls, and an endless round of visits to neighboring plantations.

For young Sarah Grimké, child of the aristocracy, such a life proved, for some reason, not enough to make her happy. Nor did it please the young Angelina, so headstrong, independent, even in childhood, that her mother scarcely could control her. Instead of absorbing the standard school curriculum for girls of the time——music, a touch of French, and gracious manners——the Grimké sisters demanded the right to the same education as their brothers: Latin, Greek, mathematics, philosophy, and law.

Both girls wept at the beatings and other punishments inflicted by slave owners, including even their own parents, to keep blacks humble and obedient. Sometimes Angelina would creep into the slave quarters at night to rub soothing ointment into the open wounds of slaves who had been lashed with the whip.

Sarah, and later Angelina, too, taught the slave girls assigned to them as maids how to read. In most parts of the South such an act was strictly forbidden, but as Angelina admitted with pride in her diary, "The light was put out, the keyhole screened, and flat on our stomachs before the fire, we defied the laws of South Carolina."

In 1819, when Sarah was twenty-seven, her father chose her, instead of his wife or any of her brothers, to travel with him to the North. He was ill and had been advised that a surgeon in Philadelphia might help him, but the illness proved fatal.

The trip was to change Sarah's life. Quakers whom she met in Philadelphia introduced her to their religion. She admired their seriousness of purpose, liked their opposition to slavery. She also approved of the laws passed in Philadelphia to protect free Negroes there.

Although the decision was painful, she decided to leave Charleston and go to live in Philadelphia. Perhaps in the North, she confided to Angelina, a woman might live a life not just of pleasure but of real purpose. In 1829 Angelina, then twenty-four, followed her sister to Philadelphia. Both sisters knew that, hating slavery as they did, the break with their old lives in Charleston could never be healed.

At first the Grimkés tried to live like religious Quakers. They lived simply, dressed simply, and did charity work. But that was not enough for them. Always rebellious, they insisted on speaking aloud in the usually silent Quaker meetings, where they

295

also made a point of sitting in the sections reserved for black women. To them the Quakers were doing too little, moving too slowly, in putting a stop to slavery in America. Just as they had left the Episcopal Church in South Carolina, they also split from the Quakers.

In 1835 Angelina decided to state publicly that all slaves must be freed. She wrote to William Lloyd Garrison, editor of the *Liberator*, America's angriest antislavery newspaper. Abolition of slavery, she declared in her letter, "is a cause worth dying for." Of Garrison himself, she stated that "The ground upon which you stand is holy ground."

Garrison printed Angelina's letter in the *Liberator*. Overnight Angelina and her sister became heroines of the antislavery movement. Here were the daughters of wealthy slave owners daring to describe the brutal acts they personally had witnessed and demanding that the slaves should be freed at once.

Next Angelina wrote a pamphlet, *An Appeal to the Christian Women of the South*, urging white women to join the fight against slavery——to put an end to "this horrible system of oppression and cruelty . . . and wrong," even if they had to break the law.

In Charleston the postmaster publicly burned copies of the pamphlet in the city's main square. Authorities warned Angelina and Sarah not to return home or they would be arrested.

The threat succeeded in keeping the Grimké sisters away from Charleston, but it could not stop them from speaking out. In 1836 Sarah published "Epistle to the Clergy of the Southern States." In that letter she urged southern ministers at least to stop giving their support to slavery, even if they could not offend their congregations by opposing it publicly.

Well known by then, the Grimkés decided to give their lives totally to the abolitionist movement. They joined the American Anti-Slavery Society and began to speak, as a team, to small meetings of women in New York City.

Soon these so-called parlor meetings became so popular that many ministers opened their churches to the Grimké sisters, usually on the condition that no men be present. But before long men demanded the right to hear the lectures, even though the appearance of women as public speakers was considered unwomanly. Almost everywhere, the Grimkés found themselves facing mixed audiences——larger and larger ones as their popularity grew.

It was during their triumphant tour of New England in 1838 that Angelina delivered her famous address to a session of the Massachusetts Legislature in the State House at Boston.

Angelina, tall, with piercing eyes and a strong voice, enjoyed meeting an audience. Sarah, more reserved, did most of the writing for the Grimké team. The two worked well together.

At first William Lloyd Garrison and other leaders of the abolitionist movement pleaded with them not to endanger the antislavery cause by linking it with questions of women's rights, especially the right of women to speak in public. Garrison changed his mind, however, as did Theodore Dwight Weld, who had coached Angelina in techniques of public speaking when she first joined the American Anti-Slavery Society.

Instead of avoiding the issue of women's rights, the Grimké sisters spoke out more strongly on it. They demanded not only the right to be heard, but also the right of women to vote, to help make laws, and even to serve as elected officials. Finally they demanded that women be given complete legal equality with men in such matters as divorce and ownership of property.

At one of their speeches a gang of boys threw apples at them. Spectators jeered at them. Newspapermen dubbed them "the weird sisters," or "Devilina and Grimalkin."

Nothing stopped the Grimkés. In the spring of 1838 they spoke at the Odeon Theater in Boston to mixed audiences of men and women numbering two thousand to three thousand. Clearly they had taken center stage in the antislavery movement. No other women in the country were so well known or so frequently discussed.

By now it became obvious, too, that Theodore Dwight Weld's interest in Angelina went beyond her ideas. He continued to give her lessons in public speaking. He accompanied the Grimkés on their tours. But he also had fallen in love with Angelina——and she with him.

In May 1838 they were married. The wedding party included, in the words of one guest, "a motley assembly of white and black, high and low." In direct defiance of "the horrible prejudice of slavery" the bride and groom introduced as bridesmaids and groomsmen six former slaves from the Grimké plantation. Two white and two black ministers presented prayers. At the end of the ceremony William Lloyd Garrison read the marriage certificate aloud and then passed it around the room to be signed by each guest.

Theodore and Angelina insisted that the wedding cake be made with sugar grown by free laborers. The cotton for their mattress, they proudly pointed out, had come from a farm in New Jersey, not "the usual slave-grown cotton ticking."

Two days after their wedding Angelina and Theodore left for a honeymoon. As might be expected, they spent it working for the antislavery cause. Along with Sarah, they attended the opening session of the Anti-Slavery Convention of American Women, held in Philadelphia's attractive new Pennsylvania Hall. The hall had been built especially for such occasions, since reformers, even in Quaker-dominated Philadelphia, had experienced difficulty renting space for speeches on such topics as women's rights and abolition.

On the first night of the convention, Angelina Grimké Weld rose to address a mixed audience of more than a thousand blacks and whites. Outside the hall a mob of whites gathered. As Angelina began to speak they shouted and cursed. They stamped their feet. Then they began throwing bricks and stones at the newly opened hall, shattering the windows. Glass fell to the floor, some of it at Angelina's feet.

"What is a mob?" she continued calmly.

What would the breaking of every window be? Any evidence that *we are* wrong, or that slavery is a good and wholesome institution? What if that mob should now burst in upon us, break up our meeting and commit violence on our persons— would this be anything compared with what the slaves endure?

For more than an hour Angelina spoke on as the mob groaned and roared angrily in the background. Nothing could stop her from delivering her message.

Before the meeting could begin on the next night, the mayor of Philadelphia closed the hall, fearing violence. After he left the scene, the mob surged forward. They burst into the offices of the Anti-Slavery Society there and destroyed many precious papers. Then they set fire to the hall, dedicated to free speech, burning it completely to the ground.

In the months that followed the fire Angelina and Theodore Weld did little public speaking. They began to build a family, eventually having three children. Sarah, now alone, came to live with them, first in their home in New Jersey and later in Massachusetts. She took special pleasure in caring for the Weld children.

The three also worked together on an important new collection of documents, *American Slavery As It Is: Testimony of a Thousand Witnesses*. Drawing heavily on advertisements and published accounts in southern newspapers, the study offered powerful evidence against slavery. Included were advertisements for the return of runaway slaves, identified by their owners, for example, as "stamped on the left cheek 'R' and a piece is taken off her left ear, the same letter is branded on the inside of both legs"; or, "branded 'N.E.' on the breast and having both small toes cut off."

Harriet Beecher Stowe relied heavily on the Weld-Grimké evidence in writing *Uncle Tom's Cabin*, the novel that, according to some, became a major emotional cause of the Civil War.

In time, illness and age began to limit the involvement of Sarah, Angelina, and Theodore in the antislavery cause. Still, they continued to circulate petitions against slavery. They also became interested in other reforms of the day, such as less confining clothing for women, sensible diet, and better forms of education.

After the Civil War ended the sisters learned that two of their brother Henry's sons, born of a Negro slave woman, were in the North. Without hesitation they welcomed the boys into their home and paid for their education. One son later became a prominent minister in black churches. The other became a leader in the National Association for the Advancement of Colored People (NAACP).

In 1873 Sarah Grimké died. Six years later Angelina followed her sister to the grave. Both had lived long enough to see the end of slavery in America. And although the women's rights movement had not yet triumphed, the Grimké sisters had been early leaders in drawing the nation's attention to that movement, too.

Women of ability and high character, the Grimkés turned their backs, as young adults, on what surely would have been lives of security, comfort, leisure, and wealth. Instead they chose to live lives of struggle but also of great accomplishment and——through service to others——lives filled with meaning.

The Grimké Sisters

Meet the Author

William Jay Jacobs writes about history for children and young adults. Much of his writing is about important people and events in American history. His family background led him to write about history. "My mother came to America on her own from Austria at the age of twelve. . . . My father escaped from Hungary just before being taken into that country's army. . . . America to me is more than just a place of residence. It is a passion."

Meet the Illustrator

Stephen Harrington began working as an art director for a local advertising agency after graduating from the Rhode Island School of Design in 1983. After four years, he gave it up to become a freelance illustrator, working out of his home. He has now been doing this for the last 11 years. Harrington was able to combine his two loves, art and history, while illustrating *The Grimké Sisters*. Using books from his own collection and those in the local library, he tried to create images that were visually dramatic, as well as historically accurate.

Theme Connections

Within the Selection

Record your answers to the questions below in the Response Journal section of your Writer's Notebook. In small groups, report the ideas you wrote. Discuss your ideas with the rest of your group. Then choose a person to report your group's answers to the class.

- What were some early signs the Grimké sisters showed of possessing unusual fortitude and independence?
- What did the Grimké sisters sacrifice to become leaders in the antislavery and suffragist movements?
- What connection did the Grimké sisters have to Harriet Beecher Stowe?

Across the Selections

- Compare "The Grimké Sisters" to "The Pretty Pennies Picket." What role does public speech play in each story?
- Taking a stand sometimes causes confrontation. For instance, the Grimké sisters were often faced with jeering mobs. What other confrontations have you read about in this unit? How would you compare these confrontations to those experienced by the Grimké sisters?

Beyond the Selection

- Think about how "The Grimké Sisters" adds to what you know about taking a stand.
- Add items to the Concept/Question Board about taking a stand.

Rosa Parks, The Beginning. **Artis Lane.**
Private collection.

Armor of George Clifford, third earl of Cumberland. c.1580–1585. **Unknown artist**, made in Royal Workshop at Greenwich. Steel–blue, etched, and gilded. Metropolitan Museum of Art, New York, NY.

The Uprising. c.1848. **Honoré Daumier.** Oil on canvas. The Phillips Collection, Washington, DC.

I Have a Dream

from the speech by Martin Luther King, Jr.

Born in 1929, Dr. Martin Luther King, Jr., began his career at the age of twenty-seven as the minister of the Dexter Avenue Baptist Church in Montgomery, Alabama. He later became the leader of the struggle for civil rights for African-Americans. On August 28, 1963, he made his famous "I Have a Dream" speech in Washington, D.C., where more than a quarter-million people were gathered to convince Congress to pass a civil-rights bill. In his speech, Dr. King pleaded for freedom and justice for all people.

So I say to you, my friends, that even though we must face the difficulties of today and tomorrow, I still have a dream. It is a dream deeply rooted in the American dream that one day this nation will rise up and live out the true meaning of its creed——we hold these truths to be self-evident, that all men are created equal.

I have a dream that one day sons of former slaves and sons of former slave-owners will be able to sit down together at the table of brotherhood.

I have a dream my four little children will one day live in a nation where they will not be judged by the color of their skin but by the content of their character. I have a dream today!

I have a dream that one day . . . little black boys and black girls will be able to join hands with little white boys and white girls as sisters and brothers. I have a dream today!

I have a dream that one day every valley shall be exalted, every hill and mountain shall be made low, the rough places shall be made plain, and the crooked places shall be made straight and the glory of the Lord will be revealed and all flesh shall see it together.

This is our hope. This is the faith that I go back to the South with.

With this faith we will be able to hew out of the mountain of despair a stone of hope. With this faith we will be able to transform the jangling discords of our nation into a beautiful symphony of brotherhood.

With this faith we will be able to work together, to pray together, to struggle together, to go to jail together, to stand up for freedom together, knowing that we will be free one day. This will be the day when all of God's children will be able to sing with new meaning——"my country 'tis of thee; sweet land of liberty; of thee I sing; land where my fathers died, land of the pilgrims' pride; from every mountainside, let freedom ring"—— and if America is to be a great nation, this must become true.

So let freedom ring from the prodigious hilltops of New Hampshire.

Let freedom ring from the mighty mountains of New York.

Let freedom ring from the heightening Alleghenies of Pennsylvania.

Let freedom ring from the snow-capped Rockies of Colorado.

Let freedom ring from the curvaceous slopes of California.

But not only that.

Let freedom ring from Stone Mountain of Georgia.

Let freedom ring from Lookout Mountain of Tennessee.

Let freedom ring from every hill and molehill of Mississippi, from every mountainside, let freedom ring.

And when we allow freedom to ring, when we let it ring from every village and hamlet, from every state and city, we will be able to speed up that day when all of God's children——black men and white men, Jews and Gentiles, Catholics and Protestants——will be able to join hands and to sing in the words of the old Negro spiritual, "Free at last, free at last; thank God Almighty, we are free at last."

I Have a Dream

Meet the Author

Martin Luther King, Jr., was a Baptist minister who wanted to end racial segregation in the South. He believed that people should be judged by the "content of their character" and not by their skin color. King worked hard to bring people of all races together, and he believed this could be done without violence. Because of his hard work, he earned the Nobel Peace Prize in 1964. King was the leader of the civil rights movement from the mid-1950s until 1968 when he was assassinated.

Theme Connections

Within the Selection

Record your answers to the questions below in the Response Journal section of your Writer's Notebook. In small groups, report the ideas you wrote. Discuss your ideas with the rest of your group. Then choose a person to report your group's answers to the class.

- What was Martin Luther King, Jr.'s dream?
- What does he mean by saying that a stone of hope can be hewn from a mountain of despair?
- After mentioning places like New York and Pennsylvania, why does Dr. King make a special point of mentioning places like Stone Mountain of Georgia and Lookout Mountain of Tennessee?

Across the Selections

- Dr. King's "I Have a Dream" speech is most closely connected to what other selection you've read in this unit? Why?
- Sometimes when stands are taken, the old saying is true: "The pen is mightier than the sword." To what other selections in this unit would you say this saying pertains? Why?

Beyond the Selection

- Think about how "I Have a Dream" adds to what you know about taking a stand.
- Add items to the Concept/Question Board about taking a stand.

Martin Luther King Jr.

by Gwendolyn Brooks

A man went forth with gifts.

He was a prose poem.
He was a tragic grace.
He was a warm music.

He tried to heal the vivid volcanoes.
His ashes are
   reading the world.

His Dream still wishes to anoint
   the barricades of faith and of control.

His word still burns the center of the sun,
   above the thousands and the
   hundred thousands.

The word was Justice. It was spoken.

So it shall be spoken.
So it shall be done.

Focus Questions How did Gandhi's convictions change his life?
How did his nonviolent civil disobedience influence
others around the world?

GANDHI

Nigel Hunter
illustrated by Richard Hook

MEMORIES OF THE MAHATMA

His face is familiar to people in all parts of the world, but to the people of India, Mahatma Gandhi is part of the landscape itself. In every Indian town and village, you are likely to see his image. It could be a framed portrait in the Post Office or bank or a faded photograph displayed on the crumbling wall of a back street tea shop. It could be a brightly-colored postcard clipped to the side of a street-vendor's stall; or a full-length statue set up in the restful shade of a public park or above the hurly-burly and bustle of the crossroads.

He may be pictured at his spinning wheel, absorbed in concentration, or playing with children, laughing good naturedly. Or perhaps he is drinking tea with the Viceroy. More often, he is portrayed striding purposefully forward, leading the movement for Indian independence; for freedom, peace and friendship. Millions affectionately called him *Bapu,* father of the nation. As a sign of respect he became known as Gandhiji and was also called "Mahatma" (great soul) by one of India's finest poets, Rabindranath Tagore. People in every part of India remember Gandhi.

In the southern town of Madurai, what was once a palace is now a museum dedicated to his memory. Outside, in reconstructed buildings, his modest *ashram* living conditions are shown. Inside, a display of words and pictures portrays the long, painful, triumphant march to freedom from British rule. Behind glass there are relics of Gandhi's life; photographs, letters, documents and books; a pair of spectacles, and a spinning wheel. In one cool and carefully-lit space lies an exhibit that bears witness to his sudden, shocking death: a quantity of simple homespun-cloth, white linen darkened by the stain of blood . . .

Gandhi with his granddaughters
in New Delhi.

312

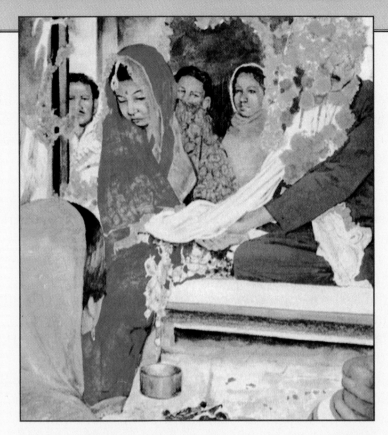

Gandhi's wedding. His head is covered with traditional decorations.

A HINDU FAMILY

When Mohandas Gandhi was born in 1869, the British Empire was at the peak of its power. The British had ruled India for almost three centuries. Certain parts of the country, ruled by princes who were loyal to the British, were allowed to continue as separate princely states. Mohandas' father was the *Diwan,* or Prime Minister, of Porbandar, a small princely state on India's western coast. It was an appointment that passed from father to son.

His first language was Gujarati; his family's religion was Hindu.

When he was thirteen, his parents arranged for him to marry. In later life, he criticized the custom of child-marriage, but at the time he readily accepted it. Mohandas' bride, Kasturbai, was also thirteen, and he soon became devoted to her. He was a very strict husband, and Kasturbai felt he restrained her too much. She was supposed to get his permission before seeing her friends, or visiting the temple. Firmly, she resisted, until he grew to accept her point of view. It was a valuable lesson to Mohandas: he learned that nonviolent persuasion could convince people that they were wrong. Years later, nonviolent resistance would prove to be a powerful weapon in the struggle for social and political reform.

313

Gandhi's family hoped that he might become a *Diwan*, like his father and grandfather before him. For this, it would be a great advantage for him to study law in England, and so he sailed from Bombay in September 1888. For nearly three years, he would be away from Kasturbai, who had just given birth to a son.

Gandhi was ill at ease in Britain at first. He had very little confidence but studied English manners, dressed expensively, and took dancing lessons, trying to fit into English society as a gentleman. While living in London, Gandhi first read the *Bhagavad Gita,* the greatest holy book of Hinduism. As a boy, he had known some of the Hindu stories, but had not held any particular religious beliefs. He had developed friendships with people of many different religions. This helped him to develop a respect for different religions, but he remained uncommitted to any particular faith. Both the *Bhagavad Gita,* and then the Christian *New Testament,* had a profound effect on him.

As soon as he had qualified in law, Gandhi returned home to India. At first, prospects as a lawyer were uncertain because of his nervousness in public. Then a chance came to work on a business dispute in South Africa. This changed his life.

The Challenge

Soon after his arrival in South Africa, while traveling to the city of Pretoria, Gandhi was forcibly ejected from a first-class train compartment. This was simply because he was Indian and the South African whites assumed that he had no right to enjoy first-class train travel. He spent the night on the station platform, considering the humiliations that the Indians in South Africa suffered daily.

Ninety thousand Indians lived and worked in South Africa under white British rule, often in appalling conditions, and many were treated almost as slaves. Only a few hundred Indians, who owned a large amount of land, enjoyed the right to vote in the South African government. For all the Indians, government restrictions were a way of life.

Continuing his journey to Pretoria, Gandhi faced more insults. On a stagecoach, he was again shocked that he was not allowed to take a place inside the coach. He was then beaten by the driver for refusing to sit on the footboard, outside the carriage.

Gandhi is ejected from a first-class train seat because he is Indian.

The journey to Pretoria spurred him into action. In the face of this racial injustice, Gandhi lost his public timidity and called a meeting to discuss the Indians' situation. From this, an organization emerged through which Indians could voice their discontent. Within a short time, Gandhi was acknowledged as a leader of the South African Indian community.

Meanwhile, the legal case that had originally brought Gandhi to South Africa was successfully resolved, largely through his own contribution. His method of solving the dispute was to appeal to what he called "the better side of human nature." To Gandhi, the point was not to achieve outright victory for one side over the other, but to bring both sides together in a mutually satisfactory arrangement. Before long, he was a highly successful lawyer.

It was at this time that Gandhi developed a belief that God was "absolute truth" and that the way to reach Him was through the concept of nonviolence.

Toward Community

Over the next twenty years, Gandhi was to lead the Indians of South Africa in their struggle for justice and equality. He developed a form of political struggle based on nonviolent civil disobedience.

In 1894, Gandhi organized a successful petition and newspaper publicity against new anti-Indian laws. He helped to set up the Natal Indian Congress, which aimed to improve life for the Indian community through educational, social and political work. Gandhi returned to his family in India, and there he publicized the injustices in South Africa and sought support to tackle the problems. When he returned to South Africa he was brutally attacked for being a troublemaker by a white mob. As he recovered at a friend's house, a crowd gathered menacingly outside and sang "We'll hang old Gandhi on the sour apple tree . . ." He managed to escape under the cover of night, disguised as a policeman, and said that he forgave his attackers.

During the Boer War (1899–1902) between Britain and the South African Boers, Gandhi formed and led the Indian Ambulance Corps, which worked for the British Army. Since he was demanding rights as a citizen, he felt he owed loyalty to the British Empire; and Britain awarded him a medal. After the war he visited India again, and renewed his contacts with the leaders of the country's growing nationalist movement.

On his return to South Africa in 1903, Gandhi started a magazine for Indians in South Africa. It was called *Indian Opinion,* and it became crucial to the campaign for equality. His lifestyle changed. He decided to give up all his possessions and established a community. Here, he detached himself from his normal family ties. Gandhi believed that to serve others, he must not distract himself with the burden of possessions or involvement with family and the pleasures of family life.

Nonviolent Rebels

A new law in South Africa required all Indians over eight years old to register with the authorities, and carry a pass at all times. Failing this, they could be imprisoned, fined, or deported. Under Gandhi's leadership, the Indians resisted this new law. He called their action *satyagraha,* which means "holding to the truth." They would not cooperate with the authorities and their resistance was to be nonviolent. Courageously, they confronted prison, poverty, hunger, and violence against them, peacefully refusing to obey the law.

In 1908, Gandhi visited London to muster support. On his return to South Africa, he was imprisoned. Still wearing prison uniform, he was taken to meet General Jan Christiaan Smuts, the South African leader. Smuts promised that if the Indians registered, he would repeal the registration law. Trusting him, Gandhi called on all Indians to register. But Smuts broke his word. In protest, Gandhi led a public burning of the registration certificates. The campaign continued, with thousands of Indians inviting arrest by refusing to register.

Gandhi spent much of his time in prison reading and writing. He discovered the works of the famous Russian writer Leo Tolstoy, and, inspired by each other's ideas, they began exchanging letters. With the help of a friend, Gandhi founded a new community called *Tolstoy Farm.* The community members grew their own food, made their own clothes and built their own homes. Gandhi himself baked bread and made marmalade, and helped to teach the children.

More new laws, including one that said only Christian marriages were legal, prompted Gandhi to step up his campaigning. Again and again he was jailed, along with thousands of others. Many people were assaulted by the police, and several died. Finally, on the main issues, Smuts gave way. With this vital experience behind him, Gandhi was ready to return to India.

Smuts confronts the prisoner Gandhi.

317

Gandhi toured India, talking to the people.

AN INDIAN FUTURE

In Bombay in 1915, Gandhi was welcomed as a hero. He no longer wore western clothing, and he chose to speak Gujarati rather than English, as English was the language of the oppressor. For a year, he toured the country, speaking on religious and social matters. He visited the community that had been started by the poet Rabindranath Tagore. Tagore shared many of Gandhi's ideals. He compared Gandhi to Buddha, because like Gandhi, he had also taught the importance of kindness to all living creatures. Outside the city of Ahmedabad, Gandhi founded the *Satyagraha Ashram,* a community committed to nonviolence and service to others.

Gandhi was determined to break down the Hindu "caste" system, which prevented the caste of Hindus who traditionally did the dirtiest work, from ever entering temples. They were called the "untouchables" because their mere touch horrified higher class Hindus. Despite opposition from Kasturbai and others who found it hard to accept, he brought an "untouchable" family into the *Ashram* and renamed them *Harijans,* meaning "Children of God."

Gandhi successfully led the workers of the province of Bihar in a nonviolent campaign against the unjust demands of British landowners. He carried out a fast, threatening to starve himself to death unless his demands were met.

His action resulted in better wages and conditions for mill workers. He also inspired farm workers who were suffering the effects of famine not to pay Government tax demands, and eventually the demands were withdrawn. He always appealed to his opponents' sense of right and wrong. Briefly, during World War I (1914–18), he helped to recruit Indian soldiers for the British Army. This seemed at odds with his belief in nonviolence; but he hoped that service to save the Empire would earn India self-rule after the war. However, Britain passed harsh new laws preventing India from becoming a self-governing country within the Empire.

Turning and Turning

When Gandhi heard about the new British laws, preventing Indian Home Rule, he called on all Indians to suspend business for a day of national, nonviolent protest, including fasting, prayer and public meetings. But troops in Delhi killed nine people, and when Gandhi tried to reach the city, he was arrested and turned back. News of this provoked rioting and violence in several places. It seemed to Gandhi that he had made a grave mistake. People still did not understand that *satyagraha* persuasion should be nonviolent. He punished himself by fasting for three days.

Then came the terrible massacre at Amritsar. On April 13, 1919, about 15,000 people had gathered together to demonstrate peacefully on the day of the Sikh New Year. Suddenly, soldiers of the British Army appeared, under the command of General Reginald Dyer. He gave the order to shoot, and for ten minutes the soldiers fired into the crowd, who were trapped in a square. Nearly 400 men, women and children were killed, and 11,000 wounded. Gandhi was horrified by the brutality of the British Army, directed at unarmed subjects of the Empire. His loyalty to the British was completely shattered. He felt they had clearly lost all right to govern.

In 1920, Gandhi became president of the All-India Home Rule League, which sought independence from the Empire. Following this, he became the leader of the Indian National Congress. He launched a massive program of non-cooperation against the British. Cotton cloth made in Britain was boycotted and clothes made of foreign material were burned on great bonfires. To symbolize getting rid of foreign influences, hand-spinning and weaving were revived throughout the country. To Gandhi, spinning represented economic progress, national unity and independence from the Empire. He himself spun daily.

HIGH IDEALS

The Indian National Congress, led by Gandhi, now called on all Indian soldiers and civilians to quit British Government service. By 1922, 30,000 people, including nearly all the Congress leaders, had been imprisoned for acts of civil disobedience. Then twenty-two policemen who had attacked the stragglers of a protest march were viciously slaughtered. Realizing that even now the nonviolent nature of *satyagraha* was not understood, Gandhi called off the campaign, and fasted again, punishing himself for the violence he felt was his fault. He was then put on trial, accused of stirring up trouble.

In court, Gandhi spoke movingly of the people's misery under British rule and of the absurd laws. He said that perhaps in reality he was innocent, but under these laws, he was guilty,

Gandhi himself enjoyed spinning every day.

so he expected the highest penalty. The judge, although he praised Gandhi "as a man of high ideals and a noble and even saintly life," sentenced him to six years' imprisonment.

Two years later, Gandhi was released. For three weeks, he fasted in protest against the increasing conflict between Hindus and Muslims. Then he turned his attention to social reforms, touring the country by train, cart, and on foot, speaking to vast crowds. Many of his followers considered him a saint, and he was showered with gifts, which he turned into funds for the cause. He taught the importance of equality for women and for people of different classes and religions. He encouraged spinning and discouraged taking alcohol or using drugs.

In 1928, a Royal Commission arrived from Britain to review the situation in India. Since it included no Indian members, it was met by protest meetings, which were broken up by the British authorities. The new proposals would have still left the country subject to British control. Now the Indian National Congress decided it could accept nothing less than complete independence.

A Pinch of Salt

The Salt March of 1930 began a new round of nonviolent protest. Gandhi walked 322 km (200 miles) to the coast at Dandi. Thousands joined the march, watched by the world's press. On the beach after morning prayers, Gandhi picked up a lump of sea salt.

Salt was taxed; legally, only the Government could extract it from sea water. Gandhi's signal prompted people all along the coast of India to defy the law by manufacturing salt. In cities and villages, illegal salt was distributed. Following this action, about 100,000 people, including Gandhi and other Congress leaders, were imprisoned. Bravely, without violence, they faced police brutality. Many were badly beaten and some died; but eventually, the campaign succeeded, and salt manufacturing was allowed.

Gandhi discussed India's future at The Round Table conference in London.

Later, Gandhi took part in The Round Table conference in Britain about the future of India. While in London, he chose to stay in an East End hostel for the poor. He visited Lancashire and made friends among the mill workers, even though many were unemployed because of the Indians' boycott of British cloth. He met politicians and celebrities, and went to tea at Buckingham Palace. Everywhere, he impressed people with his sincerity and humor. As for his manner of dress at the Palace, he said, "The King was wearing enough for both of us!"

Only a week later, when he returned to India, he was imprisoned again. Before long, 30,000 others had been arrested too. In prison, Gandhi carried out a prolonged fast against the class divisions among Hindus. He was willing to starve himself to death, if the barriers were not broken down throughout the country. People valued Gandhi's life so greatly that he succeeded in changing traditions that were thousands of years old. For the first time, temples were opened to *Harijans,* and all Hindus could eat together, drink water drawn from the same wells, and even marry each other.

After his release, Gandhi turned to educational and welfare work. He toured rural India, speaking on health care, village industries and reorganization, and about land ownership and justice.

Gandhi opposed Indian involvement in World War II (1939–44), believing now that all war was wholly wrong. Leading members of the Indian Congress, including his close friend Jawaharlal Nehru, disagreed. They were willing to cooperate with the British if they could obtain reforms that would lead to self-government. But Britain would give no promise of independence.

Under Gandhi's direction, people made speeches and signed written protests against taking part in the war. Thousands, including Nehru, were imprisoned for up to a year.

In 1942, Gandhi announced a new *satyagraha* campaign aimed directly at British withdrawal from India. Once again, he was imprisoned. While in prison, he fasted again, coming close to death, in protest against accusations that he had stirred up violence against the British. Kasturbai was one of 100,000 other prisoners. Her health was poor, and in 1944, she died. Feeling her loss keenly, Gandhi himself became ill, recovering only after his release a few months later. With the end of World War II, Indian independence came closer.

Gandhi and Nehru disagreed about Indian involvement in World War II.

Gandhi had always contested religious divisions. Most Indians were either Hindus or Muslims. In the northwest and northeast of the country, Muslims were in the majority. Their leader, Muhammad Ali Jinnah, favored the creation of a separate Muslim state there, to be called Pakistan. Congress, like Gandhi, wanted a united India. Nehru was appointed Prime Minister of a provisional Indian Government, which meant Indian rule by a Hindu for that area. Jinnah announced that the Muslim League would hold a day of action to protest. The result was horrifying violence between Muslims and Hindus, with 20,000 killed or injured.

THE PEACEMAKER

From the rural area of Bengal came reports of Muslim atrocities. Gandhi walked through the villages for four months, seeking desperately to persuade people to end the violence. But soon after, in a neighboring province, there were similar Hindu atrocities to quell.

In 1947, Lord Louis Mountbatten became the last British Viceroy of India. Reluctantly, and against Gandhi's opposition, the Indian National Congress agreed that Pakistan was to become a country in its own right, separate from India. Independence came on August 15, 1947. Gandhi was living in the poorest quarters of Calcutta, where there had been appalling bloodshed, riots and fighting between the Hindu and Muslim communities. While he succeeded in pacifying the people of Bengal, the northwest was in uproar. Millions of people were migrating across the new border separating

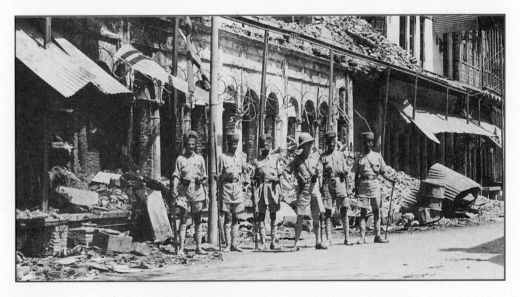

A British officer with five Indian soldiers guarding a building burnt by Muslims.

Gandhi's fast brings him near death.

"Muslim" Pakistan from "Hindu" India. Massacres were widespread, causing almost a million deaths. When violence broke out again in Calcutta, Gandhi undertook a fast "to death," refusing food until the northeast was peaceful. Then, in riot-torn Delhi, came his "greatest fast." Dramatically, it brought a pledge of peace among all the community leaders, and throughout India and Pakistan, the violence ceased.

Though millions revered him, and cherished his life so deeply, to some Hindu fanatics, Gandhi was an obstacle. On January 30, 1948, he was murdered——shot three times by an assassin who stepped from the crowd at a prayer meeting. His death caused worldwide shock and sorrow. To countless people, he was a modern-day saint, a teacher of humanity such as the world has rarely seen. As a champion of peace, his influence still remains.

Gandhi walks the streets of Delhi with a welcoming group of residents.

GANDHI

Meet the Author

Nigel Hunter's life was greatly influenced by a teacher from New England, Edgar Stillman. Stillman showed Hunter how important imaginative writing was in people's lives, and he made Hunter aware of civil rights leaders like Malcolm X, whose writings were a big influence on Hunter. Because of this, it's no surprise that Hunter's books have focused on politics, including books on Martin Luther King, Jr., the Cold War, and, of course, Gandhi. Hunter now lives with his wife near the beach in Salvador, Brazil, where he teaches English at a university.

Meet the Illustrator

Richard Hook has been a freelance artist since 1966, when he left a job as an illustrator and designer for Harmon Books. He has illustrated more than 50 books on historical topics, such as Anne Frank, Beethoven, and Louis Braille. When he's not illustrating books, Hook is spending time with his wife and three children.

Theme Connections

Within the Selection

Record your answers to the questions below in the Response Journal section of your Writer's Notebook. In small groups, report the ideas you wrote. Discuss your ideas with the rest of your group. Then choose a person to report your group's answers to the class.

- How did Gandhi's first trip to South Africa change his outlook on life?
- What kinds of sacrifices did Gandhi make for his cause?
- What does the word *satyagraha* mean? Why was it an important concept for Gandhi?

Across the Selections

- How was Gandhi's nonviolent protest similar to the nonviolent protest found in "The Pretty Pennies Picket?"
- Sometimes taking a stand involves making sacrifices. What other characters have you read about in this unit who made sacrifices?

Beyond the Selection

- Think about how "Gandhi" adds to what you know about taking a stand.
- Add items to the Concept/Question Board about taking a stand.

Focus Questions How does Nellie Bly turn the city of Pittsburgh
on its head with her newspaper articles?
Is breaking the rules a necessary part of taking a stand?

Sweeping Pittsburgh Clean

from *MAKING HEADLINES:
A BIOGRAPHY OF NELLIE BLY*
by Kathy Lynn Emerson

What Elizabeth Cochrane really wanted to do was write. A female writer was not a new idea in 1885; Louisa May Alcott had been earning a living as a novelist for nearly twenty years. Elizabeth had probably read *Little Women*. If she did, she knew that Alcott's character, Jo March, stormed a newspaper office to sell her stories.

Elizabeth may have heard tales of women who were newspaper reporters, too. By 1880, almost every major newspaper in the United States paid women to write feature articles, usually essays in letter form, and send them in through the mail. In New York City, a female writer who used the name Jenny June worked in a newspaper office on a day-to-day basis. Another young woman named Sally Joy had talked herself into a job on the Boston *Post* when she was eighteen. Still, compared to New York, Pittsburgh was a small place, and its people had old-fashioned ideas. Elizabeth might never have become a journalist if it hadn't been for a newspaper column titled "What Girls Are Good For."

This essay expressed ideas held by most men in the 1880s. The writer protested the alarming trend of hiring women to work in shops and offices, and called the employment of women in business a threat to the national welfare.

Other unfair, harshly critical remarks filled the column, too. When Elizabeth Cochrane read them, she became so angry that she sat down and wrote a letter to George A. Madden, managing editor of the Pittsburgh *Dispatch*. She didn't use her name in the letter——that wouldn't have been ladylike. Instead, she signed it "Lonely Orphan Girl" and sent it off.

Elizabeth Cochrane (Nellie Bly) as a young newspaperwoman.

George Madden was so impressed by the letter that he wanted to find the author and hire him to work on the *Dispatch*. It never entered his mind that the writer might be a woman. He pictured the writer as a young man who wanted to work for the *Dispatch*, and had deliberately taken the wrong side of the issue to get attention.

On January 17, 1885, an advertisement appeared in the *Dispatch*, asking "Lonely Orphan Girl" to contact Mr. Madden. Once more Elizabeth addressed a note to the editor, but this time she signed her own name. Mr. Madden may have groaned in dismay, imagining some old "battle-ax" with strong feminist views, but he wrote back anyway. She did, after all, write well. He said that he would be willing to consider publishing an article on "girls and their spheres in life" in the Sunday paper if she would write and submit it.

Elizabeth sent in the article as soon as she could get it written, and Madden liked it. He paid her five dollars, and published her work on January 25 under the title "The Girl Puzzle." Then, throwing caution to the wind, Madden wrote to Elizabeth once more to ask if she had any other suggestions for stories. He had no idea how she would respond, but the last thing he expected was that she would turn up several days later at the Fifth Street offices of the *Dispatch*.

Elizabeth Cochrane appeared fragile for her height of five feet five inches. She wore her chestnut-colored hair in a chignon with bangs, a youthful style in those days, and had a jaunty sailor hat on her head. In spite of the determined gleam in her wide hazel eyes, she had a meek and mild appearance. The *Dispatch's* reporters, who shared the one big city room, didn't know what to think of her.

Newspaper offices in the nineteenth century echoed with the clatter of presses from the floors below. The rooms smelled of printer's ink, gaslights, and tobacco, and were filled with a haze of cigar smoke. Chewing tobacco was popular, too, and the men were often careless when they aimed at the spittoons. The floors were filthy. In Sally Joy's city room in Boston, the more gentlemanly reporters put newspapers down so she wouldn't get her long skirts stained with tobacco juice.

Elizabeth Cochrane looked out of place in this setting. A more timid woman would have turned and fled, but her ladylike appearance masked a will of iron. She informed the gawking reporters, sitting at desks crowded together and piled high with copy paper, that Mr. Madden had sent for her. When they directed her to his desk, she introduced herself and said she had come with her ideas.

In the nineteenth century, newspaper offices such as this one
were not considered proper places for a young lady to work.

If George Madden was surprised by Elizabeth Cochrane's sudden appearance in his city room, he was shocked by the subject on which she wanted to write. Divorce, she told him, was an issue that needed to be discussed in the newspaper.

Elizabeth tried hard to persuade Mr. Madden to give her a chance. He protested at first, but finally agreed to let her prove she could do what she said she could. He sent her home to write her article on divorce, and probably thought he would never see her again.

Elizabeth, however, tackled her new project immediately. She had the notes on divorce cases that her father had made during his years as a judge, but she had been doing some research of her own as well. Since she and her mother had spent almost all of their inheritance from her father, they had changed addresses several times, each time selecting a less expensive place. By the time "What Girls Are Good For" was printed, they were living in rundown lodgings in a poor section of the city, where Elizabeth had talked to several women who had suffered because of unfair divorce laws.

All night long, Elizabeth worked on her article, writing and revising, scratching out passages and copying it over. At that time there were no word processors and no portable typewriters to make the work easier. Even in the newspaper offices, articles were composed with pen and ink. Despite the long, slow process, Elizabeth persisted until her story was just the way she wanted it. The next morning she returned to the *Dispatch* office with a final draft that was neat and easy to read. More importantly, the article said something. Mr. Madden was impressed and immediately agreed to publish the story.

George Madden was a businessman. He might have believed, as the article in his paper had said, that respectable women stayed at home until they married, or at worst went into a "woman's profession" such as teaching or nursing. Still, he knew the facts. Since the Civil War, women had been working in mills, factories, and offices. The thought of a woman in politics made him shudder, but a woman had run for president in 1884.

In spite of his doubts, Madden found himself encouraging Elizabeth Cochrane. If one thing could overcome his prejudices, it was the promise of a controversial series for his newspaper. Controversy increased a newspaper's circulation, and that was good business.

He asked for more stories, saying that if the series on divorce were a success, he would give Elizabeth a regular job and pay her five dollars a week. She accepted at once.

Madden had only one problem left. He was worried about allowing Elizabeth to use her own name. What would people say if they knew he had hired an eighteen-year-old girl to write on such a sensitive subject as divorce? What would her family say? She had respectable and old-fashioned older brothers who would not approve of her new career.

Just as Mr. Madden and Elizabeth Cochrane agreed to invent a pen name, Mr. Madden's assistant, Erasmus Wilson, began to hum a popular Stephen Foster song. Everyone knew the words:

Nelly Bly, Nelly Bly,
bring the broom along.
We'll sweep the kitchen clear, my dear,
and have a little song.
Poke the wood, my lady love,
and make the fire burn,
And while I take the banjo down,
just give the mush a turn.
Heigh, Nelly, Ho, Nelly,
listen love, to me;
I'll sing for you, play for you,
a dulcet melody.

From that day on, Elizabeth Cochrane was Nellie Bly, and Madden immediately published her articles on divorce. The subject alone was enough to make people sit up and take notice, but the newspaper-reading public of Pittsburgh was just as intrigued by the author. Who was this Nellie Bly? they wondered.

The *Dispatch* made the most of the mystery surrounding its new reporter's identity. Circulation improved dramatically as Nellie wrote more articles. In time, she came up with an idea that would set the tone for her entire newspaper career——she asked Mr. Madden if she could write about life in the slums and factories of Pittsburgh. As a reporter and a reformer, she would tell the real story of her own experiences visiting these places, from a lady's point of view. She would take an artist with her to sketch what she saw. Mr. Madden saw the circulation of the *Dispatch* going up and up . . . and agreed.

Women working in a Pittsburgh bottling factory in the early 1890s.

Nellie brought the broom along, as the song says, and set out to sweep Pittsburgh clean. It needed it. Under smoke-blackened skies, which glowed flame red at night, workers were little more than slaves to uncaring factory owners. Women in a bottle factory worked fourteen-hour days in an unheated building. Children were endangered by living in dirty, disease-ridden, fire-prone buildings in a slum called the Point.

When Nellie Bly joined the staff of the *Dispatch,* more than 156,000 people lived in Pittsburgh. Many were immigrants, drawn by jobs in the iron and steel industries. Few labor unions protected these unskilled workers, and no social service agencies existed.

Nellie brought her discoveries of social injustices to public attention through the *Dispatch.* She was not content to sit at her hard-won desk in the city room, letting others do the research. Every story was her own, from the first idea, through the investigation and writing, to her byline, or name, on the finished article.

A bottling factory was Nellie's first target. The glass industry was Pittsburgh's third largest business; some seventy factories produced half the nation's glass, and more champagne bottles than there were in France. Accompanied by her artist, she located the factory owner and told him she wanted to write an article for the *Dispatch* about his factory. Deceived by her ladylike manner and pleasant smile, he welcomed her with open arms. He thought she was offering him good, free publicity, so he told her to talk to anyone and look anywhere.

Nellie reported on crowded living conditions in the Point, a Pittsburgh slum.

Nellie talked to the workers as the artist sketched. Some of these women stood on an icy cement floor for fourteen hours at a stretch. To cope with the winter cold that seeped through the factory walls, the workers had to wrap rags around their feet, which kept their toes from freezing. Several hundred workers shared one toilet, along with a family of rats. Worse yet was the daily risk of injury from broken or exploding bottles. Since worker's compensation did not exist, an injury could result in the loss of a person's job and only source of income.

Nellie was shocked by the conditions in the factories, and she channeled all her outrage into print. She held nothing back, including names, dates, and drawings. When her article appeared in the *Dispatch*, every copy of that day's paper sold quickly at the city's newsstands.

The factory owners were enraged when they saw Nellie's articles. Letters flooded the *Dispatch* office. Although Nellie faced protests, and even threats, efforts at reform began which eventually improved conditions in the factories of Pittsburgh.

Nellie attacked the slums next. In the course of her own frequent moves, she had seen how crowded many of the city's tenement buildings were. In the Point she found a family of twelve living in one unheated room. In the rickety wooden shanties along Yellow Row, and the ramshackle cottages on the hill at Skunk Hollow, Nellie Bly asked questions and got answers. When she wrote her story, she named the slumlords, hoping to shame them into repairing their buildings.

The run-down tenement houses of Pittsburgh's Yellow Row were another of Nellie's targets.

The uproar this time was even greater than it had been after her article about the factory. Pittsburgh businessmen began to organize against the threat of Nellie Bly. They claimed she was ruining the city's reputation. Despite fourteen thousand chimneys that polluted the air, they still insisted that Pittsburgh was one of the healthiest cities in the United States. In fact, they said that people worked so hard that they didn't notice the smoke. Pollution had killed the grass and flowers, but a child who complained about the foulness of the air was told she should be "grateful for God's goodness in making work, which made smoke, which made prosperity." With that kind of thinking, no wonder the businessmen threatened George Madden with the loss of all his advertising if he didn't stop those reform-minded articles by Nellie Bly.

George Madden's business sense told him it was time to let things cool down. He gave Nellie a raise to ten dollars a week and made her society editor for the *Dispatch.* Nellie Bly began writing about the upper classes, whose parties, art, drama, and books were part of a world far removed from the city's slums.

Plays, lectures, concerts, and charity balls soon left Nellie bored and restless. "I was too impatient," she wrote, "to work along at the usual duties assigned women on newspapers." Yet nearly a year passed before she could persuade Mr. Madden to let her write serious articles again.

A modern jail, Riverside Penitentiary of Western Pennsylvania, had just been built to replace the old Western Penitentiary. It was the most up-to-date facility of its kind, and Nellie wanted to visit it. Her article would be full of praise, she argued. Why not let her cover its opening? Reluctantly, Madden agreed.

In her article, Nellie praised the new facility's separate cells for inmates and large common work and recreation areas, but she used this praise of one jail as a starting point to criticize the rest. When Madden read her attack on other Pennsylvania jails, he knew trouble lay ahead, but he decided to print the article anyway.

Meanwhile, Nellie wanted to take another look at the factories. This time she went undercover, dressing herself as a poor woman looking for a job. She was hired at the first factory where she applied, though she had no skills. Her job was to hitch cables together in an assembly line with other young women. They could be fined for talking, or even for smiling, but Nellie did manage to learn that they all suffered from headaches.

An aerial view of Pittsburgh in the late nineteenth century.

She soon understood why. The light was so dim that her head began to ache, too. Then her feet started to hurt, because she had to stand. Her hands became raw and started to bleed. Before long, she ached all over. Just like the workers in the bottle factory, these young women kept working in spite of their fear of blindness and the constant discomfort. They had to work to live.

The women's supervisor kept urging them to work faster and faster. He paced back and forth behind them, yelling out threats and foul language. Since Nellie had been brought up to have good manners, she found it difficult to listen to curses and insults for hours on end. Finally, Nellie simply walked away from the assembly line to get a drink of water. The foreman fired her.

When Nellie's two stories appeared in the *Dispatch*, the response was overwhelming. The paper's sales increased, and Nellie was criticized by just about everyone. City law enforcement officials said she wasn't qualified to judge their jails. The clergy called her shameless for visiting a men's prison without a chaperon. Again, the factory owners and businessmen of Pittsburgh threatened to withdraw their advertising. Madden raised Nellie's pay to fifteen dollars a week and sent her back to write the society page.

The other reporters of the *Dispatch* appreciated her, even if the targets of her articles didn't. "Only a few months previous I had become a newspaper woman," she wrote, and in October 1886, she became the first woman invited to join the Pittsburgh Press Club.

Sweeping Pittsburgh Clean

Meet the Author

Kathy Lynn Emerson writes for both children and adults. She credits her interest in writing to her grandfather. "Grandpa penned his memoirs when he was in his eighties, paying special attention to stories from his boyhood . . ." Some of Emerson's writing has been based on her grandfather's boyhood experiences. Her work often involves characters who must learn to be more open-minded. "If there is any single theme running through my work, it concerns the dangers of jumping to conclusions about people."

Theme Connections

Within the Selection

Writer's Notebook

Record your answers to the questions below in the Response Journal section of your Writer's Notebook. In small groups, report the ideas you wrote. Discuss your ideas with the rest of your group. Then choose a person to report your group's answers to the class.

- Why did Nellie Bly have a difficult time gaining acceptance for her articles about the social problems of the day?
- What made "Nellie Bly" a good pen name for Elizabeth Cochrane?
- Why did George Madden like publishing Elizabeth's articles?

Across the Selections

- Elizabeth Cochrane's newspaper articles allowed her to reach a large audience. What other techniques for reaching large audiences have you read about in this unit? Explain.
- In Units 2 and 3, what other characters have you encountered who were considered unladylike for being too outspoken?

Beyond the Selection

- Think about how "Sweeping Pittsburgh Clean" adds to what you know about taking a stand.
- Add items to the Concept/Question Board about taking a stand.

Focus Questions Will Sugihara help strangers even if it means putting his own family in danger? How will he decide?

PASSAGE TO FREEDOM

The Sugihara Story

Ken Mochizuki
illustrated by Dom Lee

There is a saying that the eyes tell everything about a person.

At a store, my father saw a young Jewish boy who didn't have enough money to buy what he wanted. So my father gave the boy some of his. That boy looked into my father's eyes and, to thank him, invited my father to his home.

That is when my family and I went to a Hanukkah celebration for the first time. I was five years old.

In 1940, my father was a diplomat, representing the country of Japan. Our family lived in a small town in the small country called Lithuania. There was my father and mother, my Auntie Setsuko, my younger brother Chiaki, and my three-month-old baby brother, Haruki. My father worked in his office downstairs.

In the mornings, birds sang in the trees. We played with girls and boys from the neighborhood at a huge park near our home. Houses and churches around us were hundreds of years old. In our room, Chiaki and I played with toy German soldiers, tanks, and planes. Little did we know that the real soldiers were coming our way.

Then one early morning in late July, my life changed forever.

My mother and Auntie Setsuko woke Chiaki and me up, telling us to get dressed quickly. My father ran upstairs from his office.

"There are a lot of people outside," my mother said. "We don't know what is going to happen."

In the living room, my parents told my brother and me not to let anybody see us looking through the window. So, I parted the curtains a tiny bit. Outside, I saw hundreds of people crowded around the gate in front of our house.

The grown-ups shouted in Polish, a language I did not understand. Then I saw the children. They stared at our house through the iron bars of the gate. Some of them were my age. Like the grown-ups, their eyes were red from not having slept for days. They wore heavy winter coats— some wore more than one coat, even though it was warm outside. These children looked as though they had dressed in a hurry. But if they came from somewhere else, where were their suitcases?

"What do they want?" I asked my mother.

"They have come to ask for your father's help," she replied. "Unless we help, they may be killed or taken away by some bad men."

Some of the children held on tightly to the hands of their fathers, some clung to their mothers. One little girl sat on the ground, crying.

I felt like crying, too. "Father," I said, "please help them."

My father stood quietly next to me, but I knew he saw the children. Then some of the men in the crowd began climbing over the fence. Borislav and Gudje, two young men who worked for my father, tried to keep the crowd calm.

My father walked outside. Peering through the curtains, I saw him standing on the steps. Borislav translated what my father said: He asked the crowd to choose five people to come inside and talk.

My father met downstairs with the five men. My father could speak Japanese, Chinese, Russian, German, French, and English. At this meeting, everyone spoke Russian.

I couldn't help but stare out the window and watch the crowd, while downstairs, for two hours, my father listened to frightening stories. These people were refugees—people who ran away from their homes because, if they stayed, they would be killed. They were Jews from Poland, escaping from the Nazi soldiers who had taken over their country.

The five men had heard my father could give them visas—official written permission to travel through another country. The hundreds of Jewish refugees outside hoped to travel east through the Soviet Union and end up in Japan. Once in Japan, they could go to another country. Was it true? the men asked. Could my father issue these visas? If he did not, the Nazis would soon catch up with them.

My father answered that he could issue a few, but not hundreds. To do that, he would have to ask for permission from his government in Japan.

That night, the crowd stayed outside our house. Exhausted from the day's excitement, I slept soundly. But it was one of the worst nights of my father's life. He had to make a decision. If he helped these people, would he put our family in danger? If the Nazis found out, what would they do?

But if he did not help these people, they could all die.

My mother listened to the bed squeak as my father tossed and turned all night.

The next day, my father said he was going to ask his government about the visas. My mother agreed it was the right thing to do. My father sent his message by cable. Gudje took my father's written message down to the telegraph office.

I watched the crowd as they waited for the Japanese government's reply. The five representatives came into our house several times that day to ask if an answer had been received. Any time the gate opened, the crowd tried to charge inside.

343

Finally, the answer came from the Japanese government. It was "no." My father could not issue that many visas to Japan. For the next two days, he thought about what to do.

Hundreds more Jewish refugees joined the crowd. My father sent a second message to his government, and again the answer was "no." We still couldn't go outside. My little brother Haruki cried often because we were running out of milk.

I grew tired of staying indoors. I asked my father constantly, "Why are these people here? What do they want? Why do they have to be here? Who are they?"

My father always took the time to explain everything to me. He said the refugees needed his help, that they needed permission from him to go to another part of the world where they would be safe.

"I cannot help these people yet," he calmly told me. "But when the time comes, I will help them all that I can."

My father cabled his superiors yet a third time, and I knew the answer by the look in his eyes. That night, he said to my mother, "I have to do something. I may have to disobey my government, but if I don't, I will be disobeying God."

The next morning, he brought the family together and asked what he should do. This was the first time he ever asked all of us to help him with anything.

My mother and Auntie Setsuko had already made up their minds. They said we had to think about the people outside before we thought about ourselves. And that is what my parents had always told me—that I must think as if I were in someone else's place. If I were one of those children out there, what would I want someone to do for me?

I said to my father, "If we don't help them, won't they die?"

With the entire family in agreement, I could tell a huge weight was lifted off my father's shoulders. His voice was firm as he told us, "I will start helping these people."

345

Outside, the crowd went quiet as my father spoke, with Borislav translating.

"I will issue visas to each and every of you to the last. So, please wait patiently."

The crowd stood frozen for a second. Then the refugees burst into cheers. Grown-ups embraced each other, and some reached to the sky. Fathers and mothers hugged their children. I was especially glad for the children.

My father opened the garage door and the crowd tried to rush in. To keep order, Borislav handed out cards with numbers. My father wrote out each visa by hand. After he finished each one, he looked into the eyes of the person receiving the visa and said, "Good luck."

Refugees camped out at our favorite park, waiting to see my father. I was finally able to go outside.

Chiaki and I played with the other children in our toy car. They pushed as we rode, and they rode as we pushed. We chased each other around the big trees. We did not speak the same language, but that didn't stop us.

For about a month, there was always a line leading to the garage. Every day, from early in the morning till late at night, my father tried to write three hundred visas. He watered down the ink to make it last. Gudje and a young Jewish man helped out by stamping my father's name on the visas.

My mother offered to help write the visas, but my father insisted he be the only one, so no one else could get into trouble. So my mother watched the crowd and told my father how many were still in line.

One day, my father pressed down so hard on his fountain pen, the tip broke off. During that month, I only saw him late at night. His eyes were always red and he could hardly talk. While he slept, my mother massaged his arm, stiff and cramped from writing all day.

Soon my father grew so tired, he wanted to quit writing the visas. But my mother encouraged him to continue. "Many people are still waiting," she said. "Let's issue some more visas and save as many lives as we can."

While the Germans approached from the west, the Soviets came from the east and took over Lithuania. They ordered my father to leave. So did the Japanese government, which reassigned him to Germany. Still, my father wrote the visas until we absolutely had to move out of our home. We stayed at a hotel for two days, where my father still wrote visas for the many refugees who followed him there.

Then it was time to leave Lithuania. Refugees who had slept at the train station crowded around my father. Some refugee men surrounded my father to protect him. He now just issued permission papers—blank pieces of paper with his signature.

As the train pulled away, refugees ran alongside. My father still handed permission papers out the window. As the train picked up speed, he threw them out to waiting hands. The people in the front of the crowd looked into my father's eyes and cried, "We will never forget you! We will see you again!"

I gazed out the train window, watching Lithuania and the crowd of refugees fade away. I wondered if we would ever see them again.

"Where are we going?" I asked my father.

"We are going to Berlin," he replied.

Chiaki and I became very excited about going to the big city. I had so many questions for my father. But he fell asleep as soon as he settled into his seat. My mother and Auntie Setsuko looked really tired, too.

Back then, I did not fully understand what the three of them had done, or why it was so important.

I do now.

AFTERWORD

Each time that I think about what my father did at Kaunas, Lithuania in 1940, my appreciation and understanding of the incident continues to grow. In fact, it makes me very emotional to realize that his deed saved thousands of lives, and that I had the opportunity to be a part of it.

I am proud that my father had the courage to do the right thing. Yet, his superiors in the Japanese government did not agree. The years after my family left Kaunas were difficult ones. We were imprisoned for 18 months in a Soviet internment camp; and when we finally returned to Japan, my father was asked to resign from diplomatic service. After holding several different jobs, my father joined an export company, where he worked until his retirement in 1976.

My father remained concerned about the fate of the refugees, and at one point left his address at the Israeli Embassy in Japan. Finally, in the 1960's, he started hearing from "Sugihara survivors," many of whom had kept their visas, and considered the worn pieces of paper to be family treasures.

In 1969, my father was invited to Israel, where he was taken to the famous Holocaust memorial, Yad Vashem. In 1985, he was chosen to receive the "Righteous Among Nations" Award from Yad Vashem. He was the first and only Asian to have been given this great honor.

In 1992, six years after his death, a monument to my father was dedicated in his birthplace of Yaotsu, Japan, on a hill that is now known as the Hill of Humanity. In 1994, a group of Sugihara survivors traveled to Japan to re-dedicate the monument in a ceremony that was attended by several high officials of the Japanese government.

The story of what my father and my family experienced in 1940 is an important one for young people today. It is a story that I believe will inspire you to care for all people and to respect life. It is a story that proves that one person can make a difference.

Thank you.

Hiroki Sugihara

PASSAGE TO FREEDOM

The Sugihara Story

Meet the Author

Ken Mochizuki is of Japanese descent but grew up in Seattle, Washington, with his parents and his brothers. When he meets people, Mochizuki sometimes gets asked questions like "Do you speak English?" even though he has never been to Japan and cannot speak Japanese. Mochizuki hopes that through his children's books he can "*. . . convey to young readers that they should actually get to know others, rather than assume things about them . . .*" His books show that Americans of Asian descent are part of American life and have been for a long time.

Meet the Illustrator

Dom Lee learned art in his hometown of Seoul, Korea. He grew up in a family full of artists, and his father even founded the Hyang-Lin Institute, which trains young artists. After Lee's sculpture and painting training in Korea, he found that his realistic art style was very different. He moved to New York and studied illustration. For illustrating children's books, Lee has developed his own technique. He scratches out and paints his pictures on beeswax and applies them to paper. He finds that this method is a "*. . . bridge between painting and sculpture, both of which I love.*"

Theme Connections

Within the Selection

Record your answers to the questions below in the Response Journal section of your Writer's Notebook. In small groups, report the ideas you wrote. Discuss your ideas with the rest of your group. Then choose a person to report your group's answers to the class.

- What were Polish refugees doing at the Sugihara family's gate?
- Why did the narrator's father disobey orders given to him by his government?
- Why did the narrator's father insist on writing the visas himself?

Across the Selections

- Compare "The Passage to Freedom" to "The Grimké Sisters." How are the stands taken in each story the same? How are they different?
- In "The Passage to Freedom" the narrator's father uses his government position to help others. How is this scenario different from any others you have seen in this unit?

Beyond the Selection

- Think of a time when someone has used his or her position to help you. Maybe it was a teacher or coach who helped you. Were you relieved to be helped? How did it feel? How did you express your gratitude? Take a few minutes and write about your experience, then be prepared to share your experience with the class.

Beyond the Notes

What is music? What is your favorite music——rock, jazz, classical? Music is all around us and affects each of our lives. Music means different things to different people. What does it mean to you?

WHAT IS AN

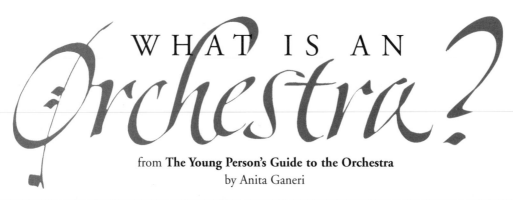

Orchestra?

from **The Young Person's Guide to the Orchestra**
by Anita Ganeri

The concert hall buzzes with voices as the audience takes their seats. Snatches of music rise from the orchestra as musicians tune their instruments. When the conductor steps on stage silence falls.

What is an orchestra?

An orchestra is a large group of musicians with instruments that play the classical music of Europe, Russia, and North America. The orchestra plays music written by a composer to make use of all the different instruments and their various sounds. When all the instruments play together, the music blends into one magnificent sound.

DID YOU KNOW?

The word *orchestra* was first used by the ancient Greeks over 2,000 years ago. It did not have the same meaning as it does today. It was the name for the dance floor in front of the stage in the Greek theater where the actors sang and danced during a play.

On June 17, 1872, in Boston, Massachusetts, Johann Strauss the Younger conducted the largest orchestra ever to play. It was made up of 987 instruments, including 400 first violins, and was accompanied by a choir of 20,000 singers.

The London Symphony Orchestra

Who's who in an orchestra?

he modern orchestra may contain more than 100 instruments, divided into four sections, or families: string, brass, percussion, and woodwind.

The conductor in charge

ith so many instruments and musicians, the conductor's role is essential. He or she stands facing the orchestra, beating time with a baton and making sure that the orchestra stays in time, in tune, and that the different instruments start and stop playing at the right times. A good conductor controls the sound of the whole orchestra. His or her interpretation of the music brings out the excitement, drama, or gentleness of the composition and makes it all the more enjoyable for the listener.

Herbert von Karajan

The string section contains violins, violas, cellos, and double basses.

The brass section contains French horns, trumpets, trombones, and tubas.

The percussion section contains drums, cymbals, gongs, triangles, xylophones, and tambourines.

The woodwind section contains clarinets, oboes, flutes, and bassoons.

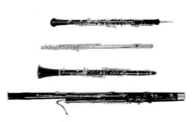

355

How Orchestras Began

The first orchestras existed about 400 years ago, but they were very different from today's orchestra. They were smaller, looser in structure, and comprised a narrower range of instruments.

Early orchestras

The earliest orchestras were simply groups of musicians, large or small, playing together on whatever instruments they had at hand. These were mainly string instruments, such as violins, violas, and cellos. No fixed rules stated which instruments should comprise an orchestra or how they should be organized. In the picture below, one of the women is playing an early string instrument called a lute. It is the oldest ancestor of the violin.

DID YOU KNOW?

In 1607, the Italian composer Claudio Monteverdi (1567–1643) used an orchestra of forty instruments to accompany his first opera, *Orfeo*. The orchestra included fifteen viols, two violins, flutes, early oboes, trumpets, trombones, two harpsichords, two organs, and a harp. These were probably the most readily available instruments at the time and not a deliberate collection.

A sixteenth-century concert

Musical movements

Classical compositions are divided into different periods, depending on the date and style of the music.

• **Baroque**—the baroque movement lasted from 1600–1750. It took its name from the grand, ornate style of architecture popular at the time. Famous baroque composers included Bach and Handel.

• **Classical**—the classical movement lasted from about 1750–1825. In music as well as architecture, it described a style that was more graceful than the baroque style. Mozart and Haydn were famous classical composers.

• **Romantic**—the nineteenth century saw the rise of the romantic movement. Music became more expressive and emotional than ever before. Romantic composers included Beethoven and Liszt.

• **Twentieth Century**—composers in Europe and America experimented with different kinds of orchestras and new "modern" sounds. Stravinsky and Mahler were twentieth-century composers.

Changing instruments

I n the seventeenth and eighteenth centuries, the variety and mix of instruments used in an orchestra changed as instrument design was improved and new instruments were invented. Early in the seventeenth century, violins replaced viols to bring a brighter, richer sound to the music. They remain the most important string instruments today.

Viol

Violin

The Golden Age

The nineteenth century was the orchestra's golden age. The range of instruments was far greater than ever before, and orchestras grew bigger and bigger.

From court to concert hall

Early orchestras were employed by the king or other members of the nobility to play at court or at private gatherings. When opera and ballet became popular in the seventeenth century, orchestras were solicited to accompany the singers and dancers. By the nineteenth century, new orchestras and auditoriums built especially for use as concert halls sprang up in Europe and the United States. The public could now pay to hear the world's finest musicians.

CHANGE OF TUNE

Composers in the nineteenth century began to write music specifically for orchestras, with different parts for different instruments. As the music became more technically demanding, the orchestra grew. With a broader range of instruments, more complex music could be written. The most important new musical form was called the symphony. This was a long work, broken into several sections called movements, designed to contrast and balance the various instruments (see p. 377).

An eighteenth-century concert given to celebrate the marriage of Louis XVI

Orchestras in the twentieth century

By the early twentieth century, some orchestras had grown very large indeed, with more than 100 musicians and possibly a choir as well. Composers such as Gustav Mahler (1860–1911) and Richard Strauss (1864–1949) wrote grand, dramatic works for them to play. Today's composers tend to write for much smaller groups or for different combinations of instruments. Modern symphony orchestras mainly play music written in the classical or romantic periods.

DID YOU KNOW?

The German composer Richard Wagner (1813–1883) wrote a series of grand operas that required very large orchestras to accompany them. He built his own opera house in Bayreuth, Germany, where the orchestra was hidden from the audience so that it did not distract their attention from the action on stage.

In Mozart's time (1756–1791), an orchestra might consist of about thirty-five musicians. In the early nineteenth century, Beethoven wrote for an orchestra of sixty. But by the late nineteenth century, orchestras were over 100 strong, including fifty to sixty string instruments.

The Royal Festival Hall, London

359

Take Your Seats

A modern orchestra is a carefully organized group of musicians, their instruments, and their conductor. The string, woodwind, brass, and percussion sections each have their own special place in the orchestra and a unique part to play.

Seating plan

In a large orchestra, the musicians are arranged in a semicircle facing the conductor and the audience. The different families of instruments are grouped together, with the loudest at the back and the quietest at the front. The principal violinist has the task of leading the other musicians.

The Royal Philharmonic Orchestra

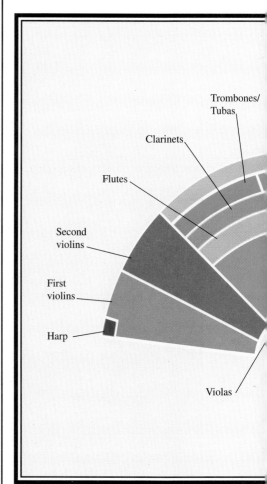

Trombones/Tubas

Clarinets

Flutes

Second violins

First violins

Harp

Violas

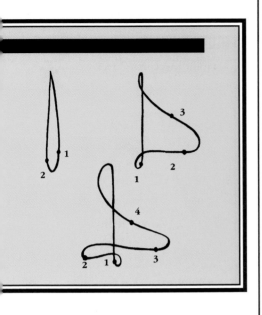

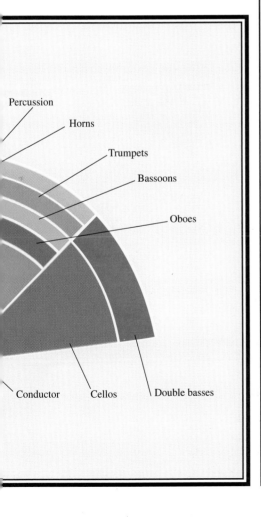

Percussion

Horns

Trumpets

Bassoons

Oboes

Conductor   Cellos   Double basses

Tuning up

All the instruments in an orchestra must play at the same pitch, otherwise they will sound out of tune. Heat and moisture can quickly cause an instrument to go out of tune, but the oboe is less affected than most. So, just before a concert begins, the oboe plays the note Middle A to which all the other instruments tune up.

Watch the conductor

Until the nineteenth century, orchestras were small enough to be directed by a violinist or from the harpsichord. However, as they got larger and the music became more complicated, a conductor was needed to keep the musicians playing together and in time. One of the first people to specialize in conducting was the German Hans Richter in 1876, but many composers, such as Wagner and Berlioz, conducted their own music. Today, every orchestra has its own conductor. He or she studies the music closely and decides exactly how it should be played before rehearsing it with the orchestra and directing the performance.

DID YOU KNOW?

The French composer Jean-Baptiste Lully (1632–1687) conducted his own works by beating time on the floor with a heavy wooden staff . . . with terrible consequences. While conducting one evening, he missed the floor and crushed his toe instead. He died of gangrene shortly thereafter.

The conductor Sir Colin Davis rehearsing with musicians

361

The String Section

In most modern orchestras, the string section is the largest group of instruments. It is made up of first and second violins, violas, cellos, and double basses.

Bring on the strings

The string section consists of instruments that all look very similar, except in size, and are played in the same way. They provide a rich, powerful body of sound in the orchestra, and are also used in solo pieces. The first violins appeared in about 1550 in Italy. They replaced another group of stringed instruments called viols. These had six strings and were played resting between the knees. A violin has four strings and is played resting under the chin. The string instruments are placed in front of the orchestra, from left to right. Many famous pieces of classical music have been written for string quartets—consisting of two violins, a viola, and a cello. This kind of music is called chamber music (see p. 376) because it can be performed in a room, or chamber, rather than a concert hall.

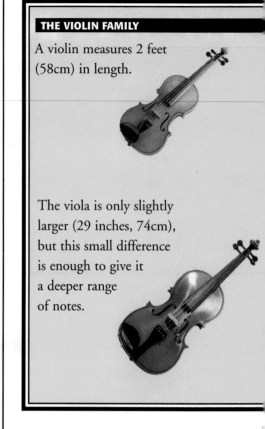

THE VIOLIN FAMILY

A violin measures 2 feet (58cm) in length.

The viola is only slightly larger (29 inches, 74cm), but this small difference is enough to give it a deeper range of notes.

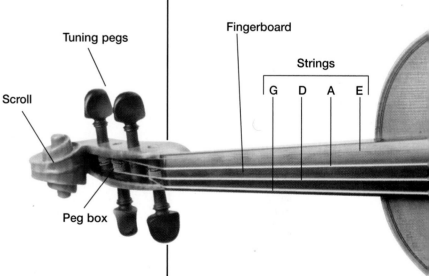

Bow—made of wood and horsehair

Fingerboard

Strings

G   D   A   E

Tuning pegs

Scroll

Peg box

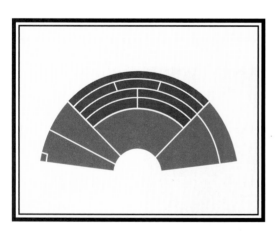

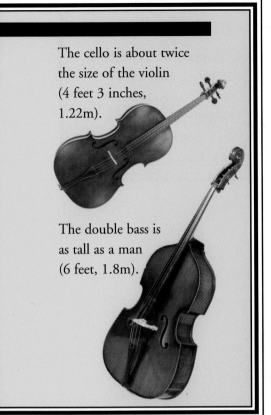

The cello is about twice the size of the violin (4 feet 3 inches, 1.22m).

The double bass is as tall as a man (6 feet, 1.8m).

How the strings are played

String instruments are played by plucking the strings or drawing a bow across them. This makes the strings vibrate and produce sound. The thicker, longer, and looser a string, the deeper the sound. The thinner, shorter, and tighter the string, the higher the sound. To produce different notes, the musician presses a string down with his finger to shorten it. The sound depends also on the instrument's size. A small violin produces much higher notes than a huge double bass. The frames, or resonators, of most stringed instruments are made from wood, which is ideal because it vibrates well. Some stringed instruments around the world also use gourds, the dried, hollowed-out husks of a large fruit, as resonators.

DID YOU KNOW?

The Italian violin maker Antonio Stradivari (1644–1737) made over 1,000 instruments, including 540 violins. These are now considered the finest of all violins and are highly prized as masterpieces.

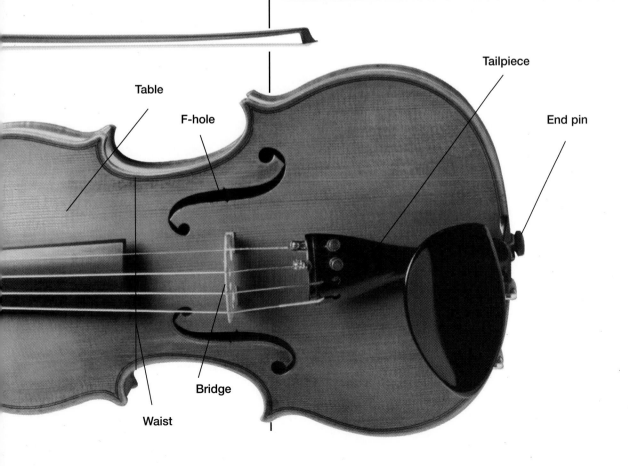

Table

F-hole

Tailpiece

End pin

Bridge

Waist

363

Deep and low

The cello, or violoncello, is a low-pitched, bass member of the string family. It is one of the most expressive of all instruments, and many pieces of orchestral music have been composed specifically for the cello, such as Sir Edward Elgar's Cello Concerto. The double bass is the deepest of all the string instruments. It is often played pizzicato (the strings are plucked), which produces a deep, resonant sound. It is played rhythmically in this way in jazz and folk music. Cellos and double basses are played in a vertical position, with the end pin resting on the floor. A cellist plays sitting down, and a double bass player sits on a high stool.

Other string instruments

Two solo instruments that have strings, but are not officially members of the string family, are the harp and the piano. A concert harp is nearly 6 feet (1.8m) high and has three pedals that change the pitch of the notes. A harpist plays with both hands, using the thumb and first three fingers. Several composers have included the gentle tones of the harp in their compositions, such as Holst's *The Planets* ("Venus").

364

The piano

The solo piano was not included as an orchestral instrument until the beginning of this century. The strings of a concert grand piano are encased in a wooden frame with a keyboard attached. When notes are played, hammers strike the strings and bounce off again, allowing a wide range of soft and loud notes to be sounded.

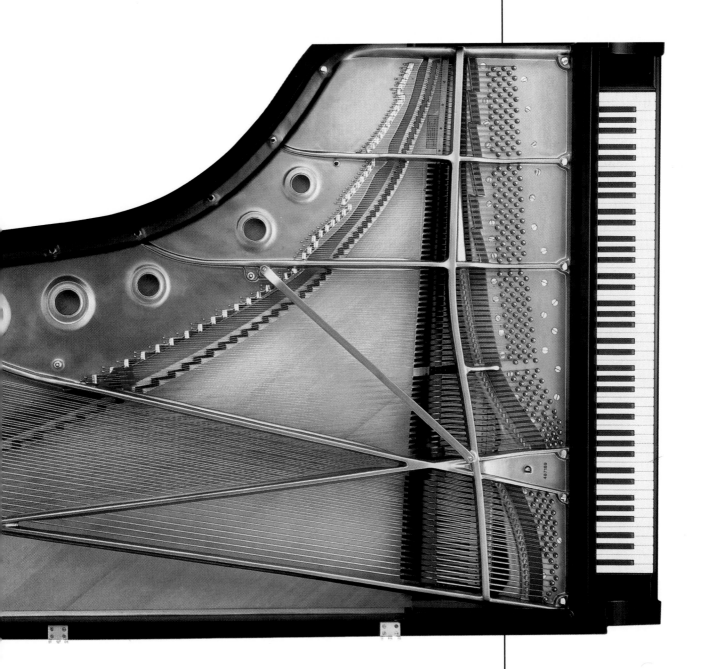

The Woodwind Section

From the tiny piccolo to the booming bassoon, the instruments of the woodwind section produce a wide range of sounds and a contrasting tone to the strings.

Woodwind sounds

The woodwind section of an average orchestra consists of one piccolo, two flutes, two oboes, one cor anglais, two clarinets, one bass clarinet, two bassoons, and one double bassoon. They sit in the middle of the orchestra, behind the violas and in front of the brass and percussion sections. First developed in the 1700s and 1800s, woodwind instruments were then made entirely of wood, hence their name. Today they are made from wood and metal. Woodwind instruments are blown to produce sound. All wind instruments are also known as *aerophones*, which means they use air to

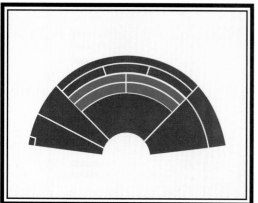

sound different notes. Woodwind instruments such as the clarinet or flute often play solos.

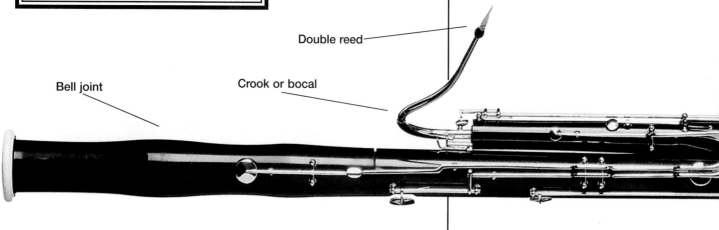

Double reed

Crook or bocal

Bell joint

Playing a woodwind instrument

A woodwind instrument is basically a long, hollow tube that you blow into or across. As you blow, the air inside the tube vibrates, producing sounds. To reach different notes, you cover or uncover the holes along the side of the tube. This makes the column (the air inside the tube) longer, to produce a lower note, or shorter, to produce a higher note. The sound also depends on the length and width of the individual instrument. The tiny piccolo makes a very high, rather shrill sound. The bassoon produces a deep, bass sound.

Mouthpieces

Most woodwind instruments, such as oboes and clarinets, have reeds (made of cane and fiberglass) in their mouthpieces. When you blow down into the mouthpiece, the reed vibrates and makes the air in the tube vibrate to produce sound. The oboe has a double reed, and these two reeds vibrate against each other to produce sound. A flute has a different type of mouthpiece. You hold the flute sideways and blow across a hole in its side to vibrate the air inside (there is more information about flutes on p. 369).

THE WOODWIND FAMILY

A flute is twice as long as a piccolo (26 inches, 67cm). The first all-metal flutes were made in the nineteenth century.

The oboe and clarinet are about the same size (25 inches, 64cm). The clarinet has a single reed; the oboe a double reed in its mouthpiece.

The mighty bassoon is 3 feet (88cm) long. Its size makes it a difficult instrument to play. The double bassoon is even bigger, and its sound is even lower.

Tenor or wing joint

Butt

The origins of woodwind instruments

Woodwind instruments of all types have a long history, and many types are still used by people all over the world. The first flutes and whistles were made about 20,000 years ago from bear, bird, and deer bones, with holes pierced in them. Panpipes are another ancient type of flute, which are still played in South American music.

Mighty pipes

A mighty organ's pipes produce sound in the same way as a simple woodwind instrument, with a different pipe for each note. An organ also has several keyboards—usually two, but a grand organ may have as many as five keyboards. When an organ key is pressed, air is sent into different-sized pipes, creating high and low notes. The lowest notes in a large organ come from pipes almost 32 feet (10m) long. Some large concert halls have a concert organ, and several composers have added organ music to their orchestral works to create a majestic sound.

The organ in the Church of St. Bartholemew in New York

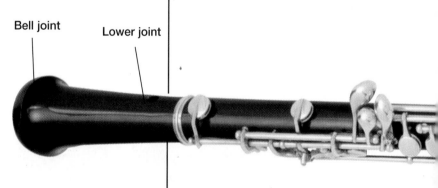

Bell joint

Lower joint

Pipes, piccolos, and flutes

Simple pipes and flutes are held upright and are "end-blown" like a recorder. In some parts of the world, pipes are blown with the nose instead of the mouth. The panpipes are a set of pipes of different lengths, bound together and blown across the tops. They get their name from the ancient Greek myths of the god Pan, who used to play them. The type of flute played in modern orchestras, however, is the "side-blown" flute, often used in military bands in the United States and Britain. The piccolo is a small version of the flute and makes a bright, shrill sound, while the flute has a soft, breathy sound. Concert flutes are usually made from metal, but some are still made from wood to produce a softer tone. A flute player is called a flautist.

THE SAX

An instrument that developed from the woodwind family is the saxophone. It was invented by a Belgian, Adolphe Sax, in 1846, and it has a single-reed mouthpiece like a clarinet, with holes in the tube that are opened and closed by keys, levers, and pads, like other woodwind instruments. The saxophone is made of brass and was intended for military bands, but it became a popular jazz instrument. A few composers have written parts for it in their orchestral work, such as Bizet's incidental music for *L'Arlesienne*.

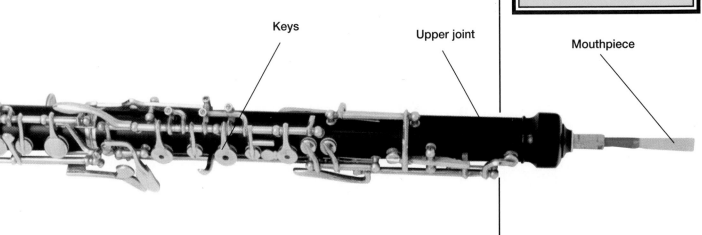

Keys

Upper joint

Mouthpiece

The Brass Section

The trumpets, trombones, horns, and tubas of the brass section provide a stirring contrast to the more delicate strings and woodwinds. They also are dramatic soloists, rising crisp and clear above the orchestra.

Fanfare of brass

For centuries, the piercing tones of trumpets and horns have been used to sound fanfares and battle and hunting calls, ringing out about the fray. In an orchestra, they produce a blaze of sound, adding a note of excitement and drama to any performance. The brass section of an average orchestra consists of four French horns, three trumpets, three trombones, and a tuba. They are positioned in the middle of the orchestra semicircle, sandwiched between the woodwind and percussion sections. Some composers have written music for a bigger brass section. Richard Wagner developed his version of the tuba, known as the Wagner tuba, for his series of operas, *The Ring of the Nibelung*.

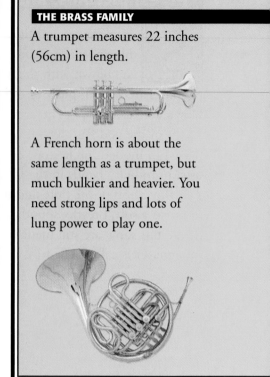

THE BRASS FAMILY

A trumpet measures 22 inches (56cm) in length.

A French horn is about the same length as a trumpet, but much bulkier and heavier. You need strong lips and lots of lung power to play one.

First valve   Second valve   Third valve

Mouthpiece

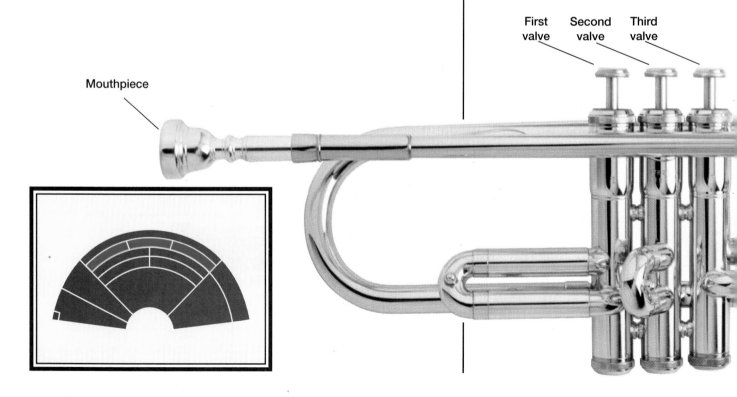

A trombone, including the slide, is 78 inches (200cm) long.

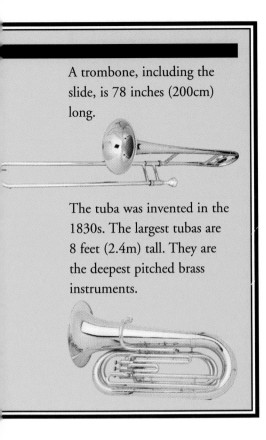

The tuba was invented in the 1830s. The largest tubas are 8 feet (2.4m) tall. They are the deepest pitched brass instruments.

Fanfare of brass

Like the woodwind family, brass instruments use air to produce sound. To play a brass instrument, you purse your lips against the mouthpiece and blow hard into it, making your lips vibrate. These vibrations travel down into the instrument to produce a sound. To play different notes, you press the piston valves down; this adds to or cuts off sections of the air column and changes the sound. (A trombone player moves a slide in and out instead.) You can also insert a plug of wood, metal, or plastic, called a *mute,* into the end of the instrument to alter or soften the sound. Horn players sometimes use their hand, instead of a mute, to change the tone.

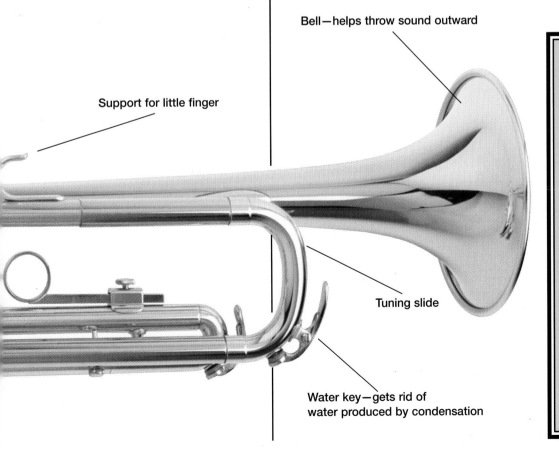

Bell—helps throw sound outward

Support for little finger

Tuning slide

Water key—gets rid of water produced by condensation

DID YOU KNOW?

A type of trumpet was found in the tomb of the Egyptian pharaoh, Tutankhamun. It is over 3,000 years old.

The serpent was a very odd instrument, invented in France in 1590. A cross between woodwind and brass, its name came from its twisting, snakelike coils. The tuba has now replaced it.

A blast of brass

The first horns were made from hollowed-out branches and animal horns. Brass horns were used to sound out hunting signals as long ago as the fourteenth century. In Haydn and Mozart's time, the trumpet was used to add strength to the orchestral sound. However, trumpets then were still *natural,* meaning without valves, so they could only produce a few different notes. The three-valve trumpet was developed in the nineteenth century. It could play all the notes of the scale. The French horn was developed from an early French hunting horn. It is two horns in one: the player's thumb works a valve that switches between two sets of coiled tubes, thus varying the pitch of the notes.

SLIDING SCALE

Trombones date back to the fifteenth century when new skills in metalwork brought improvements to all brass instruments. Beethoven was one of the first composers to include trombones in the classical orchestra, in *Symphony No. 5,* but not until the nineteenth century did trombones became regular members of the brass section.

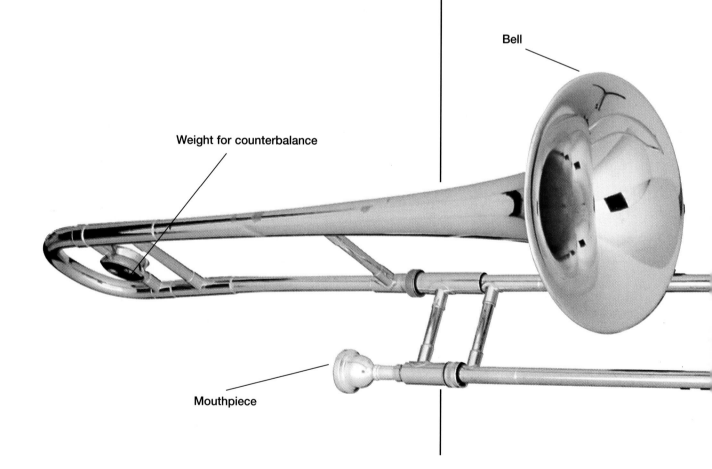

Bell

Weight for counterbalance

Mouthpiece

Bring on the band

Brass instruments are ideal for military bands because they can be easily carried in parades. The American bandmaster John Philip Sousa designed a large, deep-sounding brass instrument called a sousaphone. It twists around the player's shoulders with the bell raised high above the head, so it is ideal for playing in a marching band. Brass bands play in many different countries and include instruments such as cornets, flügelhorns, and euphoniums. Early British brass bands have existed for more than 150 years, and some British composers, such as Sir Edward Elgar and Ralph Vaughan Williams, have written music for brass bands.

A military
brass band

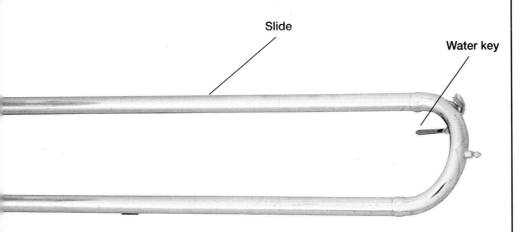

Slide

Water key

The Percussion Section

From the crash of cymbals and the beat of drums, to the shaking and rattling of bells and maracas, the percussion section is the special effects department of the orchestra.

Shake, rattle, and roll

The percussion section completes the orchestra. It is the loudest group of instruments, positioned right as the back behind the brass section. It is also the most varied group, including timpani (kettledrums), bass and side drums, tubular bells, xylophones, glockenspiels, cymbals, and triangles, together with hand bells, wood blocks, gongs, and rattles. Many percussion instruments were added to orchestras in the nineteenth century, to produce a greater range of special musical effects.

Beating drums

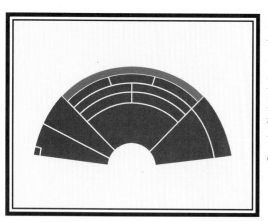

Most percussion instruments are struck in some way, with a stick or hands. When you hit a drum, the membrane, or skin, stretched over the drum's frame vibrates and sets the air inside the drum vibrating too. This produces sound. The tighter the membrane, the faster it vibrates when struck and the higher the note produced. Larger frames produce deeper notes than smaller ones, so the bigger the drum, the louder and deeper the sound.

An orchestra may have as many as six timpani, or kettledrums, beating out the rhythm or playing a drumroll.

Shell—main body or frame of drum

Struts for support

Pedal—used to change note by altering the tightness of the drumhead

Gongs and cymbals can produce great crashing sounds.

Each of the xylophone's wooden bars produces a different note.

Pitched and unpitched

Percussion instruments are divided into two groups—pitched and unpitched. Pitched instruments, such as xylophones and bells, produce definite musical notes when played. Unpitched instruments, such as tambourines, maracas, and cymbals, simply produce a soft or loud noise. The large timpani or kettledrum can be made to sound different notes by tightening the skin or drumhead. The timpanist can also use the pedal to change the note while playing.

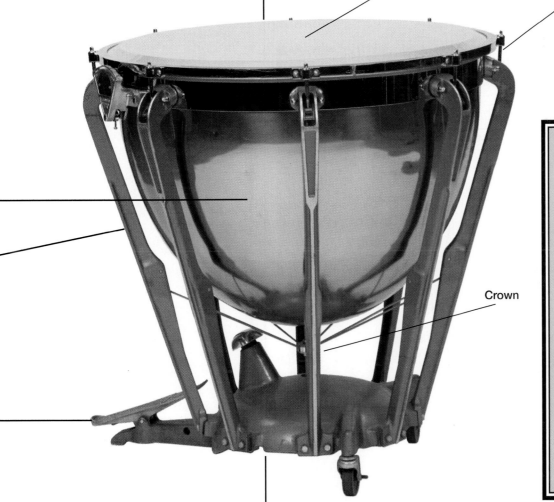

Drumhead—the membrane or skin

Tuning gauge

Crown

375

Music for Orchestras

Orchestration is the art of writing music specifically for an orchestra and its particular blend of instruments. This has produced some of the greatest works of classical music, including many famous symphonies.

Early music

At first, orchestras played music written to accompany ballets and operas. But in the early eighteenth century, composers such as Bach and Handel began writing pieces for orchestra alone. These pieces were called *concerti grossi,* or great concertos. They were written mainly for strings, contrasting a large group of players with a smaller group or a soloist.

A painting of eighteenth-century musicians

DID YOU KNOW?

The longest symphony ever written lasted thirteen hours! Called *Victory at Sea,* it was written by American composer Richard Rodgers in 1952.

Even though a symphony can last over an hour, you are not supposed to clap between movements, however well the music may have been played.

CHAMBER MUSIC

Originally written to be performed in private houses, chamber music is played by small groups of two or more instruments. Early chamber music was written for two violins, a cello, and a harpsichord, but the most well-known combination is the string quartet, which was developed in the early eighteenth century. Schubert wrote several quintets, for four strings and a piano, and Mendelssohn even wrote octets.

The age of the symphony

I n the mid-eighteenth century, composers began to write longer pieces, called symphonies, for larger orchestras. Symphony orchestras take their name from this type of music. A symphony is made up of three or four separate sections, called movements. Franz Joseph Haydn (1732–1809), who wrote over 100 symphonies, preferred four movements—a lively opening, a slow movement, a dancelike movement, and an exciting finale. In the nineteenth century, a new type of orchestral music that painted a picture or told a story became very popular. It was called *programme music* after the notes written for the audience by composers to explain what their music was about.

Settling the score

O rchestral music written on paper is called a score. It shows the parts to be played by each instrument or family. The system of signs and symbols used to write music down today dates from the twelfth century. It was devised by monks to help them record different ways of singing hymns and psalms. Modern orchestral scores are usually printed in a book. The woodwind parts are arranged at the top of the page and the strings at the bottom.

A detail from a handwritten score of music by Bach

377

Orchestras of the World

The symphony orchestra originated in Europe and largely plays Western classical music. But groups of musicians have also played together for thousands of years in other parts of the world.

The gamelan sound

The gamelan is a type of orchestra found in Indonesia. The main instruments are percussion instruments, including gongs, chimes, drums, and xylophones, with some string and woodwind instruments. There may be as many as twenty to forty musicians. Each town or village has its own local gamelan. It often accompanies traditional dancing or shadow play performances. The musicians memorize their music, then improvise around certain set melodies.

A gamelan orchestra

Indian classical music

A classical Indian group might consist of a sitar (a stringed instrument played like a guitar), *tablas* (drums), and a *sarangi* (a stringed instrument played with a bow, like a cello), or a *shahnai* (a woodwind instrument, like an oboe). The musicians do not play from a fixed score but improvise around patterns of notes, called ragas. There are hundreds of ragas designed for different times of the day and to create different moods. A raga is made up of five to seven notes, played in ascending or descending order.

South American music

Flutes and pipes such as panpipes are often played in South American music, giving a soft, dreamy sound. More unusual stringed instruments, like the harp pictured below, are played by some South American Indians, such as these Quecha Indians. Mariachi bands, consisting of violins, guitars, trumpets, and a singer, are common in Mexico.

South American Quecha Indian players

379

Instruments of the World

Musical instruments have developed all over the world to suit different cultures. Many modern orchestral instruments have their roots in the Middle East and Asia.

National instruments

The sound of certain instruments reminds us of a particular country. The clicking of castanets conjures up a picture of whirling Spanish dancers, and the twang of the sitar is unmistakably Indian. Ancient tribes from different parts of the world made instruments with their own unique sound. These could be used to send messages to other members of the tribe, rather like an early telephone system.

Musicians from the Amazon playing Urena flutes

Balalaika—a Russian instrument, like a guitar with a triangular body and three strings.

Koto—a Japanese instrument, made from a long box with thirteen strings stretched along it. It is played on the ground by plucking the strings.

DID YOU KNOW?

The *charango* is a small South American lute that traditionally was made from armadillo skin. The armadillo is now a protected animal so the instrument makers have to use wood instead.

Bagpipes have existed for more than 3,000 years. They are still a popular instrument in the Scottish Highlands of Britain. The piper blows into the mouth pipe called the chanter to inflate the bag, which is then squeezed to sound the other pipes called the drones.

380

Where in the world?

The map below shows where many different instruments come from. Although they all look quite different, they are only variations of the four families: string, woodwind, brass, and percussion. These national instruments are still handcrafted in their native countries.

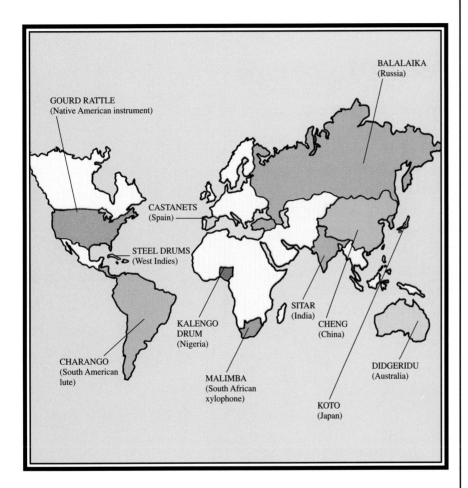

GOURD RATTLE
(Native American instrument)

BALALAIKA
(Russia)

CASTANETS
(Spain)

STEEL DRUMS
(West Indies)

SITAR
(India)

KALENGO
DRUM
(Nigeria)

CHENG
(China)

CHARANGO
(South American
lute)

DIDGERIDU
(Australia)

MALIMBA
(South African
xylophone)

KOTO
(Japan)

INSTRUMENTS OF THE WORLD

Panpipes—a set of whistlelike flutes, bound together in order of size. Each pipe produces a single note when you blow across the top. An important instrument in South American music.

Castanets—Spanish instruments, made from two small hollowed-out pieces of wood, clacked together. Used to accompany flamenco dancing.

Kalengo drum— a double-headed drum from Nigeria, used to beat out the sounds of an African language.

Didgeridu—a traditional Aborigine instrument from Australia. Made from a hollow eucalyptus branch, blown at one end.

381

WHAT IS AN
Orchestra?

Meet the Author

Anita Ganeri worked in publishing for several years before she became a freelance writer and editor of over 100 nonfiction titles for young people. Born in Calcutta, India, she studied French, German, and Hindi at Cambridge University. A fellow of The Royal Geographical Society, she has written many titles for the "Horrible Geography" book series. Ganeri lives in West Yorkshire with her husband and pets. She enjoys playing tennis and finishing her work on time.

Theme Connections

Within the Selection

Record your answers to the questions below in the Response Journal section of your Writer's Notebook. In small groups, report the ideas you wrote. Discuss your ideas with the rest of your group. Then choose a person to report your group's answers to the class.

- Why were there no conductors before the nineteenth century?
- During what period did music become more expressive and emotional?
- How do orchestras vary in different parts of the world?

Across the Selections

- In "What Is an Orchestra?" the author provides the history of the orchestra. Name other nonfiction selections you have read that provide historical facts and background.

Beyond the Selection

- Of the instruments mentioned in this selection, which have you seen or heard before? Were they part of an orchestra, or did you hear them individually? Which instrument was your favorite? Why? Get into small groups and share your thoughts. Then be prepared to share your favorite instrument with the class.

What Is Music?

from ***Music Is My Mistress***
by Edward Kennedy Ellington
illustrated by Christine Pratt

Edward Kennedy Ellington was born in Washington, D. C., in 1899.
Before he was even in high school, a friend decided that Edward should
have an elegant-sounding title. He gave Edward the nickname by which
he was known for the rest of his life: Duke. Until his death in 1974,
Duke Ellington performed music with his band. The music was jazz,
and he transformed it with a special Ellington sound that became
world-famous. For fifty years, Duke Ellington was a major force
in the music world. His influence is still felt.

What is music to you?
What would you be without music?

Music is everything.
Nature is music (cicadas in the tropical night).

The sea is music,
The wind is music,
Primitive elements are music, agreeable or discordant.

The rain drumming on the roof,
And the storm raging in the sky are music.

Every country in the world has its own music,
And the music becomes an ambassador;
The tango in Argentina and calypso in Antilles.

Music is the oldest entity.

A baby is born, and music puts him to sleep.
He can't read, he can't understand a picture,
But he will listen to music.

Music is marriage.

Music is death.

The scope of music is immense and infinite.
It is the "esperanto" of the world.

Music arouses courage and leads you to war.
The Romans used to have drums rolling before
  they attacked.
We have the bugle to sound reveille and pay homage
  to the brave warrior.

The Marseillaise has led many generations to victories
  or revolutions;
It is a chant of wild excitement, and delirium, and pride.

Music is eternal,
Music is divine.

You pray to your God with music.

Music can dictate moods,
It can ennerve or subdue,
Subjugate, exhaust, astound the heart.

Music is a cedar,
An evergreen tree of fragrant, durable wood.

Music is like honor and pride,
  Free from defect, damage, or decay.

Without music I may feel blind, atrophied,
  incomplete, *inexistent*.

385

The Nightingale

Hans Christian Andersen
translated by Eva Le Gallienne
illustrated by Nancy Ekholm Burkert

In China, you know, the Emperor is Chinese, and all his subjects are Chinese too. This all happened many years ago, but for that very reason the story should be told. It would be a pity if it were forgotten.

The Emperor had the most beautiful palace in all the world. It was built of the finest porcelain and had cost a fortune, but it was so delicate and fragile you had to be very careful how you moved about in it.

The garden was full of exquisite flowers; on the rarest and most beautiful, tiny silver bells were hung, so that people passing by would be sure to notice them. Indeed, everything in the Emperor's garden had been most ingeniously planned, and it was so large that the gardener himself didn't know the full extent of it. If you kept on walking long enough, you came to a wonderful forest with great trees and fathomless lakes. The forest grew all the way down to the deep blue sea; the trees stretched their branches over the water, and large ships could sail right under them. Here lived a nightingale who sang so sweetly that even the poor fisherman——who had so much else to attend to——would stop and listen to her as he drew in his nets at night. "How beautiful that is!" he would say; then he had to get back to his work and forget about the bird. But the next night when he came to tend his nets and heard her singing, he would say again, "How beautiful that is!"

Travelers from all over the world came to the Emperor's city. They were filled with admiration for it, and for the palace and the garden. But when they heard the Nightingale, they all exclaimed, "That's the loveliest thing of all!"

When they returned home the travelers told all about their visits, and the scholars wrote many books describing the city, the palace, and the garden——but not one of them forgot the Nightingale; they kept their highest praise for her. And those who could write poetry wrote exquisite poems about the Nightingale who lived in the forest by the deep blue sea.

These books went all over the world, and at last some of them reached the Emperor. He sat in his gold chair reading and reading, every now and then nodding his head with pleasure when he came to an especially magnificent description of his city, his palace, and his garden. "But the Nightingale is the loveliest thing of all!" the books said.

"What's this?" cried the Emperor. "The Nightingale? I've never heard of her! To think that there is such a bird in my Empire——in my very own garden——and no one has told me about her! I have to read about her in a book! It's positively disgraceful!"

So he sent for his Chamberlain, who was so very haughty that if anyone of inferior rank dared to address him or ask him a question, he only deigned to answer, "Peh!"——which of course means nothing at all!

"I understand there is a highly remarkable bird here called the Nightingale," said the Emperor. "They say she is the loveliest thing in my whole Empire! Why has no one told me about her?"

"I've never heard that name before," answered the Chamberlain. "She's not been presented at Court, I'm sure of that."

"I want her to come here this very evening and sing for me!" said the Emperor. "It seems the whole world knows that I possess this marvel, yet I myself know nothing about her!"

"No! I have never heard that name!" the Chamberlain repeated. "But I shall look for her, and most certainly shall find her!"

But where was he to look?

He ran up and down all the staircases, through all the halls and corridors, asking everyone he met about the Nightingale——but no one knew anything about her. At last he ran back to the Emperor and told him it must be some fantastic story invented by the people who write books. "Your Imperial Majesty shouldn't pay attention to everything that's written down. It's mostly pure imagination."

"But I read this in a book sent me by the High and Mighty Emperor of Japan——therefore it must be true! I insist on hearing the Nightingale. She must be here this very evening! I am graciously inclined toward her——and if you fail to produce her you'll all get your stomachs punched immediately after supper!"

"Tsing-peh!" cried the Chamberlain, and he started running again, up and down the staircases, through all the halls and corridors, and half the Court went with him, for they didn't want to have their stomachs punched——particularly after supper!

They inquired right and left about the marvelous Nightingale, who was known all over the world but had never been heard of by the courtiers in the palace.

At last they found a poor little girl working in the kitchen. She said, "Oh, the Nightingale! I know her well! How beautifully she sings! Every evening I'm allowed to take some scraps of food to my poor sick mother who lives down by the shore. On my way back I

feel tired and sit down to rest a moment in the forest, and then I hear the Nightingale! She sounds so beautiful that tears come to my eyes; it's as though Mother were kissing me!"

"Little kitchen maid," said the Chamberlain, "I'll see that you're given a permanent position in the palace kitchen, and you shall even be allowed to watch the Emperor eat his dinner, if only you will lead us to the Nightingale, for we have been ordered to bring her here this evening!"

So, accompanied by half the Court, they set out toward the forest where the Nightingale was usually heard singing. After they had walked some way they heard a cow mooing. "Ah! There she is!" cried the courtiers. "What a powerful voice for such a little creature! But we seem to have heard her before!"

"That's only a cow mooing," said the little kitchen maid. "We still have a good way to go."

Some frogs began croaking in the marshes.

"Lovely!" exclaimed the Court chaplain. "I hear her! She sounds just like little church bells!"

"Those are the frogs croaking," said the kitchen maid. "But we ought to hear her soon."

And then the Nightingale began to sing.

"There she is!" said the little girl. "Listen! Listen! She's up there. Do you see her?" And she pointed to a little gray bird perched high up in the branches.

"Is it possible?" said the Chamberlain. "I never thought she'd look like that! She's so drab and ordinary. . . . But perhaps the sight of so many distinguished people has caused her to lose color!"

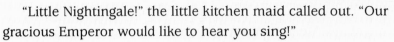

"Little Nightingale!" the little kitchen maid called out. "Our gracious Emperor would like to hear you sing!"

"With pleasure!" said the Nightingale, and sang so that it was a joy to hear her.

"It's like the tinkling of crystal bells," said the Chamberlain. "And look at her little throat——how it throbs! It seems odd that we've never heard her before. She'll have a great success at Court!"

"Shall I sing for the Emperor again?" asked the Nightingale, who thought the Emperor must be present.

"Most excellent little Nightingale!" said the Chamberlain. "It is my pleasure to invite you to appear at Court this evening, where you will delight His Imperial Majesty with your enchanting song!"

"It sounds best out in the forest," replied the Nightingale, but she consented to go willingly since it was the Emperor's wish.

The palace had been scrubbed and polished until the walls and the floors, which were made of porcelain, sparkled in the light of thousands of golden lamps. The finest flowers, those with the silver bells on them, were placed in all the corridors. There was such a coming and going, and such a draft, that all the little bells tinkled so loudly you couldn't hear yourself speak.

In the middle of the Great Presence Chamber, where the Emperor sat on his throne, a golden perch had been placed for the Nightingale. The entire Court was assembled, and the little kitchen maid, who had received the title of Assistant-Cook-to-His-Imperial-Majesty, was allowed to stand behind the door.

The courtiers were dressed in their grandest clothes and they all stared at the little gray bird, to whom the Emperor nodded graciously.

And the Nightingale sang so exquisitely that tears came to the Emperor's eyes and trickled down his cheeks. Then the Nightingale sang even more beautifully——it was enough to melt your heart. The Emperor was so delighted he wanted to give the Nightingale his gold slipper to wear around her neck. But the Nightingale declined the honor with many thanks; she felt she had been sufficiently rewarded.

"I have seen tears in the Emperor's eyes. What could be more precious to me? An Emperor's tears have a mysterious power! I have been amply rewarded!" And she sang again in that sweet, ravishing voice of hers.

"What delightful coquetry!" exclaimed the Court ladies, and they filled their mouths with water and made gurgling sounds in their throats whenever anyone spoke to them. They imagined they were nightingales too! Even the lackeys and the chambermaids admitted to being quite pleased—and that's saying a lot, for they are the most difficult people in the world to satisfy. Yes! The Nightingale was a great success!

From then on she had to remain at Court. She had a cage of her own, and was granted permission to go out twice during the day and once at night; but she had to be accompanied by twelve servants, who each held on tightly to a silk thread fastened to her leg. There wasn't much fun in that kind of an outing!

The whole city talked of nothing but the wonderful bird, and when two people met, one of them had only to say "Nightin" for the other to say "gale"; then they would sigh in perfect understanding. Eleven shopkeepers' children were named after the Nightingale—— but not one of them could sing a note, and they were tone-deaf into the bargain.

One day a large parcel arrived for the Emperor, and on it was written, "Nightingale."

"I expect it's a new book about our famous bird!" said the Emperor; but it wasn't a book at all. It was a wonderful example of the jeweler's art, lying in a velvet-lined case——an artificial nightingale that was supposed to be a copy of the real one, only it was encrusted with diamonds, rubies, and sapphires. When you wound it up, it sang one of the real Nightingale's songs and its tail moved up and down and glittered with silver and gold; around its neck was a little ribbon with the inscription, "The Emperor of Japan's nightingale is poor compared with that of the Emperor of China."

"How marvelous!" they all cried; and the messenger who had brought the artificial bird was immediately given the title of Chief-Imperial-Nightingale-Bringer.

"Now let us hear them sing together——what a duet that will be!"

So they sang together, but it didn't turn out very well, for the Nightingale sang in her own free way, while the artificial bird's song was stilted and mechanical. "The new bird is in no way to blame," said the music master. "It keeps perfect time and obeys all the rules of my special method." Then the artificial bird sang by itself and had just as great a success as the real one. And it was so much more beautiful to look at! It sparkled and shimmered like some fantastic jewel.

It sang its one and only tune thirty-three times without ever getting tired. The courtiers would have liked to hear it over and over again, but the Emperor felt it was the real Nightingale's turn to sing a bit. But where was she? No one had noticed, in all the excitement, that she had flown out of the open window, back to her own green forest.

"Here's a nice state of affairs!" cried the Emperor. The courtiers were all furious and accused the Nightingale of rank ingratitude.

"Well! After all, we still have the better of the two birds!" they said. So the artificial nightingale was made to sing again, and though they now heard the tune for the thirty-fourth time, they still hadn't quite caught on to it——for it was very difficult. The music master was loud in his praise of the artificial bird and said it was much better than the real Nightingale, for its outer covering of diamonds concealed the most delicate and intricate of mechanisms.

"You see, ladies and gentlemen——and first and foremost, Your Imperial Majesty!——the real Nightingale is totally unpredictable; she sings on the spur of the moment, and there's no way of knowing what you're going to hear. Whereas with the artificial bird everything has been regulated beforehand. You get just what you expect; there are no surprises! The mechanism can be logically explained. You can take the bird apart and examine the intricate wheels and cylinders, how one minute cog fits into another, causing it to sing. It's amazing what human skill and ingenuity are able to accomplish!"

"You're absolutely right!" they all agreed, and the very next Sunday the music master was authorized to demonstrate the bird to the common people. "They must hear it sing too," said the Emperor. So they did hear it and were so delighted they seemed quite intoxicated, as though they'd drunk too much tea——for that's what the Chinese drink, you know. They all exclaimed, "Oh!" held up their forefingers, and nodded their heads. But the poor fisherman who had heard the real Nightingale sing said, "Yes! It's pretty enough; it's a fairly good imitation, but there's something lacking——I can't explain just what it is!"

The real Nightingale was banished from the Empire.

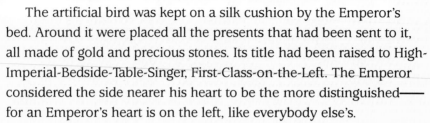

The artificial bird was kept on a silk cushion by the Emperor's bed. Around it were placed all the presents that had been sent to it, all made of gold and precious stones. Its title had been raised to High-Imperial-Bedside-Table-Singer, First-Class-on-the-Left. The Emperor considered the side nearer his heart to be the more distinguished—for an Emperor's heart is on the left, like everybody else's.

The music master wrote five-and-twenty tomes about the artificial bird, so long-winded and so learned and so full of the most complicated phrases that though everybody read them no one could understand a word; but of course they didn't dare admit it—they didn't want to appear stupid, for that would have meant having their stomachs punched, and they didn't like the thought of that!

In this way a whole year passed. By now the Emperor, the Court, and all the Chinese people knew every note and every trill of the artificial bird's song, and they enjoyed it all the more for that; now they were able to join in the singing, which of course they did. Even the street urchins sang, "Zeezee, zee! Gloo, gloo, gloo!" and the Emperor sang it too. It was all perfectly delightful!

But one evening, when the artificial bird was singing away and the Emperor lay on his bed listening to it, something went "crack!" inside the bird—a spring had broken. There was a great whirring of wheels, and the song stopped.

The Emperor leaped out of bed and sent for his personal physician, but there was nothing he could do! So a watchmaker was summoned, and after a great deal of talk and a long and careful examination, he managed to fix the mechanism fairly well, but he said it shouldn't be used too often, as many of the cogs had worn down and would be almost impossible to replace. He couldn't guarantee that the song would ever be the same again. It was a tragic state of affairs! Only once a year was the artificial bird allowed to sing—and even that put quite a strain on it. But the music master made a little speech, full of complicated words, declaring that the song was just as good as ever; and of course that settled it. Everyone agreed it was just as good as ever!

Five more years went by, and the whole country was heavy with grief—for the people were devoted to their Emperor, and now he was sick and the doctors said he hadn't long to live.

A new Emperor had already been chosen, and the people stood outside in the street and asked the Chamberlain if there was any hope of their old Emperor getting well again.

"Peh!" said the Chamberlain, and shook his head.

The Emperor lay in his huge, magnificent bed, so cold and
so pale that the courtiers thought him already dead, and they all
dashed off to pay court to the new Emperor. The lackeys ran outside
to gossip about it, and the chambermaids gave a large tea party.
Thick felt had been laid down on the floors of all the halls and
corridors to muffle the sound of footsteps; the palace was as quiet as
a tomb. But the Emperor wasn't dead yet. He lay there stiff and pale
in his magnificent bed with the long velvet hangings and the heavy
gold tassels. High up in the wall was an open window through which
the moon shone down on him and on the artificial bird by his side.

The poor Emperor could hardly breathe; he felt something heavy
weighing on his chest; he opened his eyes and saw that it was Death.
He was wearing the Emperor's gold crown, and held the gold sword
of state in one hand and the Imperial banner in the other; and from
the folds of the heavy velvet hangings strange faces peered out——
some hideous and evil, and others mild and gentle. They were the
Emperor's good and bad deeds watching him as he lay there with
Death weighing on his heart.

"Do you remember this?" they whispered to him one after
another. "Do you remember that?" And they reminded him of many,
many things——and the sweat stood out on his brow.

"I never knew about all that!" cried the Emperor. "Music! Music!" he
shouted. "Strike up the great Chinese gong and drown out their voices!"

But the voices continued, and Death nodded his head, like a real
Chinese, in agreement with all that was said.

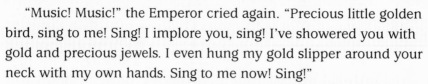

"Music! Music!" the Emperor cried again. "Precious little golden bird, sing to me! Sing! I implore you, sing! I've showered you with gold and precious jewels. I even hung my gold slipper around your neck with my own hands. Sing to me now! Sing!"

But the bird was silent. It couldn't sing unless it was wound up, but there was no one there to do it. Death kept on staring at the Emperor with his great hollow eyes, and the silence grew more and more terrifying.

Suddenly, through the window, came the sound of an exquisite song. It was the little, living Nightingale perched on a branch outside. She had heard of the Emperor's suffering and had come to bring him hope and comfort with her song. As she sang the phantoms gradually faded away, the blood began to flow more swiftly through the Emperor's feeble body, and Death himself listened and said, "Keep on singing, little Nightingale! Keep on!"

"Yes! If you will give me the golden sword! If you will give me the Imperial banner! If you will give me the Emperor's golden crown!"

And Death gave up the treasures one by one for each song the Nightingale sang. She sang of the peaceful churchyard where the white roses bloom, where the air is sweet with the scent of the elder tree, and where the green grass is moistened by the tears of those who have lost their loved ones. And, as he listened, Death was filled with a great longing to be back in his own garden, and he vanished out of the window like a cold white mist.

"Thank you, thank you!" said the Emperor. "You heavenly little bird——I know you now! I chased you out of my country, out of my Empire. And with your song you have chased the hateful dreams from around my bed; you have driven Death from my heart. How can I ever repay you, lovely bird?"

"You have repaid me," said the Nightingale. "The very first time I sang to you, you gave me your tears——I shall never forget that! Those are the jewels that gladden a singer's heart. But go to sleep now, and wake up well and strong! I'll sing to you!"

The Nightingale sang, and the Emperor fell into a deep sleep; a gentle, refreshing sleep.

When he awoke the next morning the sun was shining through the window, and he felt well and strong again; none of his servants had come back to him, for they thought he was dead, but the Nightingale was still singing.

"You must never leave me!" cried the Emperor. "You need only sing when you feel like singing, and I shall smash the artificial bird into a thousand pieces."

"Don't do that!" said the Nightingale. "It did the best it could! Keep it with you. I can't settle down and live here in the palace, but let me come and go as I like. I'll sit on the branch outside your window and sing to you, so that your thoughts may be serene and joyful; I'll sing of happy people and of those who suffer; I'll sing of the good and evil all around you which is kept hidden from you; for the little songbird flies far and wide——to the poor fisherman, and the peasant in his hut, to all those who are far away from you and from your Court. I love your heart much better than your crown, yet I venerate your crown, for there is an aura of sanctity about it! I shall come and sing for you——but one thing you must promise me!"

"Anything!" said the Emperor, who stood there in his Imperial robes, which he had put on all by himself, holding the heavy golden sword against his heart.

"I ask only one thing of you: Let no one know you have a little bird who tells you everything. It will be much better so!"

And the Nightingale flew away.

The servants and the courtiers came in to attend their dead Emperor. They were struck dumb with amazement when they saw him standing there; and the Emperor said to them, "Good morning!"

The Nightingale

Meet the Author

Hans Christian Andersen was the author of 168 fairy tales. Although best known for writing fairy tales, he also wrote novels, operas, plays, poems, and travel books. *Childlike* seems to be the word that best describes Andersen. He loved to cut animals, castles, goblins, and fairies out of paper while he talked. His story, *The Ugly Duckling*, is said to have been written because he was awkward and unattractive. Andersen must have enjoyed his life, as he once wrote, "My life is a fairy tale."

Meet the Illustrator

Nancy Ekholm Burkert loved to draw and read when she was a child. "As a child I did not see many magazines, and though I remember two or three Disney movies and the 'funnies,' my picture books provided my only source of visual art." She wrote and illustrated her first children's story when she was in the ninth grade. "I illustrate books because I enjoy 'visualizing' a literary work; illustration is like staging a play——designing the sets, the costumes, the lighting, 'casting' the characters."

Theme Connections

Within the Selection

Record your answers to the questions below in the Response Journal section of your Writer's Notebook. In small groups, report the ideas you wrote. Discuss your ideas with the rest of your group. Then choose a person to report your group's answers to the class.

- Why did the Emperor send the Chamberlain to find the nightingale?
- Why did the court women put water into their throats and make gurgling sounds?
- In what ways did the Emperor and his court prefer the artificial nightingale to the real one?

Across the Selections

- The kitchen maid describes the nightingale's music as "so beautiful that tears come to my eyes," while the Chamberlain says, "It's like the tinkling of crystal bells." With this in mind, go back and review "What Is an Orchestra?" and decide which musical instrument might produce, in your opinion, a sound that is most like the nightingale's. Explain.

Beyond the Selection

- Think about how "The Nightingale" adds to what you know about music.
- Add items to the Concept/Question Board about music.

Two Young Girls at the Piano. 1892. **Auguste Pierre Renoir.** Oil on canvas. 44 × 34 in. The Metropolitan Museum of Art, New York, NY.

Cycladic Harpest. 2500 B.C. Early Cycladic II. Island marble. 35.8 × 9.5 cm. The J. Paul Getty Museum, Malibu, California.

The Poet Fujiwara no Yasumasa playing the flute by moonlight.
1882. **Tsukioka Yoshitoshi.** Woodblock print. Private collection.

Introduction to OPERA

To sing for you would be the best way for me to introduce you to the world of opera which has been my career for almost thirty years. It was hearing voices on records when I was a boy that first brought me to opera—so in a way my career has been almost my entire life. I grew up with it the way you grow up today with Star Wars movies and games. Opera was invented by Italians, and the music and stories of the opera were part of my home life. In fact, young people in Italy and all over Europe used to trade cards with photographs of opera singers on them much the way people now trade cards with baseball players and other sports heroes.

Today it's different, and you are not likely to learn about opera unless your parents or teachers make a special effort. I have three daughters, and know from watching them grow up that most young people care about what is the newest thing—the latest hit song, the new television show, or the biggest new movie. In the last century, when most operas were written, they were truly the equivalent of the hit song, movie or show—and the effect on the people of that time was similar to the overpowering feelings we have today from the mass media. Life did not move as fast then as it does today, and to enjoy opera, you need to slow down just a bit. In that way you can hear all the beauty in the music and understand what is happening in the story.

And what marvelous stories they are! There are comic operas, and operas sad enough to make you cry. An opera can take place in any country and at any time; it can send you on a trip to ancient Egypt, to the Paris of a hundred years ago, or to a place that never existed.

Most of the world's greatest composers wrote operas, including Wolfgang Amadeus Mozart, Giuseppi Verdi, Richard Wagner, Maurice Ravel, and George Gershwin. These incredible men wrote music many years ago that can still excite and move us today. In most operas there is no spoken dialogue; all the words are sung, so the total effect is the music and words together which express what is happening along with the emotions that you can actually feel and hear in the theater.

Sometimes it is a problem that opera is sung in so many foreign languages—but believe me, even opera sung in English can sound like a different language. But if you learn the story of the opera, and take the time to listen to recordings or to watch videocassettes, you will be prepared in a better way, and your appreciation will grow as you recognize your favorite moments and feel the extraordinary power of grand opera. The more you know about opera, the more you will love it.

And then—you will want to go to a live performance. This is the most exciting: the sets and costumes, the sound of the orchestra, the experience of sharing with the rest of the audience. The next thing you know, you will be trying to go again!

The next time I am on the stage—I will look for you in the audience.

Luciano Pavarotti

as told by Leontyne Price

based on the opera by Guiseppe Verdi
illustrated by Leo and Diane Dillon

Long ago, in the faraway land of Ethiopia, there lived a Princess named Aïda. She was fair as the sunrise and gentle as starlight touching a flower. Her father, the great King Amonasro, loved her dearly.

It was a time of terrible fear and danger in Ethiopia, for the kingdom was at war with its neighbor, Egypt. Both countries raided each other's lands, killing or enslaving their enemies.

For the safety of his people, King Amonasro set strict boundaries at the borders of his country, and no Ethiopian was allowed beyond them.

The Princess Aïda was young and, locked within the palace, she grew restless. So, one morning, Aïda and her trusted friends disobeyed the King's command. They disguised themselves and slipped away from the palace guards.

It was a glorious day of freedom, out in the gentle breezes and lush green fields of their beautiful country. But Aïda wandered farther than she should have. Off on her own, enjoying the warm sun and fresh country air, she did not hear her friends in the distance when they shouted, "Aïda! Beware! Come back!"

Once again, Egyptian soldiers had invaded Ethiopia, crossing the south edge of the River Nile. Now they marched toward Aïda.

When she finally did hear her friends' warning, it was too late. Soldiers seized her. Bound with ropes and chains, Aïda, the Royal Princess of Ethiopia, was carried off to Egypt as a slave.

Aïda had learned her royal lessons well. She revealed to no one that she was the daughter of King Amonasro of Ethiopia. But her beauty and noble

404

bearing attracted great attention. So sparkling and unusual was she that the all-powerful Pharaoh, the ruler of Egypt, chose her from among thousands of captured slaves to be his gift—a personal handmaiden—to his only daughter, the Princess Amneris.

It was easy for Aïda to perform the duties of a servant, for she remembered what her own handmaidens had done. The Egyptian Princess Amneris was fascinated, for Aïda was different from any slave she had ever seen. She wanted her new handmaiden to be her closest companion.

Even with the special privileges granted to one so close to the Royal Princess, Aïda felt nothing but despair. All her life she had been the beloved daughter of Ethiopia's King, and now she was a slave to her father's enemy. She knew there was no hope of seeing Ethiopia again.

There was one source of light in her life, however. For Radames, the handsome young captain of the Egyptian Army, had fallen in love with the gentle, beautiful slave the moment he saw her. She, too, had fallen for Radames, despite his position as an enemy of her homeland.

They met often, in secret, by the Temple of Isis, and in the joy of their moments together, Radames confided his dreams to Aïda.

"I will lead the Egyptian Army to victory," he told her, "and when I return, our countries will be united, and you will become my bride and reign as the Queen of your people. It will not be long, I promise."

The day finally came when the Pharaoh was to hold court and announce the new leader of the war against Ethiopia.

Amid the majestic columns of a great hall in the palace, Egypt's High Priest, Ramfis, confided to Radames: "There are rumors that the Ethiopians plan to attack. Prepare yourself, for the Goddess Isis has chosen, and the great honor of leadership may be bestowed upon you."

All his life, Radames had dreamed of this day. If he became the new leader, he could return triumphant to free Aïda and marry her. "Ah, heavenly Aïda," he thought. "I could finally enthrone you in your native land."

Radames was deep in thought when Princess Amneris stepped from the shadows. She, too, was in love with the handsome leader, but she suspected he loved another.

Aïda suddenly appeared.

406

407

Oh, how Radames's eyes filled with passion! And when Amneris saw the look that passed between them, she was seized with suspicion and jealousy. Could Radames prefer a *slave* to the Princess of Egypt? It was intolerable! But her fury was interrupted by trumpets heralding the arrival of the Pharaoh.

A messenger came forward to give his report.

"Mighty Pharaoh, the Ethiopians have attacked. They are led by the fierce warrior King Amonasro, who has invaded Egypt!"

A thunder of anger broke out in court, and upon hearing her father's name, Aïda quietly cried out in fear.

The Pharaoh rose, and the crowd grew still.

"Radames will lead our army," he cried. "It is the decree of the Goddess Isis. Death to the Ethiopians! Victory to Egypt!" he shouted. "Return victorious, Radames!" he commanded.

"Return victorious! Return victorious!" the throng shouted, and Aïda, too, was stirred by the cry. In spite of herself, she also began to shout, "Return victorious! Return victorious!" as the court led the soldiers off to battle. Aïda was now left alone.

"Return victorious!" she called after Radames, but as her own voice echoed in the great hall, she suddenly realized she was asking for the death of her father, her mother, her friends, and all those she cherished. Yet how could she pray for the death of the man she loved?

Aïda was shocked. Her heart was torn between Radames and her loyalty to her father and Ethiopia. She fell to her knees and prayed.

"Oh, great gods of my youth!" she cried. "Pity me!"

That night, the halls of the temple rang as the priestesses chanted the sacred consecration song. The High Priest, Ramfis, led prayers to Phtha, the creator of life and mightiest Egyptian god, as he gave the great hero the sacred sword of Egypt.

"Let the sword of Radames be the strength of our nation! Let his bravery in battle crush the Ethiopians! Protect our land," they prayed, "and make Radames the most magnificent warrior of all."

"Praise to Phtha! Praise to Phtha!" the Egyptians chanted, and the priestesses danced a sacred dance to please the great god and ensure death to their enemies.

With Radames gone, time passed slowly for Aïda. But soon the prayers of the priests were granted. A special day dawned for Egypt—a day of ceremony and grandeur, of pomp and pageantry. The Ethiopians had been defeated at last.

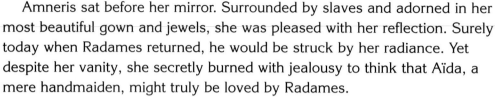

Amneris sat before her mirror. Surrounded by slaves and adorned in her most beautiful gown and jewels, she was pleased with her reflection. Surely today when Radames returned, he would be struck by her radiance. Yet despite her vanity, she secretly burned with jealousy to think that Aïda, a mere handmaiden, might truly be loved by Radames.

So Amneris decided to test her privileged slave. And when gentle Aïda entered the royal chambers, Amneris sobbed, pretending great grief.

"Oh, Aïda, Aïda!" she cried in a shaking voice. "Egypt has lost its finest warrior. Radames has been killed in battle!"

Immediately Aïda wept with the pain of one whose heart has been broken forever. There was no longer any doubt in Amneris's mind.

"It is all a lie!" she shouted. "Radames was not killed. He lives!"

Aïda's tears of sorrow turned to tears of joy.

Overcome with fury, Amneris hurled Aïda to the floor. "How dare you, a lowly slave, love the same man loved by the Princess of Egypt?"

But Aïda, too, was a Princess. She rose proudly. She was about to tell Amneris the truth, but she stopped herself. Instead, with great difficulty, she asked to be forgiven.

"Have mercy on me," she begged. "Your power is unquestioned—you have all that a person could want. But what do I have to live for? My love of Radames, and that alone."

Aïda's plea only fueled Amneris's rage. She stormed out of the chamber, leaving Aïda to fear the worst.

Flags flew, and the entire city gathered to see the grand spectacle of the victory parade led by the Pharaoh, the Princess, and the High Priest. Trumpets blared, and dancing girls threw rose petals to form a welcoming carpet before the magnificent chariot of Radames.

The handsome warrior dismounted and knelt before the royal throne. When Amneris placed a laurel wreath on his head, the crowd was wild with joy.

"Hail to the conqueror!" they roared. "Hail to Radames!"

The Pharaoh proclaimed, "Radames, you are my greatest soldier. As a reward, whatever you wish shall be yours."

When Radames rose, he saw Aïda. Amneris saw the look of love on his face, and she was consumed with jealousy. Yet he dared not ask for Aïda's hand, not at that moment in public court.

"Mighty Pharaoh," he said instead, "I ask that you allow me to call forth our prisoners of war."

410

The Pharaoh granted Radames's request, and the Ethiopians were led into the square in chains. One tall, proud man stood out above the rest. Aïda gasped. It was her father!

The crowd was shocked to see her run and embrace him, but he whispered to her, "Do not betray that I am King."

Amonasro addressed the Pharaoh. "I am Aïda's father, and I have faithfully fought for my sovereign, who died in battle. I am prepared to die for him and my country, but I beseech you to have mercy on those who have been defeated."

With outstretched arms, Aïda joined the Ethiopians. "Let the prisoners go free," she begged Radames and the Pharaoh.

So moved by her appeal, the Egyptian people joined in, and their cries urged the Pharaoh to allow the captured soldiers to be released.

"No!" the High Priest, Ramfis, cried. "The Ethiopians are still a threat and should be put to death."

"Their freedom is my wish," Radames told the Pharaoh.

"Unchain the Ethiopians!" the Pharaoh ordered. "But you, Aïda's father, must remain my prisoner as a pledge of your people's good faith."

An even greater reward was now to be bestowed upon Egypt's greatest warrior. The Pharaoh led Amneris to Radames.

"My daughter will be your bride," he proclaimed, joining their hands. "One day, you shall be Pharaoh, and together you will rule."

Radames was horrified. He dared not refuse the Pharaoh. He bowed and pretended gratitude, but his heart was filled with sorrow. Amneris looked scornfully at her handmaiden.

Aïda wept in her father's arms as the triumphant Egyptian Princess held Radames's hand and led him to the palace.

"Do not lose faith," Amonasro whispered to his daughter. "Ethiopia will soon avenge our conquerors."

It was the eve of the great wedding, and a full moon shone on the dark waters of the River Nile beside the Temple of Isis. By boat, the High Priest, Ramfis, brought Amneris to the Temple. There she was to pray that her marriage be blessed. Little did she know that Radames had sent a message to Aïda, who was waiting to meet him nearby.

Aïda sadly watched the moonlit river and longed with all her heart and soul to return to her beloved homeland. Suddenly she heard Radames approach. But when the man came closer, she was stunned to see that it was her father, King Amonasro.

412

413

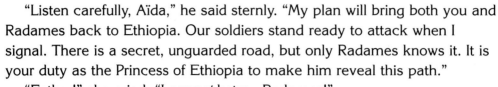

"Listen carefully, Aïda," he said sternly. "My plan will bring both you and Radames back to Ethiopia. Our soldiers stand ready to attack when I signal. There is a secret, unguarded road, but only Radames knows it. It is your duty as the Princess of Ethiopia to make him reveal this path."

"Father!" she cried, "I *cannot* betray Radames!"

With anger and disdain, King Amonasro forced her to her knees. "You are no longer my daughter! You are nothing more than a lowly slave of the Egyptians and a betrayer of your country! Have you forgotten your loved ones who were slaughtered without mercy by these, your enemies?"

"You are wrong! I am *not* and will *never* be a slave to anyone. I am the Princess of Ethiopia, and I have never forgotten my royal blood. My duty to you and to my country will always be first in my heart!"

Even as she swore to obey his command, she cried inside for what her father and her dear country would cost her. Amonasro embraced her to give her courage, and he hid in the bushes to listen.

When Radames finally came, he was breathless with love. But Aïda turned on him scornfully.

"How could you betray me and marry Amneris as your reward?"

"Aïda, you have always been my love. My passion for you is deeper than the Nile, deeper than life itself," Radames told her.

"Then show me," Aïda demanded. "You have betrayed me. And if you truly love me, you will leave Egypt tonight and flee with me to Ethiopia. Only there will we find happiness and peace."

Radames was torn. The thought of leaving Egypt was unbearable, but the thought of living without Aïda was even more painful. At last, after much persuasion, he agreed to flee.

"The roads are heavily guarded by your soldiers. How will we escape?" she asked.

"All the roads are guarded except one," he told her. "The Gorges of Napata."

"The Gorges of Napata!" a voice rang out. Amonasro sprang from his hiding place. He was ready to attack with his army.

Radames could not believe it. "You, Aïda's father, are King of Ethiopia?" He was overcome. "I have sacrificed my country for my love of you!" he cried to Aïda.

"Come with us now," Amonasro told Radames. "You and Aïda will reign happily in Ethiopia."

But as the King took Radames's hand to lead him away, a shout rang out in the darkness. "Traitor!"

It was Amneris. She and the High Priest had come from the temple and had overheard the plot.

"Traitor!" she screamed again.

Amonasro leapt to kill Amneris with his dagger, but Radames ran between them to shield her.

"Go quickly!" he warned Aïda and Amonasro, and the King ran, dragging Aïda with him.

Radames stood before Amneris and the High Priest. He did not try to escape. Instead, he threw down his sword.

"I surrender!" he cried. "I am your prisoner!"

The treason of Radames shocked and infuriated all of Egypt. Guards locked him in the deepest dungeon in the palace. Soon his trial would begin, and he would be sentenced to a horrible death.

Amneris was in a state of grief. Her love for Radames had not diminished. Deep in her heart, she knew he had not meant to betray his country. Her own jealousy had made the mighty warrior a prisoner. She longed to beg her father, the Pharaoh, to release him, but she knew Radames still loved Aïda. She also knew soldiers had killed Amonasro, but Aïda had escaped and was still alive—somewhere.

In desperation, Amneris commanded the guards to bring Radames to her. She humbled herself and pleaded with him to forget Aïda.

"I will find a way to set you free, free to marry me and share the throne of Egypt," she said. "But you must never see Aïda again."

Radames refused. "You are Princess of Egypt, my country; and you have all that anyone could ask for. Yet I will always love Aïda, and there will never be room in my heart for anyone else."

The more Amneris begged him, the more strongly he refused.

When the priests came to take Radames, Amneris was in a rage of anger and jealousy, and she made no attempt to stop them. But when he left, she fell to the ground in tears, cringing as she heard the priests loudly accuse Radames of betrayal.

"Traitor! Traitor!" the High priest, Ramfis, shouted again and again, but Radames never uttered a word to defend himself. Louder and louder the cruel accusations were hurled at him.

Amneris prayed to Isis and the other gods of Egypt to show mercy and save the man she loved, but the gods were silent.

The tribunal of priests pronounced Radames guilty of treason and sentenced him to be buried alive.

As the priests passed from the trial, Amneris flung herself before the High Priest. She insulted him and threatened revenge, but her cries were in vain.

"Radames, the traitor, will die," he said coldly.

Only the priests and guards were allowed to watch Radames walk into the deepest vault below. They sealed the last opening, shutting out all light and the last breath of fresh air. Alone, waiting quietly for death, Radames thought only of Aïda. He would never see her sparkling eyes and gentle smile again.

Suddenly, in the darkness, he heard Aïda's voice. At first, Radames thought it was a dream. But no—she had escaped and was hiding in the vault, waiting for him.

"Aïda, my love, you are too young and too beautiful to die."

Radames pushed in vain, trying to open the vault.

But Aïda gently placed her arms around him. With a tender kiss, she told him to stop.

"Remember, we will never be separated again. For eternity, we will be together."

And with all the love in the world, they held each other close—so close—as if they would never part.

Above their tomb, dressed in black, Princess Amneris prayed to the gods to forgive her and to grant heavenly rest to Radames, her love.

The gods granted her wish, but not as she hoped. For as she prayed to the gods and wept, a peaceful death had come to the Ethiopian Princess Aïda and Radames, the greatest warrior of Egypt. Finally they were together—forever in each other's arms.

Aïda

Meet the Storyteller

Famous opera singer, **Mary Violet Leontyne Price** is better known as Leontyne Price. Her interest in music began at an early age, when she began taking piano lessons at age five. By accident, Price played the first role of *Aïda* when another singer became critically ill. Her career blossomed and she eventually appeared in 118 Metropolitan Operas. After Price retired, she wrote *Aïda: A Picture Book for All Ages.* Since retiring she has also performed at presidential inaugurations and sung before the Pope.

Meet the Illustrators

Leo and Diane Dillon first met while they were students at Parsons School of Design. During an exhibition in which each had a painting on display, they both admired the other's talent; yet, because of their competitive natures, they became instant rivals. The artists eventually united their talents, marrying and freelancing as a team. They have worked in a variety of media including pastels, watercolor, acrylic, black ink, airbrush, woodcuts, crewel, and plastic and liquid steel (which created a stained-glass effect). "Over the years we've come to accept that trial and error is part of the process," explains Leo. "Technique is to the graphic artist what words are to the writer."

420

Theme Connections

Within the Selection

Record your answers to the questions below in the Response Journal section of your Writer's Notebook. In small groups, report the ideas you wrote. Discuss your ideas with the rest of your group. Then choose a person to report your group's answers to the class.

- Why was Aïda made the personal handmaiden to the Pharaoh's daughter?
- What ruined Radames's plan to return to Ethiopia and marry Aïda?
- Why did Amneris do nothing to save Radames when the priests came to take him away?

Across the Selections

- "What Is an Orchestra?" went beyond the notes by explaining the instruments that are behind the notes, and "Aïda" has gone beyond the notes by giving you the story behind an opera. Combine what you have learned in both selections, and consider which instruments you would use if you were to set "Aïda" to music. What kind of music would they play?
- At the end of "The Nightingale," the nightingale says she will sing for the emperor every day but that she must remain free and not be kept in the palace. How is this insistence on freedom similar to Radames's insistence that he loves Aïda and not Amneris?

Beyond the Selection

- Think about how "Aïda" adds to what you know about music.
- Add items to the Concept/Question Board about music.

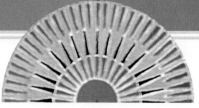

The Sound of Flutes

retold by Henry Crow Dog
illustrated by Paul Goble

Well, you know our flutes, you have heard their sound and seen how beautifully they are made. That flute of ours, the *Siyotanka*, is a very peculiar instrument. It is made for only one kind of music——love music. In the old days, the young men would sit by themselves, maybe lean against a tree in the dark of the night, hidden, unseen. They would make up their own special tunes, their courting songs.

We Indians have always been shy people. A young man hardly could screw up his courage to talk to a *wincincala*——the pretty girl he was in love with——even if he was a brave warrior who had already counted coup upon an enemy.

There was no privacy in the village, which was only a circle of tipis. No privacy in the family tipi either, which was always crowded with people. And, naturally, you couldn't just walk out into the prairie, hand in hand with your girl, to say sweet words to each other. First, because you didn't hold hands——that would be very unmannerly. You didn't show your affection——not by holding hands anyway. Second, you didn't dare

422

take a walk with your wincincala because it wasn't safe. Out there in the tall grass you could be gored by a buffalo, or tomahawked by a Pawnee, or you might run into the U.S. Cavalry.

The only chance you had to meet the one you loved was to wait for her at daybreak when the young girls went to the river or brook with their skin bags to fetch water. Doing that was their job. So, when the girl you had your eye on finally came down the water trail, you popped up from behind some bush, and stood so that she could see you——and that was about all you could do to show her that you were interested——stand there grinning foolishly, looking at your moccasins, scratching your ear, humming a tune.

The wincincala didn't do much either, except get very red in the face, giggle, fiddle with her waterbag, or maybe throw you a wild turnip. The only way she could let you know that she liked you, too, was for her to take a long, long while to do her job, looking back over her shoulder a few times, to peek at you.

So the flutes did all the talking. At night, lying on her buffalo robe in her father's tipi, the girl would hear the soulful, haunting sound of the Siyotanka. She would hear the tune made up especially for her alone, and she would know that out there in the dark a young man was thinking about her.

Well, here I am supposed to relate a legend and instead I am telling you a love story. You see, in all tribes, the flute is used as an expression of a young man's love. It has always been so. And whether it is Sioux, or Pawnee, or Cheyenne, or Shoshone, the flute is always made of cedar wood and shaped like the long neck and the head of a bird with an open beak. The sound comes out of the beak. There is a reason for this, and that's where the legend comes in.

Once, untold generations ago, the people did not know how to make flutes. Drums, rattles, bull-roarers, yes——but no flutes. In these long-past days, before the white man came with his horse and firestick, a young hunter went out after game. Meat was scarce, and the people in his village were hungry. He found the tracks of an elk and followed them for a long time. The elk is wise and swift. It is the animal that possesses the love-charm. If a man has elk medicine, he will win the one he loves for his wife. He will also be a lucky hunter.

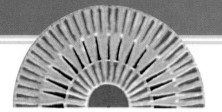

Our poor young man had no elk medicine. After many hours, he finally sighted his game. The young hunter had a fine new bow and a quiver made of otterskin full of good, straight arrows tipped with points of obsidian——sharp, black, and shiny like glass. The young man knew how to use his weapon——he was the best shot in the village——but the elk always managed to stay just out of range, leading the hunter on and on. The young man was so intent on following his prey that he hardly took notice of where he went.

At dusk the hunter found himself deep inside a dense forest of tall trees. The tracks had disappeared, and so had the elk. The young man had to face the fact that he was lost and that it was now too dark to find his way out of the forest. There was not even a moon to show him the way. Luckily, he found a stream with clear, cold water to quench his thirst. Still more luckily, his sister had given him a rawhide bag to take along, filled with *wasna*——pemmican——dried meat pounded together with berries and kidney fat. Sweet, strong wasna——a handful of it will keep a man going for a day or more. After the young man had drunk and eaten, he rolled himself into his fur robe, propped his back against a tree, and tried to get some rest. But he could not sleep. The forest was full of strange noises——the eerie cries of night animals, the hooting of owls, the groaning of trees in the wind. He had heard all these sounds before, but now it seemed as if he were hearing them for the first time. Suddenly there was an entirely new sound, the kind neither he nor any other man had ever experienced before.

It was very mournful, sad, and ghostlike. In a way it made him afraid, so he drew his robe tightly about him and reached for his bow, to make sure that it was properly strung. On the other hand, this new sound was like a song, beautiful beyond imagination, full of love, hope, and yearning. And then, before he knew it, and with the night more than half gone, he was suddenly asleep. He dreamed that a bird called *Wagnuka*, the redheaded woodpecker, appeared to him, singing the strangely beautiful new song, saying, "Follow me and I will teach you."

When the young hunter awoke, the sun was already high, and on a branch of the tree against which he was leaning was a redheaded woodpecker. The bird flew away to another tree and then to another, but never very far, looking all the time over its shoulder at the young man as if to say "Come on!" Then, once more the hunter heard that wonderful song, and his heart yearned to find the singer. The bird flew toward the sound, leading the young man, its flaming red top flitting through the leaves, making it easy to follow. At last the bird alighted on a cedar tree and began tapping and hammering on a dead branch, making a noise like the fast beating of a small drum. Suddenly there was a gust of wind, and again the hunter heard that beautiful sound right close by and above him.

Then he discovered that the song came from the dead branch which the woodpecker was belaboring with its beak. He found, moreover, that it was the wind which made the sound as it whistled through the holes the bird had drilled into the branch. "*Kola*, friend," said the hunter, "let me take this branch home. You can make yourself another one." He took the branch, a hollow piece of wood about the length of his forearm, and full of holes. The young man walked back to his village. He had no meat to bring to his tribe, but he was happy all the same.

Back in his tipi, he tried to make the dead branch sing for him. He blew on it, he waved it around——but no sound came. It made the young man sad. He wanted so much to hear that wonderful sound. He purified himself in the sweat lodge and climbed to the top of a lonely hill. There, naked, resting with his back against a large rock, he fasted for four days and four nights, crying for a dream, a vision to teach him how to make the branch sing. In the middle of the fourth night, Wagnuka, the bird with the flaming red spot on his head, appeared to him, saying, "Watch me." The bird turned into a man, doing this and that, always saying, "Watch me!" And in his vision the young man watched——very carefully.

When he awoke he found a cedar tree. He broke off a branch, and working many hours hollowed it out delicately with a bowstring drill, just as he had seen Wagnuka do it in his vision. He whittled the branch into a shape of a bird with a long neck and an open beak. He painted the top of the bird's head red with *washasha*, the sacred vermilion color. He prayed. He smoked the branch with incense of burning sage and sweet grass. He fingered the holes as he had watched it done in his dream, all the while blowing softly into the end of his flute. Because this is what he had made——the first flute, the very first *Siyotanka*. And all at once there was the song, ghostlike and beautiful beyond words, and all the people were astounded and joyful.

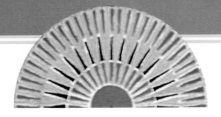

In the village lived an *itancan,* a big and powerful chief. This itancan had a daughter who was beautiful, but also very haughty. Many young men had tried to win her love, but she had turned them all away. Thinking of her, the young man made up a special song, a song that would make this proud wincincala fall in love with him. Standing near a tall tree a little way from the village, he blew his flute.

All at once the wincincala heard it. She was sitting in her father's, the chief's, tipi, feasting on much good meat. She wanted to remain sitting there, but her feet wanted to go outside; and the feet won. Her head said, "Go slow, slow," but her feet said, "Faster, faster." In no time at all she stood next to the young man. Her mind ordered her lips to stay closed, but her heart commanded them to open. Her heart told her tongue to speak.

"Koshkalaka, washtelake," she said. "Young man, I like you." Then she said, "Let your parents send a gift to my father. No matter how small, it will be accepted. Let your father speak for you to my father. Do it soon, right now!"

And so the old folks agreed according to the wishes of their children, and the chief's daughter became the young hunter's wife. All the other young men had heard and seen how it came about. Soon they, too, began to whittle cedar branches into the shapes of birds' heads with long necks and open beaks, and the beautiful haunting sound of flutes traveled from tribe to tribe until it filled the whole prairie. And that is how Siyotanka the flute came to be—— thanks to the cedar, the woodpecker, the wind, and one young hunter who shot no elk but who knew how to listen.

The Sound of Flutes

Meet the Storyteller

Henry Crow Dog, a Plains Indian, did not write *The Sound of Flutes*. It is a Native American legend that has been handed down through several generations of his people. Henry Crow Dog told this legend and others to a friend who wrote them down. The legends have been collected in a book called *The Sound of Flutes and Other Indian Legends*.

Meet the Illustrator

Paul Goble is a writer and illustrator of Native American books. He was raised in England with a love of the outdoors. As a child Goble enjoyed drawing and hearing stories about pirates, wildlife, and Native Americans. Still interested in Native Americans as an adult, he took his son to the United States to visit Sioux, Crow, and Shoshoni reservations. Goble believes television and movies may give children mistaken ideas about Native Americans. He decided to write and illustrate children's books so he could tell young people what Native American life was really like. Goble now lives in the Black Hills of South Dakota and is an adopted member of the Sioux and Yakima tribes.

Theme Connections

Within the Selection

Record your answers to the questions below in the Response Journal section of your Writer's Notebook. In small groups, report the ideas you wrote. Discuss your ideas with the rest of your group. Then choose a person to report your group's answers to the class.

- Why would young Native American men sit up at night composing songs?
- Where was the sound in the forest coming from?
- What did the young man do in order to learn to make a flute himself?

Across the Selections

- How is "The Sound of Flutes" similar to "What Is an Orchestra?" How is it different? Explain.
- As you saw in "The Nightingale," music can have an uplifting effect on people. How did you see this kind of effect in "The Sound of Flutes"? How was this effect similar to the one in "The Nightingale"?

Beyond the Selection

- The narrator in "The Sound of Flutes" says that flute music has always been love music for Native Americans. Now consider your own experience. What types of music can you think of that are associated with particular emotions? Why do you think these associations exist? Take a few minutes and jot down your thoughts, then be prepared to share them with the class.

Focus Questions Why does music evoke memories of other times and places? How does the poem suggest homesickness?

On Hearing a Flute at Night from the Wall of Shou-Hsiang

Li Yi

translated by Witter Bynner

illustrated by Cheryl Kirk Noll

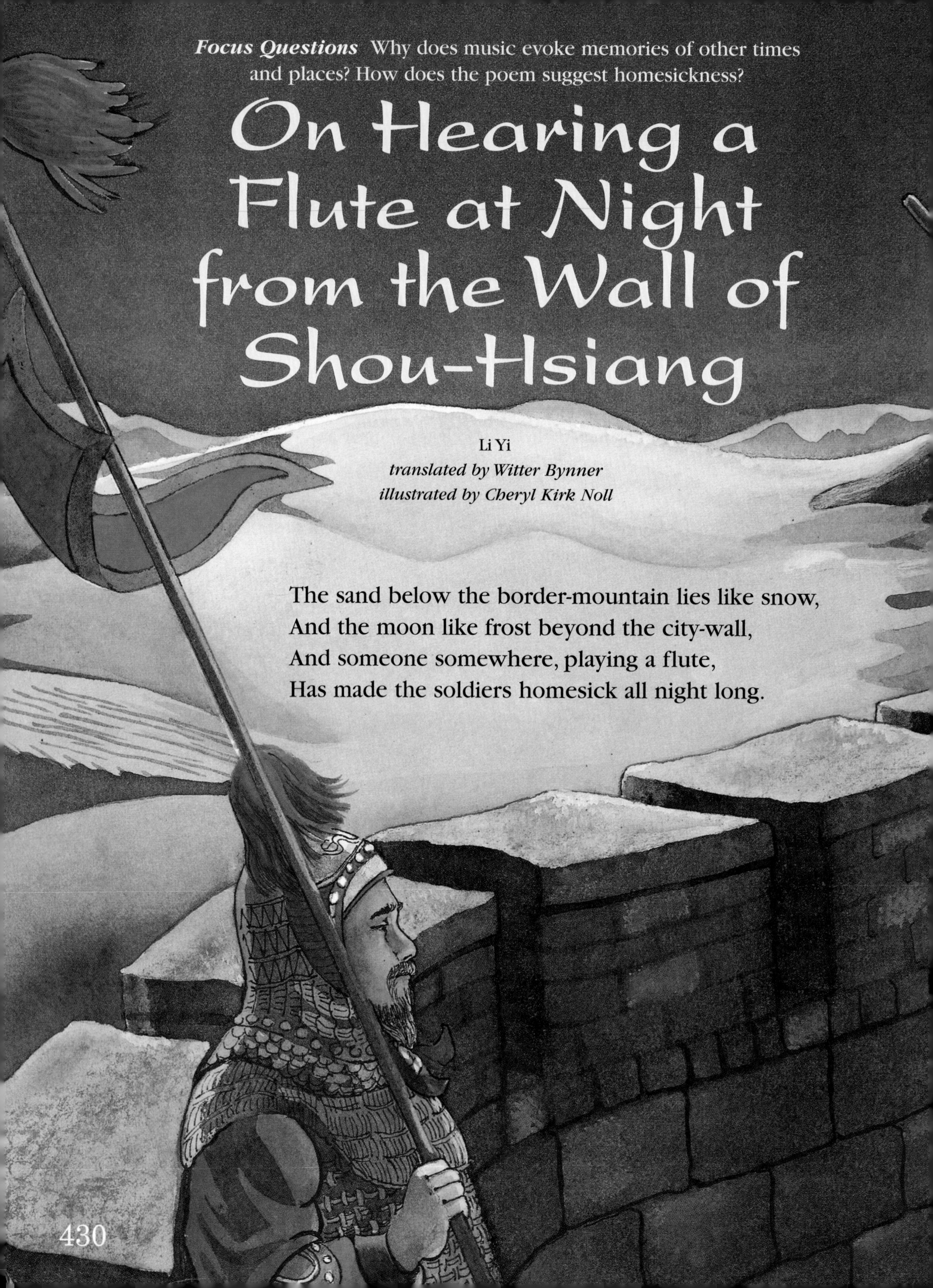

The sand below the border-mountain lies like snow,
And the moon like frost beyond the city-wall,
And someone somewhere, playing a flute,
Has made the soldiers homesick all night long.

Focus Questions How can a child's love of music be encouraged? How is Ray Charles's life influenced by music?

Ray, and Mr. Pit

from *Brother Ray: Ray Charles'*
Own Story by Ray Charles and David Ritz

Ray Charles was born in Albany, Georgia, in 1930, and spent his boyhood in the little town of Greensville, Florida. When he was five, he began to lose his sight. He was blind by the age of seven. Ray Charles has never let his blindness interfere with his passion for music, and he began performing while still a teenager. His music is often called rhythm and blues, but he embraces many forms——from country-and-western to old-fashioned ballads——fashioning them with his unique style.

And then there was music. I heard it early, just as soon as I was seeing or talking or walking. It was always there——all shapes, all kinds, all rhythms. Music was the only thing I was really anxious to get out of bed for.

I was born with music inside me. That's the only explanation I know of, since none of my relatives could sing or play an instrument. Music was one of my parts. Like my ribs, my liver, my kidneys, my heart. Like my blood. It was a force already within me when I arrived on the scene. It was a necessity for me——like food or water. And from the moment I learned that there were piano keys to be mashed, I started mashing 'em, trying to make sounds out of feelings.

Sometimes I'm asked about my biggest musical influence as a kid. I always give one name: Mr. Wylie Pitman. I called him Mr. Pit.

Now you won't find Mr. Pit in any history of jazz . . . but you can take my word for it: Mr. Pit could play some sure-enough boogie-woogie piano. And best of all, he lived down the road from us.

Red Wing Café. I can see the big ol' red sign smack in front of me right now. That was Mr. Pit's place. It was a little general store where he and his wife, Miss Georgia, sold items like soda water, beer, candies, cakes, cigarettes, and kerosene. Mr. Pit also rented out rooms.

Mama and me were always welcome there and, in fact, during one period when we were really down and out, we lived at the Red Wing Café for a while.

Mr. Pit's place was the center of the black community in Greensville, and when you walked into the café you saw two things——right off—— which shaped me for the rest of my life.

Talkin' 'bout a piano and a jukebox.

433

Oh, that piano! It was an old, beat-up upright and the most wonderful contraption I had ever laid eyes on. Boogie-woogie was hot then, and it was the first style I was exposed to. Mr. Pit played with the best of them. He just wasn't interested in a musical career; if he had been, I know he would have made it big. He just wanted to stay in Greensville and lead a simple life.

Well, one day when Mr. Pit started to playing, I waddled on up to the piano and just stared. It astonished and amazed me——his fingers flying, all those chords coming together, the sounds jumping at me and ringing in my ears.

You'd think an older cat would be put off by this young kid hangin' round. Not Mr. Pit. Maybe that's 'cause he and Miss Georgia didn't have children of their own. But for whatever reasons, the man treated me like a son; he lifted me on the stool and put me right there on his lap. Then he let me run my fingers up and down the keyboard. That was a good feeling, and forty-five years later, it still feels good.

I tried to figure out how he could make all those notes come together. I was a baby, but I was trying to invent some boogie-woogie licks of my own.

Some days I'd be out in the yard back of the house. If I heard Mr. Pit knocking out some of that good boogie-woogie, I'd drop what I was doing and run over to his place. The man always let me play.

"That's it, sonny! That's it!" he'd scream, encouraging me like I was his student or his son.

He saw I was willing to give up my playing time for the piano, so I guess he figured I loved music as much as he did. And all this was happening when I was only three.

I couldn't spend enough time with that gentleman. I was there for hours——sitting on his lap, watching him play or trying to play myself. He was a patient and loving man who never tired of me.

"Come over here, boy, and see what you can do with this pie-ano," he'd say, always helpful, always anxious to teach me something new. And when I look back now, I know he saw something in me, felt something in me, which brought out the teacher in him.

The jukebox was the other wonder. There was a long bench at Mr. Pit's place, and I had my special place, right at the end, smack against the loudspeaker. That's where I would sit for hours, enthralled by the different sounds.

Ray,
and
Mr. Pit

Meet the Authors

Ray Charles is a popular singer, pianist, and songwriter. He was born Ray Charles Robinson, September 30, 1930, in Albany, Georgia. "I was born with music inside me. From the moment I learned that there were piano keys to be mashed, I started mashing them." When he became a performer he dropped his last name because his name was so similar to that of the boxer, Sugar Ray Robinson. Charles is best known for performing soul music, although he has also had success with country-and-western music and rhythm and blues. Charles has said, "I look at music the same as I look at my bloodstream, my respiratory system, my lungs. It's something I have to do."

David Ritz was born in New York City. He is married to Roberta Plitt, a comedienne, and they have twin daughters. Ritz has worked as a copywriter, writer, and teacher.

Theme Connections

Within the Selection

Record your answers to the questions below in the Response Journal section of your Writer's Notebook. In small groups, report the ideas you wrote. Discuss your ideas with the rest of your group. Then choose a person to report your group's answers to the class.

- Why did Ray Charles devote his life to music?
- Ray Charles says that when he was a boy Mr. Pit was his greatest musical influence. Why?
- Why does Ray Charles think Mr. Pit took an interest in him?

Across the Selections

- Ray Charles says that his musical ability is simply part of who he is and likens it to an extra body part. How would you compare Ray Charles's description of himself with the nightingale you read about earlier in this unit? Would you say that what is true of Ray Charles is also true of the nightingale? Why?
- In "The Sound of Flutes," you read about how a young hunter was attracted to a sound he heard in the woods. How would you compare the reaction of the hunter to the reaction of Ray Charles on hearing Mr. Pit play the piano?

Beyond the Selection

- Think about how "Ray and Mr. Pit" adds to what you know about music.
- Add items to the Concept/Question Board about music.

What Is Jazz?

Mary L. O'Neill
illustrated by Eric Velasquez

Jazz is a swoony
Syncopated beat
In through the eardrums
Out through the feet.
Rackety, coaxie,
Blast that beat
Whop it sassy
Sound it sweet
Clap, stomp, shout,
Blow surprise,
Shoot that trumpet
Till it cries
All the teardrops
In your eyes . . .

438

The Weary Blues

Langston Hughes • *illustrated by Eric Velasquez*

Droning a drowsy syncopated tune,
Rocking back and forth to a mellow croon,
   I heard a Negro play.
Down on Lenox Avenue the other night
By the pale dull pallor of an old gas light
   He did a lazy sway. . . .
   He did a lazy sway. . . .
To the tune o' those Weary Blues.
With his ebony hands on each ivory key
He made that poor piano moan with melody.
   O Blues!
Swaying to and fro on his rickety stool
He played that sad raggy tune like a musical fool.
   Sweet Blues!
Coming from a black man's soul.
   O Blues!
In a deep song voice with a melancholy tone
I heard that Negro sing, that old piano moan——
   "Ain't got nobody in all this world,
   Ain't got nobody but maself.
   I's gwine to quit ma frownin'
   And put ma troubles on the shelf."
Thump, thump, thump, went his foot on the floor.
He played a few chords then he sang some more——
   "I got the Weary Blues
   And I can't be satisfied.
   Got the Weary Blues
   And can't be satisfied——
   I ain't happy no mo'
   And I wish that I had died."
And far into the night he crooned that tune.
The stars went out and so did the moon.
The singer stopped playing and went to bed
While the Weary Blues echoed through his head.
He slept like a rock or a man that's dead.

439

BEETHOVEN LIVES UPSTAIRS

Barbara Nichol
illustrated by Scott Cameron

On Thursday, March 29, 1827, the people of Vienna flooded into
the streets. They came to pay their respects to Ludwig van Beethoven,
the great composer, who had died three days earlier.

At three o'clock in the afternoon nine priests blessed the coffin, and
the funeral procession left Mr. Beethoven's house for the church. So dense
were the crowds that the one-block journey took an hour and a half.

I wasn't in Vienna on that famous day. I was a student of music in
Salzburg at the time. But if you had looked carefully, you might have
spotted in the crowd a little boy with a serious face. He is Christoph, my
nephew, and there was a time when he came to know
Mr. Beethoven quite well.

It was not a happy time in Christoph's life.
He was only ten years old, and his father had recently died.

The first of Christoph's letters arrived at my door in the autumn
of 1822. I was surprised that he had written. I had not seen
my nephew for some years. . . .

7 September 1822

Dear Uncle,

I hope you will remember me. It is Christoph, your nephew, who writes. As to the reasons, I will not keep you in suspense. I write, Uncle, because something terrible has happened. A madman has moved into our house.

Do you remember that when Father died, Mother decided to rent out his office upstairs? Well, she has done it, and Ludwig van Beethoven has moved in.

Every morning at dawn Mr. Beethoven begins to make his dreadful noise upstairs. Loud poundings and howlings come through the floor. They are like the sounds of an injured beast. All morning Mr. Beethoven carries on this way. After lunch he storms into the street. He comes home, sometimes long after the house is quiet for the night, tracking mud and stamping his way up the stairs above our heads.

Mother says I mustn't blame him. He's deaf and can't hear the noise he makes. But he wakes up the twins, and they start their crying. They cry all day.

Uncle, I must make this one request. I beg you to tell my mother to send Mr. Beethoven away.

Your nephew,
Christoph

10 October 1822

My dear Christoph,

I arrived home last night to find your letter on the table in the hall. Do I remember you? Of course I do!

I should tell you that I have received a letter from your mother as well. As you know, she is concerned about you and wants you to be happy. She assures me that Mr. Beethoven is peculiar perhaps, but certainly not mad.

Christoph, Mr. Beethoven will settle in soon, I'm sure. I know that life will be more peaceful before long.

Your uncle,
Karl

Having answered my nephew's letter, I left Salzburg for some weeks on matters related to my studies. In truth, I expected no further messages. The three letters that follow arrived in my absence.

22 October 1822

Dear Uncle,

I hope you will forgive my troubling you, but I am sure that you will want to hear this news. Our family is now the laughingstock of Vienna.

I opened the door this morning to find a crowd in front of our house. They were looking up at Mr. Beethoven's window and laughing, so I looked up too. There was Mr. Beethoven, staring at a sheet of music. And Uncle, he had no clothes on at all! It was a dreadful sight!

You should see him setting out for the afternoon. He hums to himself.

He growls out tunes. He waves his arms. His pockets bulge with papers and pencils. On the street the children run and call him names.

Mr. Beethoven is so famous that sometimes people stop outside our house, hoping they will see him. But if anyone asks, I say he has moved away.

Your nephew,
Christoph

29 October 1822

Dear Uncle,

I have now seen with my own eyes that Mr. Beethoven is mad. I will tell you the story in the hope that you will do something at last.

Last night, when I was getting ready for bed, I happened to look up. There were beads of water collecting on the ceiling above my head.

As usual, Mother was busy with the twins, so I climbed the stairs and crept along the hall to Mr. Beethoven's room. I looked in. He was standing there with no shirt on. He had a jug of water in his hands. He was pouring the water over his head, right there in the middle of the room, and all this time stamping his feet like he was marching or listening to a song.

You should see my father's study! Do you remember how tidy he was? Well, now there are papers lying everywhere—on the floor, on the chairs, on the bed that isn't made. There are dirty dishes stacked up and clothing crumpled on the floor. And another thing, he has been writing on the wall with a pencil!

I said nothing to Mr. Beethoven, of course. Luckily, he did not see me, and I ran back down the stairs.

Uncle, if you are thinking of coming to our aid, there could be no better time than now.

Christoph

5 November 1822

Dear Uncle,

Another week has passed, but life is no calmer here.

I've been thinking. If Mr. Beethoven were to leave, surely we could find someone nice to live upstairs. The rooms are large, and Father's patients always talked about the view of the river. Father used to carry me down to the riverbank on his shoulders, even down the steep part right behind the house.

I think that of all the places in the house, I like the outside best. I can be alone there and get away from all the noise inside. But on this day even the stray dog outside was making his pitiful voice heard.

Yours truly,
Christoph

22 November 1822

My dear Christoph,

Today I have returned home from a visit away to find three of your letters waiting. Christoph, I will admit that Mr. Beethoven does not seem to be an easy guest.

Perhaps I can help, though, by saying that as strange as Mr. Beethoven seems, there are reasons for the way he acts.

They say he is working on a symphony. And so, all day long, he is hearing his music in his head. He doesn't think, perhaps, how very strange he sometimes seems to us.

Tomorrow I am leaving Salzburg again and traveling with friends to Bonn, the city where Mr. Beethoven was born. I know I will find something to tell you about and I will be sure to write on my return.

Uncle Karl

10 December 1822

Dear Uncle,

It has now been a full three months since Mr. Beethoven moved in, but our household has not yet become like any sort of ordinary place.

Mr. Beethoven has a friend named Mr. Schindler who visits almost every day. He always says, "Poor Mr. Beethoven. He is a lonely man."

You know that Mr. Beethoven is deaf. When he has visitors, they write what they want to say in a book. He reads their message and answers them out loud. He has a low and fuzzy voice.

Mr. Beethoven's eyes are weak as well. When he works too long by candlelight, his eyes begin to ache. He sometimes sits alone, with a cloth wrapped around his head to keep out the light. He sits, not seeing and not hearing, in his chair.

Uncle, there is no hour of the day when I forget that Mr. Beethoven is in the house.

Your nephew,
Christoph

I returned to Salzburg in late January of 1823.

22 January 1823

Dear Christoph,

I have this very day returned from the place where Mr. Beethoven was born. It seems his family is well remembered there.

They say Mr. Beethoven's grandfather was a musician, in charge of all the music at the palace. And Mr. Beethoven's father was a musician, too. But Christoph, this father was an unhappy man who took to drink. Mr. Beethoven was not a happy child.

People who lived near their house remember hearing music coming from the attic late at night. Sometimes Mr. Beethoven's father would come home long after dark and get the young boy out of bed. He would make him practice his piano until dawn.

The little Beethoven would play all night, tired and cold, his face awash with tears. Finally, as the sun came up, he would go to bed to the sound of morning bells.

I will send this letter right away, in the hope that you will answer soon.

Affectionately,
Uncle

445

4 February 1823

Dear Uncle,

This afternoon a messenger arrived, bearing a note for Mr. Beethoven.

The messenger said to me, "This is from Prince Karl Lichnowsky. But the prince says that if Mr. Beethoven's door is closed, he is not to be disturbed."

Mr. Beethoven must be a terrible man if even a prince is afraid of him.

Your nephew,
Christoph

15 February 1823

Dear Christoph,

I've been thinking of your story about the prince. Christoph, I don't think the prince is afraid of Mr. Beethoven. I believe he is showing him respect. In Vienna, music is so loved that even a prince will tread carefully around a composer.

Alas, Mr. Beethoven has not returned their kindness. He has not been gentle with the fine people of Vienna, and they have done everything they can to please him. Mr. Beethoven has always had rough manners. He turns down their invitations, dresses carelessly to visit, and arrives late for their dinners.

Sometimes he is very angry if he is asked to play his music. There is one famous story of a grand lady who got down on her knees one evening to beg Mr. Beethoven to play. He refused.

And there is another tale about a prince who teased Mr. Beethoven for not playing at dinner. Mr. Beethoven flew into a rage. "There are many princes," he said, "but there is only one Beethoven."

My belief, Christoph, is that a prince has more to fear from Mr. Beethoven than has a little boy.

Affectionately,
Uncle

26 February 1823

Dear Uncle,

    No news today but this—do you remember I once told you about a stray dog who was whining on the street? He is a small and spotted dog, and I have found a way to make him stop his crying.

    Today he seemed quite pleased to share my sugar cake from lunch.

                                       Christoph

2 March 1823

Dear Christoph,

I write again so soon because I have been making inquiries on your behalf.

I spoke today with a man who once worked for Mr. Beethoven, copying out music for the players. He told me that Mr. Beethoven never stays in one home very long. He moves often—as often as three times a year.

Sometimes Mr. Beethoven wants a sunnier home, sometimes shadier. Sometimes he says he cannot live on the ground floor; then he cannot live on the top. And I hear he has been asked to leave from time to time as well.

He has a restless nature, so perhaps before too long you will have your wish and quieter people will be living upstairs.

But in the meantime, tell me . . . is it true, as I have also heard, that Mr. Beethoven has three pianos in his room?

Your uncle

Dear Uncle,

No, it is not true that Mr. Beethoven has three pianos. He has four! And you should see them! To begin with, some of his pianos have no legs. He takes the legs off to move them and so that he can play them when he is sitting on the floor. That way he can feel his playing through the floorboards, which he must do because, of course, he cannot hear.

But it's surprising that his pianos can be played at all. Many of the strings are broken and curled up. They look like birds' nests made of wire. And the pianos are stained inside from the times he's knocked the inkwell with his sleeve.

And Mr. Beethoven has all sorts of bells on his desk, and four ear trumpets to help him hear, and something called a metronome as well. It's a little box with a stick on it. The stick goes back and forth and back and forth and tells musicians how fast they should play.

Mr. Beethoven has a name for me. He calls me "the little gatekeeper" because I am always sitting outside on the step.

Yours truly,
Christoph
Gatekeeper

2 April 1823

Dear Christoph,

Your letter about Mr. Beethoven's piano has reminded me that there was a time when Mr. Beethoven was more famous for his playing than his composing.

When Mr. Beethoven first lived in Vienna, he would sit down with orchestras to play his music, without a single note written out. It was all in his head.

And the music he played! His music was so beautiful that sometimes people who were listening would start to cry. But Mr. Beethoven would laugh at them and say, "Composers do not cry. Composers are made of fire."

Now that Mr. Beethoven is deaf, of course, he plays the piano with the bumps and crashes you hear upstairs all day.

And I have another story for you, a story people tell about his deafness. One afternoon Mr. Beethoven was out walking in the woods with a friend. A shepherd was playing a flute nearby. Mr. Beethoven's friend said, "Listen!" and stopped to hear the flute. But Mr. Beethoven heard nothing. And so he knew, that day, that he was going deaf.

When Mr. Beethoven was still a young man, he began to hear humming and buzzing in his ears. At first he couldn't hear high notes. Then he couldn't hear soft voices. How frightening it must have been for him, Christoph, and how alone that man who lives upstairs must feel.

To hear Mr. Beethoven's story convinces me that I am the most fortunate man alive.

Your uncle

21 April 1823

Dear Uncle,

Do you remember my telling you that Mr. Beethoven leaves each afternoon for a walk? Did you wonder where he goes? Well, now I know, and I will tell you the story.

Mother sometimes says that instead of just staying on the front steps it would be nice if I'd spend some time inside. I used to believe she meant it until this morning.

I thought of something to play with the twins. I rolled up a bit of cardboard like an ear trumpet and put one end in little Teresa's ear. I said, "GOOD MORNING, BABY!" very loudly, and she started to scream. Mother said it hurt her. So I went outside again and sat in my usual place on the step.

Then Mr. Schindler came downstairs. He said to me, "The master needs new pencils," and off I went to the shop.

When I came back, Mr. Schindler was gone. No one was upstairs but Mr. Beethoven, and he was writing at his desk. I stamped my feet on the floor to get his attention and when he didn't notice I stamped harder until at last I was stamping as hard as I could. Then suddenly he turned around and saw me. When he laughs, he sounds like a lion.

So today I went along with him on his walk. At times Mr. Beethoven forgot that I was with him. He would hum and sometimes wave his arms. He took out his papers and made some little notes.

We walked outside Vienna into the tall woods and then past the woods and into the fields. Uncle, if you were to come to visit me, I would show you where we walked today.

Christoph

In July of 1823 the following note arrived, unfinished and unsigned. Christoph was preoccupied, I suspect, by the pleasures of summertime and was too busy for letter writing. The note was sent to me by his mother, included in a letter of her own.

30 June 1823

Dear Uncle,

   Spring has come and gone, and now it is summer. The house is quiet because tonight Mr. Beethoven has gone to Baden, where he will spend the hottest months. He will finish his symphony and then he will come back.

   Tonight as I write you it is evening, but I cannot sleep with the sun still shining through the shutters. From my room I can hear Mother playing piano as she used to when I was small.

   I have been sitting here thinking about something Mr. Schindler said. He said, "Mr. Beethoven works so hard because he believes that music can change the world."

In the autumn of 1823 Mr. Beethoven returned
to Vienna from his summer lodgings.

29 October 1823

Dear Uncle,

Mr. Beethoven has come home, and so our house is in an uproar again. Someone has given him another piano, and there was a lot of trouble getting it up the stairs.

And then last night he had a party. A lot of people went in and out very late, and the more cheerful they became upstairs, the noisier it was for us.

Finally, it was impossible to sleep. I could hear two ladies singing. I had seen them earlier, laughing on the stairs. They are called sopranos because they are singers who can sing very high.

Mr. Beethoven has a housekeeper. She says that when the sopranos come up the stairs, Mr. Beethoven rushes like a schoolboy to change his coat. And he won't let her make the coffee for them. It must be perfect, with exactly sixty beans for every cup. He counts them himself.

Uncle, I have asked Mother if you can come to visit. She said she would be delighted if you would. She thinks you would enjoy the goings-on.

Christoph

4 January 1824

Dear Christoph,

How glad I was to receive your letter. I hope you will forgive my very late reply. Did you know that your mother has written to me as well? She tells me there's a steady stream of great musicians up and down your stairs.

Since Mr. Beethoven is writing his Ninth Symphony in your very house, perhaps you will be interested in the things I have heard. According to the stories, Mr. Beethoven has felt that he is not appreciated in Vienna. He almost agreed to perform his new symphony in Berlin! I'm happy to say, though, that so many people begged Mr. Beethoven to change his mind that, luckily, he did.

And there is other news: they say the orchestra members are complaining about their parts. The bass players say their instruments aren't nimble enough for Mr. Beethoven's quick notes. The sopranos say their notes are just too high. All over Vienna the musicians are struggling with their tasks. His symphony will put to music the poem "Ode to Joy."

I hear as well that because Mr. Beethoven is deaf, he will lead the orchestra with another conductor—one who can hear—conducting alongside him.

Amid these great events, little gatekeeper, how is life at home? Do your twin sisters still torment you with their terrible shouts? Perhaps before too long I shall hear them for myself.

Uncle Karl

453

27 March 1824

Dear Uncle,

I know this will come as a surprise, but this time I write you with good news.

I was standing on the upstairs landing today when my favorite soprano came by to get tickets for the concert. At least she is now my favorite.

She had something to ask of Mr. Beethoven and she wrote her request in his book. Then she wrote another request, handed him the book, and winked at me.

He read her words and said, "Certainly. The boy and his mother will have tickets as well."

And so Mother and I will be going to the Ninth Symphony. I wrote "thank you" as neatly as I could in his book.

As for the twins, Uncle, of course they still torment me. It is what they were put on earth to do.

Now I have a new name for my sisters. I call them "the sopranos." It makes my mother laugh.

Yours truly,
Christoph

Dear Uncle,

I know now that all of us have been quite happy of late. And the way I know it is that in the past few days our happiness has vanished once again. With the symphony just two weeks away, Mr. Beethoven's moods are fierce.

Caroline, his housekeeper, is going to leave to marry the baker next door. She told Mr. Beethoven today, and he became very angry. He picked up an egg and threw it at her.

Then Mr. Schindler came rushing down the stairs like a scalded cat. He had told Mr. Beethoven that his new coat won't be ready for the concert in time. He tried to talk to Mr. Beethoven about another coat but, as Mr. Schindler said, "The master is in no mood for details."

And I have not helped matters. Today, when I was in his room, I disturbed some of his papers as I was passing by his desk. They fluttered to the floor. I am afraid these papers had been ordered in some very special way because Mr. Beethoven said, "Now I must do work again that I have already done."

Uncle, just when life was getting better, I have ruined things again.

Your nephew

28 April 1824

My dearest Christoph,

How shall I console you? Perhaps by telling you that Mr. Beethoven is famous for his temper and that his moods are not your fault.

Imagine how frustrating his life must be. Imagine how lonely to hear no voices. Imagine hearing no birds sing, no wind in the trees, no pealing of bells. Imagine: he hears no music played, not even his own!

So Mr. Beethoven has a great temper. How could he not? But if you listen to his music, you will hear that his heart is great as well, too great to be angry for long at an innocent boy.

You write me that, for the moment, your happiness has vanished. I can give you my promise, Christoph, that unhappiness has a way of vanishing as well.

Your uncle and friend,
Karl

455

The unsigned and undated note below was written in May of 1824, on the eve of the first performance of the Ninth Symphony. It arrived tucked into the letter that follows it.

Dear Uncle,

Mr. Beethoven has forgotten the incident with the papers. He squeezed my shoulder in a friendly way when he passed me in the hall this afternoon.

Now the house is quiet, and I am alone. The concert is tomorrow night, and so, of course, I cannot sleep. I think of Mr. Beethoven alone upstairs. I have not heard him stir for quite some time. I wonder what he's thinking about. I wonder if he's awake tonight like me.

Perhaps he is hearing something beautiful in his head.

7 May 1824

Dear Uncle,

Tonight I have been to the Ninth Symphony. It is very late. I have already tried to sleep, but it seems I cannot do so before I describe this night to you.

The concert looked as I expected. There was Mr. Beethoven on the stage, waving his arms as I have seen him do so many times upstairs. And there were the singers. I had seen them often too, tramping up and down our halls. And there were the musicians scowling at their charts. These sights were so familiar.

It was the music, Uncle, that took me by surprise.

And when the music ended, the audience was on its feet. Everyone was standing and cheering and clapping and waving scarves and crying and trying to make Mr. Beethoven hear them.

But he couldn't hear us and he didn't know that we were cheering until one of the sopranos took his sleeve and turned him to face the crowd. Four times the audience finished their clapping and then began to clap and cheer again. Up on the stage Mr. Beethoven bowed and bowed.

As the carriage took us home, I could hear the music in my head. But my thoughts kept turning back to Mr. Beethoven himself.

He has so many troubles, how can he have a heart so full of joy?

I cannot describe the music, Uncle. I can only tell you what the music made me think.

Uncle, how difficult Mr. Beethoven's life must be. To feel so much inside, even so much joy, must be almost more than he can bear.

Christoph

457

In June of 1824 I finally paid a visit to Vienna, to the home of my sister, her twin girls, and Christoph. It was Christoph, of course, who took the most delight in explaining the many eccentricities of the genius up the stairs. This letter, the final portion of which is now missing, is the last in which my nephew mentions Mr. Beethoven. It arrived at my home in Salzburg almost a year after my visit to Vienna.

31 March 1825

Dear Uncle,

As you know, Mr. Beethoven moved away soon after your visit. But I have seen him again and thought you might like to hear about it.

It was on the street. I saw him rushing by, humming to himself as always. I ran up and caught him by the sleeve. He looked confused at first, but then he recognized me. He said, "It's the little gatekeeper," and took my hands in his.

I took his book and asked if he was well. He had hoped his health would be better living away from the river. He told me his health has not improved. I wrote in his book that when I grow up I'm going to be a doctor like my father and then I will make him better.

He asked about Mother and the twins, and he was glad to hear that Mother is teaching piano again. And then I told him that we miss him. He squeezed my hands and looked down at the ground.

And as for other news, the twins have finally stopped their screaming. I know, however, that our good luck will not hold. I have seen them exchanging looks in their carriage and can see that they are hatching some new plan.

But Uncle! Best of all! Mother has agreed to let me keep the spotted dog. I have named him Metronome, because of his wagging tail.

BEETHOVEN LIVES UPSTAIRS

Meet the Author

Barbara Nichol lives in Toronto, Canada. Although she is best known for the numerous television dramas she has written, her humorous fiction has also appeared in magazines and books. Nichol is the director and author of the original cassette/CD of *Beethoven Lives Upstairs*.

Meet the Illustrator

Scott Cameron grew up in a forested section of Ontario, Canada. He feels the trees, squirrels, raccoons, rabbits and other plants and animals helped to shape his work. He says, *"When I look around I see bushes and vines, tall grass and tangled branches, everything that has a shaggy roughness to it."* The natural beauty that surrounds Cameron is apparent in his illustrations.

The original "Beethoven Lives Upstairs" audio cassette and compact disc, featuring dramatic storytelling, rich sound effects and more than 24 excerpts of the composer's music was written and directed by Barbara Nichol and produced by Susan Hammond's Classical Kids. "Beethoven Lives Upstairs" is published by The Children's Group Inc.
www.childrensgroup.com

Theme Connections

Within the Selection

Writer's Notebook Record your answers to the questions below in the Response Journal section of your Writer's Notebook. In small groups, report the ideas you wrote. Discuss your ideas with the rest of your group. Then choose a person to report your group's answers to the class.

- Why does Christoph write that he wishes Beethoven did not live upstairs?
- Why did Beethoven remove the legs from his pianos and rest them on the floor?
- According to Christoph's uncle, when did Beethoven first notice he was going deaf?

Across the Selections

- Beethoven was a famous composer of the Romantic period of art and music. Now that you've read about him, go back to "What Is an Orchestra?" and review what you learned there about orchestras of Beethoven's time. How big would an orchestra performing Beethoven's music likely have been? What new and improved instruments might have helped them play his difficult music?

Beyond the Selection

- Think about how "Beethoven Lives Upstairs" adds to what you know about music.
- Add items to the Concept/Question Board about music.

The Man Who Wrote Messiah

David Berreby
illustrated by Antonio Castro

*Barren masts swayed in the wind alongside the mist-covered
wharves of Chester, a port in western England. At the steamy, leaded
window of the Exchange Coffee House, a large, heavyset man stood
anxiously watching idle sailors stomping their feet in the cold. The
wind was still unfavorable, and once again no packet boats would be
setting out. Yet he had to get to Ireland, and soon.*

*Once, he had been the toast of Europe, its single most celebrated
composer. But by this unpromising day in November 1741, George
Frederick Handel was on the verge of financial, and perhaps even
artistic, bankruptcy. He was barely one step ahead of his creditors,
and his public had abandoned him.*

*He left the window, settled uneasily on a hard oak chair, and puffed
his pipe. It was a day made for glum reflection.*

Music had been Handel's passport to the world ever since the day
his father, a surgeon in the German town of Halle, had taken
him as a youth to the court of Duke Johann Adolf at
Weissenfels. His father wanted the boy to be a lawyer.

While the elder Handel attended to business at the court, George
Frederick, bored, wandered into the palace chapel and began
improvising on the organ. The sound of footsteps made him turn.
Standing there, watching, was Duke Johann Adolf.

"Who," the Duke asked, "is this remarkable child?" Handel's father
was summoned, and he was told that it would be a crime to make such a
prodigy into a lawyer.

George Frederick was a quick study. While still in his teens he left
Halle, first for Hamburg, then for Italy, where he mastered the art of
composing operas. By his mid-20s, he had set his sights on London, with
its lively musical life and money to spare for grand shows.

462

In 1711, *Rinaldo*, Handel's first opera in Italian for English audiences, played for a remarkable 15 nights to packed houses at the new Haymarket Theatre. It was a success such as the London musical scene had never known, and it launched Handel into society. Dukes and duchesses quit their country estates to hear the opera, and on the city's crowded streets those who had been lucky enough to get tickets whistled its tunes.

After Handel's "Te Deum" was performed at St. Paul's Cathedral to celebrate a peace treaty in 1713, Queen Anne granted Handel an annual stipend of 200 pounds. With that and his opera receipts, Handel was now probably the best paid composer in the world.

For good measure, Queen Anne's successor, King George I, added 200 pounds to the stipend. And the king also joined the company of many fashionable Londoners by investing thousands in Handel's opera company, the Royal Academy of Music.

The academy was the culmination of Handel's dream. Most musicians depended on handouts from aristocratic patrons. But Handel had learned to be both artist and entrepreneur. Even as he composed, he recruited investors, engaged singers, and performed various administrative duties. As long as his operas pleased the people, they would buy tickets, and the academy would turn a handsome profit.

Investing in Handel seemed a safe bet. At performances of *Amadigi* in 1715, the public kept clamoring to hear arias repeated until finally the theater management banned repetitions so the show could end before dawn. At the opening of *Radamisto* in 1720, unruly crowds fought to get at seats.

Those were the glory days, when all London buzzed with stories of how Handel had refused to be intimidated by patrons or celebrated singers. One tenor had threatened to jump headfirst into a harpsichord if Handel did not alter a tune. "That," the composer replied, "would be vastly more entertaining than your singing." And when a soprano announced she would not sing her part the way he'd instructed, Handel told her she would, or he would drop her out a window. Then he picked her up and headed for the nearest sill.

But by the mid-1720s, Handel's fortunes began fading. Audiences dwindled, and in 1728 the academy had to declare bankruptcy. Also that year, poet John Gay offered *The Beggar's Opera*, a parody of Italian opera, sung in English. It was a huge hit, and spawned a fad for shows with catchy music and English lyrics. The new craze was another nail in the coffin of Handel's Italian repertory.

But he kept on composing and doggedly producing his operas. In 1737 stress and overwork brought on an attack of the "palsy," which took away the use of four fingers of his right hand. Letters expressing concern about his decline flew across England and to the Continent. The future Frederick the Great of Prussia wrote his royal cousins in England, "Handel's great days are over, his inspiration is exhausted and his taste behind the fashion."

It was a desperate Handel who left England that summer for a cure at the famous hot springs of Aachen in Germany. There, he sat each day in the bubbling water. Little trays floated by bearing simple meals and snacks. It was a pleasant place, and it cheered him.

He had not been there long when one afternoon he left the baths and dressed quickly. Several hours later, he had not returned for his next treatment. The nuns who tended the spa grew concerned. Then, from the abbey church, came a burst of glorious music. Habits flying, the nuns ran to investigate. There was Handel, his health unaccountably restored, happily improvising on the organ.

But the return of Handel's health was not accompanied by a return of his operas to public favor. He was deep in debt, and his savings were exhausted by past operatic ventures.

For several years, he barely kept his head above water by giving concerts, as opera after opera failed. By the summer of 1741 Handel, age 56, must have wondered if the time had come to give up the stage altogether.

One morning a servant brought a thick bundle of papers, wrapped in parchment. It was a text assembled by one of Handel's wealthy admirers, a part-time poet named Charles Jennens.

Jennens had been trying for years to interest Handel in setting his words to music. He had already sent Handel a dramatization of the Biblical story of Saul and David. Handel wrote an oratorio, a sort of stripped-down opera performed by singers in ordinary clothes without scenery, but it was not a success. How could it be? No special effects, no grand costumes.

Handel surveyed this new script. Like Jennens's earlier effort, its plot was taken from the Bible. But this was different. The text actually *was* the Bible. Jennens had skillfully assembled Old and New Testament quotations into a stirring narrative of Christ's birth, sacrifice, and resurrection. He had called the piece *Messiah*.

It began with a prophecy from Isaiah, promising deliverance: "Comfort ye, my people." Here were words of solace so simple and familiar that they seemed to draw melody from Handel as easily as he breathed. He was deeply inspired.

The Lord Lieutenant of Ireland had invited Handel to Dublin to present a work for charity. Here was an occasion that would at least benefit those in greater need. Handel set to work.

He composed confidently. He began the *Messiah* on August 22, and 23 days later he was done. This music had given him something more precious than box-office appeal——it had given him hope.

465

Handel roused himself, paid his bill, and left the Chester coffeehouse. He wandered back to the Golden Falcon Inn. It was a far cry from the palaces and spas to which he had been accustomed. As he entered his small room, he was again fighting despair. After so monumental an effort, was his music to be stopped by the exigencies of wind and tide? He went to bed with a troubled mind, trying to rekindle the hope that the miraculous composition had engendered in him.

The next morning the wind had changed.

Dublin's music-lovers were expecting something extraordinary. Handel had been rehearsing his new work for months, and now the leading newspaper was requesting that at the opening performance ladies not wear hoops in their skirts and "gentlemen come without their swords" to permit an extra 100 people to fit into the theater on Fishamble Street.

It was a hot, noisy crowd that Handel saw as he sat down at the harpsichord on April 13, 1742. He looked at his small force of instrumentalists and nodded. Without further ceremony, on the serene tones of its opening sinfonia, the *Messiah* entered the world.

Before it was over, the music had moved Dubliners to tears. Reviewers were ecstatic.

The next performance was so enthusiastically attended that panes of glass were removed to keep the hall from overheating. Best of all, the work proved a windfall for charity. Four hundred pounds went to hospitals and infirmaries, and 142 prisoners were freed from prison after the *Messiah* paid their debts.

But the London première of the *Messiah* on March 23, 1743, was a different story. Sermons were preached against it. Was the Bible a text to be sung by actors for mere entertainment? And the audience that *did* seek entertainment was disappointed by the lack of action and showy arias. Later, these opera zealots hired thugs to beat people who went to see Handel's works.

No matter, thought Handel. His renewed inspiration extended to other pieces. *Samson, Judas Maccabaeus,* and the *Music for the Royal Fireworks* were all successes. He also had failures. But with renewed faith, he went about writing the best music he could. When friends commiserated about the empty seats at a performance of *Theodora,* Handel shrugged and replied, "The music will sound the better."

Through thick and thin, Handel stubbornly clung to his beloved *Messiah*, offering it every year for charity during the last decade of his life. London audiences began to flock to the performances. When King George II heard the oratorio for the first time, the story goes, he could not contain his enthusiasm. As trumpets rang out in the great Hallelujah chorus, he rose to his feet. A stir went through the audience and, in a rustle of silks and clanking of swords, everyone else stood up. To this day, when the joyous strains of this chorus are heard, audiences in the English-speaking world stand.

The mysteriously powerful inspiration that gave birth to the *Messiah* restored Handel's wavering confidence and helped save him from ruin and obscurity. Though late in life he went blind, he still composed and played the organ. It was after the blind composer had conducted a performance of *Messiah* that he fainted and had to be carried home. He lingered through the night of Good Friday, April 13, 1759——17 years to the day after the *Messiah*'s Dublin première. In the early-morning hours, George Frederick Handel died.

But to the delight of listeners of all faiths throughout the world, his *Messiah* lives.

467

The Man Who Wrote Messiah

Meet the Author

David Berreby writes mostly about science and behavior, linguistics, and social psychology. He has been writing most of his life. "It's just one of those things that I have always done." He was influenced by a writing teacher who taught him "about how to see, how to notice things. He taught us to pay attention." Berreby says that writing isn't "throwing something down on paper" and being content with it. "It's doing it again and again until it's right." To be a good writer, he says you need to be very observant, and you need "persistence, absolute stubborn persistence." He lives in Brooklyn, New York.

Meet the Illustrator

Antonio Castro is a largely self-taught artist who blends past and present with versatility. He has achieved recognition as one of the three best graphic artists in the El Paso, Texas, area. He has had his art exhibited in galleries and museums in El Paso, Texas, Juarez, Mexico, and recently in the Jose Luis Cuevas museum in Mexico City. He has created illustrations depicting the history of the city of El Paso, Fort Bliss, and the state of Texas. He has illustrated dozens of children's books, magazine and album covers, posters, brochures, and commemorative coins and jewelry.

Theme Connections

Within the Selection

Record your answers to the questions below in the Response Journal section of your Writer's Notebook. In small groups, report the ideas you wrote. Discuss your ideas with the rest of your group. Then choose a person to report your group's answers to the class.

- Why did Handel pursue a career in music instead of law as his father wished?
- Where did Handel get the idea to write *Messiah*?
- In what ways did writing *Messiah* help Handel?

Across the Selections

- What similarities do you see between Handel and the nightingale you read about earlier in this unit?
- In "Beethoven Lives Upstairs," you get an idea of what Beethoven was like as a person. Having read "The Man Who Wrote *Messiah*," what impressions do you have of Handel as a person? How would you compare Beethoven and Handel?

Beyond the Selection

- In "The Man Who Wrote *Messiah*," you read that Handel was inspired to write *Messiah*. Think of a time when you felt inspired to create something. What did you create? What inspired you to create it? Would your creation have been the same if you had created it without being inspired? What difference did your inspiration make? Get into small groups and share your stories. Be prepared to share your story with the class.

Ecology

Plants, animals, water, earth, air, people——we are all part of the ecology of the world. How do we affect each other? What can we do to help each other? Why is it important?

Focus Questions Do humans have greater rights to the land, air, and water than do plants and animals? How would people's lives and attitudes change if they lived within a wildlife habitat?

Protecting Wildlife

by Malcolm Penny

Introduction

It is dawn in the rain forest of Madagascar. An unearthly howl arises from among the trees. It is joined by another, then several more. Soon a chorus is ringing through the forest, making a weird harmony in the morning mist.

The singers are lemurs, a primitive group of animals related to monkeys. This particular species, called the indri, regularly greets the dawn by calling from the borders of its territory. Soon the indris will begin to feed, pulling branches to their mouths, biting off leaves and fruit.

They are tall, slender animals, covered in dense fur—— brown, with silver-gray arms and legs. They move between the trees in long, athletic leaps in an upright position. When they drop to the ground to cross a clearing, they hop on both feet together, with their arms outstretched.

Indris survive only in a few remaining patches of Madagascar's rain forest.

Some of the females have babies riding on their backs. Indri females bear their single babies only every three years: indris are very slow breeders. They are also very rare.

Some time after dawn, other voices are heard in the forest. Soon, there is the sound of chopping, and smoke drifts through the clearings. The local human inhabitants are preparing a new field to grow crops. They have already removed the larger trees for timber and fuel; now they are felling and burning the undergrowth to clear the land. This technique is called slash and burn.

The new vegetable plot will last only for two or three years before the soil becomes sandy and loses all its fertility. Then the people will move on to clear a new area of forest. There are similar situations all over the world, where protecting wildlife has become an urgent problem.

The Malagasy people brought this style of agriculture with them when they came to Madagascar from Malaysia about 1,500 years ago. It worked well in the ancient forests they left behind: fields they abandoned soon recovered, going back to forest within a few years. The forests of Madagascar cannot recover in the same way, and after centuries of this method of agriculture there is little left of them——just bare hills where nothing but cattle can flourish.

The result is that the people are hungry, as the dusty soil is swept from the hills by heavy rain; and the indri, along with the other species of lemurs, are practically homeless. A few small groups of them survive in carefully protected patches of forest.

Where once hills were forest covered, only dry grasslands are left.

Protecting Trees

473

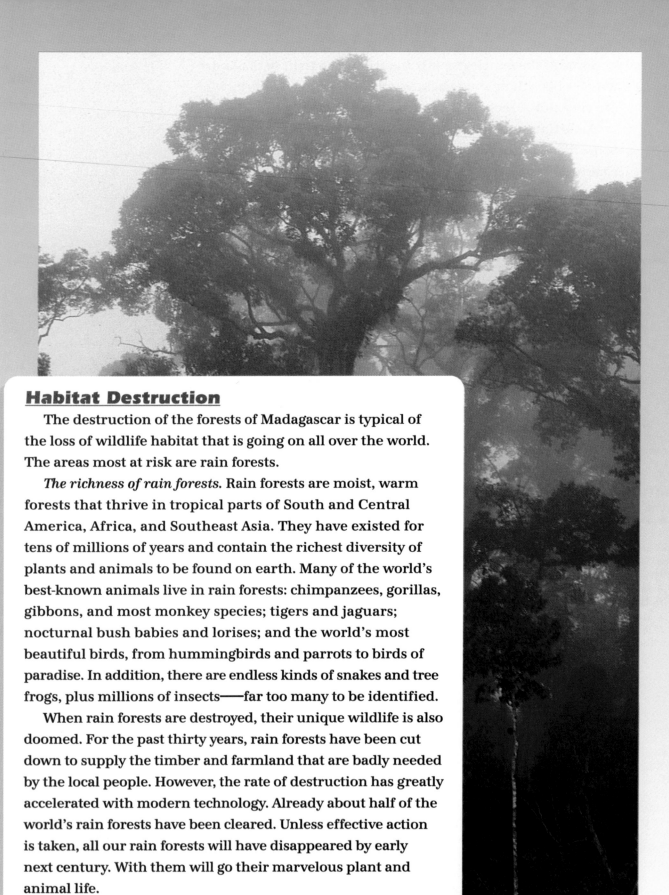

Habitat Destruction

The destruction of the forests of Madagascar is typical of the loss of wildlife habitat that is going on all over the world. The areas most at risk are rain forests.

The richness of rain forests. Rain forests are moist, warm forests that thrive in tropical parts of South and Central America, Africa, and Southeast Asia. They have existed for tens of millions of years and contain the richest diversity of plants and animals to be found on earth. Many of the world's best-known animals live in rain forests: chimpanzees, gorillas, gibbons, and most monkey species; tigers and jaguars; nocturnal bush babies and lorises; and the world's most beautiful birds, from hummingbirds and parrots to birds of paradise. In addition, there are endless kinds of snakes and tree frogs, plus millions of insects——far too many to be identified.

When rain forests are destroyed, their unique wildlife is also doomed. For the past thirty years, rain forests have been cut down to supply the timber and farmland that are badly needed by the local people. However, the rate of destruction has greatly accelerated with modern technology. Already about half of the world's rain forests have been cleared. Unless effective action is taken, all our rain forests will have disappeared by early next century. With them will go their marvelous plant and animal life.

Clouds and mist are trapped by trees in the rain forest of Sabah in Malaysia. In this way, the rain forest creates its own climate.

Bison once roamed the prairies of North America in vast numbers. Today only a few are left: these grazing bison are protected in Yellowstone National Park, Wyoming.

Floods caused by deforestation in the foothills of the Himalayas make people homeless in Bangladesh, far downstream.

The dangers of erosion. A rain forest is sometimes called "a desert covered with trees." While the trees are standing, their roots hold the soil in place, where it is fed by the leaves and other debris falling from above. When the trees are gone, the soil has nothing to feed it. It becomes loose and sandy, and will soon be eroded, washed away by the heavy tropical rainstorms.

Erosion is one of the most serious threats to all farmland, especially in the tropics. As the rainwater carries the soil away, it forms channels that get deeper and deeper until they reach the underlying rock. The soil is carried down rivers until they reach the sea. As they flow more slowly, the rivers drop the soil in the form of silt. This chokes the riverbed and increases the danger of floods.

The loss of grasslands. Most habitat destruction arises from the need for farmland to feed the world's rapidly increasing human population. Grasslands may be destroyed as a wildlife habitat when they are fenced off and sprayed with weedkillers, in order to raise cattle and grow corn. On the American prairies, for example, large grazing animals, such as deer and buffalo, are no longer able to move freely in search of food. Smaller animals, such as insects, and reptiles and birds that feed on them, are made homeless when the "weeds" are killed.

Other habitats are being destroyed as well. In many parts of the world, wetlands, such as ponds and marshes, are drained to make farmland or commercial forestry plantations. Rivers are dredged, improving the drainage of the surrounding land,

but at the same time destroying the habitat of creatures that live among reedbeds and in shallow streams. Land reclamation, especially beside estuaries, has made farmland out of what were once the feeding and roosting places of millions of birds.

It is vital that sufficient crops are grown to feed people. In developing countries it is hard to grow enough food crops, while in Europe there is a glut of food, leading to surplus grain and milk. Excess food in the U.S. is stored, sold to other countries, or fed to livestock. Many environmentalists agree that, in areas of overproduction, it would be better to reduce farmland and leave areas to become natural grassland and woodland for wild animals.

Hunting and Killing

Humans have always killed other animals to eat. In a few places this is still part of everyday life: Indians in the Amazon jungles, Bushmen in Botswana, and some tribes of Inuit in North America and the Commonwealth of Independent States still hunt in the traditional way for food and raw materials.

Wetland plants like marsh rose-mallow have become much rarer, as most of the damp meadows in which they grow have been drained to make farmland.

Puffins, shags, and kittiwakes nest safely on remote cliffs, but their numbers in the Shetland Islands have been severely reduced by a loss of the sand eels.

Most people no longer have to hunt for food. Nevertheless, hunting still causes the death of many millions of wild animals every year. Many animals are killed by farmers to protect their crops and their livestock. These "enemies" of the farmer range in size from elephants and tigers to beetles and greenflies.

Most of the wild animals killed every year are fish. Because the demand for fish rises as the human population increases, some fisheries are in danger of running out. The fishery around South Georgia, one of the Falkland Islands in the South Atlantic Ocean, is the latest area to be affected by overfishing.

Sand eels——small fish that are collected by trawling in shallow northern waters——have suffered badly from overfishing. This has affected the large bird populations that depend on them for food during their breeding season. Arctic terns, skuas, and puffins in the Shetland Islands, to the north of Scotland, have all fallen sharply in numbers. In 1981, there were 54,000 kittiwakes in the Shetlands; by 1988, there were only a few hundred left.

Hunting for sport. There is another kind of unnecessary hunting. Many people, all over the world, enjoy hunting and killing wild animals as a sport. Not very long ago, it was considered very brave and sporting to go out into the bush of Africa, or the jungles of India, to shoot lions, elephants, or tigers. Today, most people consider this type of hunting barbaric and destructive, and it has almost completely stopped. All the same, especially in North America, the shooting of wild animals is big business, with a whole industry devoted to

477

making and selling guns and special clothing for hunters. The number of animals that may be killed is carefully controlled by the authorities.

Victims of our vanity. The very worst kind of killing is poaching: hunting protected animals because they are worth a lot of money. Spotted cats are protected all over the world, but because there are still some people who like to wear their beautiful skins as coats, there are others who will hunt and kill the rarest leopard or cheetah to supply the market.

In the Far East, rhinoceros horn is regarded as a powerful medicine. In one Arab country, North Yemen, it is used to make the handles of the ceremonial daggers worn by adult men. These people are prepared to pay enormous sums of money for rhino horns. A North Yemeni ceremonial dagger with a rhino horn handle can cost over $50,000. Chinese pharmacists can sell powdered or flaked horn for as much as $5,500 per pound. Knowing this, it is easy to understand why the black rhino is hunted so extensively in Africa north of the Zambezi River.

Surprisingly, there are still people who think it is chic to wear the skins of spotted cats, mainly because they are very expensive. Until such people change their minds, animals like the Asian snow leopard will continue to be very rare because they are hunted for their coats.

478

Protecting Rhinos

The steam produced by this power station in the U.S. is harmless, but the fumes from the fossil fuels burned at the station cause acid rain.

Pollution

The oldest and most common form of air pollution is smoke. Coal fires and factory chimneys fill the air with soot, blackening buildings and causing thick fog in damp weather. Now burning forests add to the pollution.

All burning fuel releases carbon dioxide. The layer of carbon dioxide in the earth's atmosphere is becoming thicker, so that it traps heat that would otherwise escape into space. This is known as the "greenhouse effect," and scientists suspect it is causing the earth to become warmer. There is a danger that the polar ice caps might start to melt, causing the sea level to rise. If this happens, it will alter the climate, especially the distribution of rainfall. Wildlife as well as people will be in great danger. If the climate changes abruptly, they will be unable to adapt quickly enough to survive.

The fumes from burning fossil fuels contain oxides of sulfur and nitrogen, which react with damp air to make sulfuric and nitric acids. Often, the fumes drift downwind until they come to a place where the air is damp; then they form acids and fall as rain. Acid rain can kill fish in lakes and rivers, and has been blamed for causing the death of trees over large areas of the northern U.S., Canada, Europe, and Scandinavia.

The atmosphere at risk. A very dangerous form of air pollution is caused by CFCs, or chlorofluorocarbons, which are used in some aerosols, refrigerators, and polystyrene fast-food cartons. They drift up into the ozone layer, far above the earth's surface, and break down the ozone molecules. The ozone layer protects the earth from the harmful effects of sunlight. As it becomes thinner, more ultraviolet light will come through. This will help to raise the earth's temperature, already elevated because of the greenhouse effect. It will also increase the risk of skin cancer among people. Its effect on animals and plants is hard to predict.

The radioactive fuel used in nuclear power stations gives off radiation that is extremely dangerous if it escapes into the air. Even small amounts can damage human cells, causing cancer and interfering with the development of unborn babies. The effects of radiation on wildlife are not known, but it seems most likely that they will be very similar to those on human beings. Certainly, large numbers of sheep in Britain, and reindeer in Lapland, are still radioactive following the 1986 accident at the Chernobyl nuclear power station in the Commonwealth of Independent States. This released a dangerous level of radioactivity into the atmosphere, which drifted over much of Europe.

An ocean of chemicals. Water pollution, like air pollution, is made more serious now by the numbers of people involved, and the types of harmful substances that they produce.

Oil pollution has very serious effects on wildlife. It poisons fish and coastal animals like crabs and shellfish, and also clogs the feathers of seabirds. When the birds preen the oil from their feathers, it poisons them. Most oil spills are accidental, but some are deliberate, for example

Oil spilled into the sea kills thousands of birds every year. Only a few are cleaned, like these penguins in South Africa.

480

Harvest mice flourish in fields of wheat. They suffered in the past from the use of pesticides and from modern harvesting machinery, which cuts the crop very close to the ground and destroys their nests. Now it appears their population is recovering.

when a tanker captain washes out his tanks at sea. Such actions are illegal, but they save time and money, and they can be carried out far at sea, out of sight of land.

The greatest threat to the marine environment is no longer oil pollution. Industrial chemicals have been invented that are far more poisonous and long-lasting. Among them is a group known as PCBs (polychlorinated biphenyls), which are used for various industrial processes. These very strong chemicals can be destroyed by burning, but because this is expensive, they are most often buried in dumps on land, or allowed to pass down rivers into the sea.

PCBs are directly poisonous, but they also weaken the immune system of many animals, so that they become vulnerable to diseases which they would normally resist. The seal plague in the North Sea and the Baltic, first noticed in 1988, was probably made much worse because many of the seals were affected by PCBs.

Poisonous pesticides. Wild animals and plants are also harmed by pesticides and weedkillers, because these substances do not only kill the pests they are intended to, but other creatures, too. The strong chemicals contained in pesticides have harmed many insects, like butterflies, while weedkillers have killed off plants on which caterpillars feed.

Pesticides can harm many animals because they are passed along the food chain. For example, a field mouse may eat grains of wheat treated with pesticide. The pesticide chemicals are not used up, but stored in the mouse's body. If the mouse is caught by a barn owl, the harmful chemicals will be passed on to the owl. Since barn owls catch many mice, they will in time receive a poisonous dose of pesticides. The accumulated chemicals harm their eggs and the owlets that hatch from them.

Reserves and National Parks

The idea of protecting large areas of wild land was first put into practice in the U.S. in 1872, when Yellowstone National Park was opened. Since then, national parks have been founded in almost every country in the world.

When Yellowstone was founded, wildlife in the Rocky Mountains was not in any danger. The park was set up to protect the extraordinary landscape of geysers and sulfur springs, so that visitors could marvel at it forever. The fact that it was full of wildlife, including buffalo, grizzly bears, and herds of elk, was a secondary consideration.

Later, national parks were established to protect particular species of animals, usually from overhunting. The first of these was in Italy, when in 1922 the king gave his hunting preserve at Gran Paradiso to the nation, to protect the alpine ibex. Since then, most parks have been established to protect the whole environment, including all its animals and plants.

The future of national parks. For a national park to be a success, there must be a balance between the needs of the local people and those of the animals. A good example is Royal Chitwan National Park in Nepal. It is partly forest and partly

Ibex were one of the first animals to be given protection in a national park. The national park of Switzerland not only protects ibex but also provides a safe home for many other alpine animals and plants.

Protecting Bears

The millions of water birds that live in the Everglades National Park include spoonbills, egrets, and herons.

elephant grass over 6 feet tall. Tigers and one-horned rhinoceroses live there, together with two different species of crocodile. However, the park is surrounded by villages, whose people need firewood from the forest and grass from the plain, to build houses and feed cattle.

To save arguments, the local people are allowed into the park at certain times of year to collect grass. The park staff collect dead wood from the forest, and driftwood from the rivers, for the villagers to use as fuel. The villagers are encouraged to plant "firewood forests" around the edge of the park to provide a renewable fuel supply. The park is safe, and the people no longer feel it is taking land that they need.

One of the oldest and largest national parks in the U.S., the Florida Everglades, is suffering from a similar conflict. The park relies on a steady flow of clean water from the north. Unfortunately, the water is also needed for agriculture. More and more people are moving to Florida, and it is necessary to drain land to build houses and to provide people with water. This drainage removes some of the water from the edges of the park. The water that comes from the farmland is often polluted with fertilizer. This polluted water enters the tidal swamp, causing an excessive growth of some green algae.

Eventually the algae will cover the water, removing all oxygen from it. If the problem is not solved soon, the Everglades will be lost, with all its wonderful scenery, and the millions of superb birds, snakes, and alligators that live there.

The Everglades is considered so important that it has been declared a World Heritage Site, a matter of concern to the whole world. Some other World Heritage Sites are Mount Everest, the Grand Canyon, the Serengeti in Africa, and Lake Ichkeul in Tunisia, an important wetland used by migrant birds.

National parks are vital to the whole world, because they will be the only way for future generations to know what the world looked like before farmland and cities took over. Many of them are also the last home of animals that used to be common.

In Africa, the only hope for the black rhinoceros is to be protected in national parks, with armed guards to keep the poachers away. Biologists have discovered ways of making rhinoceroses breed more quickly, by adjusting the numbers in each park.

A black rhinoceros mother and her calf have been rescued from farmland, transported by truck, and released into Etosha National Park, Namibia. Such efforts are often necessary to protect endangered rhinoceroses from poachers.

Changing Our Behavior

The best hope for the black rhino is for people to change their beliefs about the value of its horn, so that the trade in daggers and medicines collapses. Many other changes in beliefs and behavior will be necessary if the natural world is to survive for much longer.

The program to persuade villagers in Nepal to plant trees for firewood is being carried out, not only on the plains near Royal Chitwan National Park, but also in the foothills of the Himalayas. As more trees are planted there, the land will become more stable, instead of being washed away down the rivers, and there will be less danger of flooding in faraway Bangladesh.

Pollution can be reduced as well, for example, by discouraging people from using pesticides and artificial fertilizers on farmland. Today a growing number of people are realizing that soil can be enriched, and pests controlled, by organic methods. Such methods are less suited to large-scale farming, but farmers can use less-harmful chemicals.

The use of CFCs has already been greatly reduced, and there are moves to ban the manufacture and use of most of the PCBs, which have caused so much damage to the environment in the short time since they were invented.

Scientists are working hard to find other ways of providing energy. "Alternative energy sources," as they are called, include wind and water power, and solar energy. Finding alternative energy sources is important for two reasons: they will reduce the pollution from burning fossil fuels, and they will postpone the time when the fossil fuels are used up.

Saving the rain forests. The destruction of rain forests can also be reduced, by changing the way in which people clear the land, and by using the land better when it has been cleared. The main problem with rain forest soil is that it is very soft, made up of leaves that have fallen over thousands of years. If the trees are cleared with heavy machinery, this fragile soil is squashed flat. It quickly becomes waterlogged, and bad for growing plants. If the trees are cleared by people on foot, the soil survives much better.

To help the forests and their animals to survive, it would be better if the clearings were much smaller, leaving "corridors" of forest between them. The animals would still have somewhere to live, and the trees would still be there to produce seeds. Thus the clearings would recover more quickly when the soil was no longer suitable for growing crops.

There are plans to slow down the destruction of rain forests in countries as far apart as Mexico and Madagascar, but at present they are on a small scale. It is important that more areas of rain forest be protected, while there are still some worthwhile areas of forest left.

This patch of Brazilian rain forest was the home of the rare golden lion tamarin.

What You Can Do

There are many organizations that exist to safeguard the environment. By joining and supporting a local group, you can let the authorities know that you, too, are concerned with what is happening to the natural world.

Conservation does not have to be a public matter: it can be personal, too. On a walk in the country, for example, a good motto is "Look, don't touch." In some nature reserves there may be a sign that says "Take only photographs, leave only footprints." If everyone followed this advice, there would be much less damage to the plants and animals that make the countryside such a marvelous place.

Making room for wildlife. If you have a garden or yard, you can make your own nature reserve. To encourage butterflies, for example, you could plant a shrub called Buddleia or "butterfly bush." Butterflies love the nectar from its sweet-scented flower spikes.

You can encourage many butterflies to breed, too, by growing various plants and flowers. Among cultivated annuals, plants that grow for only one season, are alyssum, marigolds, and verbena. Some choices of cultivated perennials, plants that grow for several years, include butterfly weed, daisies, phlox, and primroses. Wild, prickly thistle or nettles are also good choices. Avoid using chemical weedkillers.

In the countryside, ditches and ponds are often drained, or become polluted by fertilizers and weedkillers. By creating a pond in your garden, you can provide an alternative home for frogs and many freshwater insects, including beautiful dragonflies.

You can also help wild birds in winter. Bird feeders and bird baths are especially valuable to birds in winter, when food is scarce and water may be frozen. Once birds know that food and water are available in your garden, or on the terrace of your apartment, many different species may come to feed there. When small birds visit a garden in winter, they help to control pests by eating the eggs of aphids that lie under the bark of trees.

If we successfully conserve the rich wildlife we still have now, the world will be a much nicer place in the future.

Protecting Frogs

487

Protecting Wildlife

Meet the Author

Malcolm Penny has been on wildlife expeditions and has worked as a producer of wildlife documentaries for television. Penny has written many books about animals and is a successful natural history author.

Theme Connections

Within the Selection

Record your answers to the questions below in the Response Journal section of your Writer's Notebook. In small groups, report the ideas you wrote. Discuss your ideas with the rest of your group. Then choose a person to report your group's answers to the class.

- Why is a rain forest sometimes referred to as "a desert covered with trees?"
- What are PCBs? Why are they a threat to the environment?
- What problems face the Florida Everglades?

Across the Selections

- Now that "Protecting Wildlife" has you thinking about ecology, look ahead in this unit and ask yourself, What are the different facets of ecology? Is ecology concerned with just the environment? Or is ecology concerned with only the preservation of animals? Explain what you think ecology is. Then, as you progress through this unit, periodically check back to see how accurate your answer was.

Beyond the Selection

- Think about how "Protecting Wildlife" adds to what you know about ecology.
- Add items to the Concept/Question Board about ecology.

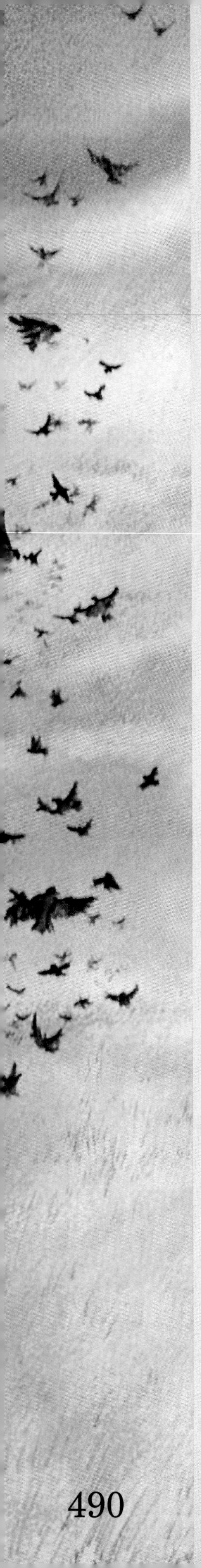

Focus Questions How does Fleischman's use of the first person underscore the desolation of this lonely passenger pigeon? Why did the passenger pigeon become extinct?

The 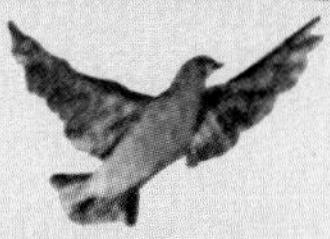 *Passenger* Pigeon

Paul Fleischman
illustrated by Diane Blasius

We were counted not in	
	thousands
nor	
	millions
but in	
billions.	*billions.*
	We were numerous as the
stars	stars
	in the heavens
As grains of	
sand	sand
at the sea	
	As the
buffalo	buffalo
	on the plains.

When we burst into flight

      we so filled the sky

that the
sun
was darkened

      sun

      and
day
      day
      became dusk.

Humblers of the sun   Humblers of the sun
we were!   we were!
The world
inconceivable   inconceivable
      without us.

Yet it's 1914,
and here I am
alone   alone
      caged in the Cincinnati Zoo,

the last
      of the passenger pigeons.

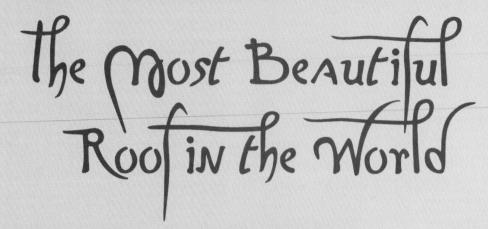

The Most Beautiful Roof in the World

EXPLORING THE RAINFOREST CANOPY

Kathryn Lasky
photographs by Christopher G. Knight

MEG LOWMAN climbs trees. She has climbed trees since she was a little girl in search of insects, leaves, and flowers, and now it is her job. Meg is a rainforest scientist, and her specialty is the very top of the rainforest, the canopy.

During the past ten years Meg has spent at least five days a month in the treetops, which adds up to six hundred days. And this does not include the approximately ten days every month she spends at the base of trees looking up. Meg wants to know about the relationships between plants and insects in the canopy. She is especially interested in herbivory, leaf and plant eating by insects and other animals. She wants to know which insects eat which leaves and how their feeding affects the overall growth of the rainforest. To answer these questions she must spend a great deal of time either up a tree or back in her laboratory, studying samples. Meg's lab is at the Marie Selby Botanical Gardens, a rainforest research center in Sarasota, Florida, where she is director of research and conservation.

Meg cannot remember a single day in her life when she wasn't either looking at or studying a plant, leaf, flower, or insect—except possibly those days when she went to the hospital to give birth to her two sons, Edward and James. Since Meg was six, she has been fascinated by the natural world. As a child she had a bird's nest collection, a rock collection, a shell collection, an insect and butterfly collection, and a bud collection. Her bedroom was stuffed with outdoor treasures. Her great love was flowers; in the fifth grade she was the only child in her class to enter the state science fair. She made a wildflower collection and won second prize.

492

A special permit allows Meg to collect many rare specimens,
some of which she keeps in the Selby greenhouse.

WHEN MEG was ten years old, she was intrigued by two women: Rachel Carson, one of the first environmentalists, who studied and wrote about the delicate relationships in the web of life, and Harriet Tubman, the most famous "conductor" of the Underground Railroad. Threading through the countryside and deep woods on long, frightening nights, Harriet Tubman guided countless African Americans out of slavery to freedom. Meg read that she often navigated by feeling for the moss that grew on the north sides of trees. But it was not only moss that she had to look for. She had to know which berries and nuts could be eaten, which could make the difference between starvation and survival. She had to know how to find a swamp to plunge into when slave-hunting dogs bore down; the sulfurous mud and slime could disguise a human scent and confuse the dogs. She had to be attuned to the environment in order to guide her people on their perilous journey. Harriet Tubman, says Meg, was a pioneer field naturalist, one of the first women field naturalists in this country.

DEEP IN BELIZE, in Central America, there is a place called Blue Creek. Almost every month nearly 40 inches (102 centimeters) of rain falls. Blue Creek is considered one of the most humid places on the entire planet. In this shadowed world, pierced occasionally by slivers of sunlight, are more varieties of living things than perhaps any other place on earth. Within a 16 foot (five-meter) square there can be upward of two hundred different species of plants.

And there are animals, too. Bats swoop through the canopy. Vipers coil among buttress roots, waiting in ambush. A rare and mysterious tree salamander slinks into the petals of an orchid. Poison dart frog tadpoles swim high above the forest floor in the tanks of bromeliads.

The rainforest is a timeless, uncharted world, where mysteries abound and new or rare species appear like undiscovered islands. Within the tangled vines under the rotting bark of fallen trees, caught in the slime and mold of decaying vegetation and fungi, life teems with ceaseless energy. When a tree falls, the stump rots, bark loosens, and new creatures move in and take over the altered habitats. It is the very diversity of the rainforest that allows life to thrive everywhere, to spring back with a rush of opportunistic species to fill the gaps.

MEG LOWMAN believes that science is the machinery that runs the earth. She explains, "I think that science is really the way things work, and that's exciting. It is important to understand the bigger picture of our planet and where we live, how it functions, what we do with it, and how that will have impact."

When Meg wants to have a close look at the machinery, she goes to the rainforest, and recently she has been coming to Blue Creek. Meg worries about the machinery. Although it seems invincible, although she can track a new swarm of ants rushing into a tree notch to fill a gap that was not there the previous day, she wonders how strong the machine really is. How many species can be removed before it will break?

Viewed from an airplane, the top of the rainforest at Blue Creek looks like a field of gigantic broccoli. The bright green florets are actually the emergent growth of the very tallest trees. The crowns of these trees extend above the canopy in the layer known as the pavilion. The pavilion is to the canopy as a roof is to a ceiling. From the emergent growth to the floor of the rainforest is a drop of 150 feet (46 meters) or more. Meg wants to go to the canopy, a layer below the emergent one. At Blue Creek a canopy walkway designed by specialists in rainforest platform construction has been built.

As the place where most photosynthesis occurs and where 95 percent of the biomass is produced, the canopy is the "powerhouse" of the rainforest.

Meg is up at first light. It is drizzling, but she will not wear rain gear. It is too hot. She has beans and rice for breakfast because this is all that is available. For her boys she has brought along Cheez Whiz and crackers because they are tired of beans and rice. Unless the Mayan people who live in the nearby village come into the forest with chickens or melons, the menu does not vary. She kisses the boys good-bye and leaves them with her brother, Ed, who helped build the walkway. She puts on a hard hat and climbs into her safety harness. The harness has two six-foot lengths of rope attached. At the end of the ropes are Jumars, or ascenders. Jumars are used in technical rock climbing. The metal U-shaped device has a hinged and grooved gate that allows the rope to slide up as one climbs but locks instantly with downward motion. To descend, the climber must manually push the gate open to allow the rope to slide through.

"Bye, Mom," James waves as he watches his mother begin her climb at the base of the *Ormosia*, or cabbage bark tree.

"Remember, it's our turn next," calls Edward as he watches his mom climb higher.

Meg inspects her equipment as she prepares for another day of work in the canopy.

This walkway will allow Meg to roam the rainforest canopy.

THE BOYS have accompanied their mother to rainforests all over the world. Now, for the first time, Meg feels they are old enough to go up with her into the canopy. She has ordered special child-size harnesses for them. They are excited, but first their mother has work to do—traps to set for insects, leaves to tag, drawings to make, flowers to count. It will be many hours before they can join her. In the meantime, they can swim in the creek and explore a secret cave that their uncle promises to take them to.

Meg is fast. Within a few short minutes she has ascended 80 feet (24 meters). Then the metal ladders fixed to the *Ormosia* tree run out; for the next 15 feet (4.5 meters) the real climbing begins. Metal staples project from the tree trunk. These are the footholds. For the unpracticed they are scary. They seem spaced too far apart for easy stepping. There is rhythm. A climber must clip the safety lines securely to wires strung above and then step. Clip, step, unclip one Jumar. Clip, step, unclip again. It is a mosaic of hand- and footwork until Meg is perhaps 95 feet (29 meters) above the ground and approaching the first platform. Meg swings herself onto the platform with the seeming ease of a spider monkey negotiating canopy vines. Now she is at the beginning of the walkway.

THE WALKWAY itself is Y-shaped. The main stem of the Y spans nearly one hundred feet (thirty meters) across Blue Creek to the other bank. Once across, the arms of the Y diverge into two separate walkways that tie into trees on the opposite bank of the creek. There is a major observation platform at the junction of the Y's arms and then others, higher up, that provide views at different levels.

When viewed from below, the canopy appears to be one big maze of tangled vines and foliage, but within the canopy there are a variety of distinct regions. Some might be sunny, some shadier; in some areas the branches of a tree grow at steep angles, while in another region they grow more horizontally. At some points in the canopy there is what researchers call crown shyness, by which they mean the spacing between the crowns of the trees. This spacing influences what lives where in the canopy, providing pathways for toucans and macaws and other creatures that fly. For those creatures that swing or glide or climb, there are the "emerald highways" strung together by vines and lianas that lace the tops of the trees together into a web for commuting life.

Meg has now crossed the creek. She is climbing to the first observation platform, 110 feet (33.5 meters) above the ground. She can hear monkey chatter just above her. She stops, balances on a staple, and looks straight up. There is a sudden dark streak against the sky. Two spider monkeys spring through the branches. They move in fluid loops and arcs, dancing in a tangled rhythm as they alternately grasp with hands, feet, and tail. The space between the branches changes with each new grip, making a shifting geometry against the sky of sliding rectangles, split-second parabolas, and drifting squares. The first monkey pauses at the end of a limb.

Spider monkeys prefer the middle layers of the canopy. The capuchins are often found in the lower levels, and the howler monkeys that bellow at dawn like distant foghorns live at the very top.

The canopy provides ample space for animal inhabitants, such as this howler monkey.

498

MEG BEGINS taking "snapshots" of leaf-eating activity. Last month she had marked every leaf on several branches with a number. She now checks to see how much of each leaf has been eaten.

"Leaf number five is zero percent. Number three is fifty percent. Leaf number four is zero percent, with three minings," Meg calls out to a graduate student assistant, who writes the figures down in a notebook. Mining occurs when an insect eats through just one layer of the leaf's surface, which results in a browning pattern. There might also be galls on a leaf to be noted. In this way Meg acquires her snapshot of leaf-eating activity on particular trees in certain regions of the canopy. She will later compare these figures and notations with

Mesh bags isolate leaves from insect predators—and help Meg refine her experiment.

what she already knows about the hatching periods of certain insect populations. She has a hunch that the hatchings are synchronized to occur when certain leaves flush, or first grow, and are at their most tender for eating. Through many years of research, Meg has seen a pattern, and her theory is that the newest leaves are the tastiest for insects. Within a matter of two months, 25 percent of the leaf will probably be eaten. The rate slows down as the tender young leaves grow older and tougher.

Meg and her assistant work for the better part of an hour making snapshots of eaten leaves. She then gets out a few mesh bags. It is necessary for a scientist not only to observe ongoing processes but to ask new questions that might only be answered by setting up experiments that often interrupt natural processes. With the mesh bags Meg is going to begin an exclusion experiment. She will tie each bag onto a branch, protecting its leaves from insect predators. Nearby will be another branch without a bag (called a control). She wants to know if by excluding one variable (the leaf-eating insects), the new growth will differ. If there is a barrier, those new leaves will not be eaten, but will this cause even more new leaves to flush out? Or does the fact that a branch's new leaves are being consumed stimulate the tree to produce more?

MEG CLIMBS higher into the canopy. The light twinkles brightly. Above her is a cascade of orchids. Suddenly, through the avenues of emerald light, like winged rainbows two macaws sweep through the canopy. The very air seems splattered with their brilliant color. The birds fly in silence, but the spider monkeys screech in alarm. Branches shake. The bright pair settles in a nearby kapok tree. There might be a nest with chicks in it, for this is the time when the young hatch. Or the pair might be foraging in the surrounding mahogany and kapok trees for fruits and nuts. The beaks of macaws are among the most powerful in the world; macaws can crack almost any nut or seed and also deliver the most wicked of bites. The two birds suddenly explode from the tree like a burst of fireworks and go to another tree nearby. Meg thinks that they are most likely foraging for food to bring to their young. They deliver the food by first chewing it up until it is a pulpy mass that they then swallow and store in a food pouch. When they return to their young, they will regurgitate this food into the mouths of their chicks. Soon they fly off. Meg wishes James and Edward could have seen them.

Meg continues climbing up. She reaches the third platform, 115 feet (35 meters) aboveground. This platform is built in the spreading branches of a *Nargusta* tree. Two lianas snake out along one branch, seeming to choke it in their twisted grip. From this platform she has a good view of four ant gardens she is monitoring as well as of two very special bromeliads.

First she peeks in on the ant gardens. They appear to be almost hanging, with their tendrils of plant roots and vines swaying in the still air. They are actually firmly based on the branches of trees.

Macaws scout the canopy in search of food for their young.

"Ah, there's a new one just beginning!" Meg exclaims as she focuses her viewing scope. At the V where one branch joins another, there appears to be a clump of dirt with several small spear-shaped leaves, similar to those of a Christmas cactus, projecting. This, in fact, is the foundation for the little treetop farms so carefully tended by several different species of ants.

(below) Meg advances to a higher level of the platform.
(right) Among the many beautiful sights Meg encounters on her climb are orchids.

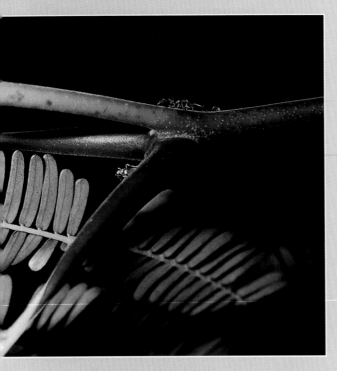

(left) This ant protects the bull-horn acacia tree from epiphytic growth, while these ants (right) merely visit tree branches in search of leaves.

Mᴇɢ ᴄʟɪᴘꜱ her Jumars into some extending cable so she can go higher and get closer to the ant gardens. She wants to observe a mature one that fairly bristles with plant life. Meg counts at least six different kinds of seedling plants here, ranging from orchids to cacti. A *Peperomia* plant forms its base. The ant gardens are magnets for epiphytic growth. Epiphytes, unlike vines or lianas, usually start growing from the canopy down. They need the tree for support. They root on the bark or soil found on the tree. They often begin when a bird excretes a seed from overhead, or as in this case, when the ants themselves drag in bits of plant materials. The bits take root, the seeds sprout. The little ant farmers tend them night and day, and in return they feed off the glucose and proteins that the plants contain in their succaries, the sugary deposits made by the plants' metabolic processes. Scientists think that the ant gardens themselves may be of benefit to more than just the ants, that these gardens help the tree itself by allowing it to capture more solar energy and to trap atmospheric nutrients that might slip off a bare trunk.

(left) Butterflies perch on bromeliads (right), whose leaves
are a point of interest for many creatures in the canopy.

THERE ARE many such interlocking relationships within the
rainforest, and ants often play a major role. Sometimes epiphytic
growth can become too much and literally strangle a tree. The
bull-horn acacia tree has a very effective defense against epiphytic
growth. With its hollow stems it cannot tolerate the stranglehold of
many epiphytes. Therefore, it has become the home for a special breed
of ants that live in its stems and protect it fiercely. Whenever the tree
is even slightly disturbed, the ants charge out of a pinhole on the thorn
and attack. In return they feast on the sugar in the tree.

Other ants visit the canopy but live underground in great fungus
factories. The leafcutter ants do their farming in reverse, trudging up
to the canopy day and night to cut dime-size disks. They then hoist
the pieces overhead and carry them back down to underground
chambered caverns. In the dark damp maze of tunnels and caves,
the leaves begin to grow mold and fungi, which in turn feed the ants.
The long, silent lines of tiny, quivering green disks move across the
rainforest floor. If you peer closely, you notice that on each disk rides
an even smaller ant. This one protects the carrier ant from attacks by
deadly micro wasps. For lateral protection alongside the column
march lines of larger soldier ants. Each leaf disk, no bigger than a dime
and only a fraction of a gram in weight, must get to the fungus factory.

503

Once there, other ants will check the leaves to see if they are right for the kind of fungus the ants are producing. If they are not, the disks are discarded and the ants must turn around and climb one hundred or more feet (thirty meters) into the canopy again in search of the right kind of leaf.

Meg carefully edges her way toward a bromeliad, another kind of epiphyte. An owl butterfly alights on a leaf, then flutters off. A dragonfly hovers like a small jeweled helicopter. At the end of this branch lies a world within a world, a pond within the canopy, a pool hovering midair within a bromeliad.

Bromeliads have spiky leaves, which form a fibrous hollow tank. The outer leaves are bright green, but often the inner leaves are a fiery red and erupt like tongues of flame from a volcano. Rather than lava, however, there is water, and within the water there is life—the larvae of mosquitoes and the tiny tadpoles of a frog, temporarily using the plant's pond as a nursery. The tadpoles, hatched on the ground, slithered onto their mother's back. She then began the long climb in the canopy in search of one of these water nurseries.

Snakes and tarantulas live within the maze of the bromeliad.

Other creatures lurk in the overlapping leaves of the bromeliad. In this bromeliad Meg finds no frogs. Maybe the frog and its tadpoles have been eaten by the little venomous snake she spots coiled among the outer leaves. Perhaps sensing her presence, it slips out of the bromeliad and scrolls across a nearby philodendron leaf—and then holds perfectly still. With its pretty chain-patterned skin, it appears like a beautiful necklace flung out of nowhere. There is a blur of movement in the corner of Meg's eye. A sudden dark design appears from deep within the bromeliad. It is a tarantula. It bristles at this disturbance, climbs toward the bark of the tree, and comes to rest like black embroidery against the bright green leaves.

There is one more bromeliad on this branch. Meg makes her way toward it and peers in. Out creeps a small tree salamander. Meg is excited. She recognizes it as a very rare lungless salamander. She has only heard about them and seen perhaps one or two pictures. Because of their rareness and their inaccessibility in the canopy, these salamanders with their suction-cup feet are one of the canopy's most mysterious inhabitants. No one knows how they breed, what they eat, or how they live. Meg backs away quickly. She does not want to disturb the creature. She hopes it will return to the maze of bromeliad leaves from which it emerged. This is the surprise she has been looking for to show her boys.

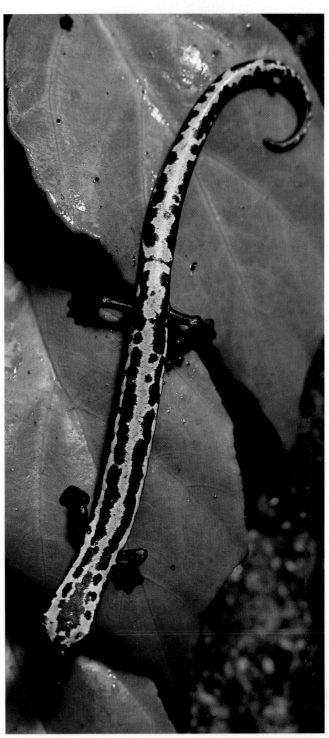

In one bromeliad, Meg is fortunate enough to discover a rare lungless salamander.

The Most Beautiful Roof in the World

Meet the Author

Kathryn Lasky grew up telling stories. *"When I was growing up, I was always thinking up stories. . . . I was a compulsive story maker."* Although she was a great story maker, she kept her stories a secret because she did not think being a writer would be a good career. She continued to write as a hobby while she was a teacher. With encouragement from her parents and her husband, Christopher Knight, she decided to publish her first book *Agatha's Alphabet*. Today she writes for both adults and children, and she has written more than fifty books.

Meet the Photographer

Christopher G. Knight became interested in photography when he was thirteen. He began his career by photographing a forty-seven page article for *National Geographic*. He teamed up with his wife, Kathryn Lasky, to create children's nonfiction books. Knight also runs a film company that produces documentaries that can be seen on many PBS television programs.

Theme Connections

Within the Selection

Record your answers to the questions below in the Response Journal section of your Writer's Notebook. In small groups, report the ideas you wrote. Discuss your ideas with the rest of your group. Then choose a person to report your group's answers to the class.

- Why did Meg as a child admire Rachel Carson and Harriet Tubman?
- What is an ant garden?
- Why is Meg excited to find a tree salamander?

Across Selections

- In "Protecting Wildlife," you read a description of how rainforests have been destroyed in Madagascar. How does "The Most Beautiful Roof in the World" add to your appreciation of this destruction? Was the forest canopy more complex than you expected it to be?

Beyond the Selection

- Think about how "The Most Beautiful Roof in the World" adds to what you know about ecology.
- Add items to the Concept/Question Board about ecology.

Mount Shuksan and Alpine Lake, North Cascades National Park.
Photo by Alan Kearney/ENP Images.

Dust Bowl. 1933. **Alexander Hogue.** Oil on canvas. National
Museum of American Art, Smithsonian Institution,
Washington, DC.

African Elephants. **Charles Tournemine.** Museé d'Orsay,
Paris.

Alejandro's Gift

Richard E. Albert
illustrated by Sylvia Long

Alejandro's small adobe house stood beside a lonely desert road.

Beside the house stood a well, and a windmill to pump water from the well. Water for Alejandro and for his only companion, a burro.

It was a lonely place, and Alejandro welcomed any who stopped by to refresh themselves at the well. But visitors were few, and after they left, Alejandro felt lonelier than before.

To more easily endure the lonely hours, Alejandro planted a garden. A garden filled with carrots, beans, and large brown onions.

Tomatoes and corn.

Melons, squash, and small red peppers.

Most mornings found Alejandro tending the garden, watching it grow. These were times he cherished, and he often stayed for hours, working until driven indoors by the desert heat.

The days went by, one after another with little change, until one morning when there was an

510

unexpected visitor. This visitor came not from the desert road, but from the desert itself.

A ground squirrel crept from the underbrush. Moving warily over the sand, it hesitated and looked around. Alejandro paused, keeping very quiet as the squirrel approached the garden. It ran up to one of the furrows, drank its fill of water, and scampered away. After it left, Alejandro realized that for those few moments his loneliness had been all but forgotten.

And because he felt less lonely, Alejandro found himself hoping the squirrel would come again.

The squirrel did come again, from time to time bringing along small friends.

Wood rats and pocket gophers.

Jackrabbits, kangaroo rats, pocket mice.

Birds, too, became aware of Alejandro's garden.

Roadrunners, gila woodpeckers, thrashers.

Cactus wrens, sage sparrows, mourning doves, and others came in the evening to perch on the branches of a mesquite bush, or to rest on the arms of a lone saguaro, before dropping down for a quick drink before nightfall.

Occasionally, even an old desert tortoise could be seen plodding toward the garden.

Suddenly, Alejandro found that time was passing more quickly. He was rarely lonely. He had only to look up from his hoe, or from wherever he might be at any moment, to find a small friend nearby.

For a while this was all that mattered to Alejandro, but after a time he wasn't so sure. He began asking himself if there was something more important than just making himself less lonely. It took Alejandro little time to see there was.

He began to realize that his tiny desert friends came to his garden not for company, but for water. And he found himself thinking of the other animals in the desert.

Animals like the coyote and the desert gray fox.

The bobcats, the skunks, the badgers, and long-nosed coatis.

The peccaries, sometimes called *javelinas,* the short-tempered wild pigs of the desert.

The antlered mule deer, the does, and the fawns.

Finding enough water was not a problem. With his windmill and well, Alejandro could supply ample water for any and all. Getting it to those who needed it was something else.

The something else, Alejandro decided, was a desert water hole.

Without delay, Alejandro started digging. It was tiring work, taking many days in the hot desert sun. But the thought of giving water to so many thirsty desert dwellers more than made up for the drudgery. And when it was filled, Alejandro was pleased with the gift he had made for his desert friends.

There was good reason to suppose it would take time for the larger animals to discover their new source of water, so Alejandro was patient. He went about as usual, feeding his burro, tending the garden, and doing countless other chores.

Days passed and nothing happened. Still, Alejandro was confident. But the days turned to weeks, and it was still quiet at the water hole. Why, Alejandro wondered, weren't they coming? What could he have done wrong?

513

The absence of the desert folk might have remained a mystery had Alejandro not come out of the house one morning when a skunk was in the clearing beyond the water hole. Seeing Alejandro, the skunk darted to safety in the underbrush.

It suddenly became very clear why Alejandro's gift was being shunned.

Alejandro couldn't believe he had been so thoughtless, but what was important now was to put things right as quickly as possible.

Water hole number two was built far from the house and screened by heavy desert growth. When it was filled and ready, Alejandro waited with mixed emotions. He was hopeful, yet he couldn't forget what had happened the first time.

As it turned out, he was not disappointed.

The animals of the desert did come,
each as it made its own discovery.
Because the water hole was now sheltered
from the small adobe house and the desert
road, the animals were no longer fearful.
And although Alejandro could not see through the desert growth
surrounding the water hole, he had ways of knowing it was no
longer being shunned.

By the twitter of birds gathering in the dusk.

By the rustling of mesquite in the quiet desert evening telling of
the approach of a coyote, a badger, or maybe a desert fox.

By the soft hoofbeats of a mule deer, or the unmistakable sound of
a herd of peccaries charging toward the water hole.

And in these moments when Alejandro sat quietly listening to the
sounds of his desert neighbors, he knew that the gift was not so
much a gift that he had given, but a gift he had received.

The Southwestern region of the United States is made up of Colorado, Arizona, New Mexico, and Utah. A variety of wildlife can be found in its varied habitats. The following glossary lists some of the animals and plants shown in this book.

The **Arizona Pocket Mouse** eats many kinds of seeds and can hibernate when food cannot be found.

Badgers have distinctive black-and-white "masks" on their faces. They live in family groups in underground burrows. Few animals will attack the badger because of its fierce temperament.

The **Black-Tailed Jackrabbit** has very large ears, which help keep it cool in hot weather. It also has very large feet, which help it run quickly.

Bobcats get their name from their stubby "bobbed" tail. They are found only in North America, where they are the most common wildcat. They eat small mammals, such as rabbits, mice, and squirrels. The bobcat barks hoarsely when threatened.

Botta's Pocket Gopher spends most of its time in underground burrows, some of which can be as long as 150 feet. Botta's Pocket Gophers live by themselves, often fighting other gophers they meet.

The **Cactus Wren** is the largest North American wren—growing up to 9 inches long. It lives in nests in clumps of mesquite on desert hillsides.

Coatis (**kwa**-tees) are short-legged animals that can grow up to two feet long. They eat lizards and insects, but are known for eating fruit, often stripping fruit trees bare. Coatis travel in large groups.

The **Collared Peccary** (**peck**-a-ree) resembles a wild pig but has a snout that points upward. It eats cacti—especially prickly pear, which it devours spines and all. During the midday heat, peccaries often sleep in hollows in the ground.

Costa's Hummingbird is a purple-throated hummingbird no more than $3\frac{1}{2}$ inches long. As it hovers over flowers, its wings beat so fast they make a humming sound. Hummingbirds are the only birds that can hover.

Coyotes can run as fast as 40 miles per hour and leap as far as 14 feet. They run with their tails down, unlike wolves, which run with their tails straight behind them.

The **Curve-Billed Thrasher** is about the size of a robin. It has a long, curved bill and red eyes. It lives in cactus deserts and eats insects.

The **Desert Tortoise** stores water in a pouch beneath its shell. It hibernates underground from October to March. Desert Tortoises can grow up to 15 inches long.

The **Elf Owl** is the smallest American owl and is no bigger than a sparrow. It lives in saguaro deserts and feeds on large insects.

Gambel's Quail lives in desert thickets. The bird has a loud, crackling call, and a large teardrop-shaped feather on its head.

The **Gila Woodpecker** nests in holes in giant saguaro cacti. Its feathers are patterned in black and white stripes. Males have a small red cap, while females and young birds have plain brown heads.

The **Gray Fox** is mostly active at night, but can sometimes be seen during the day looking for food. They are the only canids (the family of wolves, foxes, coyote, and dogs) that can climb, and they often rest in trees.

The **Greater Roadrunner** is a tall bird (20 to 24 inches) that rarely flies, running instead on strong feet. It eats a wide variety of small animals, including snakes, lizards, and scorpions.

Harris's Antelope Squirrel lives in low deserts. Its pale coloring helps it blend with the environment. Antelope Squirrels get most of the water they need from the food they eat.

Merriam's Kangaroo Rat is the smallest kangaroo rat in the United States. It lives in scrublands, feeding mostly on the seeds of mesquite and other desert plants.

Mesquite (mess-**keet**) is a spiny tree that grows in large thickets in the Southwest and Mexico.

The **Mourning Dove's** name comes from its melancholy cooing, which is its mating call. Mourning doves can be found all over North America.

Mule Deer have large ears and are one of the most common animals of the desert. Their diet consists of grasses, twigs, and cactus fruits. Mule Deer can run up to 35 miles per hour, and can jump as far as 25 feet.

The **Phainopepla** (fay-no-**pep**-la) is a tropical bird with an elegant crest on its head. It eats mistletoe berries and insects, which it snatches right out of the air.

Sage Sparrows are small brown birds with white eye rings. They are found in dry foothills and sagebrush.

The **Saguaro** (sah-**gwar**-oh) is a cactus that can grow up to 60 feet tall. It provides fruit for many desert creatures, and bears white flowers.

The **White-Throated Wood Rat** usually lives in the base of a cactus, and it uses the cactus needles to hide the entrance to its home.

Alejandro's Gift

Meet the Author

Richard E. Albert wrote and sold many "pulp westerns" early in his writing career but spent most of his life working as an engineer. After his retirement he began writing for children. He was 83 when he wrote *Alejandro's Gift*.

Meet the Illustrator

Sylvia Long has recently started illustrating children's books after working several years as a fine artist. Her love of the outdoors and animals has been an inspiration for her wonderful illustrations. Two of the four books she has illustrated have become best sellers, *Fire Race* and *Ten Little Rabbits*.

Theme Connections

Within the Selection

Record your answers to the questions below in the Response Journal section of your Writer's Notebook. In small groups, report the ideas you wrote. Discuss your ideas with the rest of your group. Then choose a person to report your group's answers to the class.

- Why was Alejandro lonely?
- What was Alejandro's gift and to whom did he give it?
- What was flawed about the first watering hole Alejandro dug?

Across the Selections

- Having read "Alejandro's Gift," compare the way Alejandro interacts with nature with the way Meg interacts with nature in "The Most Beautiful Roof in the World." In what ways are their experiences in nature the same? In what ways are they different?
- In "Protecting Wildlife," you read about some things that people can do to help save the environment. Do you think what Alejandro did would make a good addition to that list of suggestions? What do you think the author of "Protecting Wildlife" would think of Alejandro's gift?

Beyond the Selection

- Think about a time when you did something that benefited the environment. Maybe you helped clean up a park, or maybe you helped your parents put up a bird feeder. Whatever it was, take a few minutes and write about it. How did it make you feel to do something good for nature? What were the results of your actions? How might things have been different had you never taken action? Once you have written your story, be prepared to share it with the class.

A Natural Force

by Laurence Pringle

A lightning bolt flashes in the summer night. It sizzles and spirals down a tree trunk. Wisps of smoke rise from dead pine needles on the forest floor. Flames glow in the night, and a forest fire begins.

The fire spreads quickly. Flames leap up to the crowns of trees, which explode into fireballs. Overhead the fire leaps from tree to tree. A wall of flames moves through the woods, gaining speed. The forest fire seems like a terrible beast with a mind of its own. It roars; it changes direction. It hungrily sucks oxygen from the air and kills almost everything in its path.

Some of the fastest wild animals are able to escape. The unlucky and the less swift perish——burned to death or robbed of oxygen by the fire. Sometimes a dying rabbit becomes an agent of the fire; its fur ablaze, it dashes crazily through the woods, setting fires as it goes.

At last the fire comes to an end. It dies because of rain, or the efforts of firefighters, or a combination of factors. But the land is blackened, studded with tree skeletons, littered with dead animals. The soil is vulnerable to terrible erosion, and many years pass before the land heals itself with new plant growth and wildlife.

This scene of death and destruction exists in the imaginations of millions of people——*and seldom anywhere else.* Each year there are more than 100,000 forest fires in the United States. Most are started by people, either accidentally or on purpose. Some are started by lightning. Most lightning-caused fires go out, by themselves, after burning less than a quarter acre of land. And most forest fires of any size are beneficial to plants and animals.

522

Their good effects have been recognized for many years in the Southeastern United States. Each year forest managers there routinely set ablaze two million acres where pine trees grow. In the West, some wildfires are now allowed to burn for months in national parks and forests. This practice upsets people who feel that all forest fires are "bad."

Whether a forest fire is "bad" or "good" depends on many factors. No one advocates that fires be allowed to burn homes or valuable timber. But fire has been a natural force on land for millions of years, not just in forests but on prairies and savannahs (grasslands mixed with trees and shrubs). Fire became part of our planet's environment as soon as there was vegetation dry enough to be lit by lightning. From then on, periodic fires have been as natural as rain over much of the Earth's land surface. Rain can sometimes be destructive. So can fire. But a great deal of the Earth's plant and animal life has been "born and bred" with fire and thrives under its influence.

After many years of suppressing forest fires at all costs, ideas about them are changing. In the past few decades scientists have learned a lot about ecology——the study of relationships between living things and their environment. Now they are learning about ecopyrology——the ecology of fire.

Northwestern foresters deliberately set surface fires in order to help the growth of new trees.

Crown fires are inevitable in some Western forests where fuel has accumulated over many years.

The study of fire ecology is complex and fascinating because there are many kinds of forests and many kinds of fires. To understand the natural role of fire, scientists observe current fires and also investigate fires that occurred centuries ago.

They learn about past fires by examining fire scars. When a fire injures a tree's zone of growing cells (the cambium) and the wound heals, a mark that is eventually covered by bark is left. This scar can be seen later, when the tree is cut down. A cross-section near the tree's base reveals many of the fire scars that formed during the tree's life.

Studies of these scars show that fire was a normal occurrence in most of the original forests of North America. In California, scientists discovered that fires have happened about every eight years since the year 1685——as far back as they could date the cedar trees studied. They also found that few fire scars had formed after 1900, when people began preventing forest fires.

Ecologists have concluded that low-intensity fires, burning along the ground, were common in Western forests of ponderosa pine and sequoia. They also occurred frequently in Southeastern pine forests. With the exception of swamps and other year-round wet environments, fire used to be a regular happening in many parts of North America.

In many forests of the Pacific Northwest and Northern Rockies, fires were less frequent and usually more intense. Flames reached the crowns of trees, which were often killed or damaged. Forest managers have accepted the idea that crown fires are inevitable in parts of the West. The cool, dry climate prevents much decay of dead leaves and other natural litter on the forest floor. Plenty of fuel is available when ideal fire weather occurs, as it does in these northern forests every fifty to one hundred years or so.

Since fires have been a part of forest environments for many thousands of years, many plants have adapted to survive them. These plants might be called "fire species." Among them are the major forest trees of the Northern Rockies: ponderosa pine, white pine, lodgepole pine, larch, and Douglas fir.

These trees have especially thick bark, which can withstand fire damage better than the bark of other species. Fire species also include such plants as aspen, willow, and pine grass, which send up many sprouts after suffering fire damage.

One group of Western shrubs, known as *Ceanothus,* is especially dependent on fire. It includes redstem, wedgeleaf, snow brush, and deer brush. *Ceanothus* shrubs are three to nine feet tall and thrive where plenty of sunlight reaches the forest floor. Once damaged by fire, the shrubs produce abundant new sprouts. Furthermore, *Ceanothus* seeds must be exposed to high temperatures in order to sprout.

Ordinarily, vital moisture cannot get through the hard seed coat to the embryo plant inside. Heat from the fires causes the seed coat to open permanently. The seedling can then develop when conditions are right. After a forest fire, ecologists have counted as many as 242,000 *Ceanothus* seedlings on an acre of land.

Ceanothus shrubs thrive where fires occur. Western deer and elk feed on the shrubs, especially in wintertime.

Seed pods opening after a fire. A ponderosa pine seedling flourishes on a forest floor where, once, the leaves were burned and seeds fell directly onto the soil.

The reproduction of jack pine, lodgepole pine, and some other evergreens depends partly on forest fire. These species have sticky resins that hold together the scales of their seed-bearing cones. The cones remain on the trees for many years, storing thousands of pine seeds. In time, a fire releases them. A temperature of about 122 degrees Fahrenheit is needed for the resins to melt so that the seeds can pop out onto the ground.

Fire also burns away all or most of the leaves and other natural litter. Many more seedlings grow from such an exposed seedbed than from a surface covered with a deep layer of leaves.

In a plant community that depends on periodic fire, not all species are well-adapted to it. Some take over if fire is kept out of the forest. Without fire, pines in the Southeast are gradually replaced by such deciduous trees as oaks. If no fire occurs for many years in a lodgepole-pine forest in the Rocky Mountains, the old pines are eventually replaced by Engelmann spruce and fir trees. The entire plant community changes unless a forest fire halts the process. A fire would kill many spruce and fir trees, which are less able to withstand the damage than lodgepole pine. And the fire would help release the seeds that represent a new generation of lodgepole pines.

Ponderosa pine is another fire species. It covers thirty-six million acres of Western land, from Nebraska to the Pacific Ocean and from Mexico to Canada. The large needles of ponderosa pine seem designed to encourage fire. Many needles are dropped each year. Because of their size they do not pack down much, and so they dry quickly. They also contain resins. Thus, the needles decay slowly and burn easily.

527

As long as ponderosa-pine forests have occasional surface fires, the trees thrive and grow in grassy, parklike stands. A ponderosa-pine forest without fire is doomed. When young pines are not thinned out by fire, they grow so close together they are called "dog hair thickets." These thickets are a tremendous crown-fire hazard. Biologists sometimes call these dense stands of trees "biological deserts," because there is so little variety of life in them.

Without fire, white fir and Douglas fir gradually replace the ponderosa pines. The entire forest environment changes. Fir trees have dense crowns, which allow little light to reach the forest floor. Grasses and other surface plants dwindle in numbers and variety——and so do the animals that depend on them. Ecologists have concluded that fire is vital for the survival of beauty and variety in ponderosa-pine forests.

Fire obviously plays a key role in allowing some major plant communities to thrive. Just as there are plant fire species, there are also animal fire species. Elk and deer rely heavily on *Ceanothus* shrubs for winter food in the West. Their health and numbers depend in part on forest fires, which cause *Ceanothus* to thrive. Periodic fires also affect the availability of aspen, a favorite food of moose.

A lack of occasional fires in pine woods may produce a dog hair thicket of young trees.

Elk in Wyoming feed on willow and cottonwood, plants that produce new sprouts after a fire.

The very survival of the endangered Kirtland's warbler seems to depend on fire. About four hundred of these tiny, colorful birds nest in part of Michigan and nowhere else in the world. They are also known as jack-pine birds, because they build nests under or near young jack pines. This species may never have had a very big range. However, its numbers have declined because of fire control in Michigan jack-pine forests. In an attempt to prevent the Kirtland warblers from dying out, foresters now deliberately plan and set some fires to maintain the kind of nesting habitat needed by them.

Forest fires seldom kill wildlife. Most of them do not occur during the season when birds and other animals have young in nests or dens. Many kinds of animals seem able to sense a fire and its direction, and they move out of its way. Even slow-moving creatures like snakes usually escape.

Every forest fire is different and may have different effects. During most of the fire's life it moves slowly. Rain, lack of wind, or lack of fuel may bring the fire almost to a halt for several days. (Some have been known to smolder all winter long, then resume burning in the spring.) Fires have a daily rhythm too, slowing at night when winds usually die down.

A fire's biography may include a wind-pushed rapid spread when some slow-moving animals are overtaken. It may also burn with great heat in certain areas and suffocate some animals hidden in burrows. Overall, however, wildlife populations are not usually harmed.

Deer, elk, and other large mammals often feed calmly near a surface fire. Usually fire fighters, not flames, are what frighten them away. Foresters working in Southern pine woods report that hawks are attracted by smoke. It may be a signal to them that rodents and other prey are on the move. Eagles and other predatory birds in Africa have also been observed catching insects, lizards, and rodents that are flushed from hiding places by an advancing fire.

Wildlife is attracted to freshly burned land too. Mice and other seed-eating rodents appear in great numbers after a forest fire, sometimes to the dismay of foresters who are concerned about getting a new crop of seedling trees.

For elk, deer, and other plant-eating animals, the end of a forest fire marks the beginning of a period of plentiful and nutritious food. Plants that grow after a fire are usually richer than normal in protein, calcium, phosphate, potash, and other nutrients.

In some ways the burning process is like the process of decay speeded up. As leaves and twigs decay, nutrients are released slowly, over a period of months or years. When leaves and twigs burn, the

Red squirrels and deer mice find abundant seeds after a forest fire. These plentiful seed-eating mammals are hunted by hawks and other predators.

This photograph was taken immediately after the Elk Creek Fire in Yellowstone National Park in 1988.

The same place, photographed a year later, is covered by plant growth that was nourished by nutrients from ashes.

nutrients are released quickly. From the soil they are gradually recycled into the roots of plants. This sudden dose of nutrients shows up in plant tissues for about two years after a forest fire.

Whether the new growth is shrub sprouts, new grasses, or other plants, it is nutritious, tender, and perhaps better-tasting than normal. Elk have been observed eating new sprouts of plants that they usually avoid when the plants are older.

A forest fire also produces a more varied "menu" of plants. The burning away of dead leaves, release of nutrients, and increased sunlight on the forest floor help create an environment in which a great variety of plants can grow. After a forest fire swept through an Idaho Douglas-fir forest, ninety-nine different kinds of plants appeared where only fifty-one species had been found before.

Ecologists suspect that periodic forest fires have other good effects. Woodsmoke seems to inhibit the growth of fungi, which sometimes harm living trees. Fire also affects populations of insects, including some pests, which spend part of their lives in the leafy litter of forest floors.

Forests and forest fires vary a lot. Scientists still have much to learn in order to understand and manage the fires that affect the forested one-third of the United States. There is no doubt, however, that the return of periodic fires will be good for most forests and their wildlife.

A Natural Force

Meet the Author

Laurence Pringle is a freelance writer, editor, and photographer. He taught science and worked for *Nature and Science* magazine before beginning his freelance writing career. Pringle writes science books for children and sometimes illustrates his books with photographs he has taken. He feels that writing is "incredibly hard." He would rather spend his time working on photography. He has contributed to *Highlights for Children* and *Ranger Rick* magazines. His interests include reading, movies, and sports.

Theme Connections

Within the Selection

Record your answers to the questions below in the Response Journal section of your Writer's Notebook. In small groups, report the ideas you wrote. Discuss your ideas with the rest of your group. Then choose a person to report your group's answers to the class.

- What does the word *ecopyrology* mean?
- Why is lodgepole pine more resistant to fire than spruce or fir trees?
- Why are predatory birds, such as hawks, attracted to the smoke of forest fires?

Across the Selections

- In "Protecting Wildlife," you read about the value of preserving the environment. In "A Natural Force," though, the author says that forest fires are good, even though they destroy some of the environment. How can this be? Explain the benefits of a forest fire.

Beyond the Selection

- Think about how "A Natural Force" adds to what you know about ecology.
- Add items to the Concept/Question Board about ecology.

Poem for the Ancient Trees

by Robert Priest

I

am young and
I want to live
to be old
and I don't want to
outlive these trees—this forest.
When my last song is gone
I want these same trees
to be singing on—newer green songs
for generations to come
so let me be old—let me grow
to be ancient
to come as an elder
before these same temple-green sentinels
with my aged limbs
and still know a wonder
that will outlast me.
O I want
long love
long life.
Give me
150 years
of luck.
But don't
let me
outlive
these trees.

535

Focus Questions How do the toxins introduced into the environment affect the animal species? What is required to save a single endangered species from extinction?

Saving the Peregrine Falcon

Caroline Arnold
photographs by Richard R. Hewett

High above a tall bank building in downtown Los Angeles, a peregrine falcon soars in the air looking for food below. The peregrine falcon is a wild bird that we do not normally think of as a city dweller. Yet the peregrine is at home among the high-rise buildings, which in many ways are like the cliffs and mountains where peregrines usually live. Window and roof ledges make good places to perch and to lay eggs, and the streets below are filled with pigeons, starlings, sparrows, and other small birds that peregrines like to eat. Today more and more peregrines are becoming part of city life as part of a special program to try to save this beautiful and powerful bird from extinction.

For centuries the peregrine was prized by kings and falconers who used it to hunt. Bird lovers too have always admired the peregrine. Yet a few years ago it was feared that soon there would be no more peregrines. Man's pollution of the environment with the poison DDT had interfered with

536

the birds' ability to produce babies. The total number of peregrines was growing smaller each year. In 1970 there were only two known pairs of nesting peregrines in California. Until the 1940s, when DDT began to be used, there had been nearly two hundred. In the eastern United States the peregrine had already become extinct by 1970. Only with man's help could the peregrine be saved.

Peregrine falcons are found all over the world. The scientific name for those found in the United States is *Falco peregrinus anatum*. Other falcons living in the United States are the gyrfalcon, the prairie falcon, the merlin, and the kestrel. Although the numbers of these other falcons have been reduced by man, none of them were endangered like the peregrine.

Falcons are similar in many ways to birds in the hawk family. When flying, however, a falcon has pointed wings, which are better suited to speed, whereas a hawk has wide-spread wing feathers, which are better suited to soaring.

You can recognize an adult peregrine because it appears to wear a large black moustache. Both males and females have the same color markings but, as with all hawks and falcons, the female is larger and stronger than the male. A female peregrine is usually about twenty inches long and weighs about thirty ounces. A male is about fifteen inches long

and weighs about eighteen ounces. The male is sometimes called a tiercel from the French word meaning "third" because he is about a third smaller than the female peregrine.

Falcons, like hawks, eagles, and owls, catch and eat other animals. They are predators. The peregrine specializes in a diet of birds. In the United States, peregrines used to be called duck hawks because they were seen around marshes and occasionally hunted ducks.

The peregrine's body, like those of other predatory birds, is well adapted for hunting. Its strong feet and sharp talons are ideal for catching and carrying, and its beak is designed for tearing. The peregrine's eyesight is so keen that it has been compared to a person being able to read a newspaper a mile away! A soaring peregrine can see a bird hundreds of feet below.

After spotting a bird, the peregrine points its head down, tucks in its wings and feet, and transforms its body into the shape of a speeding bullet. As it begins to dive, it pumps its wings to increase its speed up to 200 miles per hour! When the peregrine reaches its prey, it grabs it with its feet, then quickly kills it by breaking its neck. The peregrine then either carries the dead bird to a protected place and eats it, or brings it back to the nest to feed hungry babies.

Baby peregrines are usually called chicks, although a chick in a wild nest is also called an eyas.

Some of the smaller birds that peregrines in the United States eat spend the winter in Central and South America. There they eat grains and insects that have been sprayed with DDT. DDT is a poison used by farmers to kill insects that are harmful to crops. When the birds eat food with DDT on it, the poison is stored in their bodies. Later, when the peregrines eat these birds, they eat the poison too. The more birds the peregrines eat, the more DDT they store.

Scientists in the United States have found that DDT causes birds to lay eggs with shells that are too thin. When they measure the shells of hatched or broken eggs, they find that the thinnest shells are those with the most DDT in them. When parent birds sit on these eggs to keep them warm, the thin shells often break. Thin-shelled eggs also lose moisture faster than thick-shelled eggs. Often the chick growing inside the egg dies because the egg dries out too much. By helping the eggs with thin shells to hatch, scientists can combat some of the effects of DDT.

Most wild peregrines nest on high ledges on rocky cliffs. These nest sites are called eyries. A pair of peregrines makes a nest in an eyrie by scraping clean a small area in the stones or sand. In the scrape the female usually lays three eggs. Scientists carefully watch each peregrine nest. Then if they feel that the eggs are unlikely to hatch without help, they borrow them for a while, but first they let the birds sit on the eggs for five days. This seems to improve the eggs' chances of hatching in the laboratory. To get the eggs to the laboratory, scientists had to find a way to extract the eggs from the nest without scaring off the parent peregrines.

Because the cliffs where peregrines nested were so steep, only a mountain climber could reach a nest. When he approached the nest, the angry parents screeched and swooped at him. The mountain climber quickly and carefully put each speckled egg into a padded box. He then replaced the eggs he had taken with plaster eggs which look just like real peregrine eggs. These fake eggs would fool the parent birds. After the mountain climber left, the parents would return to the nest and sit on the plaster eggs as if they were their own.

It was important to keep the parent birds interested in the nest. After the eggs had hatched, the mountain climber would bring the babies back so that the parents could take care of them.

When the mountain climber returned to the top of the cliff, he put the eggs into a portable incubator. The incubator would keep them safe and warm on their ride back to the laboratory.

During the extinction scare, Brian Walton and the staff of the Santa Cruz Predatory Bird Research Group (SCPBRG) would collect eggs and release birds throughout the western United States. The laboratory at the SCPBRG center was used for hatching eggs and caring for the newly hatched peregrine chicks.

In the laboratory each egg was carefully weighed. Then it was held in front of a bright light in a dark room. This is called candling. When an egg is candled, the shadow of the chick growing inside and a lighter area at the large end of the egg can be seen. The lighter area is called the air pocket.

Then the egg was placed on a rack inside an incubator. The incubator keeps the egg warm and moist. Each day the egg would be weighed and candled again. As the chick grew, water slowly evaporated from the egg, making room for the air pocket to get bigger. The egg's weight shows how much water it is losing. If it was losing water too quickly, the incubator could be made more moist.

Wild birds turn their eggs constantly as they move around in the nest. But in the laboratory, people must carefully turn each egg four or five times each day. This prevents the growing chick from sticking to the inside of the eggshell. If the eggs are not turned, they will not hatch.

Sometimes eggs were found with shells so thin that they had already begun to crack. Then people in the laboratory would try to repair them with glue. Sometimes eggs were also waxed to prevent them from losing moisture. Everything

possible was done to make sure that each egg hatched into a healthy peregrine chick.

The eggs were kept in the incubator until they were 31½ days old. Then they were carefully watched for the first signs of hatching.

Each chick has a hard pointed knob on the top of its beak. This is called an egg tooth. The chick pushes against the inside of the shell with its egg tooth and breaks the shell.

The first crack in the egg is called the pip. When the pip appears, the egg is moved to a special hatching chamber. There the egg will take 24 to 48 hours to hatch. During that time somebody watched it all the time. Some chicks are too weak to break out of their shells. Then the scientists were there to help them.

Often two eggs begin to hatch at about the same time. Then they were put next to each other in the hatcher. When a chick is ready to hatch, it begins to peep inside its shell. The two chicks can hear each other peep. This seems to encourage them to move around and break their shells. Sometimes where there was only one egg, the scientists would make peeping sounds for the chick to hear.

Starting at the pip, the chick slowly turns, pressing its egg tooth against the shell. Soon the crack becomes a ring around the shell. Then the chick pushes its head against the

top of the shell, and the shell pops open. After hatching, the egg tooth is no longer needed, and in a week or so it falls off.

The newly hatched chick is wet and its down feathers are matted together. A cotton swab was used to clean the feathers. If necessary, ointment was put on the chick's navel to prevent infection. In the shell the chick gets nutrients from the yolk through its navel. Normally, by the time a chick hatches, the yolk has been totally absorbed and the navel has closed.

In the wild, a mother bird broods her chicks by sitting on top of them to keep them warm and dry. In the laboratory, the dry chick was placed with one or more other chicks in a small container called a brooder. A heater kept the chicks warm. The chick would rest in the brooder for eight to twelve hours. Then it would be ready for its first meal.

In the wild, the father peregrine hunts birds and brings them back to the nest. Then he and the mother peregrine tear off small bits of meat to feed each chick. The hungry chicks beg for food by peeping and opening their mouths wide.

Bird meat was also used to feed chicks in the laboratory. Usually the chicks were fed quail, although adult birds were also fed pigeon and chicken meat. First the meat was put through a meat grinder to break it into small pieces. The newly hatched chicks were then fed tiny pieces with tweezers. For somewhat older chicks the ground meat could be squeezed through a bag with a nozzle.

Like many birds, falcons have pouches in their necks to store food. These are called crops. Food first goes to the crop and then to the stomach. A bird feeder knew that a chick had had enough when the crop began to bulge.

During the day, young peregrine chicks need to be fed every three to five hours. At night they sleep eight hours between feedings.

Even though the peregrine chicks were cared for by people, it is important that they remain wild. During the first week or so, the chicks cannot see very well. Then it does not matter if people feed them directly. But as they get older, their contact with people must be limited.

Young animals identify with the other animals they see during the first weeks of life. This is called imprinting. Most young animals see only their parents in early life, and they imprint on them.

Peregrines raised in the laboratory that were returned to the wild had to be imprinted on adult peregrines. One way to help them do this was to feed them with a peregrine-shaped puppet. The puppet fooled the peregrine chicks and they behaved as if it were a real bird.

When a peregrine chick was three days to a week old, it was put into the nest of an adult bird that has been imprinted on people. At the SCPBRG center, adult birds were kept in barnlike buildings. Each large, open-air room in these buildings had bars across the top to let in air and light. Each room also has perches and nesting ledges for the birds.

Unfortunately there were not enough adult peregrines at the center to care for all the hatched chicks. Another more common bird, the prairie falcon, is very much like the peregrine, and it was often used as a substitute parent for very young peregrine chicks. During the breeding season, a female prairie falcon would care for adopted peregrine chicks. She would keep them warm and feed them as if they were her own. When the chicks were one to two weeks old, they were put into nests of peregrines which were not imprinted on people. Then, at the age of three weeks, the young peregrines were ready to go back to wild nests.

Before a bird would go back to the wild, a metal band was put on its leg. The band identified the bird and helped people keep track of it as it grew up.

Then the chicks were put into a special wooden pack and taken to the nest site. There the mountain climber put the pack on his back and climbed to the nest. He removed the plaster eggs and put in the young chicks. Then he left as quickly as possible. He did not want to disturb the parent birds any more than necessary.

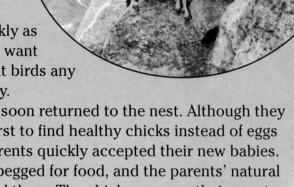

The parent birds soon returned to the nest. Although they were surprised at first to find healthy chicks instead of eggs in their nest, the parents quickly accepted their new babies. The hungry chicks begged for food, and the parents' natural response was to feed them. The chicks were on their way to growing up as wild peregrines.

Most wild birds do not breed well in captivity. They are easily disturbed by people and by loud noises. At the SCPBRG the birds rarely saw people, although people could see the birds through tiny peepholes.

In the bird buildings a radio was constantly played. The sound blocked out most noises from outside. The radio also helped the birds become used to people's voices. Then they were less likely to be startled when people made noises outside their chambers.

Pairs of peregrine falcons at the SCPBRG center built nests and bred just as birds do in the wild. Their chicks could be released to help increase the number of wild peregrines.

Both in the wild and in captivity, peregrines normally raise only one nest of chicks each year. If the eggs are destroyed,

however, the birds will lay a second set. In the wild, peregrine eggs might be eaten by other birds or animals. At the center, scientists purposely took away the first eggs from each pair of breeding falcons and hatched them in an incubator. The birds then laid another set of eggs. In this way each pair of birds could produce twice as many chicks as usual.

During its six weeks in the nest, a peregrine grows from a fluffy chick covered with soft down to a fully feathered bird the size of its parents. These first juvenile feathers are a mottled brown color. The peregrine will get its adult feathers at the beginning of its second year.

Three-week-old peregrine chicks were put into known wild nests that have parent birds on them when possible. But because there were so few peregrines left in the wild, soon all the wild peregrine nests were filled. Some peregrine chicks were put into wild prairie falcon nests. Others were released on their own when they were old enough to fly.

In the wild, a young peregrine is ready to fly at the age of six weeks. Then it leaves the nest and tries to hunt for food. At first it is not a very good hunter. Its parents will help it and continue to feed it. When juvenile peregrines from the laboratory were put into the wild, they had no parents to help them. Then people must help them instead.

Usually the birds were released near cliff tops or mountain ledges far away from where people live. They were placed in a box at the release site when they were about five weeks old. Sometimes the box had to be carried to the release site by a helicopter.

547

The box had bars across one side, but the people involved tried to stay out of the birds' sight. From behind, they dropped meat into the box for the birds. Then after a week, the box was opened and the birds were allowed to fly free.

People stayed at the site and put food out each day until the birds learn to take care of themselves. This could take four to five weeks. When the birds no longer needed to return to the release site for food, the people's job was finished.

In addition to its identification band, each bird also wore a small radio transmitter. The radio made beeping sounds which could be heard with a radio receiver. During the first few weeks on its own, a bird sometimes got lost or in trouble. Then people could find it by tracking the beeps over the radio receiver. After a few weeks the transmitter would no longer be needed, and it would fall off the bird.

Most birds were set free in wild places where peregrines once lived but are now gone. It was hoped that the new peregrines would stay there, build nests, and bring up chicks of their own.

Some peregrines were released in cities, and they seem to have adapted well to city life. Los Angeles, New York, Washington, Baltimore, Edmonton, London, and Nairobi are just some of the cities around the world where peregrines live. Some live on the ledges of office buildings. Others have

built nests on tall bridges. In England peregrines lived for many years in the spire of Salisbury Cathedral.

In cities peregrines were usually released from the tops of tall buildings. As in the wild, people stayed and fed the birds until they could take care of themselves. After a pair of peregrines had claimed a building ledge as a nest site, scientists sometimes built a nest there for the birds. They may even have put a fake egg into the nest. They hoped that this would encourage the birds to begin laying their own eggs.

Peregrines usually do not mate and have young until their third year. In their first breeding years in the wild, peregrines can raise their own chicks. But as the birds get older and store more and more DDT in their bodies, their egg shells will become dangerously thin.

Peregrines must survive many dangers before they are old enough to produce their own chicks. Many hurt themselves when they collide with man-made objects such as fences or telephone and electric wires. Others are shot by unthinking people. Centers like the SCPBRG help sick and wounded peregrines.

The peregrine falcon is a beautiful bird, and it would have been sad to let it become extinct simply through ignorance or carelessness. Many animals that once roamed the earth are now gone because man destroyed or polluted their environments. For the present, the peregrine falcon has been saved from extinction. Through the work of many people around the world its numbers are increasing each year. If you are lucky, maybe where you live, you can see one of these magnificent birds soaring high in the sky.

Saving the Peregrine Falcon

Meet the Author

Caroline Arnold is a well-known writer of nonfiction science and nature books for children. Her books help children learn about the life cycles, habitats, and histories of many amazing animals. She discovered her love of nature at an early age and still remembers how excited she would be when she found a fossil or saw an animal in the wild. "As I write about animals, dinosaur bones, and other scientific subjects, my goal is to convey that same sense of discovery."

Meet the Photographer

Richard Hewett had his own darkroom by the time he was twelve years old. He is best known for his collaboration with Caroline Arnold on a series of children's science books. When Arnold and Hewett work together to create a book, they believe that the text and the photographs are equally important.

Hewett's photograph of a bloodhound named Stretch hangs in the Metropolitan Museum in New York City.

Theme Connections

Within the Selection

Record your answers to the questions below in the Response Journal section of your Writer's Notebook. In small groups, report the ideas you wrote. Discuss your ideas with the rest of your group. Then choose a person to report your group's answers to the class.

- What is the difference between a peregrine falcon and a hawk?
- How exactly does DDT harm the peregrine falcon?
- What does *imprinting* mean? How were peregrine chicks tricked into imprinting on adult peregrines?

Across the Selections

- In "Alejandro's Gift," you saw how Alejandro put the animals at ease by digging a second water hole farther away from his house. Similarly, the people who tended to the chicks of peregrine falcons were careful to not let the chicks see them too much. These peoples' behavior suggests that saving the environment sometimes requires humility and selflessness. What do you think? How can humility and selflessness help save the environment?

Beyond the Selection

- Having read about people helping the peregrine falcon, think about a time when you helped an animal. Maybe you did something extensive, like nursing an injured animal back to health, or maybe you did something less extensive, like feeding an alley cat or having a small pet. Whatever your experience, think about how it felt to nurture an animal. How was your experience similar to the one you just read about? How was it different? Get into small groups and share your experiences. Then be prepared to share them with the class.

Focus Questions What upset the balance of the ecosystem on Borneo?
Will parachuting cats on the island solve the problem?

THE DAY THEY PARACHUTED CATS ON BORNEO

A DRAMA OF ECOLOGY
Charlotte Pomerantz
illustrated by Jose Aruego

This play is based on an actual event reported in the New York Times, *November 13, 1969.*

Cast in order of appearance and disappearance

I The Island of Borneo

II Malaria

III DDT

IV Mosquitoes

V Cockroaches

VI Caterpillars

VII Lizards

VIII More Lizards

IX Cats

X The Rivers

XI Rats

XII Helicopters

XIII Parapussycats

XIV More Parapussycats

XV Still More Parapussycats

XVI The Roof Beams

XVII The Farmer

XVIII The Ecologist

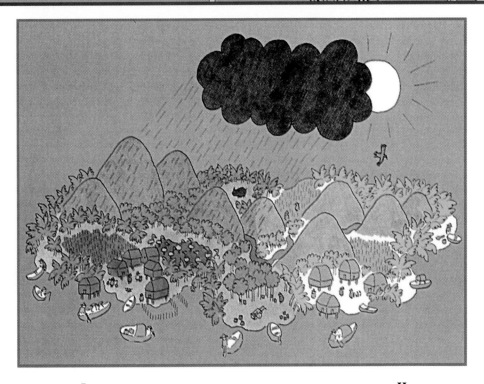

I

I am the island of Borneo,
Where the farmer—poor farmer—bends low,
   bends low.
I have honey bears, rhinos, and tiger cats,
Great falcons, flamingoes, and foxy-faced bats.
I have gold and quicksilver, rubber and rice,
Cane sugar and spice—but not everything nice:
     A land of harsh ridges and savage
      monsoon,
     Of jungles as dark as the dark of the
      moon.
     Land of thundering rains and earthquakes
      and heat,
     Where the farmer's life is more
      bitter than sweet.
     Land of mosquitoes, which
      carry with ease
     The dreaded malaria, scourge
      and disease.

II

I am malaria, dreaded disease.
I cause men to ache and to shake and to freeze.
Three hundred million a year do I seize.
One million I kill with remarkable ease.
But I'm not the big killer I used to be
In the good old days before—ugh!—DDT;
'Cause that stuff kills mosquitoes—one,
   two, three . . .

**And the death of them is
the death of me.**

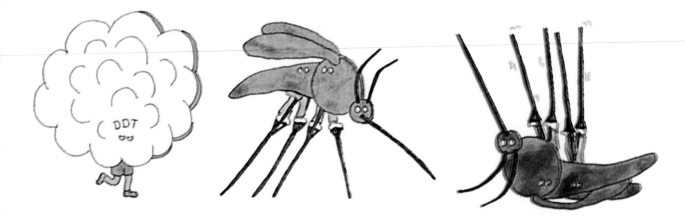

If you don't know what ecology means, you'll soon find out.

Postscriptum: we died.

III

My name is dichloro-diphenyl-trichloroethane,
Which you've got to admit is a heck of a name.
But, perhaps, some of you have heard tell of
  me
By my well-known initials, which are DDT.
An organo-chlorine insecticide,
I come in a powder or liquified.
I'm death to mosquitoes outside or inside.
I was brought here by copter to Borneo,
Where the farmer—now hopeful—bends low,
  bends low.
My job is to kill that cruel killer of man:
A worthy and wise ecological plan.

IV

We are the mosquitoes who roam day
  and night,
Bringing death to the farmer with one
  small bite.
We like the farmer's hut—it buzzes with life.
There's the farmer, of course, his kids and
  his wife.
The caterpillars chew on the roof beams there,
While the geckoes, or lizards, roam
  everywhere.
There are lots of cockroaches, and always
  some cats
Who pounce on the lizards and scare away
  rats.
All of us are busy—busy looking for food.
Sometimes we eat each other, which may
  seem rather crude.
But imagine yourself in that hut, and I bet
You would rather eat someone than find
  yourself et.

Now suddenly—zap!—there is no place to hide,
For they sprayed all the huts with insecticide.
That's the end of our tale.

You'd have to be eaten to know how it feels.

V

We are the cockroaches, homeloving pests.
In most people's huts we are unwelcome guests.
When we all got sprayed with that DDT stuff,
The mosquitoes got killed—not us. We're
  too tough.
We just swallowed hard and kept right on
  a-crawling,
Despite the rude comments and vicious
  name-calling.

People are so anti-roach.

VI

We're the hungry caterpillars of Borneo,
Where the farmer—also hungry—bends low,
  bends low.
We live on the roof beams, eating and
  thatching.
We make all our meals out of roof beams and
  thatching.
    Nosh-nosh, nibble-nibble, munch-munch-
      munch,
    For breakfast, supper, high tea and lunch.
Our life is as pleasant as green tea and roses,
Except when the lizards (gulp) poke in their
  noses
    Then nosh-nosh, nibble-nibble, munch-
      munch-munch,
    The lizards ate half our cousins for lunch.
Those four-legged reptiles ruin our meals . . .

At night the caterpillars
and the roaches
Walk right up to us and say,
Buenas Noches.

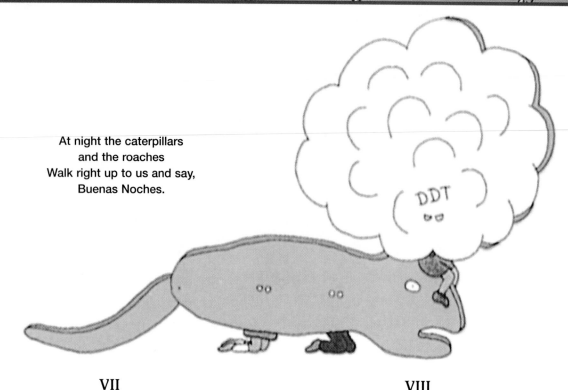

VII

We are the lizards, or geckoes, by name.
To the farmer we're useful, we're charming,
    we're tame.
Over the floors, walls and roof beams we
    roam,
Of every tropical home sweet home.
For us, cockroaches are scrumptious to eat.
Almost as tasty as caterpillar meat.

VIII

Then the copters sprayed, and we lost our
    appetite.
Now we laze away the days, we snooze the
    balmy night.
For every roach we eat, though they *do* taste
    yummy,
Adds DDT to our little lizard tummy.
And makes our tiny nervous system sluggish
    and slow.
We geckoes—leaping lizards!—got no get-up-
    and-go.
    It's true we're not dying of DDT,
    But a slooow gecko ain't nooo gecko,
    As the caterpillars can plainly see.
We watch them eating roof beams like there's
    no tomorrow,
While we lizards hold our tummies in pain
    and sorrow.

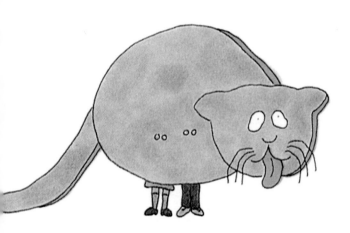

Be careful of the lizard you eat.
The life you take may be your own.

IX

We're the cats on the island of Borneo
Where the farmer—who loves us—bends low,
    bends low.
Eating all those lizards, or geckoes, by name,
Is turning out to be (sigh) a dying shame,
'Cause those lizards are poisoned from tail
    to head,
And killing those lizards is killing us dead.
We poor cats got a massive overdose.
What's left to say
(Sob)
Except *adios*.

Whoever thought that little man could affect
us mighty rivers? But the rain has washed the
DDT into our waters, and our tenants, the
friendly fish, are feeling pretty rocky.

X

We're the rivers, the rivers of Borneo.
We watch little man come and go, come and go.
We watched him kill mosquitoes with
    pesticide.
Saw the roaches poisoned, though not one
    cockroach died
Till . . .
The hungry lizards ate them, one by one
    by one.
Oh what a feast they had—it seemed like good
    clean fun.
But every roach they ate, though they *did* taste
    yummy,
Added DDT to their little lizard tummy.
Then the lizards were filled with deadly
    pesticide.
They felt pretty punchy, though not one
    lizard died
Till . . .
The hungry cats devoured them, one by one
    by one.
Oh what a feast they had—it seemed like good
    clean fun.
But every liz they ate, though they *did* taste
    yummy,
Killed the cats by poisoning their DD Toxic
    tummy.
Now this poor old island is steeped in
    poison air.
Our waters, too, are poisoned. Little man,
    take care!

XI

We're the rats on the island of Borneo,
We never had it so good—heigh—dee—ho.
When the cats who had swallowed the geckoes
    lay dying,
We crawled in by thousands from forests
    outlying.
        When the farmers saw us, they raised an
            anguished cry:
        "Rats bring plague! Fly in help, or we shall
            surely die.
        Help us, men of science, help us kill the
            rats;
        For the DDT you sprayed has killed off all
            our cats!"
"Borneo for rent," we sang. "Inquire, please,
    within.
When the cats die off from DDT, we rats—
    move—in."

It was, all told,
a rather unusual assignment.

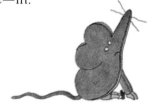

And then the helicopters came...

XII

We're the copters who've just flown in
    thousands of cats
And chuted them down on the armies of rats,
On the plague-threatened island of Borneo,
A bright green jewel in the blue sea below.

Once we came with DDT; now we come with
    cats.
Once we sprayed mosquitoes; now we'll fix
    the rats.
Looks like no one really thought the whole
    thing through . . .
Soon all the cats and rats will have a deadly
    rendezvous.

XIII

We're the parapussycats they parachuted
    down
On every cat-killed, rat-filled little village
    and town
On the dead-cat, dread-rat island of Borneo,
Where the farmer—strictly catless—bends low,
    low, low.

It's better than hanging
around fish markets.

XIV

When we parapussycats were dropped to the
    ground,
What a feast we had—there were rats all
    around.
Everywhere you looked there were rats and
    rats and rats
Pursued by our élite corps of parapussycats.
We chased the rats for days, till most of them
    had fled,
And those who didn't run fast enough were—
    biff bam!—dead.

XV

The good farmers gave us a ticker-tape parade.
They heaped us with ivory, gold and silk
    brocade.
They said they would grant us our most
    fantastic wish—
So we asked them for five hundred kettles of
    fish.
We were wined, we were dined, we slept in
    king-size beds,
Till we heard a strange creaking just over our
    heads . . .
KA-RASH!

But let the roof beams
tell their own story.

XVI

We're the roof beams of thatched huts in
  Borneo,
Where the farmer—enduring—bends low,
  bends low.
If a man, now and then, did some roof
  patching,
Replaced chewed-up beams and half-eaten
  thatching,
We could keep out the wind, the rain, and
  the sun,
And shelter a man when his labors were done.
Despite caterpillars, we roof beams stayed
  strong,
And the lizards, by eating them, helped us along.
For the lizard, you see, was the number-one
  killer
Of the beam-eating (nosh-nosh) cater- (nosh-
  nosh) pillar.

Now we mourn the little lizards—may they rest
  in peace—
While the greedy caterpillars (burp) get more
  and more obese.

XVII

Good day, I'm a farmer in Borneo,
Where the coconut palm and the mango grow.
Here are honey bears, rhinos, and tiger cats.
Great falcons, flamingoes, and foxy-faced bats.
Here are gold and quicksilver, rubber and rice,
Cane sugar and spice—but not everything nice:
    When they sprayed my hut with insecticide,
    My rat-catching cat soon sickened and
      died.
    When the rats crawled in, I was filled
      with fear:
    The plague can kill more than malaria here.
    When my roof beams caved in, I moved
      next door,
    Until *their* roof beams collapsed to the floor.
But please do not think I wish to offend,
For DDT is the farmer's good friend.
Still, perhaps you'll allow a poor man to say,
He hopes men of science will soon find a way
To kill the mosquitoes till all, all are dead—
But save the roof beams which are over my
  head,
As well as my most useful rat-catching cat.
How grateful I'd be if you'd only do that!
    Then, men of science, I would not
      complain.
    But now I must look to my roof—I smell
      rain!

560

XVIII

I am an ecologist. Ecology is the study of living things in relation to the world around them—everything around them—air, water, rocks, soil, plants, and animals, including man.

If a tree is cut down, I try to find out what will happen to the birds in the nests, the squirrels in the branches, the insects at the roots. I know that the roots of the tree hold the earth, that the earth holds the rainwater, and that the rainwater keeps the soil moist, so that plants can grow. I am concerned if too many trees are cut down, for then the rain will run off the surface of the soil, making the rivers rise, overflow their banks and flood the land. This is the kind of thing an ecologist thinks about.

Borneo is a huge island in Southeast Asia—the third largest in the world and bigger than all of Texas. It straddles the equator, which is why the climate is hot and steamy. Someone has said that there are two seasons in Borneo—a wet season and a less wet season.

The people are mainly Malays and Dyaks. The Malays, who live near the coast, are rice farmers and fishermen. Some work on rubber plantations or in the oil fields, for Borneo is rich in oil. Inland are high mountain ranges, where most of the Dyaks live. Until recently, they were headhunters—the wild men of Borneo—and they still hunt with blowguns and poisoned darts. The women grow rice, yams, and sugarcane in tiny forest clearings.

Most of Borneo is part of the Republic of Indonesia. Some of it belongs to Malaysia, and a tiny part is an independent state called Brunei. It is an island of dense tropical forests, where vines grow as high as a thousand feet, where orangutans swing through the trees, and where the giant long-nosed proboscis monkey can grow as tall as a man. There is also a great variety of insects, including the anopheles mosquito. This mosquito carries malaria and is the reason I was sent to Borneo.

Mosquitoes breed in wet places, and there are many swamps and rain holes in Borneo. In the old days, we used to fight mosquitoes by draining swamps, when possible, and by spraying a thin film of oil on stagnant waters during the breeding season. Those who could afford to, put screens on doors, windows, and openings to keep the mosquitoes out. All this helped to keep malaria down, but millions of people still got sick.

Then, during World War II, a scientist discovered that a certain chemical compound, called dichloro-diphenyl-trichloroethane—DDT for short—was a marvelous insect killer. The discoverer, Dr. Paul Mueller of Switzerland, received the Nobel Prize for his discovery.

In Borneo, we sprayed the walls and insides of the huts with DDT. You know what happened: we killed the mosquitoes—and ended up with no cats. We had not realized how much DDT can accumulate in the fatty tissues of animals. Even a tiny amount of DDT in food or drinking water, with repeated meals, builds up and up until the quantity is large enough to poison a large animal, such as a cat.

As you know, with the cats dead, the rats took over and brought the threat of plague. So cats were flown in to stop the rats. Then, just when matters seemed under control—the roofs fell down. This is but a small example of the complex and subtle connections and balances which exist among all living things.

Because of the poisonous effects of DDT, it has been banned or restricted in the United States, the Commonwealth of Independent States, and other industrial countries. In December, 1969, at a world conference of the Food and Agricultural Organization (a body of the United Nations), an attempt was made to ban the use of DDT all over the world.

But the majority of scientists, representing the nonindustrial countries, refused to go along with the ban. They knew DDT was dangerous to health, but they needed it to control malaria and other diseases, and to protect food crops from insect destruction. The alternatives to DDT are expensive, and the nonindustrial countries, which contain about eighty percent of the world's population, cannot afford them, for they are very poor.

The wealthy nations pointed out that the danger of pesticides is everyone's responsibility, for when you pollute the atmosphere, and the waters which flow to the oceans, everyone suffers. Ecologically, the nations of the earth are one.

The poor nations replied that the wealthy nations are not faced with malaria epidemics, wholesale destruction of the food supply, and mass starvation. They can afford to worry about the future of the environment. The poor nations can only think of day-to-day survival. Seventy-five per cent of the people in the world go to bed hungry, and the great majority of them are in the poor, nonindustrial countries.

Ecologists from underdeveloped countries, faced with starvation and disease, can only choose the lesser evil—DDT. But the real answer to their problem is to find new solutions. Work is going forward on drugs for the prevention of malaria. Unfortunately, some of these drugs have bad side effects. Others are not effective for all kinds of malaria. And all drugs are very expensive.

A more fruitful road is for scientists to seek an insecticide that kills mosquitoes and nothing else. Scientists have discovered that under crowded conditions, some mosquitoes release a toxic chemical that kills young mosquitoes. If they can isolate and synthesize that chemical, it would be a great step forward in malaria control.

Another possibility, which shows considerable promise, is to breed a variety of mosquito which leaves seventy-five per cent of the female eggs unfertilized. Released among other mosquitoes, this new strain transmits its infertility to all the offspring. Thus each generation would breed fewer and fewer mosquitoes.

We've been talking about DDT and the farmers of Borneo, but ecological problems are extremely varied and serious, and they cover the whole world. For example, the fumes of automobile exhausts have greatly increased the number of people who get lung diseases. Atomic radiation has increased the incidence of certain types of cancer. The hot water from power plants, when poured into lakes and rivers, kills the fishes.

There is pollution by lumber mills in Lake Baikal in the Commonwealth of Independent States. There is too much sewage in the canals of Amsterdam and Venice. The Danube is no longer blue. One can no longer swim in the Rhine in Germany, or in the Seine in Paris, or in our own Hudson River. Whole stretches of beaches in Italy, South America, England, and the United States have been polluted with oil slicks from the sea.

This is bad enough, but if the oil spills continue, worse will follow: a thin film of oil will spread over all the oceans. This will cut down the sunlight which very tiny plants, called diatoms, need both to reproduce and to live. These tiny plants, billions and billions of them, are the source of food for all the fishes of the sea. Further, these tiny plants use sunlight to combine with water to form carbon dioxide (used as food by them) and oxygen which is released into the air. Eighty percent of all the oxygen in the world comes from these tiny plants. If sunlight is cut down and the amount of oxygen is reduced, the whole animal kingdom, including man, will suffer.

We need to know these things, so that we can do something to keep the air and water clean for all the people, as well as for all the animals and plants in the world. The ecologist should not protect the farmer against malaria with one hand and bring the roof down on his head with the other. But the answer is not for the ecologist to do nothing, but to be wiser about what he does. This is the moral of Borneo.

THE DAY THEY PARACHUTED CATS ON BORNEO

Meet the Author

Charlotte Pomerantz has had articles, poems, and stories published in several magazines for children and adults. As a child she remembers writing stories for enjoyment. "As far back as I can remember, I have liked to write, with no thought of being a writer." Pomerantz continued writing throughout high school and college and found success writing children's stories after her own children were born. They "provided rich, raw material. . . . I started making notes of what they said. . . . I recommend the keeping of a journal to all who would write and remember."

Meet the Illustrator

Jose Aruego is a well-known illustrator of children's books. He was born into a family of lawyers in the Philippines. It was assumed he would also become a lawyer, so he attended law school. After working as a lawyer for three months, Aruego realized he was not happy. He really wanted to go to art school to become a cartoonist, so that is what he did. After graduating, he sold his cartoons to magazines such as *The Saturday Evening Post* and *The New Yorker*. After he married and had a child, he began writing and illustrating books for children. Aruego has written or illustrated more than 60 children's books and has won many awards for his illustrations.

Theme Connections

Within the Selection

Record your answers to the questions below in the Response Journal section of your Writer's Notebook. In small groups, report the ideas you wrote. Discuss your ideas with the rest of your group. Then choose a person to report your group's answers to the class.

- Why were cats flown into Borneo?
- Why did people's roofs fall down?
- What does the author say is the moral of Borneo?

Across the Selections

- As you saw in this selection, a very delicate balance exists in the environment. In one fashion or another, each creature depends on each other creature. What other selections have you read in this unit that highlight this delicate balance? Give examples.

Beyond the Selection

- Think about how "The Day They Parachuted Cats on Borneo" adds to what you know about ecology.
- Add items to the Concept/Question Board about ecology.

A Question of Value

Why are some things worth more than other things? Can things that cost very little money be valuable? What do you consider valuable?

KING MIDAS

A Golden Tale Told by
John Warren Stewig
Pictured Through the Mind of Omar Rayyan

Once upon a time there lived a king of Phrygia. His name was Midas. He was fonder of gold than of anything in the world, except for his daughter, Marygold.

In earlier days, when Marygold was in a cradle and the queen still alive, King Midas would sit in his garden and smell his beautiful roses. But now he only gazed at them, wondering how much they'd be worth if each rose petal were made of gold.

The king became so obsessed that he could no longer bear to see or touch any object that wasn't gold. He took to spending most of his time in the dungeon beneath the castle, examining all his treasures.

Though Midas considered himself happy, he knew he would never be completely content until the whole room was filled with gold.

One day when the king was admiring a pile of golden coins in the dungeon, a shadow fell upon them. Midas looked up and saw a stranger.

The king had bolted the door. No mere human could have entered the dungeon. Might this visitor be some sort of god? Perhaps he had come to do Midas a favor? What could that be, unless it was to help multiply the king's treasure?

The stranger gazed around the room. "You are indeed a wealthy man, my friend," he observed. "I doubt whether any four walls in all the earth contain as much gold as you have here."

"I have done pretty well," Midas agreed. "But this is merely a trifle, only a small portion of the world's gold."

"What!" exclaimed the stranger. "Then you are not content? What would satisfy you?"

"I am weary of the time and trouble it takes to collect my treasures," said Midas. "I wish that everything I touch might turn to gold."

The stranger's smile grew so bright that sunlight seemed to fill the room. "You have thought of a brilliant wish, the Golden Touch. But will this satisfy you?"

"How could it fail?" asked the king.

"And you will never regret possessing it?"

"Nothing could make me happier," answered Midas.

"Be it as you wish," agreed the stranger. "Tomorrow at sunrise you will have the Golden Touch." The stranger became brighter still, and Midas closed his eyes so as not to be blinded. When he opened them again, the stranger was gone.

The next day, before the sun reached over the hills, King Midas awoke. He stretched out his arm and laid a finger on the chair beside his bed. But the chair remained ebony. Had he only dreamed about the visitor?

He lay back in bed, growing sadder and sadder. Soon, a sunbeam shone through the window and onto the bed covering. Midas watched in amazement as the linen fabric changed into woven gold. The Golden Touch had come with the first sunbeam.

The king jumped out of bed and ran around the room, grasping everything within reach. He seized a bedpost and it turned into fluted gold. He pulled aside a window curtain and the tassel grew gold and heavy in his hand. He picked up a book and it changed into a bundle of thin gold plates.

From his pocket he took a handkerchief that Marygold had hemmed. It, too, changed to gold. But the king wished his daughter's handiwork had remained the same as when she had given it to him.

Next Midas picked up his spectacles. The moment he touched them, the glass turned to metal. This is a bother, he thought. Now I can't see through them. No matter. My own eyes will serve ordinary purposes, and little Marygold will soon be old enough to read to me.

As Midas descended the royal staircase, the balustrade became a bar of burnished gold. He lifted the door latch, which immediately turned from brass to gold, and went into his garden. Here Midas found a number of beautiful roses in full bloom, but as he hurried from bush to bush, touching each flower and bud, even the worms in the hearts of some were turned to gold. By the time this work was complete, the serving maid summoned the king to breakfast.

There, spread out on the table, was a breakfast fit for a king. As Midas adjusted his newly gold napkin, he heard Marygold crying.

"Come here, my dear. Tell me what is wrong."

Marygold held out a rose. It had recently been luscious red, soft and sweet smelling. Now it stood stiffly on its golden stem.

"Father," Marygold sobbed, "I went to cut roses for you. But all of them are spoiled."

"Sit down and have breakfast, my dear. You can easily sell this magnificent rose to buy many ordinary ones."

As Midas poured himself coffee, the pot changed into gold, too. Dining on a breakfast service of gold is rather more extravagant than even I am used to, the king thought to himself. Then he lifted the cup. The instant his lips touched the coffee, it became molten gold and hardened to a lump!

Next he took one of the steaming muffins, but had scarcely broken it when it changed from golden cornmeal into golden metal. Almost in despair, he picked up a boiled egg, which underwent the same change.

King Midas next snatched a small potato and crammed it into his mouth, attempting to swallow it in a hurry. But the Golden Touch was too nimble for him. He found his mouth full, not of mealy potato, but of solid metal. He roared aloud and jumped up, stomping around the room.

Marygold asked, "Dear father, what is the matter? Have you burned your mouth?"

"Ah, dear child," groaned Midas, "I don't know what is to become of your poor father." The king was already exceedingly hungry. How would he feel by lunchtime? By supper? How many days could he survive without starving to death?

These questions so troubled Midas that he began to doubt whether gold was, after all, the most desirable thing in the world. He groaned aloud. Marygold came to comfort him, throwing her arms around his knees. Midas bent down to kiss his daughter, whose love was worth a thousand times more than the gold he had gained.

"My precious Marygold," he cried.

But there was no answer. Alas, what had Midas done? The moment his lips touched Marygold's forehead, her sweet rosy face became glittering yellow, with yellow teardrops on her cheeks.

Heartsick, Midas looked up and saw the stranger standing near the door.

"Well, Midas," the stranger asked, "how do you enjoy the Golden Touch?"

"I am miserable."

"How so? Have you not turned everything you desire into gold?"

"But I lost what my heart loved most," Midas replied.

"So you've made a discovery," observed the stranger. "Which is of more value: the Golden Touch or a cup of cold, clear water?"

"Oh, blessed water," responded Midas. "It will never moisten my parched throat again."

"The Golden Touch," continued the stranger, "or a crust of bread?"

"A piece of bread," answered Midas, "is worth all the earth's gold."

"The Golden Touch," inquired the stranger, "or your own loving daughter?"

"Oh my child, my child," answered Midas. "I would not have given the tiny dimple in her chin for this whole world in gold."

"You are wiser now than yesterday, King Midas," said the stranger. "Tell me, do you sincerely wish to rid yourself of the Golden Touch?"

"It is hateful to me," answered Midas.

A fly settled on his nose, but fell to the floor like a small metallic button, for it too had become gold. Midas shuddered.

"Go then," directed the man, "and plunge into the River Pactolus, which glides past your garden. Take a vase of the same water and sprinkle it over any object you desire to change into its former condition."

King Midas bowed low to the stranger. By the time he lifted his head, the stranger had vanished.

The king lost no time in snatching up a great earthen pitcher, which in the process changed to brilliant gold. He hastened to the river and, without pausing to remove even his shoes, plunged into the water.

Midas dipped the pitcher into the water and was glad to see it change back to the same honest clay it had formerly been. Seeing a violet at the side of the riverbank, Midas touched it and was delighted that the flower retained its purple color.

579

He rushed to the palace and immediately poured water over Marygold. She began to sputter, astonished to find herself dripping wet and her father pouring water on her head.

Marygold did not know what had happened, since she remembered nothing after Midas had hugged her. Her father did not think it was necessary to tell his child how foolish he had been. Instead, he led her into the garden, where together they sprinkled water over each of the rosebushes. Surrounded by the roses' perfume and colors, Marygold and her father walked back to the castle.

For as long as King Midas lived, two things reminded him of the Golden Touch: the sand of the River Pactolus sparkled like gold and Marygold's hair retained a golden tinge he had never noticed before. When King Midas grew old, he delighted in telling Marygold's children this story. Stroking their hair, which was also a rich shade of gold, he would declare, "Ever since that morning, I cannot stand the sight of gold, except in your hair."

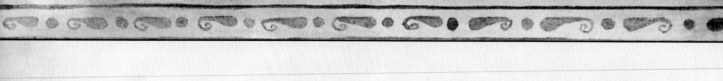

KING MIDAS

Meet the Author

John Warren Stewig has written more than thirty books, plays, and articles. He is best known for his biographies, which have introduced children to American heroes such as George Carver, Sitting Bull, and Clara Barton. Stewig has spent his life involved in children's literature and likes to help teachers develop their students' creativity and imagination.

Meet the Illustrator

Omar Rayyan was born in Jordan and traveled throughout the Middle East with his family during childhood, doodling and painting the sights around him, particularly animals. Rayyan creates illustrations for t-shirt designs, covers for magazines and books, and logos for businesses. Illustrating for children's literature, however, allows Rayyan to express fully his artistic passion. *"When your art is based on fantasy, folklore, fairy tales, you get freedom to break the rules a bit, twist the rules a bit,"* he says. Rayyan's paintings and drawings have been displayed at conventions throughout the country for nearly ten years.

Theme Connections

Within the Selection

Record your answers to the questions below in the Response Journal section of your Writer's Notebook. In small groups, report the ideas you wrote. Discuss your ideas with the rest of your group. Then choose a person to report your group's answers to the class.

- What reason does Midas give the stranger for wanting to turn everything he touches into gold?
- At what point does Midas begin to wish he didn't have the Golden Touch?
- How is Midas a changed man at the end of the story?

Across the Selections

- Near the end of "King Midas," the stranger tells the king, "You are wiser now than yesterday, King Midas." Take a moment to look ahead in this unit and begin thinking about what you value. What is important to you?

Beyond the Selection

- King Midas liked gold and mistakenly thought his life would be better if it had more gold in it. What indulgent things do you like? Maybe you like candy, or maybe you like going to the movies. What would happen, though, if your life had no moderation? How would your life be different if it were changed like King Midas's was? Get into small groups and discuss the issue. Be prepared to share your conclusions with the class.

A Brother's Promise

by Pam Conrad
illustrated by Alan Reingold

I

Annie watched Geoffrey's every move. Her brother looked very different since he had gone away to art school in Paris. He was almost a stranger, with his new mustache and fancy clothes. She watched him butter his bread while he spoke to their parents, and she imitated the way he smoothed the butter and folded his slice of bread in half.

Her father was speaking in a loud, booming voice. "The *Times* said last week that this Statue of Liberty gift may be a hoax played on the American people by the French. They say it's possible the statue doesn't even exist."

"But, Father," Geoffrey objected, "I've seen it with my own eyes." Annie watched his cheeks flush with excitement. "It towers over the houses on a small Parisian street. It's wonderful! The reason it hasn't arrived here yet has nothing to do with the French people. The problem is with the American people, who haven't collected any money for a pedestal."

"You mean," said Annie, "that when we build the pedestal, they will send over the whole statue?"

"And not until then," Geoffrey answered.

"How long have the statue's hand and torch been here in Madison Square?" she asked. She thought of it rising over the trees just a few blocks away. It had been there nearly all her life, and she was used to it. Until now, until there was talk of sending it back to Paris because there was no pedestal.

"Let's see," her father said, stroking his thick mustache and gazing into the chandelier. "The hand and the torch came over in 1876 for the United States Centennial Exposition in Philadelphia—where, I might add, its presence did little to encourage donations for a pedestal—and in 1877 it was brought here to New York. How old was Annie, dear?" he asked, turning to his wife.

584

She was pouring Geoffrey more coffee, holding her heavy lace sleeves away from the urn. "Annie was about five, I believe, and now she's twelve, so the statue must have been here for seven years."

"Are you really twelve already, Annie?" Geoffrey asked, suddenly noticing her and smiling across the table. It was that smile that made him so familiar again.

"You missed my birthday as usual, Geoffrey," she teased. "Otherwise you'd know how old I am. Besides, I'm ten years younger than you are, so you should never forget."

"Oh, but I forget how old *I* am," he said, teasing her.

Annie rolled her eyes. "Well, have you forgotten the way to Madison Square?"

"Probably," he replied.

They grinned at each other. Annie was glad he was home, even for just a visit. Now she wanted to go to the Square and up into the torch with him. "Would you like me to lead you there?" she asked.

"Sounds wonderful!" Geoffrey folded his napkin and put it next to his plate. "If you'll excuse us, Mother, Father, we're off to the statue."

"For one last look," Annie added, "before the hand is returned forever to Paris just because the stingy Americans won't make a pedestal for her."

"Don't say that, Annie," Geoffrey objected, pushing his chair quietly under the table. "Nothing is forever."

Geoffrey walked around the table and offered her his arm. "Well, let's go see her, shall we, mademoiselle? Get your wrap, and we're off."

II

It was a cold blustery morning as Annie and Geoffrey ran down the polished front stoop of their home and started toward Madison Square. Annie kept her cold hands tucked deep inside her furry muff, and she grew sadder and sadder as they walked along.

"What if Father is right, Geoffrey? What if the hand goes back to Paris? We'll never see it again."

"That won't happen," Geoffrey said. "I have a feeling. I just know that someday the Statue of Liberty will be here in New York Harbor, holding a torch in one hand and a tablet in the other. I *know* it's going to happen. You believe it, too, Annie. Your torch will be back, and not just the torch, but the entire lady, as gigantic a statue as you have ever seen, lighting the harbor and welcoming ships and people from all over the world."

They walked quickly in the winter wind, until they could see the torch and the hand in the middle of the Square. It was a sight Annie had seen nearly every day for the last seven years, but when she saw it with Geoffrey it was always better.

"Look at that, Annie. Can you imagine the size she will be? A nose as tall as you are? Eyes this big?" He motioned with his hands. "What a wonderful day it will be when she's finally in the harbor!"

Annie smiled. "Can you remember the first time we went up inside the torch, Geoffrey? Do you remember?"

"Of course. Mother was furious at me for taking you up." He shook his head. "I can still see her horrified face as her little Annie stood on the railing—held tightly by me, I might add—waving her doll and calling, 'Momma! Momma!'" He tossed back his head and laughed. "You were so funny!"

"Do you know that's the first memory I have in my whole life?" she said. "It's the very first thing I remember—being up in that torch with you holding on to me, and seeing Mother and Father like little people on the ground below us."

"I'm glad," Geoffrey said softly. "That's a wonderful first memory."

Annie felt tears burn her eyes. "Oh, but it's not fair! I don't want it to go back to Paris! I don't want to lose it. We've had so much fun here. What if it never comes back?"

"Nonsense!" said Geoffrey, as they approached the stone base of the statue that loomed three stories above them. They entered the base and started up the narrow staircase that was lit by gas lamps. At the top, they stepped onto a railed, circular walkway. Geoffrey pulled his silver spyglass out of his vest pocket and let her peer through it up and down Fifth Avenue and Broadway. The wind was howling through the metalwork, and the noise of the horse-and-carriage traffic filtered through the park's lining of bare trees.

They shared the spyglass between them, as they had so many times in the past, each quiet in thought. Annie was sure that this was the last time she would stand like this in the great torch overlooking her city. She had an awful feeling that something terrible was going to happen. Something terrible that she couldn't stop. She sighed and leaned on the railing.

"Oh now, now," Geoffrey said, patting her shoulder. "No sadness today. Try not to think of this as the end, but as the beginning."

"The beginning?" asked Annie.

"The beginning of what this all was originally intended to be, a beautiful statue in the harbor."

"It will never happen," she said.

"Let's make a pact," he said. "I, Geoffrey Gibbon, swear that I will return to this torch someday with you. I promise that one day we'll stand in this very spot, only it will be higher, much higher, nearly a hundred and fifty feet in the sky, overlooking the harbor and all of the city and country of New York, and *that* will be a great day."

"Describe it to me, Geoffrey," she said quietly.

"We'll stand in this very spot," he began, "and when we look over the edge, we'll look down into the statue's huge face. We'll stand right here and see our country spread out before us—the seas, the hills, the people everywhere celebrating and happy."

Annie smiled and looked at him, glad he was home. "You say things so nicely, Geoffrey."

"Now *you* promise," he said.

Annie straightened up and squared her shoulders. "I, Annie Gibbon, promise to come back to this very spot, wherever this spot may be, whenever that may be, with you, Geoffrey. And it will be a great day."

They smiled at each other, and Annie felt all her worries lift from her shoulders, like birds flying away. Then some people came up onto the walkway beside them.

"Do you believe this monstrosity?" one of them said. "Have you ever seen such a ridiculous lighthouse?"

Annie and Geoffrey looked at each other. He winked, and his mustache twitched ever so slightly.

III

It was almost a year since Geoffrey had returned to Paris, and the American papers were brimming with news of a campaign to bring the statue to America at last. Happily, Annie let the wind sweep her across the cobblestone street, weaving her in and out of the slow-moving carriages, and then let it push her up the polished stone steps of her home. Her one hand was jammed into her fur muff, and the other clutched a copy of the day's *New York World*.

The heavy door opened easily, and as she unwound her scarf from around her neck, she began calling, "Mother! Father!" Annie stomped into the parlor, flashing the newspaper at her parents, who sat unusually still on the velvet lounge by the fireplace. "It's really coming! We're really going to get the whole statue, and Geoffrey and I will go up into the torch again, just like he promised, only this time it will be in the harbor, not in the park.

"Imagine!" she cried. "No one thought Americans could raise the money to build the pedestal, but according to the *New York World* pennies and nickels are pouring in from all over."

"Annie," her mother said softly.

Annie rustled the day's newspaper in front of her. "They have a goal of one hundred thousand dollars to raise, and they just might be able to do it."

"Annie," her mother repeated.

"I'm so excited," Annie continued. "I'm going to earn some money and make my contribution. Have you any idea what this means? Geoffrey was right after all.

"Oh, I must write to Geoffrey! He will be so excited! He knew it! He knew it all along!" She looked from her mother to her father for the first time, and then she saw that her mother had been crying and her father was pale.

"Please, Annie," her mother said, her voice shaky and uncertain.

"What is it, Mother?" she asked. "What's wrong?"

"It's Geoffrey, dear," her mother whispered. "Your brother is dead." Annie's mother dropped her head into her hands and began to cry.

"What are you talking about? What do you mean?"

Her father's voice was choked and soft. "He's been killed in an accident, Annie. I can't believe it."

Annie felt frozen to the ground. Her ears were ringing. Her arms grew numb. "What happened?"

"It seems he was visiting with some people in Germany, riding in some kind of motorized vehicle. It went out of control. He was killed instantly."

"How do you know this?" Annie shouted, not wanting to believe she'd never see her brother again.

Her father pointed to the parlor table in front of him, to a letter beside a box. It had been posted in Germany, and like all Geoffrey's letters it had unusual and colorful stamps, but the handwriting was unfamiliar.

Annie read over the letter—the accident, the death—to the closing. "I extend my deepest sympathy. I'm sending a package to Annie, whom Geoffrey spoke of with deepest affection. It's one of his possessions that I feel he would have wanted her to have. Sincerely, Walter Linderbaum."

Annie reached out and touched the brown box beside the letter. She lifted it and gently unwrapped the paper. It was a wooden box. She pried it open and inside, nestled in cork, was Geoffrey's spyglass. Dear Geoffrey's rare and beautiful spyglass, etched in silver, trimmed in polished wood. She could almost feel the wind howling through the railings of the statue's hand, almost hear the noise of the horse-and-carriage traffic filtering through the trees. She held the spyglass up to her eye and looked out the window through the fine lace curtains. She looked and looked and looked until she could no longer see past her tears.

590

IV

In a few weeks, Annie wrote this letter to the publisher of the *New York World* newspaper.

Dear Mr. Pulitzer,

I am sending this money for the Statue of Liberty Pedestal Fund. I live near Madison Square, and I used to visit the torch with my older brother, Geoffrey. Geoffrey was an art student in Paris, and he told me all about the statue and how the man who built the Eiffel Tower in Paris also built the foundation of the Statue of Liberty. He told me how the statue towers over the buildings in Paris, and how he used to look at it and imagine it in New York Harbor. We even made a solemn promise to meet in the torch when it was finally here again. He was always completely certain that she would be here one day.

I want to make sure of it. You see, my brother died this year, and although he can't keep his promise to me, I can still keep mine. I've been to see a local pawnbroker, and I sold Geoffrey's rare antique spyglass made of silver and wood that we used for looking around New York City, from up inside the torch. I'm sad to sell it, but I'm sure he'd understand. Please take this money in Geoffrey Gibbon's memory. And please build a pedestal.

Respectfully yours,

Annie Gibbon

Annie Gibbon

Annie's letter was published in the *New York World*, and its heartfelt message touched off a series of contributions in memory of beloved relatives. Annie was proud to see the fund grow bigger every week until, finally, Joseph Pulitzer declared the fund to be complete, and the construction of the pedestal on Bedloe's Island was to begin at last.

V

October 28, 1886, was a cold, drizzly day, but was declared a holiday, and New York was astir with excitement. Even though the city was in a festive mood, Annie felt uneasy. Her parents had promised to take her to Bedloe's Island to see the statue that had finally arrived and had been assembled on its glorious pedestal, but Annie wasn't sure she wanted to see it. It wouldn't be the same without Geoffrey. If he couldn't see it, maybe she shouldn't see it either, she thought. But she got into the carriage with her mother and father and headed for the pier, where they would take a boat over to the island.

Annie was quiet in the carriage as she watched the holiday crowds out the window. Her mother patted her hand reassuringly. "I guess we all miss Geoffrey this day," her mother said. "He would have enjoyed this."

"Oh, yes," sighed Annie, watching the American and French flags on the fronts of buildings. "This should be Geoffrey's day. He saw the statue in Paris, and he should be here today."

They were all quiet and sad and rode in silence until they reached the pier. Her father found the people who would take them across. Annie boarded a boat with her parents, and they started out toward Bedloe's Island. The harbor was afloat with every kind of boat—from ferryboats and freighters to yachts, scows, and battleships. The steam from all the steamships put a cloud over the harbor, but everywhere there was music—"Yankee Doodle Dandy," the "Marseillaise"—and the laughter of people celebrating.

Annie stood shivering by the railing of the boat. Looming ahead, standing majestically in the center of the harbor, was the shape of a gigantic lady holding a torch in one hand and a tablet in the other.

"You believe it, too, Annie," she could almost hear Geoffrey saying. "The Statue of Liberty will be here in New York Harbor—the entire lady, lighting the harbor and welcoming ships and people from all over the world." Tears filled Annie's eyes. She was suddenly glad she had come.

"Look," she whispered. "Look at her, Geoffrey."

Annie had never seen so much excitement and merriment in her life. President Grover Cleveland was there, with bands and dignitaries, and there were speeches and songs and cheers and patriotic excitement. She and her parents joined the crowd and listened to the speeches. She was especially excited when Joseph Pulitzer took the stand and gave his speech. He talked about the American people who had finally come through. He talked about the great crews that had built the pedestal, the wonderful French people who had sent the statue to us. He called it the greatest gift one nation ever gave another. The crowd cheered and laughed, and Joseph Pulitzer beamed with pride as if he had brought the statue over single-handedly.

Then, just when it seemed he was through, he looked over the crowd thoughtfully and shouted out, "By the way, is Annie Gibbon here today?"

"What?" her mother gasped.

Annie froze in disbelief. "Annie Gibbon?" Joseph Pulitzer called once again.

"Here I am!" Annie cried, waving from her place in the crowd.

"Come up here, Annie!" He laughed, and the crowd parted for her. She made her way to the podium, barely knowing what she was doing, barely believing this was really happening. Mr. Pulitzer reached out his hand and guided her up the steps. He kept her at his side and spoke to the crowd.

"I don't know if you folks remember, but Annie wrote a letter to me that we published in the *World* a while ago. Isn't that right, Annie?" he said, turning to her and smiling.

She nodded numbly.

"Well, I'm so glad you're here. You see," he said, turning back to his audience, "she lost her brother last year, a brother who loved the Statue of Liberty. He'd actually seen it in Paris, and Annie sold his special spyglass and sent the money to the Pedestal Fund in his memory. And that led many others to do the same thing."

A few people clapped, and Annie looked down at their faces.

"Annie, I have a surprise for you." He turned around, and someone handed him a long, thin wooden box. "When I read your letter, I sent my people out to all the pawnshops in your area. I said to myself, 'Joseph, when the statue comes over, that little girl is going to have her spyglass back. Yes, she is.' Now you take this spyglass and climb to the top of that lady and take a good look around, Annie."

People were laughing and clapping, and Joseph Pulitzer was nearly bursting with himself. But all Annie could see was the familiar box in her hand. Carefully she opened it, not believing, but, yes, Geoffrey's spyglass was nestled in the box, waiting for her. The band began to play, and Annie looked up into the face of Joseph Pulitzer. "Thank you," she whispered.

VI

Annie's parents walked her to the base of the statue, where they hugged her and let her go up alone. Holding the spyglass box tightly in her hand, she started up the stairway. The inside of the statue was immense, studded with bolts and held together with girders and supports. She remembered how once Geoffrey had carried her up the stairs in the torch. How huge the torch had seemed then, but it was nothing like this! She climbed and climbed and climbed, 161 steps, never stopping at a rest station, and not even stopping at the observation room in the crown.

Then Annie entered the part of the statue that was so familiar to her. She began to climb up into the raised arm. Her hand touched the cold metal wall; her feet sounded lightly on the stairs. She was alone. Up and up, until at last she stepped out onto the circular walkway around the base of the torch. She felt as if she had arrived home, but only for an instant, and then her breath was whisked away. She had known she would not see Fifth Avenue and Broadway, but there was no way she could have prepared herself for what was before her. She was certain if she reached up she could have touched the gray clouds, yet she clasped the railing tightly with her gloved fingers. The wind whipped around her, whistling through the gratings, and the earth stretched out in all directions.

"Describe it to me, dear Annie," she thought she heard a voice say.

Her words were blown away by the wind, but she began slowly. "When I look over the edge, I can see down into the statue's beautiful face. Her nose is strong and straight, and I can see her lips, proud and

determined. The spikes of her crown are huge and studded with bolts. In her hand is a tablet that reads 'July 4, 1776.' I am standing in the torch that symbolizes the light of freedom, and before me I can see my country spread wide and far, the seas, the hills, and the people everywhere celebrating and happy. I can hear the band, and I can see battleships and steamships, and in the distance I see buildings and steeples. On the ground, I can see people like tiny ants."

She smiled, raised her spyglass to her eye, and scanned the crowds below. "I can't even find Mother and Father." Then she turned the spyglass to the horizon. "It's the haziest of days, Geoffrey. It's difficult to see. I'll have to come back again one day." She smiled. "Yes, I'll come back on a clear day, when I can see the hills and the distant horizon. There will be more days, many more, and I'll come back again and again. I promise. You were right, Geoffrey. This is a great day."

Annie stayed as long as she could, until the wind and the cold seemed to be buffeting her from every direction, and then she started down. On her way home, skimming across the harbor in the boat, Annie turned back to the statue and watched her there in the twilight. A few fireworks had gone up in the foggy night, and everywhere boats were lit with bright lights and lanterns.

And then slowly, very slowly, the torch in the great lady's hand began to glow. It was dim at first, and then brighter, until it glowed with a fierce and proud light. Annie watched, and she was certain that from across the dark waters of the harbor the torch light faintly, but surely, winked at her.

A Brother's Promise

Meet the Author

Pam Conrad started writing poems when she was seven years old. She wrote so many poems when she was little that her father published a private collection of them called *Tea by the Garden Wall* when she was only twelve. Many of her books today reflect a part of her life because she writes books *". . . when all of a sudden little parts of my life begin to take on strange, new significance . . . a story begins to unfold."* In the same way her parents encouraged her, Conrad is helping her daughter become a writer. They are hoping that one day they will write a children's book together.

Meet the Illustrator

Alan Reingold began his career as an illustrator after graduating from The Rhode Island School of Design. Since then, he has been commissioned to illustrate cover and interior art for domestic and international magazines. His realistic images can also be seen on movie posters, in national ad campaigns, and on book covers. Reingold's first *Time* magazine cover hangs in the permanent collection of The National Portrait Gallery in Washington, D.C. Reingold teaches illustration at Parsons School of Design.

Theme Connections

Within the Selection

Record your answers to the questions below in the Response Journal section of your Writer's Notebook. In small groups, report the ideas you wrote. Discuss your ideas with the rest of your group. Then choose a person to report your group's answers to the class.

- What was preventing the Statue of Liberty from being properly assembled and displayed in New York Harbor?
- What did Geoffrey and Annie promise to each other?
- How did Annie keep her promise?

Across the Selections

- "A Brother's Promise" emphasizes the importance of family and the bonds formed between family members. "King Midas" also involves a strong bond between family members. How are the two situations the same? How are they different?
- What does it mean to make a promise? "A Brother's Promise" seems both to ask and answer this question. Keeping a promise means being true to your word. What other selections have you read in previous units in which someone was true to his or her word?

Beyond the Selection

- Think about how "A Brother's Promise" adds to what you know about value.
- Add items to the Concept/Question Board about value.

Focus Questions Can a gift be worth less than its monetary value? How do the miner's reasons for giving a gift to the king differ from those of his brother?

A Gift for a Gift

edited and adapted by Eric Protter
illustrated by David Wenzel

"Honesty is the best policy" is one of the most popular and lasting of all folktale themes. The original version of this story is attributed to Saxony, and it dates from the 17th century. The author is unknown.

A mighty king once lost his way while hunting alone in a forest, and late at night, when he was cold and weary and hungry, he at last reached the hut of a poor miner. The miner was away digging for coal, and his wife didn't realize that the gentleman who rapped on her door and begged for a night's lodging was the king himself.

"We are very poor," she explained, "but if you will be content, as we are, with a plate of potatoes for dinner and a blanket on the floor for a bed, you will be most welcome." The king's stomach was empty; his bones ached; and he knew that on this dark night he would never find his way back to his castle. And so he gratefully accepted the woman's hospitality.

He sat down to dinner with her and greedily ate a generous portion of steaming potatoes baked in an open fire. "These are better than the best beef I've ever eaten," he exclaimed. And still smacking his lips, he stretched out on the floor and quickly fell fast asleep.

Early the next morning the king washed in a nearby brook, and then returned to the hut to thank the miner's wife for her kindness. And for her trouble he gave her a gold piece. Then he was on his way to his palace.

When the miner returned home later that day his wife told him about the courteous, kind and distinguished guest who had stayed overnight in their home. Then she showed her husband the gold piece he had given her. The husband realized at once that the king himself must have been their overnight guest. And because he believed that the king had been far too generous in his payment for their humble fare and lodging, he decided to go at once to present his majesty with a bushel of potatoes——fine, round potatoes, the very kind the king had enjoyed so much.

The palace guards refused at first to let the miner enter. But when he explained that he wanted nothing from the king—— that in fact, he had come only to give the king a bushel of potatoes——they let him pass.

"Kind sire," he said when he finally stood before the king, "last night you paid my wife a gold piece for a hard bed and a

plate of potatoes. Even if you are a great and wealthy ruler, you paid much too much for the little offered you. Therefore, I have brought you a bushel of potatoes, which you said you enjoyed as much as the finest beef. Please accept them. And should you ever pass by our house again, we will be happy to have the opportunity to serve you more."

These proud and honest words pleased the king, and to show his appreciation he ordered that the miner be given a fine house and a three-acre farm. Overjoyed by his good luck the honest miner returned home to share the news with his wife.

Now it so happened that the miner had a brother——a wealthy brother who was shrewd, greedy, and jealous of anyone else's good fortune. When he learned of his brother's luck, he decided that he too would present the king with a gift. Not long before, the king had wanted to buy one of the brother's horses. But because he had been asked to pay an outrageously high price, the king had never bought the animal. Now, thought the avaricious brother, he would go to his sovereign and make him a gift of the horse. *After all*, he reasoned, *if the king gave a three-acre farm and a house to my brother in return for a mere bushel of potatoes, I will probably get a mansion and ten acres for my gift.*

He brushed the horse and polished its harness, and then rode to the palace. Past the sentries he walked, directly into the king's audience chamber.

"Gracious sir," he began, "not long ago you wanted to buy my horse, but I placed a very high price on it. You may have wondered why I did so, great king. Let me explain. I did not want to sell the horse to you. I wanted to *give* it to you, your majesty. And I ask you now to accept it as a gift. If you look out your window you will see the horse in your courtyard. He is, as you know, a magnificent animal, and I am sure that not even you have such a fine stallion in your royal stables."

The king realized at once that this was not an honest gift. He smiled and said, "Thank you, my friend. I accept your kind gift with gratitude. And you shall not go home empty-handed. Do you see that bushel of potatoes there in the corner? Well, those potatoes cost me a three-acre farm and a house. Take them as your reward. I am sure that not even you have a bushel of potatoes in your storeroom with so high a value on them."

What could the greedy brother do? He dared not argue with the king. He simply raised the heavy sack to his shoulders and carried it home, while the king ordered the horse put in his stables.

A Gift for a Gift

Meet the Editor

Eric Protter has lived in four countries. He has written, among other books, *A Treasury of Folk and Fairy Tales*, *Explorers and Explorations*, and *Monster Festival*.

Meet the Illustrator

David Wenzel spent many hours as a child filling up sheet after sheet of paper with sketches and characters. At one point he created a series of illustrations depicting the characters from his two favorite childhood books, Lewis Carroll's *Alice in Wonderland* and *Through the Looking Glass*. He has been working full time as an illustrator since graduating from Hartford Art School in 1975. Wenzel has worked on many projects, rated versions of *Treasure Island* and *The Hobbit*. To this day, he is still inspired by the stories and illustrations he finds in books.

Theme Connections

Within the Selection

Record your answers to the questions below in the Response Journal section of your Writer's Notebook. In small groups, report the ideas you wrote. Discuss your ideas with the rest of your group. Then choose a person to report your group's answers to the class.

- Why did the king accept the hospitality of the poor miner's wife?
- Why did the miner take the king a bushel of potatoes?
- Why did the king not reward the miner's brother as well as he had hoped?

Across the Selections

- Compare "A Gift for a Gift" with "King Midas." What are the lessons to be learned from each story?
- In "King Midas," the mysterious stranger has the power to grant peoples' wishes. Which character from "A Gift for a Gift" is most like this stranger? How are the two characters different?

Beyond the Selection

- Think about how "A Gift for a Gift" adds to what you know about value.
- Add items to the Concept/Question Board about a value.

***El Pan Nuestro.* Diego Rivera.** Mural. Education Secretariat, Mexico City, Mexico.

Mrs. James Smith and Grandson. 1776.
Charles Wilson Peale. Oil on canvas.
National Museum of American Art,
Smithsonian Institution, Washington, DC.

The Gleaners. 1857.
**Jean-François
Millet.** Oil on canvas.
33 × 44 in. Musée
d'Orsay, Paris.

The Gold Coin

Alma Flor Ada
translated by Bernice Randall ● *illustrated by Neil Waldman*

Juan had been a thief for many years. Because he did his stealing by night, his skin had become pale and sickly. Because he spent his time either hiding or sneaking about, his body had become shriveled and bent. And because he had neither friend nor relative to make him smile, his face was always twisted into an angry frown.

One night, drawn by a light shining through the trees, Juan came upon a hut. He crept up to the door and through a crack saw an old woman sitting at a plain, wooden table.

What was that shining in her hand? Juan wondered. He could not believe his eyes. It was a gold coin. Then he heard the woman say to herself, "I must be the richest person in the world."

Juan decided instantly that all the woman's gold must be his. He thought that the easiest thing to do was to watch until the woman left. Juan hid in the bushes and huddled under his poncho, waiting for the right moment to enter the hut.

Juan was half asleep when he heard knocking at the door and the sound of insistent voices. A few minutes later, he saw the woman, wrapped in a black cloak, leave the hut with two men at her side.

608

Here's my chance! Juan thought. And, forcing open a window, he climbed into the empty hut.

He looked about eagerly for the gold. He looked under the bed. It wasn't there. He looked in the cupboard. It wasn't there, either. Where could it be? Close to despair, Juan tore away some beams supporting the thatch roof.

Finally, he gave up. There was simply no gold in the hut.

All I can do, he thought, is to find the old woman and make her tell me where she's hidden it.

So he set out along the path that she and her two companions had taken.

It was daylight by the time Juan reached the river. The countryside had been deserted, but here, along the riverbank, were two huts. Nearby, a man and his son were hard at work, hoeing potatoes.

It had been a long, long time since Juan had spoken to another human being. Yet his desire to find the woman was so strong that he went up to the farmers and asked, in a hoarse, raspy voice, "Have you seen a short, gray-haired woman, wearing a black cloak?"

"Oh, you must be looking for Doña Josefa," the young boy said. "Yes, we've seen her. We went to fetch her this morning, because my grandfather had another attack of——"

"Where is she now?" Juan broke in.

"She is long gone," said the father with a smile. "Some people from across the river came looking for her, because someone in their family is sick."

"How can I get across the river?" Juan asked anxiously.

"Only by boat," the boy answered. "We'll row you across later, if you'd like." Then turning back to his work, he added, "But first we must finish digging up the potatoes."

The thief muttered, "Thanks." But he quickly grew impatient. He grabbed a hoe and began to help the pair of farmers. The sooner we finish, the sooner we'll get across the river, he thought. And the sooner I'll get to my gold!

It was dusk when they finally laid down their hoes. The soil had been turned, and the wicker baskets were brimming with potatoes.

"Now can you row me across?" Juan asked the father anxiously.

"Certainly," the man said. "But let's eat supper first."

Juan had forgotten the taste of a home-cooked meal and the pleasure that comes from sharing it with others. As he sopped up the last of the stew with a chunk of dark bread, memories of other meals came back to him from far away and long ago.

By the light of the moon, father and son guided their boat across the river.

"What a wonderful healer Doña Josefa is!" the boy told Juan. "All she had to do to make Abuelo better was give him a cup of her special tea."

"Yes, and not only that," his father added, "she brought him a gold coin."

Juan was stunned. It was one thing for Doña Josefa to go around helping people. But how could she go around handing out gold coins——*his gold coins?*

When the threesome finally reached the other side of the river, they saw a young man sitting outside his hut.

"This fellow is looking for Doña Josefa," the father said, pointing to Juan.

"Oh, she left some time ago," the young man said.

"Where to?" Juan asked tensely.

"Over to the other side of the mountain," the young man replied, pointing to the vague outline of mountains in the night sky.

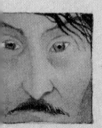

"How did she get there?" Juan asked, trying to hide his impatience.

"By horse," the young man answered. "They came on horseback to get her because someone had broken his leg."

"Well, then, I need a horse, too," Juan said urgently.

"Tomorrow," the young man replied softly. "Perhaps I can take you tomorrow, maybe the next day. First I must finish harvesting the corn."

So Juan spent the next day in the fields, bathed in sweat from sunup to sundown.

Yet each ear of corn that he picked seemed to bring him closer to his treasure. And later that evening, when he helped the young man husk several ears so they could boil them for supper, the yellow kernels glittered like gold coins.

While they were eating, Juan thought about Doña Josefa. Why, he wondered, would someone who said she was the world's richest woman spend her time taking care of every sick person for miles around?

The following day, the two set off at dawn. Juan could not recall when he last had noticed the beauty of the sunrise. He felt strangely moved by the sight of the mountains, barely lit by the faint rays of the morning sun.

As they neared the foothills, the young man said, "I'm not surprised you're looking for Doña Josefa. The whole countryside needs her. I went for her because my wife had been running a high fever. In no time at all, Doña Josefa had her on the road to recovery. And what's more, my friend, she brought her a gold coin!"

Juan groaned inwardly. To think that someone could hand out gold so freely! What a strange woman Doña Josefa is, Juan thought. Not only is she willing to help one person after another, but she doesn't mind traveling all over the countryside to do it!

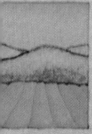

"Well, my friend," said the young man finally, "this is where I must leave you. But you don't have far to walk. See that house over there? It belongs to the man who broke his leg."

The young man stretched out his hand to say good-bye. Juan stared at it for a moment. It had been a long, long time since the thief had shaken hands with anyone. Slowly, he pulled out a hand from under his poncho. When his companion grasped it firmly in his own, Juan felt suddenly warmed, as if by the rays of the sun.

But after he thanked the young man, Juan ran down the road. He was still eager to catch up with Doña Josefa. When he reached the house, a woman and a child were stepping down from a wagon.

"Have you seen Doña Josefa?" Juan asked.

"We've just taken her to Don Teodosio's," the woman said. "His wife is sick, you know——"

"How do I get there?" Juan broke in. "I've got to see her."

"It's too far to walk," the woman said amiably. "If you'd like, I'll take you there tomorrow. But first I must gather my squash and beans."

So Juan spent yet another long day in the fields. Working beneath the summer sun, Juan noticed that his skin had begun to tan. And although he had to stoop down to pick the squash, he found that he could now stretch his body. His back had begun to straighten, too.

Later, when the little girl took him by the hand to show him a family of rabbits burrowed under a fallen tree, Juan's face broke into a smile. It had been a long, long time since Juan had smiled.

Yet his thoughts kept coming back to the gold.

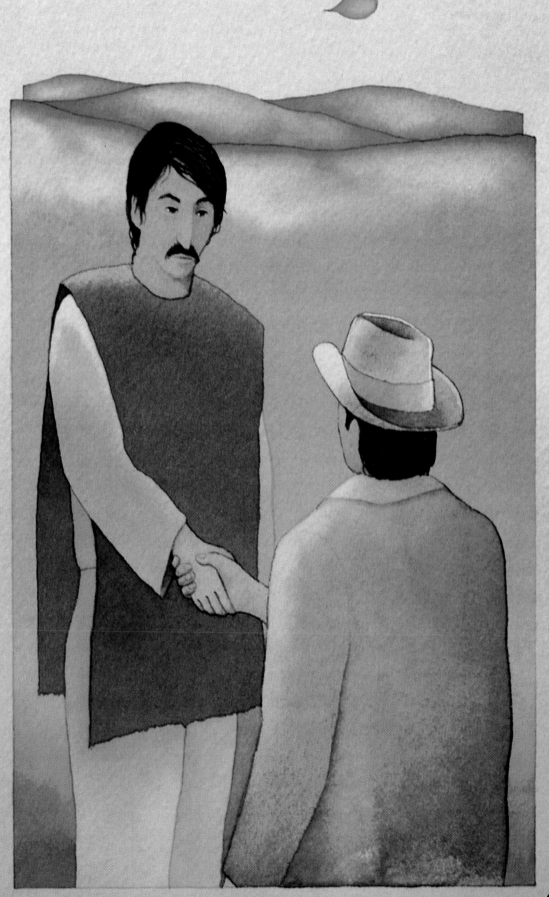

The following day, the wagon carrying Juan and the woman lumbered along a road lined with coffee fields.

The woman said, "I don't know what we would have done without Doña Josefa. I sent my daughter to our neighbor's house, who then brought Doña Josefa on horseback. She set my husband's leg and then showed me how to brew a special tea to lessen the pain."

Getting no reply, she went on. "And, as if that weren't enough, she brought him a gold coin. Can you imagine such a thing?"

Juan could only sigh. No doubt about it, he thought, Doña Josefa is someone special. But Juan didn't know whether to be happy that Doña Josefa had so much gold she could freely hand it out, or angry for her having already given so much of it away.

When they finally reached Don Teodosio's house, Doña Josefa was already gone. But here, too, there was work that needed to be done . . .

Juan stayed to help with the coffee harvest. As he picked the red berries, he gazed up from time to time at the trees that grew, row upon row, along the hillsides. What a calm, peaceful place this is! he thought.

The next morning, Juan was up at daybreak. Bathed in the soft, dawn light, the mountains seemed to smile at him. When Don Teodosio offered him a lift on horseback, Juan found it difficult to have to say good-bye.

"What a good woman Doña Josefa is!" Don Teodosio said, as they rode down the hill toward the sugarcane fields. "The minute she heard about my wife being sick, she came with her special herbs. And as if that weren't enough, she brought my wife a gold coin!"

In the stifling heat, the kind that often signals the approach of a storm, Juan simply sighed and mopped his brow. The pair continued riding for several hours in silence.

Juan then realized he was back in familiar territory, for they were now on the stretch of road he had traveled only a week ago—though how much longer it now seemed to him. He jumped off Don Teodosio's horse and broke into a run.

This time the gold would not escape him! But he had to move quickly, so he could find shelter before the storm broke.

Out of breath, Juan finally reached Doña Josefa's hut. She was standing by the door, shaking her head slowly as she surveyed the ransacked house.

"So I've caught up with you at last!" Juan shouted, startling the old woman. "Where's the gold?"

"The gold coin?" Doña Josefa said, surprised and looking at Juan intently. "Have you come for the gold coin? I've been trying hard to give it to someone who might need it," Doña Josefa said. "First to an old man who had just gotten over a bad attack. Then to a young woman who had been running a fever. Then to a man with a broken leg. And finally to Don Teodosio's wife. But none of them would take it. They all said, 'Keep it. There must be someone who needs it more.'"

Juan did not say a word.

"You must be the one who needs it," Doña Josefa said.

She took the coin out of her pocket and handed it to him. Juan stared at the coin, speechless.

At that moment a young girl appeared, her long braid bouncing as she ran. "Hurry, Doña Josefa, please!" she said breathlessly. "My mother is all alone, and the baby is due any minute."

"Of course, dear," Doña Josefa replied. But as she glanced up at the sky, she saw nothing but black clouds. The storm was nearly upon them. Doña Josefa sighed deeply.

"But how can I leave now? Look at my house! I don't know what has happened to the roof. The storm will wash the whole place away!"

And there was a deep sadness in her voice.

Juan took in the child's frightened eyes, Doña Josefa's sad, distressed face, and the ransacked hut.

"Go ahead, Doña Josefa," he said. "Don't worry about your house. I'll see that the roof is back in shape, good as new."

The woman nodded gratefully, drew her cloak about her shoulders, and took the child by the hand. As she turned to leave, Juan held out his hand.

"Here, take this," he said, giving her the gold coin. "I'm sure the newborn will need it more than I."

621

The Gold Coin

Meet the Author

Alma Flor Ada credits her family with giving her a love of stories. "My father told me stories he invented to explain to me all that he knew about the history of the world." Ada has written many textbooks and children's stories and enjoys translating stories, written by other authors, from English to Spanish.

Meet the Translator

Bernice Randall is editorial director of Santillana Publishing Company. She has worked for several other publishing companies in the past. She also teaches a workshop at Stanford Publishing Course.

Meet the Illustrator

Neil Waldman illustrates children's books. He always wanted to paint and draw as a child. "I sensed, as a small child, that finger paints and coloring books were more than just fun. They were important tools that lead to a road of joy, discovery, and fulfillment."

Theme Connections

Within the Selection

Record your answers to the questions below in the Response Journal section of your Writer's Notebook. In small groups, report the ideas you wrote. Discuss your ideas with the rest of your group. Then choose a person to report your group's answers to the class.

- Why do people keep seeking the services of Doña Josefa?
- What changes does Juan begin to notice in his physique after he has spent some time working in peoples' fields?
- At the end of the story you learn that Doña Josefa has only one gold coin. What must she have meant, then, when Juan overheard her saying, "I must be the richest person in the world?"

Across the Selections

- In "The Gold Coin," Juan experiences a change of heart. Which other characters have you encountered in this unit who have experienced a change of heart? Which of these other characters do you think is most like Juan? Explain.
- Juan's change of heart is complete when he gives the gold coin back to Doña Josefa at the end of the story. Something similar happens in "A Gift for a Gift" when the miner gives the gold piece back to the king. How are the two situations alike? How are they different?

Beyond the Selection

- Think about how "The Gold Coin" adds to what you know about value.
- Add items to the Concept/Question Board about value.

THE No~GUITAR BLUES

from *Baseball in April and Other Stories*
by Gary Soto
illustrated by José Miralles

The moment Fausto saw the group Los Lobos on "American Bandstand," he knew exactly what he wanted to do with his life——play guitar. His eyes grew large with excitement as Los Lobos ground out a song while teenagers bounced off each other on the crowded dance floor.

He had watched "American Bandstand" for years and had heard Ray Camacho and the Teardrops at Romain Playground, but it had never occurred to him that he too might become a musician. That afternoon Fausto knew his mission in life: to play guitar in his own band; to sweat out his songs and prance around the stage; to make money and dress weird.

Fausto turned off the television set and walked outside, wondering how he could get enough money to buy a guitar. He couldn't ask his parents because they would just say, "Money doesn't grow on trees" or "What do you think we are, bankers?" And besides, they hated rock music. They were into the conjunto music of Lydia Mendoza, Flaco Jimenez, and Little Joe and La Familia. And, as Fausto recalled, the last album they bought was The Chipmunks Sing Christmas Favorites.

But what the heck, he'd give it a try. He returned inside and watched his mother make tortillas. He leaned against the kitchen counter, trying to work up the nerve to ask her for a guitar. Finally, he couldn't hold back any longer.

"Mom," he said, "I want a guitar for Christmas."

She looked up from rolling tortillas. "Honey, a guitar costs a lot of money."

"How 'bout for my birthday next year," he tried again.

"I can't promise," she said, turning back to her tortillas, "but we'll see."

Fausto walked back outside with a buttered tortilla. He knew his mother was right. His father was a warehouseman at Berven Rugs, where he made good money but not enough to buy everything his children wanted. Fausto decided to mow lawns to earn money, and was pushing the mower down the street before he realized it was winter and no one would hire him. He returned the mower and picked up a rake. He hopped onto his sister's bike (his had two flat tires) and rode north to the nicer section of Fresno in search of work. He went door-to-door, but after three hours he managed to get only one job, and not to rake leaves. He was asked to hurry down to the store to buy a loaf of bread, for which he received a grimy, dirt-caked quarter.

He also got an orange, which he ate sitting at the curb. While he was eating, a dog walked up and sniffed his leg. Fausto pushed him away and threw an orange peel skyward. The dog caught it and ate it in one gulp. The dog looked at Fausto and wagged his tail for more. Fausto tossed him a slice of orange, and the dog snapped it up and licked his lips.

"How come you like oranges, dog?"

The dog blinked a pair of sad eyes and whined.

"What's the matter? Cat got your tongue?" Fausto laughed at his joke and offered the dog another slice.

At that moment a dim light came on inside Fausto's head. He saw that it was sort of a fancy dog, a terrier or something, with dog tags and a shiny collar. And it looked well fed and healthy. In his neighborhood, the dogs were never licensed, and if they got sick they were placed near the water heater until they got well.

This dog looked like he belonged to rich people. Fausto cleaned his juice-sticky hands on his pants and got to his feet. The light in his head grew brighter. It just might work. He called the dog, patted its muscular back, and bent down to check the license.

"Great," he said. "There's an address."

The dog's name was Roger, which struck Fausto as weird because he'd never heard of a dog with a human name. Dogs should have names like Bomber, Freckles, Queenie, Killer, and Zero.

Fausto planned to take the dog home and collect a reward. He would say he had found Roger near the freeway. That would scare the daylights out of the owners, who would be so happy that they would probably give him a reward. He felt bad about lying, but the dog was loose. And it might even really be lost, because the address was six blocks away.

Fausto stashed the rake and his sister's bike behind a bush, and, tossing an orange peel every time Roger became distracted, walked the dog to his house. He hesitated on the porch until Roger began to scratch the door with a muddy paw. Fausto had come this far, so he figured he might as well go through with it.

He knocked softly. When no one answered, he rang the doorbell. A man in a silky bathrobe and slippers opened the door and seemed confused by the sight of his dog and the boy.

"Sir," Fausto said, gripping Roger by the collar. "I found your dog by the freeway. His dog license says he lives here." Fausto looked down at the dog, then up to the man. "He does, doesn't he?"

The man stared at Fausto a long time before saying in a pleasant voice, "That's right." He pulled his robe tighter around him because of the cold and asked Fausto to come in. "So he was by the freeway?"

"Uh-huh."

"You bad, snoopy dog," said the man, wagging his finger. "You probably knocked over some trash cans, too, didn't you?"

Fausto didn't say anything. He looked around, amazed by this house with its shiny furniture and a television as large as the front window at home. Warm bread smells filled the air and music full of soft tinkling floated in from another room.

627

"Helen," the man called to the kitchen. "We have a visitor." His wife came into the living room wiping her hands on a dish towel and smiling. "And who have we here?" she asked in one of the softest voices Fausto had ever heard.

"This young man said he found Roger near the freeway."

Fausto repeated his story to her while staring at a perpetual clock with a bell-shaped glass, the kind his aunt got when she celebrated her twenty-fifth anniversary. The lady frowned and said, wagging a finger at Roger, "Oh, you're a bad boy."

"It was very nice of you to bring Roger home," the man said. "Where do you live?"

"By that vacant lot on Olive," he said. "You know, by Brownie's Flower Place."

The wife looked at her husband, then Fausto. Her eyes twinkled triangles of light as she said, "Well, young man, you're probably hungry. How about a turnover?"

"What do I have to turn over?" Fausto asked, thinking she was talking about yard work or something like turning trays of dried raisins.

"No, no, dear, it's a pastry." She took him by the elbow and guided him to a kitchen that sparkled with copper pans and bright yellow wallpaper. She guided him to the kitchen table and gave him a tall glass of milk and something that looked like an *empanada*. Steamy waves of heat escaped when he tore it in two. He ate with both eyes on the man and woman who stood arm-in-arm smiling at him. They were strange, he thought. But nice.

"That was good," he said after he finished the turnover. "Did you make it, ma'am?"

"Yes, I did. Would you like another?"

"No, thank you. I have to go home now."

As Fausto walked to the door, the man opened his wallet and took out a bill. "This is for you," he said. "Roger is special to us, almost like a son."

Fausto looked at the bill and knew he was in trouble. Not with these nice folks or with his parents but with himself. How could he have been so deceitful? The dog wasn't lost. It was just having a fun Saturday walking around.

"I can't take that."

"You have to. You deserve it, believe me," the man said.

"No, I don't."

"Now don't be silly," said the lady. She took the bill from her husband and stuffed it into Fausto's shirt pocket. "You're a lovely child. Your parents are lucky to have you. Be good. And come see us again, please."

Fausto went out, and the lady closed the door. Fausto clutched the bill through his shirt pocket. He felt like ringing the doorbell and begging them to please take the money back, but he knew they would refuse. He hurried away, and at the end of the block, pulled the bill from his shirt pocket: it was a crisp twenty-dollar bill.

"Oh, man, I shouldn't have lied," he said under his breath as he started up the street like a zombie. He wanted to run to church for Saturday confession, but it was past four-thirty, when confession stopped.

He returned to the bush where he had hidden the rake and his sister's bike and rode home slowly, not daring to touch the money in his pocket. At home, in the privacy of his room, he examined the twenty-dollar bill. He had never had so much money. It was probably enough to buy a secondhand guitar. But he felt bad, like the time he stole a dollar from the secret fold inside his older brother's wallet.

Fausto went outside and sat on the fence. "Yeah," he said. "I can probably get a guitar for twenty. Maybe at a yard sale——things are cheaper."

His mother called him to dinner.

The next day he dressed for church without anyone telling him. He was going to go to eight o'clock mass.

"I'm going to church, Mom," he said. His mother was in the kitchen cooking *papas* and *chorizo con huevos*. A pile of tortillas lay warm under a dishtowel.

"Oh, I'm so proud of you, Son." She beamed, turning over the crackling *papas*.

His older brother, Lawrence, who was at the table reading the funnies, mimicked, "Oh, I'm so proud of you, my son," under his breath.

At Saint Theresa's he sat near the front. When Father Jerry began by saying that we are all sinners, Fausto thought he looked right at him. Could he know? Fausto fidgeted with guilt. No, he thought. I only did it yesterday.

Fausto knelt, prayed, and sang. But he couldn't forget the man and the lady, whose names he didn't even know, and the *empanada* they had given him. It had a strange name but tasted really good. He wondered how they got rich. And how that dome clock worked. He had asked his mother once how his aunt's clock worked. She said it just worked, the way the refrigerator works. It just did.

Fausto caught his mind wandering and tried to concentrate on his sins. He said a Hail Mary and sang, and when the wicker basket came his way, he stuck a hand reluctantly in his pocket and pulled out the twenty-dollar bill. He ironed it between his palms, and dropped it into the basket. The grown-ups stared. Here was a kid dropping twenty dollars in the basket while they gave just three or four dollars.

There would be a second collection for Saint Vincent de Paul, the lector announced. The wicker baskets again floated in the pews, and this time the adults around him, given a second chance to show their charity, dug deep into their wallets and purses and dropped in fives and tens. This time Fausto tossed in the grimy quarter.

Fausto felt better after church. He went home and played football in the front yard with his brother and some neighbor kids. He felt cleared of wrongdoing and was so happy that he played one of his best games of football ever. On one play, he tore his good pants, which he knew he shouldn't have been

wearing. For a second, while he examined the hole, he wished he hadn't given the twenty dollars away.

Man, I coulda bought me some Levi's, he thought. He pictured his twenty dollars being spent to buy church candles. He pictured a priest buying an armful of flowers with his money.

Fausto had to forget about getting a guitar. He spent the next day playing soccer in his good pants, which were now his old pants. But that night during dinner, his mother said she remembered seeing an old bass guitarron the last time she cleaned out her father's garage.

"It's a little dusty," his mom said, serving his favorite enchiladas, "but I think it works. Grandpa says it works."

Fausto's ears perked up. That was the same kind the guy in Los Lobos played. Instead of asking for the guitar, he waited for his mother to offer it to him. And she did, while gathering the dishes from the table.

"No, Mom, I'll do it," he said, hugging her. "I'll do the dishes forever if you want."

It was the happiest day of his life. No, it was the second-happiest day of his life. The happiest was when his grandfather Lupe placed the guitarron, which was nearly as huge as a washtub, in his arms. Fausto ran a thumb down the strings, which vibrated in his throat and chest. It sounded beautiful, deep and eerie. A pumpkin smile widened on his face.

"OK, *hijo*, now you put your fingers like this," said his grandfather, smelling of tobacco and aftershave. He took Fausto's fingers and placed them on the strings. Fausto strummed a chord on the guitarron, and the bass resounded in their chests.

The guitarron was more complicated than Fausto imagined. But he was confident that after a few more lessons he could start a band that would someday play on "American Bandstand" for the dancing crowds.

THE No-GUITAR BLUES

Meet the Author

Gary Soto wasn't interested in books or school as a child. While he was in school, he read a poem that expressed emotions he also felt. Soto realized he wanted to express his feelings by writing. He now writes poetry, essays, and fiction and produces short 16mm films.

Meet the Illustrator

José Miralles was born in Barcelona during the Spanish Civil War. He always wanted to be an artist, and at sixteen years old he published his first illustrations in a Barcelona newspaper. After completing his studies in art, Miralles went on to illustrate for many other publications. His work has appeared in magazines and books worldwide. Some of his favorite subjects are history, religion, and children.

Theme Connections

Within the Selection

Record your answers to the questions below in the Response Journal section of your Writer's Notebook. In small groups, report the ideas you wrote. Discuss your ideas with the rest of your group. Then choose a person to report your group's answers to the class.

- Why does Fausto go out to rake peoples' lawns?
- What does Fausto do that makes him feel guilty?
- What does he do with the money to make his conscience feel better?

Across the Selections

- Compare "The No-Guitar Blues" with "A Gift for a Gift." How is Fausto similar to the miner's brother? How is he different?
- In "A Gift for a Gift," the miner is rewarded for his honesty. Fausto, on the other hand, is not rewarded for his honesty, but his honesty still affects the outcome of his story. How is the role that honesty plays in both stories similar?

Beyond the Selection

- In "The No-Guitar Blues," you read about how Fausto wanted a guitar. What is something you have badly wanted? Why did you want it so badly? What did you do to get it? Get into small groups and share your stories with each other. Then choose one or two stories from your group to share with the class.

THE COURAGE THAT MY MOTHER HAD

Edna St. Vincent Millay
illustrated by Fabricio Vanden Broeck

The courage that my mother had
Went with her, and is with her still:
Rock from New England quarried;
Now granite in a granite hill.

The golden brooch my mother wore
She left behind for me to wear;
I have no thing I treasure more:
Yet, it is something I could spare.

Oh, if instead she left to me
The thing she took to the grave!—
That courage like a rock, which she
Has no more need of, and I have.

The Coin

Sara Teasdale
illustrated by Fabricio Vanden Broeck

Into my heart's treasury
I slipped a coin
That time cannot take
Nor a thief purloin—
Oh, better than the minting
Of a gold-crowned king
Is the safe-kept memory
Of a lovely thing.

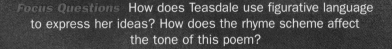

The Quiltmaker's Gift

Jeff Brumbeau
watercolors by Gail de Marcken

There was once a quiltmaker who kept a house in the blue misty mountains up high. Even the oldest great, great grandfather could not recall a time when she was not up there, sewing away day after day.

Here and there and wherever the sun warmed the earth, it was said she made the prettiest quilts anyone had ever seen.

The blues seemed to come from the deepest part of the ocean, the whites from the northernmost snows, the greens and purples from the abundant wildflowers, the reds, oranges, and pinks from the most wonderful sunsets.

Some said there was magic in her fingers. Some whispered that her needles and cloth were gifts of the bewitched. And still others said the quilts really fell to earth from the shoulders of passing angels.

Many people climbed her mountain, pockets bursting with gold, hoping to buy one of the wonderful quilts. But the woman would not sell them.

"I give my quilts to those who are poor or homeless," she told all who knocked on her door. "They are not for the rich."

On the darkest and coldest nights, the woman would make her way down the mountain to the town below. There she would wander the cobblestone streets until she came upon someone sleeping outside in the chill. She would then take a newly finished quilt from her bag, wrap it around their shivering shoulders, tuck them in tight, and tiptoe away.

Then the very next morning, with a steaming cup of blackberry tea, she would begin a new quilt.

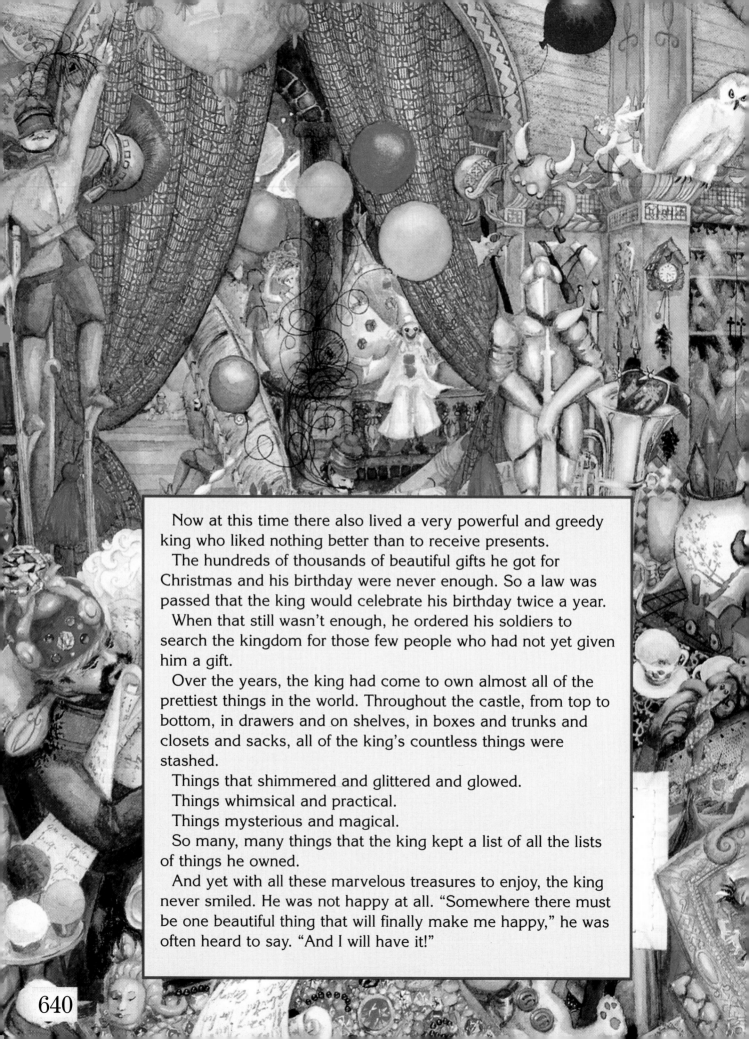

Now at this time there also lived a very powerful and greedy king who liked nothing better than to receive presents.

The hundreds of thousands of beautiful gifts he got for Christmas and his birthday were never enough. So a law was passed that the king would celebrate his birthday twice a year.

When that still wasn't enough, he ordered his soldiers to search the kingdom for those few people who had not yet given him a gift.

Over the years, the king had come to own almost all of the prettiest things in the world. Throughout the castle, from top to bottom, in drawers and on shelves, in boxes and trunks and closets and sacks, all of the king's countless things were stashed.

Things that shimmered and glittered and glowed.

Things whimsical and practical.

Things mysterious and magical.

So many, many things that the king kept a list of all the lists of things he owned.

And yet with all these marvelous treasures to enjoy, the king never smiled. He was not happy at all. "Somewhere there must be one beautiful thing that will finally make me happy," he was often heard to say. "And I will have it!"

641

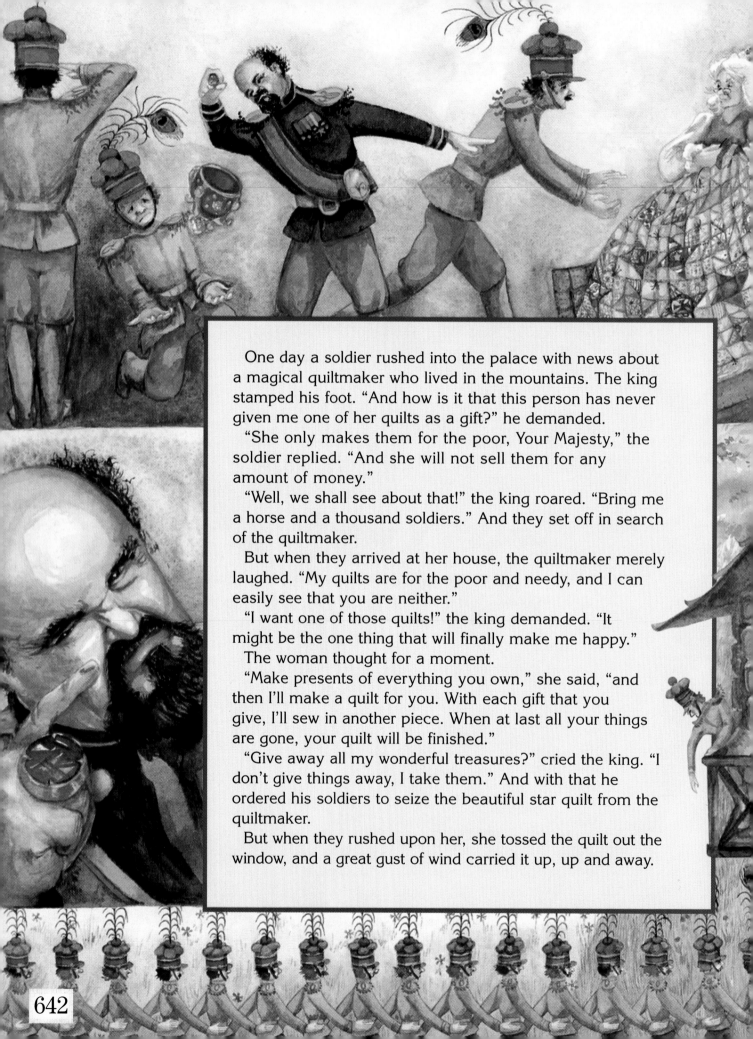

One day a soldier rushed into the palace with news about a magical quiltmaker who lived in the mountains. The king stamped his foot. "And how is it that this person has never given me one of her quilts as a gift?" he demanded.

"She only makes them for the poor, Your Majesty," the soldier replied. "And she will not sell them for any amount of money."

"Well, we shall see about that!" the king roared. "Bring me a horse and a thousand soldiers." And they set off in search of the quiltmaker.

But when they arrived at her house, the quiltmaker merely laughed. "My quilts are for the poor and needy, and I can easily see that you are neither."

"I want one of those quilts!" the king demanded. "It might be the one thing that will finally make me happy."

The woman thought for a moment.

"Make presents of everything you own," she said, "and then I'll make a quilt for you. With each gift that you give, I'll sew in another piece. When at last all your things are gone, your quilt will be finished."

"Give away all my wonderful treasures?" cried the king. "I don't give things away, I take them." And with that he ordered his soldiers to seize the beautiful star quilt from the quiltmaker.

But when they rushed upon her, she tossed the quilt out the window, and a great gust of wind carried it up, up and away.

643

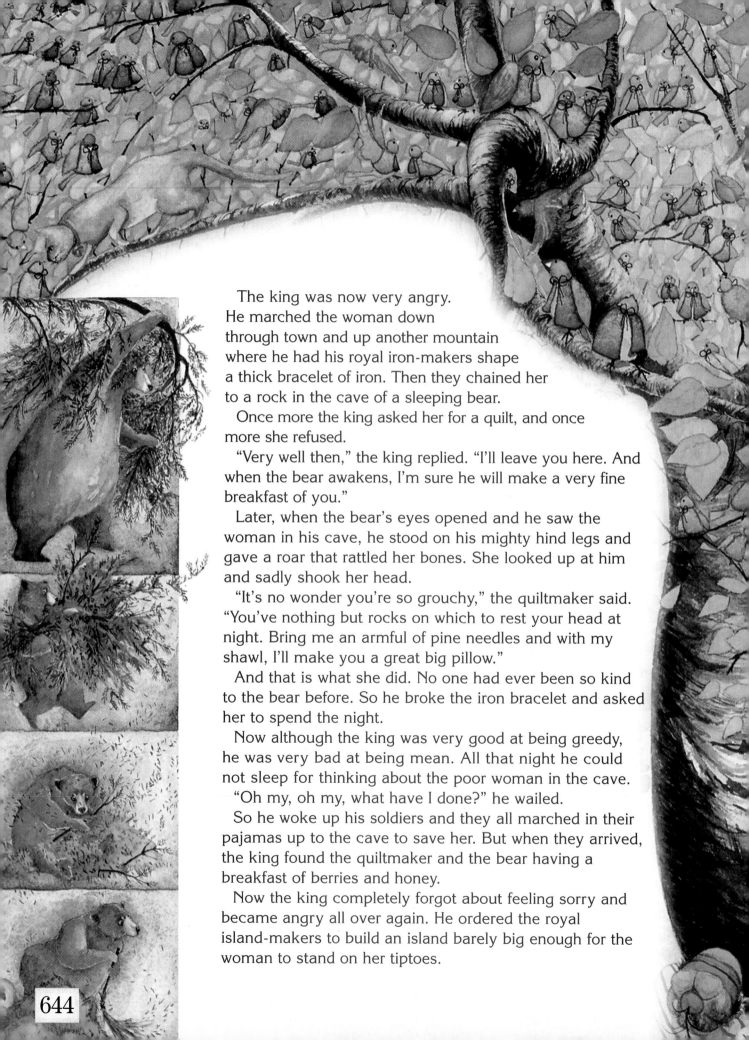

The king was now very angry.
He marched the woman down
through town and up another mountain
where he had his royal iron-makers shape
a thick bracelet of iron. Then they chained her
to a rock in the cave of a sleeping bear.

Once more the king asked her for a quilt, and once more she refused.

"Very well then," the king replied. "I'll leave you here. And when the bear awakens, I'm sure he will make a very fine breakfast of you."

Later, when the bear's eyes opened and he saw the woman in his cave, he stood on his mighty hind legs and gave a roar that rattled her bones. She looked up at him and sadly shook her head.

"It's no wonder you're so grouchy," the quiltmaker said. "You've nothing but rocks on which to rest your head at night. Bring me an armful of pine needles and with my shawl, I'll make you a great big pillow."

And that is what she did. No one had ever been so kind to the bear before. So he broke the iron bracelet and asked her to spend the night.

Now although the king was very good at being greedy, he was very bad at being mean. All that night he could not sleep for thinking about the poor woman in the cave.

"Oh my, oh my, what have I done?" he wailed.

So he woke up his soldiers and they all marched in their pajamas up to the cave to save her. But when they arrived, the king found the quiltmaker and the bear having a breakfast of berries and honey.

Now the king completely forgot about feeling sorry and became angry all over again. He ordered the royal island-makers to build an island barely big enough for the woman to stand on her tiptoes.

Once again the king asked her for a quilt, and once again she said no.

"Very well," the king replied. "Tonight when you're too tired to stand, and lie down to sleep, you'll drown." And the king left her alone on the tiny island.

Shortly after he left, the quiltmaker saw a sparrow flying across the great lake. A cold, fierce wind was blowing and it did not look like the poor bird would make it to shore. The quiltmaker called to him and he stopped to rest on her shoulder. The poor, tired sparrow was shivering, so the woman quickly made him a coat from scraps of her purple vest.

When he was warmed and the wind had stopped, the bird blew off. But he was very grateful to the quiltmaker for what she had done.

Soon the sky darkened as the air filled with a huge cloud of sparrows. Thousands of wings beating together, they swooped down, lifted the woman in their little beaks, and carried her safely to shore.

Again that night, the king could not sleep for thinking about the woman alone on the island.

"Oh my, oh my, what have I done?" he moaned.

So he woke up his sleepy soldiers again and they marched in their pajamas down to the lake to set the woman free. But when they arrived, she was sitting on a tree limb sewing tiny purple coats for all the sparrows.

"I give up!" the king shouted. "What must I do for you to give me a quilt?"

"As I said," the woman answered, "give away all of the things you own and I'll sew a quilt for you. And with each gift that you give, I'll add another piece to your quilt."

"I can't do that!" cried the king. "I love all my wonderful, beautiful things."

"But if they don't make you happy," the woman replied, "what good are they?"

"That's true," the king sighed. And he thought about what she had said for a long, long time. So long that weeks went by.

"Oh, all right," he finally muttered, "if I must give away my treasures, then I must!"

The king went to his castle and searched from top to bottom for something he could bear to give away.

Frowning, he finally came out with a single marble. But the boy who received it smiled so brightly in return, the king went back for more things.

Eventually, he brought out a pile of velvet coats and went about the town, giving them to people dressed only in rags. All were so pleased that they marched up and down the street in a grand parade.

Still, the king did not smile.

Next the king fetched a hundred waltzing blue Siamese cats and the dozen fish that were clear as glass.

Then the king ordered his merry-go-round with the real horses to be brought out. Children cried with delight and cartwheeled around him.

And just the smallest of smiles began to show on the king's face.

The king looked about him and saw the dancing and merry-making and all the happiness his gifts had brought. A child took hold of his hand and pulled him into the dance. Now the king really smiled and even laughed out loud.

"How can this be?" he cried. "How can I feel so happy about giving my things away? Bring everything out! Bring it all out at once!"

Meanwhile, the quiltmaker kept her word and started making a special quilt for the king. With each gift that he gave, she added another piece to his quilt.

So the king kept on giving and giving.

When at last there was no one left in town who had not received something, the king decided to go out into the world and find others who might be in need of his gifts.

But before he left, the king promised the quiltmaker he would send a sparrow back to her each and every time he gave something away.

Morning, noon, and night, the wagons rolled out of town, each piled high with the king's wonderful things. And for years and years, messenger sparrows flew to the quiltmaker's windowsill as the king slowly emptied his wagons, trading his treasures for smiles around the world.

On and on the quiltmaker worked, and piece by piece the king's quilt grew more and more beautiful.

Finally, one day a weary sparrow flew into her window and perched on her needle.

She knew then and there that it was the last messenger, so she put a final stitch in the quilt and started down the mountain in search of the king.

648

After a long search, she finally found him. The king's royal clothes were now in tatters and his toes poked out of his boots. Yet his eyes glittered with joy and his laugh was wonderful and thunderous.

The quiltmaker unfolded the king's quilt from her bag. It was so beautiful that hummingbirds and butterflies fluttered about. Standing on tiptoe, she tenderly wrapped it around him.

"What's this?" cried the king.

"As I promised you long ago," the woman said, "when the day came that you, yourself, were poor, only then would I give you a quilt." The king's great sunny laugh made green apples fall and flowers turn his way.

"But I am not poor," he said. "I may look poor, but in truth my heart is full to bursting, filled with memories of all the happiness I've given and received. I'm the richest man I know."

"Nevertheless," the quiltmaker said, "I made this quilt just for you."

"Thank you," replied the king. "I'll take it, but only if you'll accept a gift from me. There is one last treasure I have left to give away. All these years I've saved it just for you." And from his rickety, rundown wagon the king brought out his throne.

"It's really quite comfortable," the king said. "And just the thing for long days of sewing."

From that day on the king often came to the quiltmaker's house in the clouds.

By day the quiltmaker sewed the beautiful quilts she would not sell, and at night the king took them down to the town. There he searched out the poor and downhearted, never happier than when he was giving something away.

649

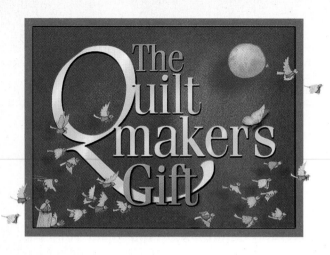

Meet the Author

When **Jeff Brumbeau** set out to write *The Quiltmaker's Gift*, he knew he wanted to write a story about generosity. He selected the quilt as a symbol for the theme of giving and caring because to him, the quilt offers both practical warmth and artistic beauty. Brumbeau hopes this story will inspire readers to think about their own patterns of accumulating. He says, *"Instead of always wanting more, maybe we can all start looking at ways to live with a little less and start learning to share whatever we have with others."*

Meet the Illustrator

Gail de Marcken has traveled all around the world with her husband, who is a director in the Peace Corps. A lifelong painter, de Marcken incorporated her own life experiences in some of the illustrations for *The Quiltmaker's Gift*. *"The king's gifts are given away and used in many of the places we have lived,"* she says.

Theme Connections

Within the Selection

Record your answers to the questions below in the Response Journal section of your Writer's Notebook. In small groups, report the ideas you wrote. Discuss your ideas with the rest of your group. Then choose a person to report your group's answers to the class.

- Why would the quiltmaker not sell her quilts?
- What does the quiltmaker tell the king he must do if she is to make him a quilt?
- How has the king's appearance changed by the end of the story?

Across the Selections

- At the end of the selection, the king claims to be the richest man he knows. How is his wealth at the end of the story different from his wealth at the beginning of it? Where else in this unit have you seen a statement like the king's? Who said it, and who does this character most closely resemble in "The Quiltmaker's Gift?"
- True generosity lies in giving away things that matter. Think about Annie in "A Brother's Promise." How is her generosity similar to the king's? How is it different?

Beyond the Selection

- What is the greatest gift you have ever given someone? Was the gift you gave something with special meaning for you, or did it have special meaning for the person to whom you gave it? Perhaps it meant a lot to you both. Take several minutes to write about your gift. How did it feel to give it? What distinguishes it as the greatest gift you have ever given? Be prepared to share your story with the class.

Pronunciation Key

a as in **a**t

ā as in l**a**te

â as in c**a**re

ä as in f**a**ther

e as in s**e**t

ē as in m**e**

i as in **i**t

ī as in k**i**te

o as in **o**x

ō as in r**o**se

ô as in b**ough**t and r**aw**

oi as in c**oi**n

o͝o as in b**oo**k

o͞o as in t**oo**

or as in f**or**m

ou as in **ou**t

u as in **u**p

ū as in **u**se

ûr as in t**ur**n; g**er**m, l**ear**n, f**ir**m, w**or**k

ə as in **a**bout, chick**e**n, penc**i**l, cann**o**n, circ**u**s

ch as in **ch**air

hw as in **wh**ich

ng as in ri**ng**

sh as in **sh**op

th as in **th**in

th́ as in **th**ere

zh as in trea**s**ure

The mark (′) is placed after a syllable with a heavy accent, as in **chicken** (chik′ ən).

The mark (′) after a syllable shows a lighter accent, as in **disappear** (dis′ ə pēr′).

Glossary

A

ablution (ə blōō´ shən) n. A cleansing.

abolition (ab´ ə lish´ ən) n. The termination, or ending, of something.

abolitionist (ab´ ə lish´ ən ist) n. A person who wanted to end slavery.

abrupt (ə brupt´) adj. Sudden; without warning.

accelerate (ak sel´ ə rāt´) v. To increase speed.

access (ak´ ses´) n. Permission or ability to enter, approach, communicate with, or pass to and from.

accompany (ə kəm´ pə nē) v. To play along with musically.

accumulate (ə kyōō´ myə lāt´) v. To gather more and more; to pile up.

acrylic (ə kril´ ik) n. A synthetic, or human-made, liquid that dries clear and hard like plastic.

adapt (ə dapt´) v. To adjust to new or different conditions.

adherent (ad hir´ ənt) n. One who believes or follows.

adobe (ə dō´ bē) n. Sun-dried brick.

advance (əd vans´) v. To bring or move forward.

advocate (ad´ və kāt´) v. To speak in favor of; to support.

aerosol (âr´ ə sôl´) n. A liquid sealed under pressure in a can with a gas. When a button on the can is pressed, the liquid sprays out.

aggravate (ag´ rə vāt´) v. To annoy.

alkali (al´ kə lī´) n. A chemical compound or element that forms salts and neutralizes acids.

ally (a´ lī´) n. Someone who works with another as a helper.

alpine ibex (al´ pīn ī´ beks) n. A wild mountain goat from a high mountain area.

alter (ôl´ tər) v. To change; to make different.

ambassador (am bas´ ə dər) n. A representative; one who represents something.

ambrosia (am brō´ zhə) n. Something delicious to smell.

amethyst (am´ ə thist) n. A purple or violet gem.

amiably (ā´ mē ə blē) adv. Being friendly or helpful.

amphitheater (am´ fə thē´ ə tər) n. An area with flat ground surrounded by rising hills or cliffs.

ample (am´ pəl) adj. More than enough; plenty.

amply (am´ plē) adv. Sufficiently; plentifully; enough.

anoint (ə noint´) v. To apply oil or ointment as part of a religious ceremony; to make sacred in a ceremony.

anonymously (ə no´ nə məs lē) adv. Without being identified or named.

anthropologist (an´ thrə pol´ ə jist) n. A scientist who studies the various physical aspects or cultural features of human beings.

antislavery (an´ tē slā´ və rē) adj. Against slavery.

anvil (an´ vil) n. The iron block on which a blacksmith hammers and shapes metal.

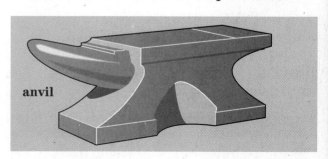

anvil

appreciation (ə prē´ shē ā´ shən) n. Recognizing the benefits of something.

archaeologist (är kē ol´ ə jist) n. A person who studies the life and culture of people of the past.

aria (är´ ē ə) n. A song that is sung by one person in an opera.

aristocracy (ar´ ə stok´ rə sē) n. The upper class.

aristocrat (ə ris´ tə krat´) n. An upper-class person.

armor (är´ mər) n. A covering that protects the body during fighting.

arroyo (ə roi´ ō) n. A small gulch or gulley.

artifact (är´ ti fakt) n. Any object made by humans; a name usually given to items made a long time ago.

artisan (är´ ti sən) n. A skilled craftsman.

ascend (ə send´) v. To climb up, rise. In music, scales with notes that go higher in pitch.

ascent (ə sent´) n. The act of rising or moving upward; climb.

asinine (as´ ə nīn´) adj. Silly; stupid.

associate (ə sō´ sē āt) v. To relate or compare to something else.

astuteness (ə stoot´ nəs) n. Cleverness; shrewdness.

atmosphere (at´ məs fēr) n. The air that surrounds the earth.

audacious (ô dā´ shəs) adj. Extremely daring; recklessly brave.

augment (ôg ment´) v. To add to; to increase; to enlarge.

Word History

The word **augment** comes from the French word *augmenter.* This French word goes back to a Latin word meaning "to increase."

aura (or´ ə) n. A certain quality; an atmosphere surrounding something.

authorize (ô´ thə rīz´) v. To make legal; to give legal power to.

Word Derivations

Below are some words derived from the word *authorize.*

authorized	authorizing
unauthorized	authorization

avaricious (av´ ə rish´ əs) adj. Greedy.

avert (ə vûrt´) v. To prevent or change the probable outcome of; to ward off.

awash (ə wôsh´) adj. Filled with, flooded with.

awl (ôl) n. A pointed tool for poking holes in things.

B

bade (bād) v. A past tense of **bid:** To command.

balustrade (bal´ ə strād´) n. A railing with upright supports.

barren (bar´ ən) adj. Bare.

bass (bās) n. The lowest part in the musical range; the lowest range of the male singing voice.

beacon (bē´ kən) adj. Used to signal.

belabor (bi lā´ bər) v. To beat; to hit.

bellow (bel´ lō) v. To yell or cry out in a deep voice.

beseech (bi sēch´) v. To beg.

besiege (bi sēj´) v. Under attack, to surround with armed forces.

bestow (bi stō´) v. Given, granted to.

biceps (bī´ seps) n. A muscle in the upper arm.

biologist (bī ol´ ə jist´) n. A scientist who studies living things, both plant and animal.

blackguard (blag´ ärd) n. A scoundrel; a bad person.

blockade (blo´ kād) n. A line of military troops or ships that prevents the passage of people or vessels through a certain area.

bolt (bōlt) *n.* A roll of fabric.

boogie-woogie (bŏŏg´ ē wŏŏg´ ē) *n.* A type of jazz played on the piano.

boycott (boi´ kot) *v.* To refuse to do business with someone.

Word History

The term **boycott** originated in 1880 when Irish tenants refused to do business with Charles C. Boycott, an English land agent who would not reduce rents and who tried to have these tenants evicted.

---

brandish (bran´ dish) *v.* To shake; to wave.

brimstone (brim´ stōn´) *n.* Sulfur, a yellow mineral substance with a sharp odor.

brooch (brōch) *n.* A pin that is highly decorated, worn as jewelry.

brood (brŏŏd) *v.* To sit on eggs in order to hatch them.

buckle (buk´ əl) *n.* A bend or bulge.

Buddhist (bŏŏ´ dist) *n.* One who follows the teachings of Gautama Buddha.

buenos noches (bwe´ nōs nō´ ches) *n. Spanish.* Good night.

bull-roarer (bŏŏl´ ror´ ər) *n.* A strip of wood on a string that is twirled around one's head to make a roaring sound.

bush baby (bŏŏsh´ bā´ bē) *n.* A primate of Africa with large eyes and ears, woolly fur, and a bushy tail.

C

calculation (kal´ kyə lā´ shən) *n.* The result of counting, computing, or gauging something.

calypso (kə lip´ sō) *n.* A style of jazz from the West Indies.

canister (ka´ nə stər) *n.* A tank that holds compressed gas.

canopy (kan´ ə pē) *n.* The highest part of a forest where leaves are the thickest.

caravan (câr´ ə van´) *n.* A group of people traveling together through a desert or hostile region.

carbide (kär´ bīd) *n.* A compound made with carbon and another element.

Carthaginian (kär´ thə ji´ nē ən) *adj.* Relating to or having to do with Carthage, which was an ancient city and state of North Africa near present-day Tunis.

chamber (chām´ bər) *n.* 1. A room in a royal palace, especially a bedroom. 2. An enclosed space.

chamberlain (chām´ bər lin) *n.* An important official in a royal court.

champion (cham´ pē ən) *n.* One who defends others.

chaperon (shap´ ə rōn´) *n.* A person who stays with a young, unmarried woman in public.

chaplain (chap´ lin) *n.* A religious leader in a royal court.

charity (châr´ i tē) *n.* Generosity, helpfulness.

cherish (châr´ ish) *v.* To value and enjoy; to hold dear.

chignon (shēn´ yon) *n.* A twist or knot of hair worn at the nape of the neck.

chimney (chim´ nē) *n.* A narrow crack in rock or ice.

chorizo con huevos (chō rē´ sō kōn we´ vōs) *n. Spanish.* Sausage with eggs.

cicada (si kā´ də) *n.* A large insect that makes a shrill sound.

circulate (sûr´ kū lāt) *v.* To distribute, to spread out.

circulation (sûr´ kyə lā´ shən) *n.* The number of newspapers sold to readers.

cite (sīt) *v.* To state as proof or as an example.

civil disobedience (siv´ əl dis´ ə bē´ dē əns) *n.* The refusal to obey certain laws in order to eventually change those laws.

civilization (siv´ ə lə zā´ shən) *n.* A culture, society, or group of human beings who have developed education, agriculture, trade, science, art, government, and so on.

classical (kla´ si kəl) *adj.* Music or art created in the late eighteenth and nineteenth centuries.

cliff dwelling (klif dwel´ ing) *n.* A home that is built on a cliff ledge or is built inside a cave in the side of a hill.

clung (klung) *v.* Hold on to tightly, like a hug.

Pronunciation Key: at; l**ā**te; c**â**re; f**ä**ther;
s**e**t; m**ē**; **i**t; k**ī**te; **o**x; r**ō**se; **ô** in b**ou**ght;
c**oi**n; b**ŏŏ**k; t**ōō**; f**or**m; **ou**t; **u**p; **ū**se; t**û**rn; **ə**
sound in **a**bout, chick**e**n, penc**i**l, cann**o**n,
circ**u**s; **ch**air; **hw** in **wh**ich; ri**ng**; **sh**op;
thin; **th**ere; **zh** in trea**s**ure.

cog (kog) *n.* The part of a gear that sticks
out like a tooth; a tiny part of a machine.

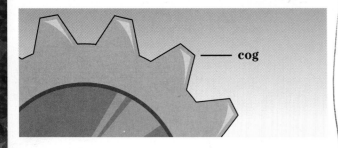

cog

colossal (kə lo′ səl) *adj.* Of incredible size or
power; great.

concept (kon′ sept) *n.* An idea.

condescending (kon′ də sen′ ding) *adj.*
Acting as if one is coming down to the level
of a person thought of as inferior.

conjunto (kōn hōōn′ tō) *n. Spanish.* A set;
an ensemble.

conserve (kən sûrv′) *v.* To preserve; to keep.

Word History

The word **conserve** is a French word that
comes from two Latin terms: *com-*, which
means "with" or "together," and *servare*,
which means "to keep."

contagious (kən tā′ jəs) *adj.* Spreading by
touch or by contact.

contest (kən test′) *v.* To struggle against.

continuity (kon′ tən ōō′ ə tē) *n.* Something
that exists without interruption.

contraption (kən trap′ shən) *n.* A device, a
gadget.

controversy (kon′ trə vûr′ sē) *n.*
Disagreement; strife.

convert (kən vûrt′) *v.* To change.

coquetry (kō′ ki trē) *n.* Flirting.

corps (kor) *n.* A group of individuals working
together under a common direction.

corridor (cor′ ə dōr) *n.* A narrow strip of
land; passageway.

cosmopolitan (koz′ mə po′ lə tən) *adj.*
Having people, ideas, and elements from
many parts of the world.

cosmos (koz′ məs) *n.* The world or universe.

couch (kouch) *v.* To lower a weapon and
hold it ready for attack.

coup (kōō) *n.* A daring deed in battle,
especially touching an enemy without
being harmed.

court (kort) *v.* To seek to win a pledge of
marriage from.

courtier (kor′ tē ər) *n.* A person in
attendance at a royal court.

cradleboard (krād′ l bord′) *n.* A wooden
frame that Native American women wore
on their backs to carry their babies.

crayfish (krā′ fish′) *n.* A freshwater
shellfish like a small lobster.

creditor (kred′ i tər) *n.* One to whom money
is owed.

creed (krēd) *n.* A statement of belief.

cremate (krē′ māt) *v.* To burn to ashes.

crescent (kres′ ənt) *n.* A curved shape like a
new moon.

croon (krōōn) *v.* To sing in a low,
moaning tone.

crop (krop) *n.* A pouch in the necks of birds
where food is stored before it is eaten.

crown (kroun) *n.* The leaves and the live
branches of a tree.

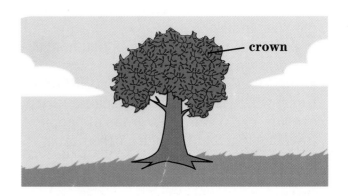

crown

culmination (kul´ mə nā´ shən) *n.* The end; the finish.

curious (kyoor´ ē əs) *adj.* 1. Strange. 2. Interesting. 3. Prying; inquisitive; wanting to know.

curtail (kər tāl´) *v.* To cut short; to put a stop to.

curvaceous (kûr vā´ shəs) *adj.* Having curves.

D

dank (dangk) *adj.* Damp; moist.

DDT **D**ichloro**d**iphenyl-**t**richloroethane: An insecticide; a substance used to kill insects.

deceitful (di sēt´ fəl) *adj.* Misleading; cheating.

deciduous (di sij´ oo əs) *adj.* Falling off or shedding yearly. Deciduous trees shed their leaves every year.

decipher (di sī´ fûr) *v.* To decode.

decree (di krē´) *n.* A political order or law.

deign (dān) *v.* To lower oneself.

delirium (di lēr´ ē əm) *n.* A state of excitability; a madness.

delude (di lood´) *v.* To mislead; to deceive.

deport (di port´) *v.* To banish; to expel from a country.

Word Derivations

Below are some words derived from the word *deport.*

deported	deportation
deportable	deportee

depression (di presh´ ən) *n.* A shallow hole or a dent.

descend (di send´) *v.* To go down, lower. In music, scales with notes that go down in pitch.

descent (di sent´) *n.* The act of inclining downward or moving from higher to lower.

despise (di spīz´) *v.* To look down on; to scorn.

deter (di tûr´) *v.* To hold back; to prevent.

devour (di vour´) *v.* To eat quickly.

dictate (dik´ tāt) *v.* To prescribe; to command.

dignitary (dig´ ni târ ē) *n.* A person who holds a position of honor or status.

diminish (di min´ ish) *v.* To reduce, to decline, to make smaller.

diplomat (di´ plō mat) *n.* A person who works with and deals with other countries and who usually lives in that country.

disbursement (dis bûrs´ mənt) *n.* Money spent.

discern (di sûrn´) *v.* To understand differences by using one's intellect or senses.

discord (dis´ kord) *n.* Disagreement.

discordant (dis kor´ dnt) *adj.* Harsh; jarring.

disdain (dis dān´) *n.* Contempt; the act of looking down upon someone.

disparage (di spar´ ij) *v.* To belittle; to run down.

dispel (di spel´) *v.* To drive away; to banish.

distinguished (dis ting´ gwisht) *adj.* Marked by status or greatness.

distract (di strakt´) *v.* To draw one's attention away.

Word History

The word **distract** comes from two Latin terms: *dis-*, which means "apart," and *tract*, which means "to draw."

distressed (dis trest´) *adj.* Feeling pain or misery.

document (dok´ yə mənt) *n.* A written proof or testimony.

down (doun) *n.* Very soft or fine feathers.

dredge (drej) *v.* To scoop mud from a channel.

drudgery (dru´ jə rē) *n.* Work that is boring and tiring.

dulcet (dul´ sit) *adj.* Pleasant; soothing.

dumb (dum) *adj.* Unable to talk.

durable (door´ ə bəl) *adj.* Lasting; long-wearing.

dwindle (dwin´ dəl) *v.* To become less.

Pronunciation Key: at; l**ā**te; c**â**re; f**ä**ther; set; m**ē**; **i**t; k**ī**te; **o**x; r**ō**se; **ô** in b**ou**ght; **coi**n; b**oo**k; t**oo**; f**o**rm; **ou**t; **u**p; **ū**se; t**û**rn; **ə** sound in **a**bout, chick**e**n, penc**i**l, cann**o**n, circ**u**s; **ch**air; **hw** in **wh**ich; ri**ng**; **sh**op; **th**in; **th**ere; **zh** in trea**s**ure.

E

ebony (eb´ ə nē) *n.* A dark, heavy wood from Africa.

eccentric (ik sen´ trik) *adj.* Odd; peculiar.

eccentricity (ek sen tris´ ə te) *n.* Deviation from normal behavior.

ecstatic (ek stat´ ik) *adj.* Extremely joyful; intensely happy.

eerie (ēr´ ē) *adj.* Scary, creepy.

elated (i lā´ tid) *adj.* Joyfully excited.

elder (el´ dər) *n.* An older, respected member of a group.

elevator (el´ ə vā´ tər) *n.* A flap on a wing of an airplane that is raised or lowered to raise or lower the plane's nose.

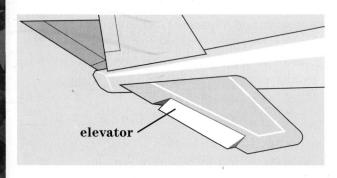

elevator

élite (i lēt´) *adj.* The best.

embalmer (em bäm´ ər) *n.* A person who preserves dead bodies.

embedded (im bed´ id) *v.* To find within.

emergent (i mûr´ jent) *adj.* A tree that rises above the surrounding forest.

encase (in cās´) *v.* To enclose or put in a case.

encrusted (en krust´ id) *adj.* Covered with.

endangered (en dān´ jərd) *adj.* At risk of becoming extinct; in danger of being killed off.

endure (in door´) *v.* To tolerate; to get through something without giving up.

engage (en gāj´) *v.* To employ; to hire.

engender (en jen´ dər) *v.* To produce; to cause.

enhance (in hans´) *v.* To improve the quality of.

enlightened (en līt´ nd) *adj.* Informed; educated.

enterprising (en´ tər prī zing) *adj.* Willing to try something new or that requires an energetic, problem-solving attitude; creative.

enthralled (en thrôld´) *adj.* Charmed; fascinated.

enthrone (in thrōn´) *v.* To put someone in a position of influence or authority.

entity (en´ ti tē) *n.* Something that exists on its own.

entrails (en´ trālz) *n.* The organs inside the body.

entrepreneur (än´ trə prə nûr´) *n.* A person who starts a business that usually involves risk.

Word History

Entrepreneur is a French word that comes from another French word, *entreprendre*, which means "to take on."

epistle (i pis´ əl) *n.* A letter; a message.

equivalent (i kwiv´ ə lənt) *n.* Equal.

erratic (i rat´ ik) *adj.* Changeable; not reliable.

eruption (i´ rup shən) *n.* When lava explodes out of a volcano.

esperanto (es´ pə rän´ tō) *n. usually capitalized.* A language that was invented in hopes that all the people in the world could speak the same language.

estuary (es´ choo er´ ē) *n.* A river mouth; where a river meets the sea.

etch (ech) *v.* To produce a design by making furrows on a hard surface.

ewer (ū′ ər) *n.* A pitcher or jug.

ewer

excavate (eks′ kə vāt′) *v.* To dig out.

Word History

The word **excavate** comes from two Latin terms: *ex-*, which means "out of" or "from" and *cavate*, which means "to make hollow."

---

exhibition (ek′ sə bi′ shən) *n.* A public showing.

exigency (ek′ si jən sē) *n.* Urgency; the need to act immediately.

expedition (eks pə di′ shən) *n.* A group of people on a trip for specific purpose.

exploration (eks plə rā′ shən) *n.* Trips where people search or explore.

expose (iks′ pōz) *v.* Show to someone.

exquisite (ik skwiz′ it) *adj.* Having special or rare beauty.

extensively (ik sten′ siv lē) *adv.* Widely; to a great extent.

extent (ik stent′) *n.* The size; the amount.

extinct (ik stingkt′) *adj.* Not now existing.

eyrie (âr′ ē) *n.* Nest site on a rocky cliff.

F

falconer (fôl′ kə nər) *n.* A person who hunts by using falcons or hawks, both powerful birds of prey.

fanatic (fə nat′ ik) *n.* A person who is carried beyond reason by feelings or beliefs.

fare (fâr) *n.* Food.

fast (fast) *n.* A period of time when a person chooses to not eat food as a way to protest.

fathomless (fath′ əm lis) *adj.* Extremely deep; bottomless.

feminist (fem′ ə nist) *adj.* Agreeing with equal rights for women.

fetter (fet′ ər) *n.* A chain binding the ankles.

flatiron (flat′ ī′ ərn) *n.* An iron that is not electric, used to press clothes.

flue (flo̅o̅) *n.* A chimney; a shaft for letting gases or fumes float out of a building.

fluted (flo̅o̅′ tid) *adj.* Having rounded grooves.

foe (fō) *n.* An enemy; an opponent.

forage (for′ ij) *v.* To search for food in leaves or on the ground.

foremost (for′ mōst′) *adj.* The most important.

fortunate (for chə nət) *adj.* Lucky.

frankincense (frang′ kin sens′) *n.* A substance with an aroma, burned as incense or used as perfume.

fraud (frôd) *n.* Someone who pretends to be something that he or she isn't; an imposter.

freeway (frē′ wā′) *n.* A highway.

frieze (frēz) *n.* An ornamental border around the walls of a room or the outside of a building.

frost heave (frôst′ hēv′) *n.* An area of soil that is raised due to the freezing of the moisture within the soil.

fungi (fun′ jī) *n.* A plural of **fungus** (fung′ gəs): A group of spongy plants that get their food from other dead or living plants; mushrooms, molds, and the like.

furl (fûrl) *v.* To roll up, as a flag or sail.

furrow (fûr′ ō) *n.* A depression made by a plow; a groove.

G

galley (gal′ ē) *n.* A ship's kitchen.

garnet (gär′ nit) *n.* A deep red gem.

Pronunciation Key: at; l**ā**te; c**â**re; f**ä**ther; set; m**ē**; **i**t; k**ī**te; **o**x; r**ō**se; **ô** in b**ou**ght; c**oi**n; b**ōō**k; t**ōō**; f**o**rm; **ou**t; **u**p; **ū**se; t**û**rn; **ə** sound in **a**bout, chick**e**n, penc**i**l, cann**o**n, circ**u**s; **ch**air; **hw** in **wh**ich; ri**ng**; **sh**op; **th**in; **th**ere; **zh** in trea**s**ure.

gatekeeper (gāt´ kē pûr) *n.* A person who guards the entrance of a place.

Word History

The word **garnet** comes from the French word *grenat*, which means "red like a pomegranate." This word can be traced back to the French words *pomme* and *grenate*, which mean "seedy apple." A pomegranate is a thick-skinned red fruit about the size of an orange.

gibbon (gib´ ən) *n.* A small ape.

gingerly (jin´ jər lē) *adv.* Cautiously; warily.

glance (glans) *v.* To glide off an object instead of hitting it full.

glower (glou´ ər) *v.* To look or stare with sullen annoyance or anger.

glut (glut) *n.* An excess; too much of something.

Godspeed (god´ spēd´) *n.* Good luck; success.

good and honest faith (good´ and on´ est fāth´) *n.* Lawfullness of purpose.

guitarron (gi tä ron´) *n. Spanish.* A large guitar.

gypsum (jip´ səm) *n.* A soft white mineral, or nonliving substance, that occurs in nature. The type of gypsum used in carvings and building is known as alabaster.

H

habitat (hab´ i tat´) *n.* The natural surroundings of a plant or animal; native environment.

Hail Mary (hāl´ mâr´ ē) *n.* A Roman Catholic prayer.

halflight (haf´ līt´) *n.* Dimmed light.

hamlet (ham´ lit) *n.* A small village.

handmaiden (hand mā´ dən) *n.* A woman who assists or serves someone else; a servant.

harpsichord (härp´ si kord´) *n.* A musical instrument like a small piano but with a more delicate sound.

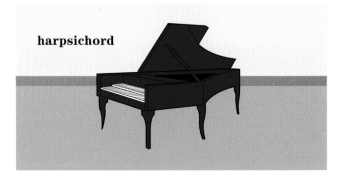

harpsichord

henna (hen´ ə) *n.* A reddish-orange dye.

hermit (hûr´ mit) *n.* Someone who lives alone and stays away from others.

hew (hū) *v.* To cut with an axe.

hijo (ē´ hō´) *n. Spanish.* Son.

hoax (hōks) *n.* A trick, an attempt to fool someone.

hobble (ho´ bəl) *v.* To make unable to walk by tying the legs together.

hoe (hō) *n.* A garden tool that has a thin flat blade with a straight edge used to break up ground.

hogan (hō´ gôn) *n.* The rounded log and mud dwelling of the Navajo.

homage (hom´ ij) *n.* Duty; loyalty; devotion.

home-cooked (hōm kookt) *adj.* Food prepared at home, usually eaten with family.

horde (hord) *n.* A large group of nomads.

hospitality (hos pi tal´ i tē) *n.* Kindness, care.

human nature (hū´ mən nā´ chûr) *n.* The way people usually act.

husk (husk) *v.* To remove the outer leaves of an ear of corn.

I

ibis (ī´ bis) *n.* A large wading bird with a long bill that curves downward.

imam (i mom´) *n.* A prayer leader.

immortal (i mor´ tl) *adj.* Living forever.

imperial (im pir´ ē əl) *adj.* Relating to an empire or emperor.

impoverished (im pov´ ər isht) *adj.* Very poor.

improvise (im´ prə vīz´) *v.* To write music without planning by just playing on an instrument.

inclined (in klīnd´) *adj.* Tending to be in favor of.

inconceivable (in´ kən sē´ və bəl) *adj.* Unbelievable; impossible to imagine.

incorporate (in korp´ ûr āt) *v.* To combine or include into one unit.

incubator (in´ kyə bā´ tər) *n.* An enclosure in which eggs are hatched by being kept at the right conditions.

indispensable (in´ di spen´ sə bəl) *adj.* Necessary; essential.

influence (in´ flōō ens) *n.* To inspire, to give someone a reason for doing something.

inevitable (in ev´ i tə bəl) *adj.* Certain; sure.

inexistent (in´ ig zis´ tənt) *adj.* Not living; not being.

inferior (in fir´ ē ər) *adj.* Less than acceptable; not as good as others.

Word History

The word **inferior** comes from the Latin word *inferus*, which means "lower."

---

infertility (in´ fûr til´ i tē) *n.* The inability to bear young.

infinite (in´ fə nit) *adj.* Having no limits; endless; immense.

ingenuity (in jə nōō´ i tē) *n.* Cleverness.

ingratitude (in grat´ i tōōd´) *n.* A lack of thankfulness.

initial (in nish´ əl) *adj.* At the beginning; first.

inkwell (ink´ well) *n.* A container for ink.

insatiable (in sā´ shə bəl) *adj.* Unable to be satisfied; endless.

inscription (in skrip´ shən) *n.* The writing on a document.

insensitive (in sen´ si tiv) *adj.* Not caring; not feeling sympathy.

insist (in sist´) *v.* To demand.

insistent (in sis´ tənt) *adj.* Demanding; grabbing the attention of someone.

insulation (in sə lā´ shən) *n.* Padding or layers used to keep things warm.

intent (in tent´) *adj.* Fixed upon or bent upon; attentive to.

internment (in tûrn´ ment) *v.* To confine or impound, especially during a time of war.

interpretation (in tûr prə tā´ shən) *n.* The way someone feels written music should be played.

intoxicated (in tok´ si kā´ tid) *adj.* Highly excited.

intricate (in´ tri kit) *adj.* Made of many parts.

inundation (in´ ən dā´ shən) *n.* A deluge; a flood.

issue (i´ shū) *v.* Give out to someone.

J

jaeger (yā´ gər) *n.* A dark-colored seabird that is a hunter of other birds' prey, especially that of gulls.

jaeger

jukebox (jūk´ boks) *n.* A machine that plays music when money is inserted.

K

keen (kēn) *adj.* Fine; sharp.

ken (ken) *n.* Knowledge; understanding.

kittiwake (kit′ ē wāk′) *n.* A cliff-nesting gull of the northern seas.

km Kilometer.

knight (nīt) *n.* A soldier in armor and on horseback, working on behalf of a feudal lord or a king or queen.

kohl (kōl) *n.* A dark powder, used as eyeliner or eye shadow.

L

lackey (lak′ ē) *n.* A footman; a manservant.

laden (lā′ dən) *adj.* Loaded with, carrying a heavy weight or a lot of items.

lamentation (lam′ ən tā′ shən) *n.* A vocal expression of grief or mourning.

lapis lazuli (lap′ is laz′ oo lē) *n.* A deep blue, semiprecious gemstone.

lateral (la′ tə rəl) *adj.* Toward the side, sideways.

laurel (lor′ əl) *n.* A small, European evergreen tree with dark, glossy green leaves.

lave (lāv) *v.* To wash; to bathe.

lectern (lek′ tərn) *n.* A podium; a tall, narrow piece of furniture with a slanted top, which a speaker stands behind.

Word History

The word **lectern** comes from a French word that can be traced to a Latin word that means "to read."

lector (lek′ tər) *n.* A person who acts as a reader of Bible selections during a church service.

liana (lē ä′ nə) *n.* A climbing vine found in rainforests that roots itself in the ground.

license (lī′ səns) *v.* To permit by law.

lichen (lī′ kən) *n.* A simple plant that grows on rocks and tree trunks.

liquefy (li′ kwə fī) *v.* To make as a liquid.

logically (loj′ i kə lē) *adv.* In a reasonable way.

loom (loom) *v.* To appear larger than its surroundings.

loris (lor′ is) *n.* A slender primate with no tail.

lotus (lō′ təs) *n.* A kind of water lily that grows in Egypt and Asia.

M

magma (mag′ mə) *n.* The molten material that pours out of a volcano and hardens to become rock.

malaria (mə lâr′ ē ə) *n.* A disease marked by fevers, caused by the bite of certain mosquitoes.

Word History

The word **malaria** comes from the two Italian words *mal* and *aria*, which mean "bad air."

maritime (mâr′ ə tīm′) *adj.* Relating to the sea.

Marseillaise (mär′ sə lāz′) *n.* The national anthem of France.

mason (mā′ sən) *n.* A builder in stone, bricks, and tile.

mass (mas) *n. often capitalized.* The chief service of the Roman Catholic Church.

master (mas′ tûr) *n.* One having chief authority.

mealy (mēl′ ē) *adj.* Soft and dry.

melancholy (mel´ ən kol´ ē) *adj.* Sad; moody.

mesa (mā´ sə) *n.* High, flat land like a plateau, but smaller.

metabolic (me tə bä´ lik) *adj.* Relating to the conversion of food into energy.

metronome (me´ trə nōm) *n.* A machine that keeps rhythm for musicians.

mildew (mil´ dōō´) *v.* To grow a coating of fuzzy mold.

mingle (min´ gəl) *v.* To interact with others; to mix together socially.

mottled

Word Derivations

Below are some words derived from the word *mingle*.

mingled   mingling   intermingle

mirage (mi räzh´) *n.* Something that appears but is not really there.

mock (mok) *v.* To make fun of; ridicule.

modest (mo´ dəst) *adj.* Having a moderate opinion of oneself.

molten (mōl´ tən) *adj.* Liquid.

monopoly (mə no´ pə lē) *n.* Owned and controlled by only one person, group, or company.

monsoon (mon sōōn´) *n.* A wind that blows across south Asia seasonally, bringing heavy rains.

monstrosity (mon stros´ i tē) *n.* A bad example of something, something very different than normal.

moonstone (mōōn´ stōn´) *n.* A pearly blue stone.

moonstruck (mōōn´ struk´) *adj.* Crazed as a result of the moon's influence.

moral (mor´ əl) *n.* The lesson taught by an experience.

mosque (mosk) *n.* The building in which Muslims worship publicly.

motley (mot´ lē) *adj.* Many-colored.

mottled (mot´ ld) *adj.* Spotted or blotched with different colors or shades.

mournful (morn´ fəl) *adj.* Sad, upsetting.

myriad (mir´ ē əd) *n.* An immense number.

myrrh (mûr) *n.* A fragrant, bitter resin used in medicine, perfumes, and incense.

N

nary (nâr´ ē) *adj.* Not any.

nationalist (nash´ ə nl ist´) *adj.* Patriotic; supporting one's country.

nimble (nim´ bəl) *adj.* Quick, agile.

nocturnal (nok tûr´ nl) *adj.* Awake or active at night.

nomad (nō´ mad´) *n.* Someone with no permanent home who moves from place to place within a given area during different seasons.

noncommittal (non´ kə mit´ l) *adj.* Having no point of view; giving no opinion.

nosh (nosh) *v. informal.* To snack; to eat snacks.

Word History

Nosh is a Yiddish word that dates back to a German word that means "to eat on the sly."

O

obelisk (ob´ ə lisk) *n.* A tall stone monument that is narrower at the top.

obese (ō bēs´) *adj.* Fat; overweight.

oblivion (ə bliv´ ē ən) *n.* The state of being unknown or totally forgotten.

Pronunciation Key: a**t**; l**ā**te; c**â**re; f**ä**ther; s**e**t; m**ē**; **i**t; k**ī**te; **o**x; r**ō**se; **ô** in b**ou**ght; **coi**n; b**oo**k; t**oo**; f**o**rm; **ou**t; **u**p; **ū**se; t**û**rn; **ə** sound in **a**bout, chick**e**n, penc**i**l, cann**o**n, circ**u**s; **ch**air; **hw** in **wh**ich; ri**ng**; **sh**op; **th**in; **th**ere; **zh** in trea**s**ure.

obscurity (əb skyoor´ i tē) *n.* The state of being unknown.

observatory (əb zûr´ və tor´ ē) *n.* A place that is designed for astronomers to study the stars.

obsidian (ob si´ dē ən) *n.* Black glass that comes from volcanos.

oppressor (ə pres´ sûr) *n.* Someone in power who abuses that power to hurt or abuse other people.

oratorio (or ə tor´ ē ō) *n.* A long vocal concert, done without costumes or acting.

outing (ou´ ting) *n.* A trip for pleasure.

ozone (ō´ zōn) *n.* A form of oxygen with three atoms in each molecule instead of the usual two, often present in the atmosphere after a thunderstorm.

ozone layer (ō´ zōn lā´ ûr) *n.* The layer of the atmosphere that protects the earth from the sun's rays.

P

palanquin (pal´ ən kēn´) *n.* An enclosed structure stretched across four poles in which a person rides while four people carry the poles.

pallor (pal´ ər) *n.* Paleness.

palsy (pôl´ sē) *n.* Paralysis; numbness.

papa (pä´ pä´) *n. Spanish.* A potato.

parabola (pə ra´ bə lä) *n.* Something that curves, forming a shape like a bowl.

passion (pa´ shən) *n.* Emotion.

patron (pā´ trən) *n.* One who supports an artist by giving money.

patron saint (pā´ trən sānt´) *n.* A saint who is the special guardian of a person or group.

patronage (pā´ trə nij) *n.* The attitude that one is granting a favor.

peal (pēl) *v.* To utter or give forth sound loudly.

peculiar (pə kūl´ yûr) *adj.* Strange, different, weird.

pedestal (pe´ dəs təl) *n.* The base on which a statue rests.

perch (pûrch) *n.* A resting place, a place or roost where a bird stands.

peril (per´ il) *n.* Being at risk or in danger.

perilous (per´ i lus) *adj.* Dangerous, full of peril.

perpetual (pər pech´ oo əl) *adj.* Lasting forever or for a long time.

pesticide (pes´ tə sīd´) *n.* A chemical used to destroy insect pests.

petition (pə tish´ ən) *n.* A written request to the government.

phenomenal (fi no´ mə nəl) *adj.* Amazing; incredible.

picket (pik´ ət) *n.* A line of people standing in front of someting.

picket line (pik´ ət līn) *n.* A line of people protesting in front of a building or company.

pilgrim (pil´ grəm) *n.* Someone who travels to a foreign land.

piñon (pin´ yən) *n.* A kind of pine tree with seeds that can be eaten.

pip (pip) *n.* The first crack in a bird's egg.

plait (plāt) *v.* To twine or braid.

plateau (pla tō´) *n.* A tract of high, flat land; a tableland.

pneumonia (noo mō´ nyə) *n.* A disease of the lungs caused by infection or irritation.

poach (pōch) *v.* To kill or hunt animals illegally.

polecat (pōl´ kat) *n.* A skunk.

polystyrene (pol´ ē stī´ rēn) *n.* A clear plastic or a stiff foam used to make objects or used as insulation.

poncho (pon´ chō) *n.* A cloak with an opening for the head.

porcelain (por´ sə lin) *n.* A white ceramic material that can almost be seen through.

porter (por´ tər) *n.* A person who carries supplies.

postscriptum (pōst skrip´ təm) *n.* A note attached to the end of a letter as one final message.

pound (pound) *n.* A unit of money in England.

predator (pred´ ə tər) *n.* An animal that hunts and kills other animals for its food.

predatory (pred´ ə tor´ ē) *adj.* Preying on other animals for food.

prehistoric (prē´ hi stor´ ik) *adj.* Belonging to a time before history was written down; very early in the history of humans.

prejudice (pre´ jə dəs) *n.* An unsupported negative opinion or attitude toward a person or group, often based on stereotypes.

première (pri mēr´) *n.* The first public performance of a work.

preserve (pri sûrv´) *v.* To save from destruction or decay.

presume (pri zōōm´) *v.* To take for granted; to suppose.

Word Derivations

Below are some words derived from the word *presume.*

presumed	presuming	presumedly

---

prodigious (prə dij´ əs) *adj.* Enormous; monstrous.

prodigy (prod´ i jē) *n.* A child with extraordinary talent.

profound (prə found´) *adj.* Of deep meaning.

proposed (prə pōzd´) *v.* To put forward a plan for possible future action.

prose (prōz) *n.* Written language that is not verse.

prostrate (pros´ trāt) *adj.* Lying flat.

pueblo (pweb´ lō) *n.* A group of adobe dwellings set into cliffs and reached by ladders.

puffin (puf´ in) *n.* A diving seabird with a beak like a parrot.

pumice (pum´ is) *n.* Light, porous lava.

purloin (pər loin´) *v.* To steal.

Q

quarry (kwor´ ē) *v.* To dig stone out of an open pit.

quell (kwel) *v.* To overcome by force; to crush.

queue (kū) *n.* A line.

R

radioactive fuel (rā dē ō ak´ tiv fyōōl) *n.* Energy or fuel that comes from the decay of atoms.

rally (ra´ lē) *v.* To inspire or motivate a group to support a given cause.

rank (rangk) *adj.* Absolute; complete.

ransack (ran´ sak) *v.* To search a place looking for things to steal; to plunder; to pillage.

ration (ra´ shən) *n.* Food supply.

ravel (ra´ vəl) *v.* To separate or undo.

ravishing (rav´ i shing) *adj.* Extremely beautiful.

receipts (ri sēts´) *n.* The amount received; income.

reclamation (rek´ lə mā´ shən) *n.* The act of putting land back into a pure or healthy state.

reconcile (rek´ ən sīl) *v.* To compare to; to make equal with.

reformer (ri for´ mər) *n.* A person who brings about change for the better.

refund (ri fund´) *v.* To pay back, to give money back.

regulate (reg´ yə lāt´) *v.* To adjust something to make it accurate.

Word Derivations

Below are some words derived from the word *regulate.*

regulated	regulation
regulating	regulatory

relay (rē´ lā´) *n.* A race in which each member of a team takes a turn running a certain length of the course.

relic (rel´ ik) *n.* A surviving trace of something past or dead.

rendezvous (rän´ də vōō´) *n.* An arranged meeting.

repertory (rep´ ə tōr´ ē) *n.* A theater where operas or plays are performed.

resin (rez´ in) *n.* The gummy sap of certain pine trees.

resound (ri zound´) *v.* To echo; to make a continuing sound, like ringing.

Word History

Resound comes from a French word that can be traced back to two Latin terms: *re-*, which means "again," and *sonare*, which means "to sound."

resistance (ri zis´ təns) *n.* Opposition.

restrain (ri strān´) *v.* To hold back; to control.

resurrection (rez´ ə rek´ shən) *n. usually capitalized.* The act of Christ rising from the dead.

retaining wall (ri tān´ ing wôl´) *n.* A wall constructed to keep earth from pouring over it.

reveille (rev´ ə lē) *n.* A bugle or drum signal used to call soldiers together in the morning.

revelation (rev´ ə lā´ shən) *n.* Something that had not been known before.

revenge (ri venj´) *n.* Vengeance; retaliation; the act of hurting in return for being hurt.

rickety (rik´ ə tē) *adj.* Old, worn-down.

ridicule (rid´ i kyōōl´) *v.* To make fun of; to mock.

rivet (riv´ it) *v.* To have one's complete attention.

rural (rōōr´ əl) *adj.* Having to do with the countryside.

S

sanctity (sangk´ ti tē) *n.* A sacred or holy nature.

scholar (skä´ lûr) *n.* One who studies or teaches in school.

scoff (skof) *v.* To make fun of; to treat with contempt.

screen (skrēn) *v.* To keep something from being in clear view.

scribe (skrīb) *n.* A clerk with official status.

seditious (si dish´ əs) *adj.* Disloyal; unpatriotic.

segment (seg´ mənt) *n.* A part that breaks off naturally; a distinct part of something.

seize (sēz) *v.* To grab hold of; to take possession of.

self-pity (self pi´ tē) *n.* Feeling sorry for oneself.

semaphore (sem´ ə for´) *n.* A system of signaling using flags in which the positions of the flags have different meanings.

semaphore

sentinel (sent´ nəl) *n.* Guard; soldier watching for the enemy.

sentry (sen´ trē) *n.* A soldier on guard duty.

sever (sev´ ər) *v.* To cut; to separate.

shaman (sho´ mən) *n.* A priest or priestess who uses magic.

shawl (shäl) *n.* A square piece of fabric used to cover the head or shoulders.

Sherpa (shûr´ pə) *n.* A member of the people originally from Tibet who live on the high southern slopes of the Himalayas in eastern Nepal.

shrewd (shro͞od) *adj.* Abusive, hard, ill-natured.

shrill (shril) *adj.* A high-pitched, loud sound.

shun (shun) *v.* To have nothing to do with; to ignore.

sift (sift) *v.* To pass dirt through a screen to separate items from the dirt.

sinfonia (sin fō ne´ ə) *n.* A symphony, or instrumental piece, played as an introduction to an opera or oratorio.

sirdar (sûr´ där) *n.* A person holding a responsible position; the leader of the Sherpas on a mountaineering expedition.

siskin (sis´ kin) *n.* A small bird in the finch family.

site (sīt) *n.* The place where something is or was located.

skein (skān) *n.* Yarn or thread wound in a coil.

skirt (skûrt) *v.* To go along the edge of; to go around to avoid danger.

skitter (ski´ tûr) *v.* To dart or run away quickly.

skua (sko͞o´ ə) *n.* A large brown bird that is like a gull.

smolder (smōl´ dûr) *v.* To burn slowly, without much flame, and often with much smoke.

smote (smōt) *v.* A past tense of **smite:** To strike with a hard, sudden blow.

sneer (snēr) *n.* A smile that shows scorn or hate.

solace (sol´ is) *n.* Comfort; consolation.

solar (sō´ lər) *adj.* Concerning the sun.

solder (sod´ ər) *n.* A hot, melted blend of metals used to join pieces of metal together. —*v.* To join pieces of metal together by applying a blend of melted metals at the joints.

soulful (sōl´ fəl) *adj.* Having deep feeling.

spa (spä) *n.* A health resort that has a mineral spring.

Word History

The city of Spa, Belgium, became so famous for its mineral springs that the term **spa** has been used for all health resorts with mineral springs.

spawn (spôn) *v.* To give rise to.

specimen (spe´ si men) *n.* A single sample out of a group.

spectacle (spek´ ti kəl) *n.* Something unusual or entertaining that is put on display as a curiosity; an impressive public display.

sphere (sfēr) *n.* The area or environment of a person's life.

spiritless (spir´ it lis) *adj.* Without enthusiasm.

sprocket (sprok´ it) *n.* A wheel with tooth edges that grab another moving part.

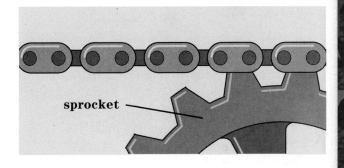

sprocket

sputter (sput´ ûr) *v.* To spit or squirt from the mouth in surprise.

spyglass (spī´ glas) *n.* A telescope.

stabilize (stā´ bə līz´) *v.* To make steady.

staff (staf) *n.* A rod; a long cane.

steep (stēp) *v.* To soak; to saturate.

stench (stench) *n.* A disagreeable odor.

steppe (step) *n.* A large area of land that is flat and treeless.

stilted (stilt´ əd) *adj.* Stiff, fake.

stipend (stī´ pend) *n.* A fixed salary.

straddle (strad´ l) *v.* To be positioned with parts on each side of something.

strategic (strə tē´ jik) *adj.* Of great importance.

stucco (stuk´ ō) *n.* Plaster for covering outer walls.

Styx (stiks) *n.* In Greek mythology, the river that dead souls crossed.

subdivision (sub´ di vizh´ ən) *n.* A piece of land broken into separate lots for houses.

sulphur or **sulfur** (sul´ fər) *n.* A yellow mineral substance with a sharp odor, used in medicine and chemistry.

summit (sum´ it) *n.* The highest point; the top.

summons (sum´ ənz) *n.* A signal that commands someone to approach.

superior (soo pēr´ ē ûr) *n.* Boss, person at work to whom you report.

suppress (sə pres´) *v.* To stop; to crush; to put down.

Word Derivations

Below are some words derived from the word *suppress*.

suppresses	suppressant
suppressing	suppression
suppressive	

sweat lodge (swet´ loj´) *n.* A building in which Native Americans cleanse themselves both spiritually and physically.

synchronize (sin´ krə nīz) *v.* To schedule an event to happen at the same time as something else.

syncopated (sing´ kə pā´ tid) *adj.* Having a shortened, quick-sounding rhythm.

synthesize (sin´ thə sīz´) *v.* To make something by putting together parts or elements.

T

talon (tal´ ən) *n.* The claw of an animal or predatory bird.

tango (tang´ gō) *n.* The music for a Latin-American ballroom dance.

tenement (ten´ ə mənt) *n.* A run-down and crowded apartment building in a poor section of a city.

tern (tûrn) *n.* A web-footed water bird that resembles a gull.

terrain (tə rān´) *n.* The roughness or smoothness of a piece of land.

textile (tek´ stīl´) *n.* Cloth; fabric.

Word History

The word **textile** was first used in English in 1626 and comes from the Latin word *textilis*, which means "woven."

thatch (thach) *n.* Straw for a roof covering.

thicket (thi´ kət) *n.* A thick growth of bushes and small trees.

thrust (thrust) *n.* The force caused by the propellers or the jets of an airplane.

thunderous (thun´ dûr əs) *adj.* Very loud.

ticker-tape parade (ti´ kər tāp´ pə rād´) *n.* A type of parade during which narrow strips of long white paper are released.

tidal (tīd´ l) *adj.* Having to do with the rise and fall of the sea.

timidity (ti mid´ i tē) *n.* Shyness; fright.

tinder (tin´ dər) *n.* Any very dry material that can be set on fire by a spark.

tinge (tinj) *n.* A light shade or color.

tome (tōm) *n.* A large book; a scholarly book.

tone-deaf (tōn´ def) *adj.* Being unable to hear or sing the correct notes in a musical piece.

toxic (tok´ sik) *adj.* Poisonous.

transform (trans form´) *v.* To change completely.

translate (trans´ lāt) *v.* To turn words from one language into a language one can understand.

transmission (trans mish´ ən) *n.* An enclosed box of gears that causes a transfer of forces from one part or machine to another.

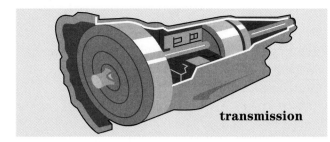

transmission

transmitter (trans mit´ ər) *n.* A device that sends out radio or television signals.

traverse (trə vûrs´) *n.* Crossing.

trawl (trôl) *v.* To catch with a large fishing net.

treacherous (tre´ chə rəs) *adj.* Having hidden dangers.

treat (trēt) *v.* To negotiate; to try to reach a settlement.

trek (trek) *n.* A trip, usually a difficult one.

tribunal (trī bū´ nəl) *n.* A group of people who decides law or judgements.

trifle (trī´ fəl) *n.* A small amount of little value.

trill (tril) *n.* A musical sound that goes quickly back and forth between two notes.

tripe (trīp) *n. slang.* Something that is worthless.

trowel (trou´ əl) *n.* A short-handled tool for spreading mortar or digging up plants.

Word History

The word **trowel** came into English usage about 600 years ago from the French word *truelle*, which goes back to a Latin word that means "ladle."

---

tundra (tun´ drə) *n.* A vast, treeless plain in the Arctic regions.

turquoise (tûr´ koiz) *n.* A semiprecious stone of bluish-green color.

U

unabashed (un´ ə basht´) *adj.* Bold; not embarrassed or ashamed.

uncharted (un chär´ tid) *adj.* Not mapped; not explored.

uncommitted (un´ kə mit´ id) *adj.* Not promised or bound to support a specific cause.

unguent (ung´ gwənt) *n.* An ointment or a salve, as a lotion.

unique (ū nēk´) *adj.* Having no equal; one of a kind.

unison (ū´ nə sən) *adj.* Together; as one.

unlikeliest (un līk´ lē əst) *adj.* The least likely.

unmannerly (un man´ ûr lē) *adj.* Rude.

upright (up´ rīt´) *n.* A type of piano.

urn (ûrn) *n.* A large vase.

V

vague (vāg) *adj.* Not clearly seen.

vainglorious (vān glor´ ē əs) *adj.* Boastful; having too much pride.

vanity (van´ i tē) *n.* Pride in appearance.

variable (vâr´ ē ə bəl) *n.* In science, something measurable that can change, out of many possible things. For example, wind, temperature, and humidity are all variables that make up weather.

vast (vast) *adj.* Extremely large; enormous.

venerate (ven´ ə rāt´) *v.* To respect or treat with reverence.

venomous (ven´ ə məs) *adj.* Poisonous.

vicious (vi´ shəs) *adj.* Dangerously aggressive, fierce.

visage (vi´ zij) *n.* The face of a person.

vulnerable (vul´ nər ə bəl) *adj.* Weak; defenseless.

W

waltz (wôlts) *v.* To move or advance in a lively manner; flounce.

warehouseman (wâr´ hous´ mən) *n.* A person who works in a building where goods are stored.

warily (wâr´ ə lē) *adv.* In a watchful, slightly uncomfortable way.

> **Pronunciation Key: a**t; l**ā**te; c**â**re; f**ä**ther;
> s**e**t; m**ē**; **i**t; k**ī**te; **o**x; r**ō**se; **ô** in b**ou**ght;
> c**oi**n; b**oo**k; t**oo**; f**o**rm; **ou**t; **u**p; **ū**se; t**û**rn; **ə**
> sound in **a**bout, chick**e**n, penc**i**l, cann**o**n,
> circ**u**s; **ch**air; **hw** in **wh**ich; ri**ng**; **sh**op;
> **th**in; **th**ere; **zh** in trea**s**ure.

warp (worp) *n.* A twist; a bend.

wash (wosh) *n.* An area of dry land that has
been shaped partly by the action of water
moving over it.

whilst (hwīlst) *conj. British.* While.

windfall (wind′ fôl′) *n.* An unexpected gain.

X

X-ray vision (eks′ rā vi′ zhən) *n.* A way of
seeing through solid substances using a ray
or beam that allows photographs to be
taken of broken bones or other unseen
objects.

Y

yucca (yuk′ ə) *n.* A plant with white flowers
and large leaves shaped like swords in
a cluster.

yucca

yurt (yûrt) *n.* A dome-shaped tent.

Z

zealot (zel′ ət) *n.* A person who shows too
much enthusiasm for a cause.

zombie (zom′ bē) *n.* A person whose actions
are mechanical and unemotional.

Macmillan) published as Broadside by Broadside Press. From GHANDI by Nigel Hunter. Reproduced by permission of Hodder and Stoughton Limited. "Sweeping Pittsburgh Clean" from MAKING HEADLINES: A BIOGRAPHY OF NELLIE BLY by Kathy Lynn Emerson. Copyright © 1989 by Dillon Press. Used by permission of the author. From PASSAGE TO FREEDOM text copyright © 1997 by Ken Mochizuki, illustrations copyright © 1997 by Dom Lee. Afterword copyright © 1997 by Hiroki Sugihara. Permission arranged with Lee & Low Books, Inc., NY, NY 10016.

BEYOND THE NOTES
From THE YOUNG PERSON'S GUIDE TO THE ORCHESTRA, copyright © 1996 by pavilion Books, copyright © 1996 by Anita Ganeri. Illustrations © 1996 by Alex Yan. Reprinted with permission of Harcourt, Inc. From MUSIC IS MY MISTRESS by Duke Ellington. Copyright © 1973 by Duke Ellington, Inc. Used by permission of Doubleday, a division of Random House, Inc. The Nightingale by Hans Christian Andersen by Eva Le Gallienne. Text copyright © 1965 by Eva Le Gallienne. Pictures copyright © 1985 by Nancy Ekholm Burkert. Selection reprinted with permission of International Creative Management. "Introduction" from SING ME A STORY, text copyright © 1989 by Luciano Pavarotti. Reprinted with permission of Herbert Breslin, Inc. All rights reserved. AIDA text copyright © 1990 by Leontyne Price, illustrations copyright © 1990 by Leo and Diane Dillon, reprinted by permission of Harcourt, Inc. From THE SOUND OF FLUTES AND OTHER INDIAN LEGENDS by Richard Erdoes. Text copyright © 1976 by Richard Erdos. Illustrations

copyright © 1976 by Paul Goble. Reprinted by permission of Random House Children's Books, a division of Random House, Inc. "On Hearing a Flute at Night" from THE JADE MOUNTAIN by Witter Bynner. Copyright 1929 and renewed 1957 by Alfred A. Knopf Inc. Reprinted by permission of Alfred A Knopf, a Division of Random House Inc. "Ray and Mr. Pit" from BROTHER RAY: RAY CHARLES' OWN STORY by Ray Charles and David Ritz, copyright © 1978 by Ray Charles and David Ritz. Reprinted with permission. "What is Jazz" from WHAT IS THAT SOUND! By Mary O'Neill. Copyright © 1966 by Mary O'Neill. © Renewed 1994 by Abigail Hagler and Erin Baroni. Reprinted by permission of Marian Reiner. "The Weary Blues" from COLLECTED POEMS by Langston Hughes. Copyright © 1994 by the Estate of Langston Hughes. Reprinted by permission of Alfred A. Knopf, a Division of Random House Inc. From BEETHOVEN LIVES UPSTAIRS by Barbara Nichol, illustrated by Scott Cameron. Published by Orchard Books, an imprint of Scholastic Inc. Text copyright © 1993 by Classical Productions for Children Limited, illustrations copyright © by Scott Cameron. Reprinted by permission of Scholastic Inc. BEETHOVEN LIVES UPSTAIRS copyright © 1993 by Classical Productions for Children Limited, illustrations copyright © 1993 by Scott Cameron. Reprinted by permission of Stoddart Publishing Co. Limited, Toronto. The original "Beethoven Lives Upstairs" audio cassette and compact disc, featuring dramatic storytelling, rich sound effects and more that 24 excerpts of the composer's music was written and directed by Barbara Nichol and produced by Susan Hammond's Classical Kids. "Beethoven Lives Upstairs" is

published by The Children's Group Inc. www.childrensgroup.com "The Man Who Wrote Messiah" Copyright © 1992 by David Berreby.

ECOLOGY
From PROTECTING WILDLIFE by Malcolm Penny. Reproduced by permission of Hodder and Stoughton Limited. "The Passenger Pigeon" TEXT COPYRIGHT © 1985 BY PAUL FLEISCHMAN. Used by permission of HarperCollins Publishers. THE MOST BEAUTIFUL ROOF IN THE WORLD by Kathryn Lasky, text copyright © 1997 by Kathryn Lasky Knight, illustrations copyright © 1997 by Christopher G. Knight, reprinted with permission of Harcourt, Inc. ALEJANDRO'S GIFT text copyright © 1994 by Richard E. Albert. Illustrations copyright © 1994 by Sylvia Long. Reprinted with permission by Chronicle Books, San Francisco, California. All rights reserved. NATURAL FIRE: ITS ECOLOGY IN FORESTS reprinted by permission of Laurence Pringle. Copyright © 1979 by Laurence Pringle. "Poem for the Ancient Trees" © Robert Priest. First published in A TERRIBLE CASE OF THE STARS Puffin (Canada) Also available as a song on Tongue n' Groove (EMI Canada) by Robert Priest. Saving the Peregrine Falcon by Caroline Arnold, photographs by Richard R. Hewett. Copyright © 1985 by Caroline Arnold. Published by Carolrhoda Books, Inc. a division of Lerner Publishing Group. Used by permission of the publisher. All rights reserved. From THE DAY THEY PARACHUTED CATS ON BORNEO, text copyright © 1971 by Charlotte Pomerantz. Reprinted with permission of Writers House LLC. All rights reserved. Illustrated by Jose Aruego.

A QUESTION OF VALUE
KING MIDAS text copyright ©

1999 by John Warren Stewig. Illustrations copyright © 1999 by Omar Rayyan. All rights reserved. Reprinted by permission of Holiday House, Inc. "A Brother's Promise" copyright © 1993 by Pam Conrad. Originally published in WITHIN REACH edited by Donald Gallo, HarperCollins, 1993. Used by permission of Maria Carvainis Agency, Inc. All rights reserved. A GIFT FOR A GIFT reprinted by permission of Eric Protter from A CHILDREN'S TREASURY OF FOLK & FAIRY TALES, edited and adapted by E. Protter. Translation copyright © 1961 By Channel Press, Inc. From THE GOLD COIN. Text copyright © 1991, by Alma Flor Ada, illustrations copyright © 1991, by Neil Waldman. Reprinted with permission of Atheneum Books for Young Readers, Simon & Schuster Children's Publishing Division. All rights reserved. "The No-Guitar Blues" from BASEBALL IN APRIL AND OTHER STORIES, copyright © 1990 by Gary Soto, reprinted by permission of Harcourt, Inc. "The Courage That My Mother Had" by Edna St. Vincent Millay. From COLLECTED POEMS, HarperCollins. Copyright © 1954, 1982 by Norma Millay Allis. All rights reserved. Used by permission of Elizabeth Barnett, literary executor. "The Coin" reprinted with the permission of Scribner, a Division of Simon & Schuster from THE COLLECTED POEMS OF SARA TEASDALE. Copyright © 1920 by Macmillan Publishing Company, renewed 1948 by Mamie T. Wheless. From THE QUILTMAKER'S GIFT by Jeff Brumbeau, illustrated by Gail de Marcken. Published by Pfeifer-Hamilton Publishers, an imprint of Scholastic Inc. Text copyright © 2000 Jeff Brumbeau, illustrations copyright © 2000 by Gail de Marcken. Reprinted by permission of Scholastic Inc.

Photo Credits

7, ©The Library of Congress/PHOTRI; **8 (1),** ©Spencer Swanger/Tom Stack & Associates, **(r)** ©Giraudon/Art Resource, NY; **9,** ©Erich Lessing/Art Resource; **11 (t),** ©The Hulton Getty/Liaison Agency, **(b)** ©Corbis-Bettmann; **12,** PhotoDisc; **14,** ©Christopher G. Knight; **15 (t),** ©Bob McKeever/Tom Stack & Associates, **(b)** ©Richard R. Hewett; **20-31,** Matt Meadows; **30 (t),** Ruth Wright Paulsen, **(b)** Renee Reichert; **48 (t),** ©Ellen Young, **(b)** Anthony Carnabuci; **62,** Mary Ann Fraser; **72,** file photo; **74,** The National Museum of Women in the Arts, Washington, D.C. Gift of Elizabeth Sita; **75 (t)**, By courtesy of The Board of Trustees of the Victoria and Albert Museum, London/ET Archive, London/SuperStock, **(b)** Giraudon/Art Resource, NY; **88 (t),** David A. Adler, **(b)** Robert Casilla; **92,** The Library of Congress/PHOTRI; **93,** Wright State University; **95 (t),** The Library of Congress/PHOTRI, **(b)** Wright State University; **96, 99, 101,** The Library of Congress/PHOTRI; **104,** Wright State University; **107,** ©Corbis/Bettmann; **108 (t),** file photo, **(b)** ©The Library of Congress/PHOTRI; **109,** The Library of Congress/PHOTRI; **110-111,** Kim Westerkov/Tony Stone Images; **112-113,** ©Gianni Dagli Orti/Corbis; **138,** ©CORBIS/David Muench; **140,** ©John Gerlach/Tom Stack & Associates; **143,** National Park Service;

Photo Credits, continued

Unit Opener Acknowledgments